ACHIEVING WORKERS' RIGHTS IN THE GLOBAL ECONOMY

ACHIEVING WORKERS' RIGHTS IN THE GLOBAL ECONOMY

Edited by Richard P. Appelbaum
and Nelson Lichtenstein

ILR PRESS, AN IMPRINT OF CORNELL UNIVERSITY PRESS
ITHACA AND LONDON

First published 2016 by Cornell University Press
First printing, Cornell Paperbacks, 2016
Printed in the United States of America

Library of Congress Cataloging-in-Publication Data

Names: Appelbaum, Richard P., editor. | Lichtenstein, Nelson, editor.
Title: Achieving workers' rights in the global economy / edited by Richard P.
    Appelbaum and Nelson Lichtenstein.
Description: Ithaca ; London : ILR Press, an imprint of Cornell University
    Press, 2016. | Includes bibliographical references and index.
Identifiers: LCCN 2015048042
ISBN 9781501700033 (cloth : alk. paper)
ISBN 9781501700040 (pbk. : alk. paper)
Subjects: LCSH: Employee rights. | Labor and globalization.
Classification: LCC HD6971.8 .A24 2016 | DDC 331.01/1—dc23
LC record available at http://lccn.loc.gov/2015048042

Cornell University Press strives to use environmentally responsible suppliers
and materials to the fullest extent possible in the publishing of its books. Such
materials include vegetable-based, low-VOC inks and acid-free papers that are
recycled, totally chlorine-free, or partly composed of nonwood fibers. For further
information, visit our website at www.cornellpress.cornell.edu.

Cloth printing   10 9 8 7 6 5 4 3 2 1
Paperback printing   10 9 8 7 6 5 4 3 2 1

This book is dedicated to the 1,138 people who lost their lives at Rana Plaza

Contents

Acknowledgments

We wish to acknowledge the people and organizations who helped make this book possible and who provided invaluable assistance along the way: the MacArthur Foundation, whose endowed chairs supported our work on workers' rights around the globe; the Rockefeller Foundation's Bellagio Center, for hosting the conference that resulted in this book, as well as our month-long residencies, where we were able to do collaborative writing on workers' rights; Gaye Tuchman, who from the beginning realized the importance of a book publication resulting from our conference; Shirley (Xueying) Han, who helped to organize our conference and managed the "supply chain" of book contributors; Fran Benson, editorial director of ILR Press at Cornell University Press; Karen M. Laun, our patient production editor at CUP; Mary Petrusewicz, our copyeditor; and Jim O'Brien, our indexer.

ACHIEVING WORKERS' RIGHTS IN THE GLOBAL ECONOMY

Introduction

ACHIEVING WORKERS' RIGHTS IN THE GLOBAL ECONOMY

Richard P. Appelbaum and Nelson Lichtenstein

The world was shocked in April 2013 when more than eleven hundred garment workers lost their lives in the collapse of the Rana Plaza factory complex
in Dhaka. It was the worst industrial tragedy in the two-hundred-year history
of mass apparel manufacture. This was an accident just waiting to happen, and
not merely because of the corruption and exploitation of workers so common
among the four million garment workers in Bangladesh. The real cause of the
disaster, as well as the low wages, poor working conditions, and voicelessness
endemic to the vast majority of workers who labor in the export industries of
the global South, arises out of the very nature of world trade and production.

Today retail-dominated supply chains, of which those commanded by executives at Walmart, Apple, Nike, Zara, and H&M are the most prominent, generate
at least half of all world trade and "employ" hundreds of millions of workers in
thousands of contract manufacturers from Shenzhen and Shanghai to Sao Paulo
and San Pedro Sula. Given their enormous power to squeeze prices and wages,
these North Atlantic brands and retailers today occupy the commanding heights
of world capitalism.

The essays collected in *Achieving Workers' Rights in the Global Economy*
offer an incisive analysis of this pernicious system alongside proposals for its
radical reform. Its contributors, many of whom have years of experience study-
ing or working with major companies, nongovernmental organizations, international regulatory bodies, and trade unions on more than four continents, explain

why so many high-profile corporate social responsibility programs have failed, why real wages have declined in much of the garment-manufacturing sector, and why unions and other forms of worker self-organization have had such difficulty establishing themselves in China, South Asia, and Central America. The concluding chapters call for cross-border regulation, worker self-empowerment, and brand and retailer legal responsibility for the wages, working conditions, and safety of all those who labor in their contract factories.

The Changing Nature of Production

Today's globalization differs from that of even a few decades past because of the big-box retail chains—the big buyers that have often displaced the large manufacturing firms that once reigned supreme as the central pillars and most consequential entities in the capitalist economy during most of the twentieth century. The Walmarts, Home Depots, and Carrefours sit atop global supply chains, along with brands such as Apple and Nike. They make the markets, set the prices, and determine the worldwide distribution of labor for that gigantic stream of commodities that flows across their counters (Lichtenstein 2009). The loss of US goods-producing manufacturing firms to low-wage countries has entailed not just cheap labor competition from abroad but also a historic shift in power within the structures of world capitalism from manufacturing to a retail sector that controls the supply chains spread around the planet.

These buyer-driven commodity chains play a pivotal role in setting up the decentralized production networks that today stand at the heart of transnational capitalism. Producer-driven supply chains, characteristic of capital-intensive industries such as automobiles, aircraft, computers, semiconductors, and heavy machinery, still exist, but their relative importance has declined since the mid-twentieth century, when multinational manufacturers played the dominant role in coordinating worldwide production networks. In contrast, the retailers and marketers who stand at the apex of the buyer-driven global commodity chains of our day are best understood as "branded marketers" who do not actually make their own products, but rather design and advertise them, thus creating a market based on product image and recognition. Actual manufacturing takes place in a worldwide set of independently owned contract factories that purchase the raw materials, recruit and pay the workers, and oversee all aspects of the production process. This system is most advanced within the world of light manufacturing, especially apparel, shoes, and consumer electronics, but the output of more complex, capital-intensive products, including high-value aviation and computer parts as well as call-center services contracted to phone companies and airlines, is rapidly becoming a link in these global supply chains.

The result of this shift has been a parallel transformation in the nature of economic governance. In the era after the Great War, social democrats on both sides of the Atlantic sought to institutionalize a "tripartite" structure in which the state, the corporations, and the unions negotiated with one another in order to reach a set of social and economic outcomes that some latter-day observers would denominate a "social compact." Although such a corporatist settlement seemed within reach during the height of the Second World War and the most fraught Cold War years that followed, in the United States it never achieved the legitimacy that would for many decades characterize class politics in Austria, West Germany, and the Nordic countries (Moody 1988; Swenson 1989; Jacoby 1997; Swenson 2002; Phillips-Fein 2010; Lichtenstein 2013). Nevertheless, it remained an aspiration, encoded and advanced most consistently by the International Labour Organization (ILO), where a "tripartite" structure was embedded within the very DNA of organizational decision making and implementation.

Today, of course, such twentieth-century industrial tripartism is in decay. In the United States collective bargaining as a mechanism for setting labor standards no longer has an effective state patron, and in Europe unionism is also in decline and state patronage is on the wane. In East Asia, the new workshop of the world, authoritarian governments of a Stalinist or militarist character have given way to hypercapitalist ruling coalitions that are just as determined to suppress working-class claims to autonomous organization and power sharing. Into this vacuum—both of industrial governance and the ideology essential to sustain it—have stepped the giant corporations of our time who have deployed the framework known as corporate social responsibility (CSR) as a new kind of tripartism in which negotiations now take place between those brands and retailers at the top of the supply chain, their contract factories in Asia and Central America, and a set of nongovernmental organizations (NGOs) whose role it is to substitute themselves for both an indifferent or weak state and the workers themselves, whose level of political and economic organization remains anemic.

This arrangement effectively makes corporations responsible for monitoring themselves, and in turn has given rise to a global compliance industry. Whereas Jill Esbenshade famously argued that in a world dominated by global supply chains a new "triangle of power" now exists, "with employers, contractors, and the government forming its points" (Esbenshade 2004a, 33; see also chapter 3), we take the argument one step further to argue that government itself is largely absent: the three points on the triangle are now the brands, their contract factories, and the set of largely Western NGOs that prod the corporations to improve

labor standards and monitor the firms hired by the brands to inspect their factories and report back (to the brands) their findings.

Self-Regulation in Global Industries

In response to these developments, and in the United States and Europe a growing anti-sweatshop movement (see chapters 2 and 14),[1] businesses have since
the late 1990s emphasized the importance of corporate social responsibility,
sustainability, fair trade, and the "triple bottom line" (profits, equitable business
practices, environmental sustainability). Leading corporations such as Nike and
Walmart have adopted codes of conduct that are intended to require their suppliers to behave according to ethical business practices as well as signal their customers that such practices are reflected in their products. The growing interest
in equitable business practices is reflected in a large number of organizations
and institutions that have been created since the 1990s, as well as the theoretical
and empirical attention that has been given to these issues in the literature and
in business school curricula (Tickle 2009). A small sampling of organizations
and institutions would include Businesses for Social Responsibility (now simply
BSR), the Fair Labor Association (FLA), the Sustainable Apparel Coalition, Green
America, and the United Nations Global Compact. Among business and management schools that emphasize corporate social responsibility issues, the top ten
would include the Ross Business School, University of Michigan; Yale School of
Management; Stanford Graduate School of Business; Mendoza Business College,
Notre Dame; Haas Business School, University of California at Berkeley; Stern
Business School, NYU; Columbia University Business School; Darden Busi-
ness School, University of Virginia; Johnson Graduate School of Management,
Cornell; and the George Washington University School of Business.

Businesses have been especially keen to emphasize sustainable environmental practices. This most likely stems from several sources: genuine ethical concern, the recognition that ecologically sustainable practices can open up new
market opportunities, concern that embarrassing revelations involving pollution or sweatshop production might hurt brand image, and the desire to cut
costs through greater efficiency (for example, when green technologies reduce
fossil fuel consumption). The policing of supply chains—at least on the environmental side—has come to be regarded as legitimate by a growing segment
of the business community. In the most widely discussed example (because of
its enormous potential impact), Walmart in 2009 notified its approximately one
hundred thousand global suppliers that they would henceforth be required to
estimate and report their carbon footprint. This would be put into an index that

would then be reported on the product's price tag, enabling consumers to take into account its ecological impact. Walmart's efforts are not only good PR but they are also good for Walmart's bottom line, since energy costs across the company's global supply chains are being reduced as a result. As the world's largest retailer, Walmart's sustainability program will certainly have a large environmental impact and provide a template competitors will feel pressure to emulate. Although businesses that have embraced environmentally sustainable practices have been accused of "greenwashing"—engaging in public-relations efforts that entail few actual changes in practices—there is some evidence that at least in this area, business's economic and social objectives can coincide: ecologically sustainable products now command a large market and cost-cutting based on any criteria is essential to efficient supply-chain management.[2]

If some businesses have clearly taken preliminary steps toward developing environmentally sustainable products, progress is far more problematic when it comes to labor issues involving wages, hours, health and safety, and the right to freedom of association. Corporations that adopt fair labor standards typically do so by deploying codes of conduct that apply to their supply chains, while avoiding the transparency and independent monitoring of actual results that would permit effective evaluation of their programs. We term this practice "bluewashing," that is, a mere rhetorical and reputational commitment toward the improvement of labor standards.

NGOs have become highly active in this area—some working with corporations to provide a variety of monitoring services for purposes of self-enforcement, others as independent monitors (or, more often, industry watchdogs) that are highly critical of the corporate ability to self-regulate. Examples of the former include the Global Social Compliance Program, Veritas, and PwC, a separate legal entity of PriceWaterhouseCoopers International. Examples of the latter are numerous: the Worker Rights Consortium (WRC), the Fair Labor Association (FLA), Maquila Solidarity Network, and the International Labor Rights Forum.[3]

Finally, some transnational governmental institutions seek to raise labor standards, but their effectiveness remains unclear. The UN Global Compact, enacted in the late 1990s, represents an essentially aspirational manifesto designed to facilitate business self-regulation on an international scale (see chapter 2). More substantial is the work of the ILO, which periodically establishes new international labor standards, normally embodied in a convention and adopted by two or more countries. But ILO standards lack effective enforcement mechanisms and so are seldom honored outside of the rich social democracies of Europe. Indeed, the United States remains an outlier, having adopted only two of the ILO's eight core labor-standard conventions. China has adopted none. Moreover, the ILO is committed to the old tripartite schema involving capital, labor, and the state, a framework, as we have seen, that has little bearing in a world where the key actors are brands, suppliers, and the organizations that brands hire to monitor their supply chains. Labor and the state are noticeably absent from this new arrangement. (The role of the ILO is discussed more extensively in chapters 2, 5, and 6.)

The Growth of Big Suppliers: A New Opportunity for Activism?

Whereas the growing importance of big buyers—major brands and retailers—in supply chains has been well documented, less appreciated is the parallel rise of giant transnational contractors, based primarily in Hong Kong, Taiwan, South Korea, and China. They operate factories primarily in East Asia (China, Vietnam, Malaysia, Singapore, and Indonesia), Mexico, and Central America, although they are beginning to appear in Africa and Latin America as well. Such "big suppliers" are themselves market makers for their own contract suppliers, exerting increasing control over key aspects of the production supply chain.[4]

In the textile and apparel industries, the consolidation of production, both at the factory and country level, is highly pronounced, having accelerated after the demise of the thirty-year Multi-Fiber Arrangement (MFA). Under the MFA's quota system, clothing production had been dispersed to some 140 countries, but when the arrangement was phased out in 2005 the consolidation of clothing production into a few larger companies and a small number of supplying countries accelerated because of the economies of scale that could be achieved and because some nations, such as China and Vietnam, had the infrastructure to efficiently sustain high levels of export production.

Examples of giant East Asia-based contractors abound. In the footwear industry, the firm Yue Yuen boasts of being "the largest branded athletic and casual footwear manufacturer in the world" (Pou Chen 2015). The company's sprawling complexes (resembling small cities) produce for Nike, adidas, Reebok, Asics, New Balance, Puma, Timberland, and Rockport, whose production occurs in side-by-side factory buildings. Yue Yuen was founded by the Tsai family in Hong Kong in 1988. They also control the Taiwanese firm Pou Chen, the largest shareholder in Yue Yuen, which has acquired Pou Chen's interest in nearly seventy companies providing raw materials, production equipment, and shoe components, along with a number of companies engaged in sportswear and casual apparel manufacturing. In the textile and apparel industries, the Taiwanese multinational Nien Hsing Textile Co. Ltd supplies such customers as The Gap, Kohl's, Levi Strauss,

Liz & Co., Target, and Oshkosh B'Gosh. It has denim mills or factories in Taiwan, Mexico, Nicaragua, Vietnam, Cambodia, and Lesotho. Yupoong Inc., a Korean multinational that has become one of the world's largest cap manufacturers, has supplied its "Flexfit" caps to markets around the world—including (in the United States), the NBA, MLB, NFL, NHL, and NCAA. And when it comes to assembling consumer electronics, the Taiwanese company Foxconn is by far the largest: grossing nearly $65 billion in sales, Foxconn is the single largest private employer in China, with 1.4 million workers in Asia, Europe, and Latin America (see chapter 9).

This consolidation of production results in an industry-driven designated supplier program in which major brands and retailers increasingly source their production from a smaller number of large multinational manufacturers. As we shall see in the cases of Nike and Apple, this creates new opportunities for public disclosure and concerted pressure to ameliorate conditions. It also begins to reproduce the social and organizational environment that existed during the heyday of union organizing in the twentieth century: large factories that are vulnerable to mass work stoppages and a supply chain that is vulnerable to such worker pressure at a variety of points from Asian ports to US trucking and distribution sites. Although these export manufacturers remain independently owned contract factories, to the extent that they account for a significant portion of their clients' products, worker or consumer action directed against the factories can have a strong impact on brand reputation and retailers that sell such well-known consumer goods.

Recent Developments May Hold Some Promise

We argue that as aspirational statements, corporate codes of conduct set a public standard to which firms can be held accountable. Even when imperfectly asserted and enforced, such an enunciation of a corporate standard opens the door to the kind of "naming and shaming" that has become an NGO specialty. Recent victories by the anti-sweatshop movement have shown that public pressure on leading brands can result in significant changes in their behavior. Although generally restricted to the university apparel sector, these victories have sent signals throughout the industry. Though very few brands have made changes that go beyond their licensed university products, well-publicized campaigns against brands such as Nike and Russell Athletic contribute to a climate of concern that is reflected in the proliferation of codes and brand alliances that at least pay lip service to enforcement (see chapter 14).

Nike provides an excellent case study. When United Students Against Sweatshops, and others who favored development of collegiate codes of conduct for companies that sold their product in university bookstores, began a boycott campaign against Nike in the early 1990s, the company claimed that more transparency—involving contract manufacturers and working conditions— would destroy their business, a claim still made by most brands and retailers today. But student activism and consumer pressure forced Nike to develop a well-formulated code of conduct and then regularly issue CSR reports. The company began to work cooperatively with the WRC and FLA and it provides a public website that is said to include all of its contractors and subcontractors.[5] Most important, Nike has moved much of its footwear production into its giant Yue Yuen factory complexes in Dongguan. Of course, without either effective unions or much state regulation, problems clearly persist in Nike's supply chain, as the authors of chapters 2, 3, and 14 discuss.

Apple provides another instructive case study. Apple is reportedly the world's most admired company; in the second decade of the twenty-first century it also became the world's most valuable company, at least as measured by stock capitalization. Components for Apple products are sourced all over the world but assembled primarily in Foxconn's Chinese factories. When revelations surfaced, beginning in 2011, about despondent workers committing suicide in Foxconn's Shenzhen factory, enormous public pressure forced Apple to join the FLA, which conducted worker audits on Apple's behalf; Foxconn also raised wages. But as is described in detail in chapter 9, these victories proved to be more illusory than real: wage and hour violations persist, and Foxconn responded in part by reducing its workforce in Shenzhen and moving production to western provinces, where wages are much lower.

It is a good thing that firms have committed themselves to the maintenance of codes of conduct that address wages and working conditions. But meaningful improvements are unlikely to occur unless retailers and brands are willing to front any higher labor costs associated with code enforcement, since supplier factories will claim (with some justification) that they are already being squeezed. Factory giants like Yue Yuen and Foxconn may be able to absorb some higher costs, but their profitability is unlikely to extend to the smaller suppliers and subcontractors. This is why factory consolidation is such an important development. The mutual reliance of big buyers and big suppliers on one another can create opportunities to apply the sort of leverage, via publicity and even boycotts, that force export manufactures to make improvements to their operations that can affect hundreds of thousands of workers after just one campaign. Such consumer pressure, over time, may help to achieve workers' rights, beginning by creating a market niche for truly labor-friendly products. But this is hardly a long-term solution, since consumer consciousness can be so unreliable and fickle.[6]

Passing (and enforcing) labor-friendly laws in supplier countries may also prove helpful, as is evidenced by Indonesia's rulings that workers at PT Kizone, abruptly shut down by its Korean owner, were entitled to legally mandated severance pay (see chapter 14). Even China, long dependent on cheap exports for amassing its mountain of foreign-reserve currencies, enacted a contract labor law in 2008 that guarantees workers some basic rights (Wang et al. 2009). China has also raised worker wages in the coastal provinces where most factory production occurs, and worker militancy has begun to make some inroads into China's state-controlled labor unions (see chapters 9, 10, and 11). Yet these developments reveal some of the problems in state-level action: rising wages and improved working conditions in a single country can lead to capital flight to less labor-friendly (and lower-cost) countries. This is currently the case with China, where low-cost production is now being offshored to Bangladesh, Vietnam, Cambodia, and many African countries.

Enforceable (and enforced) trade treaties involving the leading apparel importing countries could level the playing field, since brands would be required to comply regardless of where they produced their products. Such "social clauses" in trade agreements would, however, likely be challenged as in violation of World Trade Organization (WTO) trade liberalization requirements. In the long run, perhaps, even the WTO might change its charter to incorporate ILO core labor-standard conventions—provisions that then might be enforced by the ILO itself.

All of these efforts can contribute to selective improvements in working conditions, particularly where major brands and their large-scale suppliers are involved. CSR, though limited in crucial ways, should not be dismissed out-of-hand by anti-sweatshop activists: to the extent that it opens the door to previously hidden working conditions in global supply chains, it provides an opportunity for activists to push for that door to open still further.

Organization of This Book

The four chapters in part 1 provide a detailed look at CSR, examining why it has failed to achieve its professed objectives. In chapter 1, Scott Nova and Chris Wegemer survey the many challenges that must be confronted in achieving workers' rights in global supply chains. Nova, head of the WRC and one of the chief negotiators of the innovative Bangladesh Accord on Fire and Building Safety, graphically chronicles the efforts to achieve a meaningful (and enforceable) solution to the ever-present danger of fires and building collapses among Bangladesh's thousands of garment factories. Drawing on his experience as one of the architects of the 2013 Accord, he documents two principal challenges: remediating the physical dangers Bangladeshi workers encounter daily and overcoming the resistance of brands and retailers to incurring a legal obligation to make the necessary remediation, even if it means covering the costs themselves. The failure of voluntary CSR and the need for binding commitments (some form of "joint liability" between the brands/retailers and their contract factories) are themes that will run throughout this book.

In chapter 2, Richard Appelbaum examines the history of the CSR idea, tracing its corporate origins as well as its internationalization in approaches favored by the United Nations. During the early part of the twentieth century, when production was largely national in scope, strong unions in the United States and other industrial nations were able to achieve varying degrees of government regulations that protected workers' rights. These protections reflected a tripartite labor-capital-state system of corporate governance envisioned as early as 1919 with the birth of the ILO. But during the latter part of the twentieth century, as production went global, state regulation gave way to corporate self-regulation—private enforcement of codes of conduct that corporations adopted in the face of embarrassing revelations of labor abuses in overseas contract factories. This approach, taught in business schools, embraced universally by corporations, and reflected in the United Nations Global Compact, has failed to secure workers' rights.

In chapter 3, Jill Espenshade begins with an extensive review of some fifty studies that examine the success, failure, and challenges of codes of conduct and monitoring efforts, looking at the wide variety of practices, the role of worker participation, the importance of independence and transparency, consumer activism, government enforcement, and the relationship between brands/retailers and their suppliers. She argues that although the ultimate solution lies in strong government enforcement, "moving from checklist monitoring to contractual obligation" between brands/retailers and their suppliers can play an important role in enforcing substantive codes of conduct.

In chapter 4 Robert Ross provides research that graphically documents the failure of CSR. He begins with a historical review of the origins and development of CSR before turning to the principal critiques of its weaknesses. He then reviews the history of the many fires and building collapses in Bangladesh, the preferred lowest-cost site for many Western brands and retailers, focusing on case studies of disasters in buildings that had been preceded by favorable CSR audits and monitoring reports. He concludes with an argument for joint liability, introducing a discussion of the so-called jobbers' agreements between manufacturers (known as "jobbers") and union shops in New York City's garment industry during the 1920s and 1930s. The history and relevance of jobbers' agreements as a way forward are also discussed in detail by Mark Anner, Jennifer Bair, and Jeremy Blasi in chapter 13.

The four chapters in part 2 offer different approaches to the governance of global supply chains: greater vertical integration of production, encouraging international labor standards through the ILO, developing private transnational law, and upgrading in global supply chains. In chapter 5, Nelson Lichtenstein begins with a discussion of the degree to which the disaggregation of the vertically integrated corporation, combined with the emergence of an era of "thin" states incapable of regulating their own economies, has rendered the idea of tripartite industrial governance an antique relic of an increasingly distant time. Retail-dominated global supply chains therefore remain virtually unregulated by the nation-states that host their production facilities, while trade unions remain weak throughout the export industries of East Asia. All this has proven a challenge to the ILO even as it tries to accommodate its regulatory mission to the new architecture of corporate power. Lichtenstein therefore examines three ILO initiatives designed to salvage a measure of industrial tripartitism. The ILO itself remains skeptical of the entire CSR project, but has nevertheless established a voluntary corporate "help desk" designed to facilitate CSR initiatives that base their codes and standards on established ILO conventions. The limitations of the ILO approach are revealed in the ILO's Better Factories Cambodia program, an initiative strongly supported in its formative years by the United States.

In chapter 6, Anne Caroline Posthuma and Renato Bignami examine a CSR initiative recently introduced by the Brazilian Association of Apparel Retailers, which they argue offers the potential of bridging two prevalent regulatory gaps in global supply chains: the gap between private-sector audits and public labor inspections and the gap between first- and lower-tier suppliers. Using a global-value-chain approach, which examines the possibilities of upgrading into higher value-added production, this chapter argues that despite the many challenges that still exist in Brazil, when strong communication exists between a vigorous public labor inspectorate and the leading association of apparel retailers, it may prove possible to bridge the public/private and first-tier/lower-tier regulatory gaps that commonly exist in the promotion of labor standards in global and national value chains.

In chapter 7, Brishen Rogers examines the challenging relationship between global legal structures and global value chains through which brands operate and shape workers' responses. He shows how workers' organizations are increasingly bypassing national-level collective bargaining laws and procedures, holding brands accountable through private contractual agreements linking brands, suppliers, and workers, as seen in the Bangladesh Accord on Fire and Building Safety. Such agreements, which take the form of contracts that are enforceable through binding arbitration in national courts, may prove to be a way forward (although how they will stand up in national courts remains to be seen). More important, he argues, such contracts empower workers' organizations in creating and enforcing labor law "from below," linking workers across borders directly to brands, a topic that is further discussed in chapter 14.

In chapter 8, Gary Gereffi and Xubei Luo employ a global-value-chain framework to show that although in some cases it is possible to "capture the gains" from economic upgrading, this is not always possible. The economic dividends generated by participation in global supply chains do not necessarily translate into good jobs or stable employment. Moreover, the economic upgrading experienced by some export-oriented low-income countries has been associated with a significant deterioration of labor conditions. The authors call on governments to take several steps to improve workers' lives. These include playing a central role in addressing the risks for workers, enforcing regulations that address working conditions, and facilitating human capital development by collaborating with universities and firms to enhance workforce development.

The three chapters of part 3 examine the prospects for workers' rights in China—a country now emerging as the planet's most important manufacturing power with a proletariat numbering in the hundreds of millions. As these chapters show, workers are not quiescent in China but in various ways—always constrained by the state—have been effective in demanding and winning better working conditions and wage improvements.

In chapter 9, Jenny Chan, Pun Ngai, and Mark Selden take an insider's look at what they term China's "new working class" by focusing on the giant Foxconn factories that produce consumer electronics for Apple and many other brands. Based on an examination of reports as well as interviews with workers and managers, they argue that Apple, not Foxconn, reaps the profits from their production relationship, with a resulting downward squeeze on wages and working conditions. Workers have responded: initially with well-publicized suicides of despondent workers in Foxconn's Longhua Shenzhen factory, then with strikes and worker protests at Foxconn factories throughout China. Because China's government sees these direct actions as threatening social stability, it has forced Foxconn and other employers to raise wages, while enacting some limited policies that improve workers' lives.

In chapter 10, Katie Quan takes a hard look at recent labor struggles in southern China, focusing especially on the role of wildcat strikes, which have forced the government, and the government-controlled unions, to provide dispute-resolution mechanisms that give workers increasing voice through collective bargaining and election of union leaders. Through a series of case studies and interviews with labor activists, she shows that although these developments have the potential for increasing worker power, the Communist Party—which controls the unions—remains a barrier: wildcat strikes may be tolerated, but formal, openly declared union strikes are not. The chapter concludes with a call for increased dialogue and exchanges with US unions as a way of strengthening China's unions and fostering joint actions.

In chapter 11, Anita Chan looks at trade union elections throughout China, arguing through a series of case studies that five types of elections are reshaping labor practices there. These five fall into two broad categories: trade union elections initiated by parties other than the workers themselves (by multinationals, by foreign trade unions and NGOs, or by China's government-controlled All-China Federation of Trade Unions, the ACFTU) and elections initiated by the workers themselves (initiated and organized by workers or initiated by workers but organized by the union). These cases show that there is an emerging awareness on the part of workers of the importance of true democratic labor representation in China, something even the ACFTU now understands. Professor Chan concludes that both categories of labor activism have encountered difficulties. Where workers are passive (the first category), any gains realized can be quickly withdrawn. Where workers are active (the second category), their actions often face repression from company or regional government, resulting in a loss of momentum and few if any permanent gains. Nonetheless, she argues, in the long run, these varied experiences are ones of learning and consciousness formation that may prove invaluable for achieving workers' rights in China.

The three chapters in part 4 draw on past and current labor struggles to chart a way forward. In chapter 12, the Sustainable Apparel Coalition's (SAC) Jason Kibbey offers the apparel and footwear industry's preferred approach: strengthening CSR efforts by statistically measuring the social, labor, and environmental impacts of factory production through the use of the Higg Index. SAC is an industry-wide group of leading apparel and footwear brands, retailers, manufacturers, NGOs, and academic experts working to measure and improve the environmental and social impacts of the apparel and footwear industry. Kibbey briefly describes the history, membership, and aspirations of the SAC before turning to an extended discussion of the Higg Index itself: its origins, function, and the theory of change it embodies.

In chapter 13, Mark Anner, Jennifer Bair, and Jeremy Blasi provide a detailed look at the early jobbers' agreements in the United States, which they argue can serve as a model for achieving some form of joint liability between brands and retailers on the one hand, and their globally dispersed contract factories on the other. Examining the history of the International Ladies' Garment Workers' Union during its mid-twentieth-century heyday, they find that key elements of the original jobbers' agreements are replicable today: direct wage negotiations, stabilization of contracting relationships by registering contractors with the union, and making jobbers directly liable for labor costs beyond wages. The chapter concludes with a discussion of possible approaches to joint liability in today's global supply chains that draw on these lessons: global framework agreements negotiated between international union federations and multinational companies or global brands, university codes of conduct and student corporate campaigns, and the Accord on Fire and Building Safety in Bangladesh. They argue that effective domestic laws and international labor standards are, by themselves, insufficient: binding agreements that create joint liability are necessary to achieve meaningful (and enforceable) workers' rights.

In chapter 14, Jeff Hermanson examines current efforts to foster cross-border union solidarity and labor organizing. After first reviewing the history of labor organizing in the garment industry, he turns to current global efforts, including some in which he has been directly involved, discussing their strengths and weaknesses. The emergence of global federations of unions is one promising development. Beginning in 2012, the International Union League for Brand Responsibility has linked a number of national unions together, employing an original strategy: global campaigns against a single brand that target dozens of the brand's contract factories around the world. Although this approach is not without difficulties, Hermanson writes that it has the potential to bring rank-and-file factory workers face to face at the bargaining table with the top executives of some of the most powerful and wealthy corporations in the world.

Part I

SELF-GOVERNANCE

The Challenges and Limitations of
Corporate Social Responsibility

OUTSOURCING HORROR

Why Apparel Workers Are Still Dying,
One Hundred Years after Triangle Shirtwaist

Scott Nova and Chris Wegemer

The fire broke out at 5:30 p.m., right after the bell sounded the end of the workday. The building is 10 stories high. The Triangle Waist Company occupied the top three floors, and that is where the fire started . . . The flames spread very quickly. A stream of fire rose up through the elevators to the uppermost floors. In the blink of an eye, fire appeared in all the windows and tongues of flame climbed higher and higher up the walls, as bunches of terrified working girls stood in astonishment. The fire grew stronger, larger and more horrifying. The workers on the upper floors were already not able to bear the heat and, one after another, began jumping from the eighth, ninth and 10th floors down to the sidewalk where they died.

—*The Forverts*, March 26, 1911

Survivors have described how a fire tore through a multi-story garment factory just outside Bangladesh's capital, Dhaka, killing more than 100 of their colleagues . . . Muhammad Shahbul Alam, 26, described flames filling two of the three stairwells of the nine-floor building—where clothes for international brands . . . appear to have been made . . . Rooms full of female workers were cut off as piles of yarn and fabric filling corridors ignited. Reports also suggested fire exits at the site had locks on, which had to be broken in order for staff to escape . . . Witnesses said many workers leapt from upper stories in a bid to escape the flames.

—*The Guardian* (Burke and Hammadi), November 25, 2012

Time and again when workers speak up with concern about safety risks, they aren't listened to. And in the moment of crisis, when the fire alarm goes off or a building starts to crack, workers' voices not only fall on deaf ears, but they are actively disregarded . . . Change can happen. It is happening. But there's still a long way to go.

—Kalpona Akter, Bangladesh Center for Worker Solidarity, January 23, 2014

On March 25, 1911, on the top floors of a ten-story building on the corner of Greene Street and Washington Place in lower Manhattan, a fire broke out in a factory operated by the Triangle Shirtwaist Company. As smoke and flames rapidly spread, a lack of fire exits made escape impossible; workers desperately scrambling for egress found only locked doors. Many chose to leap to their deaths rather than succumb to the flames. One hundred and forty-six people, mostly young women in their late teens and early twenties, died in a tragedy that helped catalyze a national movement for workplace reform.

Unfortunately, we don't need a history lesson to contemplate the horror of garment workers falling to their deaths from the high floors of a burning factory. The abusive conditions, poverty wages, and shoddy garment industry safety practices that unions and social reformers decried in 1911 have not disappeared. They have been relocated. Today, leading apparel brands and retailers produce their goods in countries like Bangladesh, now the world's second-largest garment exporter, where from 2005 to 2013 nearly two thousand workers were killed in more than a dozen fires and building collapses. Each of these disasters arose from the same kind of reckless disregard for worker safety that produced the tragedy at Triangle Shirtwaist.

Thanks to decades of legislative reform and union activism, by the 1950s apparel production in the United States came to be defined by decent wages, strong unions, and enforceable safety regulations. However, as communications and transportation technology made overseas production increasing feasible, clothing brands and retailers eventually relocated the manufacturing of garments to countries that offered what the United States no longer did: workers willing to toil for poverty wages and governments willing to turn the other way while factory managers cut costs by ignoring labor standards. It is important to bear in mind that low wages, though important, were never the sole attraction; the savings that can be derived in an environment of lax-to-nonexistent regulation are also substantial.

Unconstrained by regulation, apparel producers in 1911 Manhattan did not waste money on niceties like workplace safety. Neither do their counterparts today in Bangladesh and many other garment-producing countries. Leading Western apparel brands and retailers have thus accomplished a perverse form of time travel: they have re-created 1911 working conditions for millions of twenty-first-century garment workers.

On no issue has the cost to workers been more obvious, or more tragic, than workplace safety. The garment industry has known for a century how to operate an apparel factory safely, a lesson learned in the wake of the Triangle Shirtwaist fire. Moreover, virtually every exporting country, including Bangladesh, has laws on the books that require proper building design and operation. Yet in Bangladesh, prior to recent reform efforts spurred by the Tazreen Fashions fire (November 2012) and the Rana Plaza building collapse (April 2013), it is highly likely that none of the country's 3,500 garment factories had fire exits or sprinkler systems. Hundreds were structurally unsound. No factories were found to be even close to meeting safety standards (Accord on Fire and Building Safety in Bangladesh 2014). As a result, millions of garment workers risked their lives every day merely by going to work.

This recklessness explains why, despite all of the last century's advances both in the technical understanding of building safety and in the official recognition by governments and corporations of the rights of workers, three of the four worst disasters in the centuries-long history of mechanized garment production have occurred in the three years before 2015.

Only in the wake of the worst of these, the Rana Plaza collapse, which generated weeks of worldwide media coverage highly embarrassing to leading brands and retailers, was it finally possible to persuade some of these corporations to commit to take the action necessary to make garment factories in Bangladesh safe.

In the following, we discuss why preventable mass fatality disasters continue to occur in factories producing the clothing of major Western brands and retailers more than one hundred years after the Triangle Shirtwaist fire, the actions necessary to bring an end to this long season of horror, and the initial steps taken in this direction since the Rana Plaza collapse.

How We Got Here

Although apparel brands and retailers pay ample lip service to worker rights and worker safety, dangerous and degrading working conditions are a product of their own manufacturing strategies. Today's global apparel supply chains have the following salient features: (1) brands and retailers generally eschew ownership of manufacturing capacity and instead assign their production to contract factories; (2) relations with these producers are defined by short-term contracts for specific orders of apparel with no guarantee of continued business; (3) brands and retailers usually limit their production in a given factory to a modest portion of the factory's overall output, so factory owners must piece together numerous short-term orders from a long list of current and prospective customers in order to survive; and (4) with barriers to entry into garment production low, and with large numbers of workers desperate for some form of employment, there is excess capacity on the production side, allowing brands and retailers to bargain prices, and order deadlines, downward by exploiting competition between suppliers.

These factors combine to generate intense and consistent pressure on producers to cut costs, and therefore prices, by any means available; they understand that
if they cannot meet a given customer's price demands, there is another factory,
across the street or across the world, that will. The options for reducing production costs are limited; factory owners have virtually no ability to reduce the cost
of cloth, or of power, or of sewing machines. The one cost over which they can
exert substantial control is labor.

The barrier to achieving large savings by squeezing labor—underpaying relative to the minimum wage, forcing workers to endure long hours of overtime,
cutting corners on workplace safety, firing workers who try to unionize—is that
apparel exporting countries generally have strong labor laws. In many cases, laws
concerning such issues as mandatory benefits, limits on overtime, protection for
women workers, and occupational health and safety are as strong as, or stronger
than, those in the United States. If factory owners had to follow these laws, they
would have about as much control over the cost of labor as they do over the cost
of cotton. Fortunately for them, and unfortunately for those who sew garments
for a living, governments are every bit as attuned to the priorities of foreign buyers and investors as local factory owners are. Believing, with strong historical
basis, that brands and retailers will reward those countries that keep labor costs to
a minimum and punish those that fail to do so, governments in apparel exporting
countries are notoriously willing to abdicate regulatory responsibility.

Garment factory operators therefore have both powerful incentive (relentless
pressure on price and delivery speed) and ready means (lax regulation) to reduce
production costs by running roughshod over the rights of workers. This is the
dynamic that explains the contemporary sweatshop and is at the root of every
major category of labor rights abuse in the garment sector, including the heed-
less safety practices that have advanced the macabre parade of fires and building
collapses in Bangladesh and elsewhere.

The astounding growth of garment production in Bangladesh is a testament
to the overriding importance of cost reduction to brands and retailers and their
willingness to tolerate abusive and dangerous working conditions as a means
to that end, despite their public insistence that worker rights rank high as a
corporate priority. Bangladesh offers very few advantages to brands and retailers: productivity levels have never been high, transportation infrastructure is
shambolic and has been slow to improve, political instability is a constant threat
(Berg et al. 2011). Meanwhile, the country's record on labor rights is among the
worst in the industry (Wood 2010; International Trade Union Confederation
2014; Human Rights Watch 2015a). Until the government came under significant pressure in 2013, there were no unions in Bangladesh, and in the face of
continued resistance from factory management, less than 5 percent of workers

are currently organized (Westervelt 2015). The "troublemakers" are fired, often threatened with police repression, and, increasingly, face violent retaliation (Ali Manik and Bajaj 2012).

How does a highly inefficient producer with a terrible human rights reputation become the second-largest garment exporter on the globe? It does so by offering labor costs lower, by a sizable margin, than any of its competitors—low enough to more than offset the inefficiency—and by betting that the unsavory means utilized to achieve those cost savings, and the ugly consequences for workers, will not deter brands and retailers from taking advantage.

The year before the Rana Plaza collapse, Bangladeshi garment factories exported garments worth more than $80 billion at retail, enough production to give two-dozen pieces of clothing to every person in the United States.[1] The factories employ more than 3.5 million workers in the process, over a million more than were employed in the US garment industry during its mid-twentieth-century peak. Only China, the undisputed industrial behemoth of the early twenty-first century, has a larger garment sector than Bangladesh—and, with garment-worker wages in China now high by industry standards, at $1.25 an hour, Bangladesh and other super-low-cost producers are taking over a growing chunk of China's business (BGMEA 2015).

Relentless Price Pressure

The relentless, and spectacularly successful, drive of apparel brands and retailers for lower production costs is reflected in the trend in the retail price of clothing. Between 1994 and 2014, the overall price of consumer goods in the United States increased by 87 percent; for apparel, prices *declined* by 6 percent (US Bureau of Labor Statistics 2015). This means that, after inflation, the price American consumers pay for clothing has dropped 50 percent over the last two decades.

Given the effect of low-cost imports on wages in the North, it is debatable whether saving a few hundred dollars a year in clothing costs represents a genuine benefit to Northern consumers; what is beyond dispute is that garment workers in the Global South pay for these savings in the form of depressed income and substandard conditions of work.

A recent study by the Center for American Progress and the Worker Rights Consortium found that the real wages of apparel workers in the large majority of top apparel-producing countries *decreased* substantially between 2001 and 2011; the study shows that the prevailing wage for garment workers in all of the countries was found to be a small fraction of a conservatively defined living wage (Center for American Progress et al. 2013). In Bangladesh, the minimum wage for garments workers is 32 cents an hour—*after* a 77 percent increase in

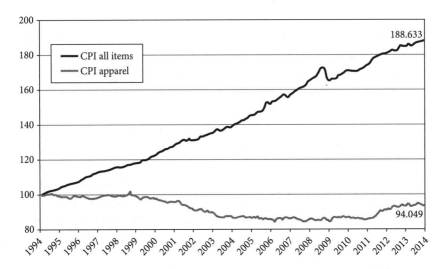

FIGURE 1.1   The falling prices of apparel relative to all consumer goods
Source: US Bureau of Labor Statistics 2015

2013, implemented in the face of mass worker protests and growing international pressure on the Bangladesh government driven by revulsion over the Rana Plaza collapse. This 32 cents an hour is less than it costs a garment worker to shelter, clothe, and feed herself, much less her dependents.

Failure of Corporate Self-Regulation

Low wages, abusive conditions, and disregard for workplace safety keep production costs low, but they also create risks for brands and retailers, as the Tazreen fire and the Rana collapse demonstrate. For apparel corporations, brand image and reputation are highly valued assets; devaluation of these assets, through association with sweatshop conditions, can yield lasting damage.

Faced with stinging criticism over conditions in their overseas factories, and forced to acknowledge that governments in the countries where they are producing do not regulate factories effectively, apparel corporations, beginning in the 1990s, publicly accepted responsibility for policing labor practices in their supply chains.[2] Today, every major apparel brand and retailer has a labor rights "code of conduct" and a factory monitoring program, involving a pledge to regularly inspect their supplier factories using either in-house personnel or contract auditors, to press factories to correct any labor rights or safety violations identified, and to stop doing business with factories that refuse to comply.

This is not regulation, it is self-regulation. These are voluntary programs; brands and retailers promise to ensure respect for worker rights and worker safety in their supply chains, but they make no binding commitments to any third party. Whether apparel corporations follow through on their pledges is at their sole discretion. The monitoring process is controlled and run by the brands and retailers; the inspectors work for them. The brands and retailers tell the inspectors what to look for, exclude those issues they choose to exclude, and act—or don't act—on the inspectors' findings as they see fit. Public pressure to live up to their official labor rights promises can, in some circumstances, be brought to bear on brands and retailers, but the brands and retailers sharply limit transparency in order to minimize the ability of advocates to do so: inspection results are kept secret (from workers as well as from the public) and the only information that gets reported is what the brands and retailers choose to report (generally, glossy paeans to the great progress ostensibly being achieved, backed up by little to no hard information).

The official goal of these programs is in conflict with the brands' and retailers' short-term economic interests: it costs more to produce under good conditions than bad conditions. Factories that observe the minimum wage, pay required overtime premiums, refrain from forcing workers to stay overnight when orders are due, provide maternity leave where the law requires it, and invest in nec-essary safety equipment will have higher production costs than factories that ignore these requirements, and will therefore need higher prices. Thus if brands are successful in compelling their factories to come into compliance with the applicable local law and the brands' own labor standards, the brands' costs will increase and profits will be reduced accordingly. The cost impact of genuine compliance is modest, but significant, and cost sensitivity is deeply ingrained in the culture of the industry. Thus if brands and retailers faithfully carry out their labor rights pledges, they will produce a result that they otherwise strive relentlessly to avoid.

Given these realities, is not surprising that these programs have failed to achieve high levels of labor rights and worker safety compliance in global apparel supply chains. When the goal of achieving the lowest production costs comes into con-flict with corporations' labor rights promises—as it does on a daily basis—there is nothing to stop companies from subordinating fundamental human rights concerns to immediate financial exigencies. Factory monitoring programs are honor systems operating in a cut-throat business, with predictable results.

The failure of the self-regulatory approach has been brought into stark-est relief by recent factory disasters. Every one of the apparel factories where dozens or hundreds of workers have died in the last several years had been repeatedly inspected under the brands' and retailers' monitoring regimes. The conflagration in September 2012 at the Ali Enterprises factory (in Karachi, Pakistan) was the worst factory fire in world history, with a death toll of more than 250. Incredibly, the factory had been certified as a safe and responsible workplace just three weeks before the fire, under Social Accountability International's factory inspection program (Walsh and Greenhouse 2012a; Walsh and Greenhouse 2012b). It was also earlier inspected by UL Responsible Sourcing, an auditing firm contracted by the German retailer Kik (CCC and SOMO 2013). The various factories in the Rana Plaza building that collapsed in April 2013 all produced for brands and retailers with factory monitoring programs, including Loblaw (owner of Joe Fresh) and Children's Place (CCC 2015). Two of the factories had undergone, and passed, inspections carried out by the industry-run Business Social Compliance Initiative (BSCI 2013). The Garib & Garib factory in Dhaka, which burned in February 2010, killing 22 people, had been audited repeatedly by H&M, a leading member of the Fair Labor Association (Hickman 2010). That's It Sportswear, another factory in Dhaka where 29 workers died in a fire in December 2010, had been monitored by all of the major brands that produced there. These include Gap, a board member of SAI and a leading participant in the Global Social Compliance Program; VF Corporation, owner of Timberland, Nautica, and other brands and a key player in Worldwide Responsible Accredited Production; and PVH Corp., one of the founders of the FLA (VF Corporation 2011; Maquila Solidarity Network 2012a). The fire at Tazreen Fashions, where at least 112 workers died in November 2012, came after years of labor audits by Walmart (the founder of the Global Social Compliance Program) and other "socially responsible" brands and retailers. Tazreen, like all of these factories, had grave safety deficiencies (Henn 2013). Yet none of the audits by Walmart or the other buyers yielded any corrective action or gave a single word of warning to the workers.

All of these factories were covered by one or more of the multistakeholder monitoring organizations. All were producing for brands and retailers that claim to be operating robust factory inspection programs. All of these tragedies were preventable. Aside from empty promises routinely issued in the wake of each disaster, the brands and retailers did not deviate from their course: continued increases in production in countries with unsafe factories and continued use of obviously inadequate inspection regimes as the only means to address worker rights and worker safety.

What is perhaps most shocking is that even after similar disasters were repeated again and again, inspectors were not even asked to look for hazards that were killing workers. The two biggest factors in the mass deaths of apparel workers—absence of properly constructed fire exits and flaws in building construction—have not even been part of the audit checklists that are used by industry monitors. For example, it is likely that none of the apparel factories in Bangladesh had proper fire exits, yet factory managers have credibly reported that this extremely hazardous form of noncompliance has never been raised in the audits that retailers have conducted in their factories (Alam 2012).

The auditing firm employees and brand personnel who conduct factory inspections do not have adequate training in fire and building safety to conduct competent assessments, a fact brands themselves have acknowledged (Greenhouse and Yardley 2012; Clifford and Greenhouse 2013). Visits to factories are too brief for inspectors to sufficiently evaluate all of the issues they claim to investigate. Even when violations are found, they have no power to address the root causes of problems; voluntary monitoring carries no influence over production, order contracts, or funding of repairs.

These programs have been in place in all major apparel producing countries for more than a decade (AFL-CIO 2013). Most factories are inspected several times a year. Despite its ineffectiveness, not only has this system remained fundamentally unchanged but its use has also proliferated. The programs are clearly not designed as a tool to protect workers, but rather serve as an alibi for brands. The problem is not technical, it is economic and political; in a price-driven, hyper-competitive, high-pressure industry like apparel, self-policing doesn't work. The result is perpetuation of a status quo where exploited workers are killed en masse with appalling regularity.

Bangladesh: The World's Sweatshop

The modern epicenter of industrial horror in today's global economy is Bangladesh. Since 2005, nearly 2,000 people have died in factory fires and building collapses in Bangladesh. Wages are the lowest anywhere in the industry: a prevailing wage of 31 cents an hour (up from 18 cents an hour last year as a result of international pressure and domestic worker organizing). The cost of living is comparatively high; the World Bank pegs the cost of living at more than one fifth that of the United States. Key protections in labor law, from pregnancy leave to limits on overtime hours, are routinely ignored. Verbal abuse of workers is standard operating procedure, and physical and sexual abuse is not uncommon. Any attempt by workers to address these issues by advocating for better conditions and wages is met with swift and harsh repression. Until the government came under significant pressure in 2013, there were no unions in Bangladesh, and in the face of continued resistance from factory management, less than 3 percent of workers are currently organized. The "trouble-makers" are fired, often threatened with police repression and, increasingly, face violent retaliation. If there is a race to the bottom, Bangladesh has won it.

In the face of this deplorable labor rights situation, brands and retailers have been pouring business *into* Bangladesh. H&M (one of the largest clothing retailers in Europe) and Walmart each buy more than $1 billion worth of apparel a year from Bangladesh; Inditex (the owner of Zara) is not far behind. With approximately 3,500 factories and 3.5 million apparel workers, it has become the second largest apparel producer in history (behind China and far above the peak of the US industry). The garment sector has grown in spite of significant disadvantages, such as political corruption, low productivity, and lack of transportation infrastructure. It is the rock-bottom prices that attract foreign business, which is made possible because of three factors: the industry's lowest wages, ruthless suppression of unions, and a breathtaking disregard for worker safety. The brands and retailers say they want improved working conditions, but they are sending an economic message to factories that is far louder and clearer: keep cutting costs and business will continue to boom. The same dynamics apply throughout the brands' and retailers' entire global supply chains, but wages and conditions are worst in Bangladesh, where workers continue to die by the hundreds in preventable disasters.

The dynamics of the apparel industry have manifested themselves so destructively in Bangladesh for a number of reasons. Regulatory efforts are weak, even compared with other developing countries. Accounting for over 80 percent of exports, the garment industry, which resists enforcement of labor standards, is tremendously influential in Bangladesh politics (Hassan 2014; Ullah Mirdha 2014). The Bangladesh National Building Code is a compelling work of fiction; it has nothing to do with the way buildings are constructed, maintained, and owned by apparel manufacturers (Housing and Building Research Institute 2015). In most other countries, apparel factories are usually warehouse-style constructions that are built out rather than up. For geographic and political reasons, Bangladesh uses tall buildings, which are particularly vulnerable to fires and structural collapse. Dangerous conditions are the norm rather than the exception.

Fires usually start because of substandard electrical wiring. Casualties result because most factories are in multistory buildings that lack adequate emergency exits and other essential safety systems (such as emergency lighting and fire extinguishers). Alarm systems are frequently faulty and sometimes require manual operation (that is, amidst a factory blaze, a worker must stay in the factory and constantly operate the alarm in order for it to sound). Exits that do exist are fraught with problems: they are usually locked (purportedly to prevent theft), unprotected and unenclosed (without fire doors), and lead to the interior of the building rather than outside. Routes are frequently (and illegally) packed with highly flammable textile goods. Stairwells act as chimneys rather than safe pathways. Workers often escape fires only because they were fortunate enough to survive a leap from a third- or fourth-story windows.

Collapses are the result of substandard construction and near-zero enforcement of the building code. Additional stories are often added to buildings after original construction. Structures have insufficient column strength to support heavy factories on higher floors. Structural flaws abound and unpermitted construction is rampant. These buildings would be ordered shut down tomorrow if they were located in the United States.

To add to the disarray, when disasters are imminent, the situations are improperly handled by factory management. Amidst fires or the buckling of foundation columns, workers are frequently told to go back to work, under pressure to avoid losing production hours or missing quotas so that contracts can be met. In numerous instances, this behavior has been responsible for increasing the death toll by orders of magnitude.

Confronting these deplorable circumstances in Bangladesh, a united front of unions and workers' rights organizations around the world designed a program to address the underlying causes of catastrophes and secure the safety of workers: the Accord on Fire and Building Safety in Bangladesh.

The Story of the Accord
Structure and Major Provisions

The Accord is a breakthrough in workers' rights. It represents a fundamental departure from the voluntary industry monitoring initiatives that have been utilized in Bangladesh for more than a decade and have utterly failed to protect the safety of workers. It is a binding agreement between corporations and worker representatives, enforceable as a legal contract, that requires the brands and retailers to pay hundreds of millions of dollars to convert death traps into safe factories (Accord on Fire and Building Safety in Bangladesh 2013). As of May 2015, more than two hundred apparel corporations have signed the agreement, including three of the world's four largest fashion retailers and two of the three largest general retailers (Accord on Fire and Building Safety in Bangladesh 2015a). Two global unions and eight Bangladeshi unions are signatories on the labor side. The Accord covers more than 1,700 factories and 2 million workers, accounting for over half of all apparel production in Bangladesh.

The program is governed by a steering committee of seven members: three chosen by retailers, three chosen by worker representative unions, and one chairperson chosen by the International Labour Organization (ILO). The committee hires a chief safety inspector and a lead training coordinator, each responsible for hiring and managing their respective teams of inspectors and trainers. There are currently thirty staff members of the Accord, with plans to expand to nearly one hundred. Retailers that participate in the Accord contribute up to $500,000 annually, proportional to their volume of orders, to fund the inspections and administration of the program (in addition to any repairs necessary). The program has a $24 million budget for the first two years to cover inspection costs ($9 million in the first year and $15 million in the second, not including costs of factory renovations). The Bangladesh Accord Foundation oversees the program and has dual headquarters in Dhaka and Amsterdam.

The initiative calls for independent fire and building safety inspections in every factory (something that has never happened in most of these buildings). Reports of each inspection must be made public. The first round of inspections, involving 1,106 factories, was completed as of October 2014 (Accord on Fire and Building Safety in Bangladesh 2014; Accord on Fire and Building Safety in Bangladesh 2015b). All safety violations must be brought to code in accordance with corrective action plans that are issued after each inspection.

Major renovations, repairs, and retrofitting are needed in most facilities. Under the Accord, retailers must ensure that factories have enough money to make the factories safe. The means of doing so is left up to the discretion of each retailer; this can include making a joint investment with the factory, providing loans, soliciting contributions from governments and donors, offering business incentives, or paying for the expenses themselves. (The total cost of upgrading Bangladeshi factories to meet existing safety standards likely exceeds $1 billion.)

Retailers must terminate contracts with factories that do not comply and help the resulting unemployed workers find gainful employment at safe factories. These policies and long-term commitments fundamentally change apparel sourcing by incentivizing adherence to safety standards.

Every factory is also required to have a health and safety committee, with at least 50 percent of the members being workers chosen democratically (by the factory's union, if there is one). Workers can confidentially lodge complaints about factory conditions to Accord inspectors (through two-way channels much more robust than "hotlines"). Workers also have the right to refuse to enter the workplace if they believe it is unsafe, without fear of discrimination or retaliation. In combination with other provisions that involve the input of worker representative unions at all levels of the program, workers do not just participate in the Accord, they can influence every part of it, from what happens on the factory floor to the highest decision-making processes.

These commitments are binding and legally enforceable. Any disputes can be resolved through an international arbitration process, the decisions legally enforceable in each retailer's home country. Although the scope and breadth of the Accord is unprecedented, such legal arrangements have historical roots, the earliest being jobbers' agreements in which the retail buyer (jobber) shares liability for the working conditions of a subcontracted facility (see chapter 13 for further discussion of the jobbers' agreement). The first of these contracts were negotiated by the International Ladies' Garment Workers' Union (ILGWU) nearly one hundred years ago, and within a few decades of their implementation, the contracts transformed working conditions of the US garment industry.

Origin of the Accord

In December 2010, 29 workers were trapped and killed in a factory blaze at the That's It Sportswear factory in Bangladesh, despite the fact that this was one of the newer buildings in Bangladesh and was viewed as state-of-the-art and one of the safest. The preceding years were plagued with similar tragedies (notably at the Spectrum Sweater, KTS Textiles, Phoenix Garment, Sayem Fashions, Garib & Garib factories). Between 2006 and 2010, 493 workers lost their lives in at least 224 separately reported factory fires (CCC 2012a). Over the years, worker rights organizations had pressed brands for fundamental changes in the wake of each disaster, but there was no movement. The relentless regularity of such horrific incidents inspired labor unions and NGOs to join together and propose a solution: a binding agreement under which brands and retailers would be contractually required to make their factories safe.

For two years, despite broad backing in the labor rights community, all brands and retailers (led by Walmart) rejected this proposal. Then in 2012 PVH Corp.—the owner of Tommy Hilfiger, Calvin Klein, and other major brands—agreed to sign, in part to minimize the embarrassment from a pending ABC News story on the December 2010 disaster (PVH 2012). Tchibo, a German retailer, signed shortly thereafter (Barrie 2012).

However, the Accord required the support of more brands to be viable and most retailers remained unmoved, despite the long series of mass fatality disasters in Bangladesh. The horrific blaze at Tazreen Fashions, one of the deadliest fires the apparel industry has ever endured, was still not enough to motivate additional brands to fundamentally change their approach to safety in Bangladesh (Eidelson 2012; Worker Rights Consortium 2012). It required a disaster of unprecedented magnitude, yielding unprecedented media coverage, to convince brands and retailers that it was in their interest to act.

The Rana Plaza collapse on April 24, 2013 changed the landscape of negotiations for workers' rights in Bangladesh. Apparel brands faced tremendous public scrutiny over the humanitarian crisis of Bangladeshi garment workers (Ali Manik et al. 2013; Fossett 2013; Johnson and Alam 2013; PBS Newshour 2013; Stillman 2013). A coalition of workers' rights groups set a deadline of May 15 for the apparel companies to take action, after which they would finalize a plan for the Accord and move forward with implementation of a safety plan. Two days before the deadline, H&M, the largest purchaser of garments from Bangladesh, and Inditex, the world's largest fashion retailer and owner of Zara, signed on to the Accord. Other companies followed suit. Within hours, C&A of the Netherlands and two major British retailers—Primark and Tesco—also signed.[3] By May 15, twenty-four companies had confirmed their participation in the Accord. The following weeks brought more signatories, and by October more than one hundred brands had joined the agreement.

Industry Maneuvering

Some major brands and retailers, particular those like Walmart, Gap, and VF Corporation that are based in the United States and have little or no history of productive cooperation with labor unions, ultimately refused to sign the Accord—instead forming a corporate-controlled organization called the Alliance for Bangladesh Worker Safety (the Alliance). The Alliance corporations rejected the enforceable commitments to worker representatives that the Accord corporations have embraced (however reluctantly), yet attempted nonetheless to defend the Alliance as a legitimate alternative to the Accord, imbued with an equivalent commitment to protecting the safety of workers.

The formation of the Alliance represented both a victory and a defeat for labor rights advocates and worker organizations. On the one hand, the Alliance includes, in official terms, a number of the same commitments that are integral to the Accord and that advocates had repeatedly demanded, and major brands and retailers invariably rejected, in the years prior to the Rana collapse: that brands and retailers would assist factories with the cost of safety renovations, that the results both of initial inspections and assessments of progress would be made public, that factories would be required to accept meaningful levels of worker participation in determining policy and practice on safety issues in the workplace. In forming the Alliance, its corporate members thus implicitly admitted that their critics had been right, and they had been wrong, about the adequacy of the industry's pre-Rana approach to worker safety. At the same time, by rejecting the third-party enforceability at the heart of the Accord, and insisting instead that the Alliance's members should be trusted to self-enforce, Walmart, Gap, VF, and their allies had ensured, in the view of labor rights advocates and unions, that these corporations would never fulfill the new commitments that the pressures created by the Rana collapse had finally forced them to make.

Looking Forward

If labor unions and NGOs are successful in enforcing the Accord, the initiative will have a profound impact on the safety of more than 2 million apparel workers and will help transform the second largest apparel industry in the world. It will also serve as a model for a new approach to protecting worker rights, demonstrating that binding, enforceable agreements that compel brands and retailers to pay for improved conditions can succeed where voluntary, corporate-controlled schemes have failed. Unfortunately, the formation of the Alliance ensures that many factories in Bangladesh remain, at least for now, outside the Accord's umbrella of protection. Workers in these factories must hope that fear of further reputational damage will be sufficient to convince the Alliance brands to honor at least some of their commitments, even in the absence of genuine enforceability.

2

FROM PUBLIC REGULATION TO PRIVATE ENFORCEMENT

How CSR Became Managerial Orthodoxy

Richard P. Appelbaum

The safety and well-being of workers across our supply chain is the Responsible Sourcing group's top priority, which is why Walmart suppliers are contractually required to sign our Standards for Suppliers before they're approved to produce merchandise for sale at Walmart. These Standards for Suppliers make clear our fundamental expectations for suppliers and factories regarding the treatment of workers and impact on the environment. Suppliers are also required to display our Standards for Suppliers in the local language in all factories where products are made for us, so workers know our expectations of suppliers and factory management.

—Walmart 2014 Global Responsibility Report, Statement on Compliance and Sourcing

Walmart, the world's largest corporation in 2015, invests in "comprehensive social audits across our global supply chain." Its factory audits—reportedly often unannounced—are conducted by "independent accredited and internationally recognized auditing firms." Factories are then said to be reaudited every six to twenty-four months, based on the results. This comprehensive auditing system is designed to verify that factories "meet or exceed" Walmart's standards, which include assurance that all labor is voluntary, prohibitions against child labor, requirements that hours are not excessive (and are consistent with local laws or regulations), and that factories provide safe and healthy working conditions (Walmart 2014).

On November 24, 2012, a fire at the Tazreen Fashion apparel factory in Dhaka, Bangladesh, claimed 112 lives and injured 200 others, making it the deadliest factory fire in the history of a country long plagued by factory fires. Workers found themselves trapped by the absence of safe and accessible fire exits, windows blocked by iron grills, a lack of adequate fire preparedness training, and the fact that the building was at the time under construction: five additional stories were being added to the original three-story structure, even as garment production continued as usual.

In this unsafe environment, ten workers perished on Tazreen's fifth floor, where they were sewing Walmart's Faded Glory shorts. Walmart, one of the many companies producing garments at the factory (Maquila Solidarity Network 2012b),[1] claimed it was unaware that its Faded Glory shorts were being sewn at Tazreen through a subcontracting arrangement. Yet the factory's owner reported that Walmart's local office had audited the factory a year earlier, finding only problems with excessive overtime. A Walmart spokesperson confirmed this, acknowledging that the company had conducted at least two inspections in 2011, but claiming that Walmart had stopped production "many months before the fire" (Yardley 2012).

How could such a disaster occur in a factory where one of Walmart's "comprehensive social audits across our global supply chain" had previously reported no fire or safety violations? Nor was the Tazreen fire an exception. Between 1990 and 2012 (the year of the Tazreen fire), nearly a thousand people perished in factory fires in Bangladesh.[2] Yet during this same period, all major corporations have embraced a commitment to socially responsible business practices. In Bangladesh and around the world, businesses have adopted codes of conduct much like Walmart's, created departments dedicated to overseeing and implementing those codes, and hired specialized firms to audit the factories throughout their supply chains to assure compliance with the codes. As I shall argue below, as well as elsewhere in this book (see especially chapters 1 and 3), most of the Bangladesh factories in which fires occurred had been given clean bills of health when audited by internationally recognized social compliance firms.

In order to account for the failures of private enforcement, it is important to understand that today's globalization differs from that of the post–World War II era because of the role now played by large retail multinationals—the "big buyers"[3] that have largely replaced the large manufacturing firms that characterized the twentieth century. The Walmarts, Targets, and Tescos now rule global supply chains, along with brands such as Apple and Nike. They make the markets, set the prices, and structure the global distribution of labor for a gigantic stream of consumer commodities. The loss of US manufacturing firms to low-wage countries has entailed not just cheap labor competition from abroad but also a shift in power within the structures of world capitalism, from manufacturing to a retail sector that today controls the supply chains that encircle the globe.

In this new world of global supply chains driven by big buyers, the brand has emerged as a key reputational asset: from Apple to Zara, firms depend on brand image as their key asset. Although today's big buyers do not make any products themselves, they do engage in two activities that are critical for success in a globally competitive world: designing ever-changing products and convincing consumers that they cannot do without them. The firms that sit atop global supply chains are best understood as "branded marketers" (Gereffi 1999), for whom image is everything. Since child labor, sweatshop conditions, and worker deaths are hardly compatible with a positive image, the reliance on branding has proven to be an Achilles heel.

Corporate Concern with Workers' Rights

Academics who write about corporate behavior have for more than a half century argued that firms should be not only be profit maximizers but good citizens as well. Corporations were more than happy to concur, with the proviso that good citizenship was not contingent on government regulation or bargaining with trade unions. Rather, corporate spokesmen argued, the best results would come from self-regulation.

In 1951 the influential management consultant Peter Drucker published *The New Society: The Anatomy of the Industrial Order*, in which he called for "plant self-government"—a form of corporatism in which workers (or at least their representatives) would govern some aspects of the workplace, partnering with management to create what he argued would result in a mutually beneficial alternative to labor-capital strife. This was a time when the United States enjoyed unrivaled global economic dominance, vertically integrated manufacturing was the dominant mode of industrial capitalism, and corporations were largely national rather than global entities—a time, in other words, when workers in sectors dominated by large corporations enjoyed a significant degree of countervailing power[4] through their unions.[5] Under these conditions—the heyday of postwar national capitalism—Drucker argued that corporations were not fundamentally driven by the profit motive but were instead political bureaucracies with responsibilities for their communities.

This view was widely shared by those academics who studied corporations and corporate power. Two years after Drucker's *New Society* appeared, the economist Howard R. Bowen published *Social Responsibilities of the Businessman*, in which he posed two rhetorical questions: "Are businessmen, by virtue of their strategic position and decision-making power, obligated to consider social consequences when making private decisions? If so, do they have social responsibilities that transcend obligations to owners or stockholders?" Bowen's response was short and simple: "the answer to both these questions is clearly yes" (Bowen 2013, 2). Then, echoing Drucker and Bowen, the economist Carl Kaysen in 1957 published an article in the prestigious *American Economic Review* proclaiming the existence of the "soulful corporation," in which management no longer focused exclusively on maximizing return but rather "sees itself as responsible to stockholders, employees, customers, the general public, and, perhaps most important, the firm itself as an institution. . . . To the employees, management owes high wages, pensions and insurance systems, medical care programs, stable employment, agreeable working conditions, a human personnel policy" (Kaysen 1957, 313).

The idea that businesses should (and could) be guided by ethical principles was given a boost during the struggle to end apartheid in South Africa during the 1970s. Reverend Leon Sullivan, a prominent black leader from Philadelphia, had joined the General Motors Board of Directors in 1971, at a time when GM was the largest corporate employer of blacks in South Africa.[6] In 1977, as part of the divestment campaign directed at the apartheid regime in South Africa, Sullivan crafted a set of ethical principles to guide the behavior of corporations (like General Motors) that were doing business in South Africa.

The original Sullivan Principles called for the end of workplace segregation, equal pay for equal work, increasing the number of nonwhites in management and supervisory positions (and providing the training required to accomplish this), improving the quality of life for nonwhites outside the workplace, and fair and equal employment practices for all workers.[7] Sullivan eventually came to endorse corporate civil disobedience against apartheid laws, the freeing of Nelson Mandela, and an end to apartheid itself. Sullivan's efforts eventually convinced more than a hundred firms to pull out of South Africa, contributing to the end of apartheid in 1993.

The Sullivan Principles reflected the view that corporations had an obligation to behave ethically, ushering in a strong moral (some would say public relations) obligation that corporations behave "soulfully," at least when it came to racial equality. This obligation was not purely ethical, however. It also stemmed from Title VII of the 1964 Civil Rights Act, which prohibited employment discrimination on the basis of race, color, religion, sex, and national origin,[8] opening a door to the possibility of government regulation. That possibility—along with the rise of anti-sweatshop activism in the following decades—led corporations to call for a "trust me" approach to labor abuses based on self-regulation and private enforcement.

Anti-Sweatshop Activism, Private Enforcement, and Reputation Management

Beginning in the 1990s, well-publicized revelations of labor abuses in Asian contract factories tarnished the images of major US brands such as Nike, Gap, and Kathie Lee (a line sold at Walmart). Anti-sweatshop campaigns put additional pressure on these companies to address the problems that were proving to be the norm rather than the exception. The emergence of firms that publicly express a commitment to behave in socially responsible ways is the direct result of revelations about corporate abuses, worker strikes, and activist campaigns that began in the 1990s and continue to the present.

As early as 1992, Levi Strauss, concerned about media exposure of working conditions in its contract factories, adopted a code of conduct and created an internal monitoring program. But Nike, the footwear giant, proved to be the first major firm to garner worldwide media attention for abuses throughout its supply chain. Reporters and activists knew about labor problems in Nike's Indonesian contract factories in the early 1990s, but Nike initially denied any responsibility, its general manager for Indonesia admitting that although he had heard of problems in a number of factories, "I don't know that I need to know . . . they are our subcontractors. It's not within our scope to investigate" (Vogel 2006, 78). Tenacious coverage of Nike's factory problems forced the company to rethink this position.

In August 1992 *Harpers Magazine* featured an article by Jeffrey Ballinger entitled "The New Free-Trade Heel: Nike's Profits Jump on the Backs of Asian Workers." The article featured Sadisah, a young Indonesian woman who worked ten hours a day, six days a week, making Nike athletic shoes. Sadisah earned 14 cents an hour, which, according to Ballinger's calculations, meant she would have to work an entire month to purchase the pair of shoes she labored over. The article, which included a photograph of Sadisah's meager paystub, also featured Michael Jordan, the basketball superstar who was at the time (and remains) a major part of the Nike brand. (The Nike Air Jordan XX8SE currently retails at $150.) Sadisah, Ballinger estimated, would have to labor 44,000 years to earn as much as Jordan's $20 million endorsement deal.

Ballinger, who headed a small NGO called Press4Change, proved to be a tireless antagonist for Nike, whose identity as a brand did not include employing young women as virtual slaves in Indonesian sweatshops. Ballinger's article was not the first revelation to embarrass Nike, however. Ballinger himself had been writing about Nike's labor problems for at least a year, and for several years Indonesian trade union publications and local newspapers had been running accounts of abuses in Nike factories. As early as 1989 a US Agency for International Development (USAID) study had already documented pervasive minimum wage violations. That year Human Rights Watch and the International Labor Rights Research and Education Fund filed a complaint with the US Trade Representative calling for a review of Indonesia's benefits under the Generalized Systems of Preferences. A series of strikes—some dealt with harshly by Indonesian authorities—generated additional bad press for Nike. By the time Ballinger's article had appeared, a US State Department report to Congress had documented minimum wage violations and Nike's Sung Hwa factory was in the midst of a protracted strike (Ballinger 2015).

In response to these events and revelations, in 1992 Nike implemented its first code of conduct, a Memorandum of Understanding and Code of Conduct for Indonesian Business Partners. The code prohibited the use of forced labor, set minimum-age standards (either fourteen years, local legal limits, or age of compulsory schooling—whichever was highest), required compliance with local legal wage and overtime standards, set a sixty-hour weekly maximum for work, and required compliance with local health and safety standards (Heuer and Ronkainen n.d.). The code did not end reported abuses in Nike factories, however.

Long before "going viral" entered the vocabulary with the arrival of social media, throughout the 1990s criticism of Nike's labor practices grew exponentially—in the popular press, television documentaries, NGO reports, films, and government studies. Anti-Nike protests, organized by the Campaign for Labor Rights and other NGOs, began in 1996 in the United States and Europe; the following year US students began protesting Nike's links with universities at Penn State, Florida State, the University of Illinois, North Carolina, Colorado, and Michigan.[9]

In response, in 1996 Nike established a department charged with addressing workplace issues in its contract factories, and two years later—faced with bad press and flagging demand—Nike CEO Phil Knight gave a well-publicized speech at the National Press Club, admitting that "the Nike product has become synonymous with slave wages, forced overtime, and arbitrary abuse. I truly believe the American consumer doesn't want to buy products made under abusive conditions." Knight pledged to increase monitoring and adopt US clean air standards for Nike's contract factories, as well as increase the minimum age to eighteen for workers in its contract shoe factories. Knight also agreed to permit monitors from independent NGOs to join its own factory auditors, and even predicted "that these are practices which the conscientious, good companies will follow in the 21st century" (Cushman 1998). The following year Nike played a key role in the creation of the Fair Labor Association (FLA), a corporate-funded NGO charged with overseeing labor practices in the garment and footwear industries.

Nike was not the only company whose labor practices created public concern during the 1990s. In 1996 the popular TV co-host Kathie Lee Gifford licensed her name to Walmart to produce the Kathie Lee line of clothing, which boasted that some of the profits went to support children's charities. Charles Kernaghan, head of the National Labor Committee (a small but highly vocal NGO focused on Central America) testified before Congress that her clothing line was being made by thirteen- and fourteen-year-old girls working twenty-hour shifts in Honduran factories. When Kathie Lee denied the charges on the *Today Show*,

Kernaghan confronted her with Wendy Diaz, one of the Honduran child factory workers. Kathie Lee broke down and cried; her lack of knowledge about where her Walmart line of clothing was produced spoke volumes about the nature of global supply chains (Strom 1996). When a US Labor Department investigation found that Walmart's Kathie Lee line was also being made under sweatshop conditions in New York City, the publicity made clear that domestic production suffered from the same problems as foreign production (Bobrowsky 1999). In 1994 Kernaghan also launched a well-publicized campaign against Liz Claiborne, which led the company to adopt a code of conduct. The following year Kernaghan took on The Gap, at the time one of the world's largest apparel retailers; one of Gap's contract factories in El Salvador, Mandarin International, had fired workers who were trying to organize a labor union. Gap ultimately agreed to allow independent monitoring of its factory (Bair and Palpacuer 2013).

The most significant scandal, however, hit even closer to home when 72 mostly female workers from Thailand were found to be working as indentured servants in a working-class Los Angeles suburb. In what came to be known as the El Monte slave-shop case, the workers had been kept in a small factory complex, behind razor wire, some for as long as seven years. Their starvation wages did not cover the cost of their indenture—the fees they had to pay to be illegally trafficked to the United States and the provisions they were forced to buy in the company store. The workers slept in crowded, unsanitary quarters—some in the same workspace as their sewing machines. Their plight became known only when one of the workers escaped. They avoided deportation only when the Asian Pacific American Legal Center's attorney, Julie Su,[10] took up their case. The workers eventually received citizenship, as well as a $2 million settlement from the firms whose garments were found hanging in the sweatshop: Montgomery Ward, Mervyns, BUM International, and LF Sportswear.[11] The settlement included no admission of wrongdoing by the firms, whose contracts were with licensed factories that were secretly funneling work to the El Monte factory—licensed factories that were part of a self-monitoring scheme called the Compliance Alliance. At the time Los Angeles was home to some 150,000 garment workers, many undocumented, and most working under sweatshop conditions.[12]

The Road to Global Workers Rights: Detours along the Way

The International Labour Organization (ILO), today a UN agency, was created in the aftermath of the First World War. It was part of a larger movement, involving governments and labor unions, to regulate labor conditions in industrial nations during the first third of the twentieth century. Organized labor was more than merely present at the ILO's founding: Samuel Gompers, head of the American Federation of Labor (AFL), chaired the 1919 Labor Commission—comprised of representatives from nine countries—that was responsible for drafting the ILO's constitution (ILO 2015a). The ILO proudly claims that it "is the only tripartite U.N. agency with government, employer, and worker representatives . . . a unique forum in which the governments and the social partners of the economy of its Member States can freely and openly debate and elaborate labor standards and policies" (ILO 2015b). This tripartite structure goes back to its origins, which envisioned a world in which labor and capital might work together in a mutually beneficial fashion, under the watchful eye of the state. Tripartism was seen as key because this arrangement seemed to best reflect the existing power relations in democratic industrial societies, thereby legitimating the resulting labor standards and collective bargaining standards. During the course of the twentieth century, both prior to and after becoming part of the newly created United Nations in 1946, the ILO enacted some 190 conventions governing workers' rights.

The UN Gets Involved

In 1977, following a decade of debate and discussion about the emerging strength of multinational corporations, the ILO drew on its workers' rights conventions when it adopted the Tripartite Declaration of Principles concerning Multinational Enterprises and Social Policy (the so-called MNE Declaration, "the first normative text concerned with this category of enterprises that was completed within the framework of the United Nations' system" (Günter 1981, p 1). The MNE Declaration, revised in 2006, notes that while multinationals "play an important part in the economies of most countries and in international economic relations . . . the advances made by multinational enterprises in organizing their operations beyond the national framework may lead to abuse of concentrations of economic power and to conflicts with national policy objectives and with the interest of the workers" (ILO 2006, 1–2). To remedy this situation it calls on all parties to respect human rights, obey local laws and regulations, promote secure and safe employment, eliminate discrimination, and in general follow ILO conventions on workers' rights. Consistent with the ILO's overall approach, however, the MNE Declaration is entirely voluntary—a set of aspirations and guidelines, laudable suggestions but lacking in any enforcement power.

By the mid-1990s it had become clear to the ILO that free trade was bringing hardship to many workers. The creation of the World Trade Organization (WTO) in 1994 had also spurred a debate over whether "social clauses," including labor standards, should be included in trade agreements (ILO 2015c).[13] Although free-trade proponents prevailed in terms of the rules governing the WTO, the ILO nonetheless in June 1998 adopted a Declaration on Fundamental Principles and Rights at Work, according to which "all Members, even if they have not ratified the Conventions in question, have an obligation arising from the very fact of membership in the Organization to respect, to promote and to realize, in good faith and in accordance with the Constitution, the principles concerning the fundamental rights which are the subject of those Conventions, namely: (1) freedom of association and the effective recognition of the right to collective bargaining, (2) the elimination of all forms of forced or compulsory labor, (3) the effective abolition of child labor, and (4) the elimination of discrimination in respect of employment and occupation" (ILO 2015d).These four fundamental rights are contained in eight core ILO Conventions.[14] Of the eight, the United States has ratified only two: the Conventions on the abolition of forced labor (no. 105) and the worst forms of child labor (no. 182).[15]

ILO Conventions do not, however, have the force of law: although they can provide aspirational standards, they lack enforcement mechanisms. Insofar as they derive from the ILO's tripartite organization, they also suffer from a twenty-first-century challenge: the ILO's underlying labor-capital-state model, grounded in the twentieth-century heyday of nationally based industrial capitalism, provides a weak framework for dealing with labor abuses. Today, global supply chains touch down in countries where independent unions are weak, nonexistent, and sometimes illegal. Governments in those countries are unlikely to enforce labor standards, either because they are corrupt or genuinely fear that strong enforcement of labor standards will result in capital flight. In short, two of the three key actors in the tripartite model—organized labor and the state—are missing in action.

THE GLOBAL SULLIVAN PRINCIPLES

Although the original Sullivan Principles were aimed at ending apartheid in South Africa, they resurfaced more than two decades later, in 1999, when Leon Sullivan and UN Secretary-General Kofi Annan announced the Global Sullivan Principles. These were intended to "support economic, social and political justice by companies where they do business; to support human rights and to encourage equal opportunity at all levels of employment, including racial and gender diversity on decision making committees and boards; to train and advance disadvantaged workers for technical, supervisory and management opportunities; and to assist with greater tolerance and understanding among peoples; thereby, helping to improve the quality of life for communities, workers and children with dignity and equality" (Leon H. Sullivan Foundation 2013).

The Global Sullivan Principles greatly extended the list of workers' rights, calling for the end of child labor, involuntary servitude, physical punishment, and other forms of abuse; the right to freedom of association; compensation sufficient to meet basic needs (what is today called a "living wage"); and full transparency with respect to implementation (University of Minnesota Human Rights Library 2015). The United Nations was now fully on board in support of workers' rights, having called for a set of principles long advocated by workers' rights activists.

The UN Global Compact and Guiding Principles on Human Rights

The United Nations took yet another step to affirm the importance of labor rights when it officially launched its Global Compact in 2000, today billed as the "largest corporate sustainability initiative in the world—with 10,000 signatories based in more than 140 countries." The Global Compact's approximately 8,000 member companies pledge to "voluntarily align their operations and strategies with ten universally accepted principles in the areas of human rights, labor, environment and anti-corruption." The four labor-related principles are the ILO's four Fundamental Principles and Rights at Work (UN Global Compact 2015a).

The Global Compact reflects in large part the efforts of the Harvard political scientist John Ruggie, whose scholarship focused on the mismatch between economic globalization and nation-based regulations and enforcement. Ruggie served as the UN Assistant Secretary-General for Strategic Planning from 1997 to 2001, a post created for him by UN Secretary-General Kofi Annan. Among his responsibilities, in addition to playing a key role in developing the UN Millennium Development Goals, was creating and then overseeing the Global Compact.

The Global Compact emphasizes that it "is not a code of conduct" but instead offers "a policy framework for organizing and developing corporate sustainability strategies." It is not legally binding, nor is it "a substitute for existing regulatory approaches," rather, it is "a purely voluntary initiative designed to promote innovation in relation to good corporate citizenship" (UN Global Compact 2015b). It costs little for a business to join the UN Global Compact: membership fees range from $250 ("suggested minimum") for companies with annual revenues below $50 million, to $15,000+ for companies whose annual revenues exceed $5 billion. Active firms are promised the benefits of information sharing across a global network of organizations, all of which profess a commitment to making the world a better place (UN Global Compact 2015c).

The UN Global Compact states explicitly that "the initiative is not designed, nor does it have the mandate or resources, to monitor or measure participants' performance . . . it is not now and does not aspire to become a compliance based initiative." If a member firm is accused by some party of "systematic or egregious abuses" that are "found not to be prima facie frivolous," the Global Compact Office may require the firm to provide a written account and work, in various ways, to remediate the problem; only in extreme cases might a firm be rendered inactive as a member. The only way a firm is likely to be rendered inactive is if it fails for two consecutive years to submit an annual "Communication on Progress," a public statement of steps taken to meet the Compact's goals (UN Global Compact 2015d).

Based on a 2012 survey of member corporations, in terms of overall sustainability efforts (which include, besides the four labor-related principles mentioned above, six other principles concerned with human rights, the environment, and corruption), the UN Global Compact *Global Corporate Sustainability Report 2013* reports that "companies are moving from good intentions to significant actions," although "supply chains are a roadblock to improved performance." Among findings related specifically to labor, 77 percent of companies report having taken some action to define their workers' right to freely form and join trade unions, and 59 percent claim they have taken steps to actually implement collective bargaining.[16]

These results suffer from the same believability problem that plagues corporate monitoring: they are self-reported by firms that have a strong interest in burnishing their image without being subject to independent verification. As we shall see later in this chapter, there is a significant gap between what businesses profess to do in terms of implementing CSR policies and the results on the ground of those efforts.

The UN Global Compact may enable firms to share their best ideas for achieving sustainable practices, but firms are under no obligation to implement those ideas, much less provide full transparency when they claim to do so. It is difficult to avoid the conclusion that however well intentioned, the UN Global Compact's main effect is to provide its members with the public-relations benefit of being a part of "the largest corporate sustainability initiative in the world."

Ruggie was later recalled by Annan in 2005 to serve as his Special Representative, charged with "identifying what international human rights standards currently regulate corporate conduct, as opposed to the conduct of states and individuals; and clarifying the respective roles of states and businesses in safeguarding these rights" (Ruggie 2013). In this position he developed set of Guiding Principles on Human Rights, unanimously endorsed by the UN Human Rights Council in 2011. The Guiding Principles set forth a series of guidelines for states and corporations to protect human rights. Like the Global Compact, they are not legally binding: "Nothing in these Guiding Principles should be read as creating new international law obligations" (OHCHR 2011). Like the Global Compact, the Guiding Principles are aspirational guidelines, something for businesses to affirm without concern about verification or enforcement.

Corporate Self-Regulation: A Growth Industry

By the second decade of the twenty-first century the adoption of corporate codes of corporate conduct had become frenetic. In 1970 almost no large corporations had codes of conduct. The number grew slowly until the 1990s, and then exploded. During the past decade the number of codes has doubled, such that 86 percent of Fortune Global 200 corporations now have codes of conduct and two-thirds report having updated their codes within the past three years. According to KPMG, a Swiss-based firm that assists companies in the "development, implementation and monitoring of their codes and compliance programs," codes are typically adopted for one of three reasons: to comply with legal requirements, create a shared company culture, and to protect or improve the corporate reputation (KPMG 2008, 3–4). Firms that fall into one of two categories typically implement CSR: oversight organizations and factory inspection companies that do the actual work.

How CSR Works

Oversight organizations are typically nonprofit NGOs whose responsibility is to provide model codes of conduct, hold training sessions, and accredit factory inspection companies to perform audits and certify compliance. There are more than a dozen such companies, introducing a vast and bewildering new lexicon of acronyms into the business vocabulary. These include (to mention some of the better-known firms) BSCI (Business Social Compliance Initiative), ETI (Ethical Trading Initiative), FLA (Fair Labor Association), GSCP (Global Social Compliance Program), ILO Better Work (a program of the UN International Labour Organization), SMETA (Sedex Members Ethical Trade Audit), SAI (Social Accountability International), SAAS (Social Accountability Accreditation Services), WRAP (Worldwide Responsible Accredited Production), and WRC (Worker Rights Consortium). Some of these firms (for example, FLA and the WRC) sometimes conduct their own monitoring as well. Oversight organizations generally share a common (and converging) set of principles regarding such issues as prohibiting child labor, forced labor, discrimination, harassment, and sexual abuse; specifying standards for maximum hours (typically forty-eight, or else as mandated by local law), as well as requiring that overtime be voluntary; and even calling for freedom of association and collective bargaining. There are some major differences as well: only the WRC, for example, requires the payment of a living wage or the full public disclosure of the results of factory audits.[17]

Factory inspection companies, which are typically for-profit businesses, visit factories and assess their compliance with the codes of conduct of the oversight organization. Depending on the type of certification system, either factories or brands initiate the process by contacting an oversight organization or one of the factory inspection companies. Because supply chains of large retailers or brands often consist of thousands of factories, only a small percentage of their factories are typically inspected; those that are chosen for inspection are often visited only once every few years. Visits from inspectors can be brief or cursory, or can last several days. There are dozens of factory inspection companies around the world, varying in size from large, multinational corporations to very small, local firms.[18] It is estimated that some fifty thousand factories employing millions of workers are audited each year, with Walmart alone accounting for some 11,500 inspections (Clifford and Greenhouse 2013). The results of audit reports are usually kept confidential, since they are proprietary information for firms that hire the auditors.

Monitoring far-flung supply chains for compliance has proven to be challenging, to say the least—and, for reasons discussed elsewhere in this book, it has not succeeded in its objectives (see especially chapters 1, 3, and 4). In recent years there have been major efforts to quantify compliance in hopes of developing industry-wide standards that would result in better outcomes. These efforts initially focused on the environmental side, but with the creation of the Sustainable Apparel Coalition (SAC) in 2010, incorporated social standards as well. The SAC is headed by Jason Kibbey, who discusses its origins and methods in chapter 12. Another effort at developing a single index, the Key Performance Indicators (KPI) Initiative, has been developed by Harvard Law School's Pension and Capital Stewardship Project. This index intended to provide a guide for socially responsible investors (IRRC Institute 2012). Indices such as the SAC and the KPI Initiative face at least two major challenges: they rely on self-reporting rather than truly independent verification and, to the extent that they involve combining different measures and scales into a single number, they may obscure significant problems by masking their underlying assumptions.

Business Schools Get on Board

Business schools have increasingly mainstreamed social and environmental concerns into their curricula as well. Every two years the Aspen Institute issues its *Beyond Grey Pinstripes* report, based on a survey of fully accredited full-time MBA programs around the world. The 2011–2012 report, which documents "how business schools are introducing and developing the concepts of social, ethical and environmental stewardship with business students," is based on surveys of 149 schools in twenty-two countries on six continents (Antarctica being the exception). Schools are given numerical ratings based on their response to the survey.[19]

Eight of the top ten schools are in the United States, with Stanford receiving top billing. York University (Canada) ranks second, and IE University (Spain) third. Among the one hundred top-ranked schools, the United States, with sixty-eight schools, is the clear front-runner in the burgeoning business of educating future business leaders in responsible stewardship. The United Kingdom is a distant second with five schools, followed by Canada and Australia (four each), Spain (three each), and Germany, France, and Mexico (two each). China,[20] Colombia, Denmark, Finland, Netherlands, Norway, Peru, Philippines, South Africa, and South Korea each have one school among the top hundred. Not all of these schools focus on the social aspects of "stewardship" and few provide an emphasis on workers' rights. Among the more than 6,000 courses surveyed, a search on the term "workers' rights" turned up only 320 courses (5 percent). Most programs appear to emphasize environmental concerns.

The Fair Labor Association: A "Multistakeholder NGO" Funded by Business

The Fair Labor Association (FLA) grew primarily out of government concern over revelations about sweatshop abuses. Robert Reich, Labor Secretary during the first term of the Clinton administration, began a government crusade against US firms' use of domestic and foreign sweatshops as soon as he took office. In 1993 Reich launched a "no sweat" campaign on the Labor Department website, and the following year authorized the Labor Department to enforce the 1938 Fair Labor Standards Act's "hot goods" provision, under which goods made in violation of wage and hour standards would be seized when they crossed state lines and were therefore subject to federal jurisdiction (Los Angeles Times 1994). When the El Monte "slave-shop" scandal occurred, Reich publicized the names of the companies involved, much to the dismay of the companies, who claimed they had no knowledge that their contracts with licensed factories had been subcontracted to the El Monte factory. His investigations also found that Walmart's Kathie Lee line was being produced under sweatshop conditions in New York City. Reich's strategy of "naming, blaming, shaming" was one of the major reasons that major firms came to a series of meetings organized by Reich.[21]

The initial meeting, in July 1996, was co-organized with a now humbled Kathie Lee Gifford. Dubbed the Fashion Industry Forum, it brought together some three hundred participants, including major brands and retailers (including Kathie Lee, Levis, Kmart, Liz Claiborne, and Walmart), representatives for labor and NGOs, and fashion celebrities. The general consensus resulting from this effort—at least on the part of industry—was to reaffirm the belief that market mechanisms, not government enforcement, was the way to go. One month later President Clinton hosted a meeting at the White House that led to the creation of the Apparel Industry Partnership (AIP). Although the AIP had a broad representation of businesses, NGOs, and two domestic unions, it necessarily lacked (given the political climate at the time) worker or NGO representatives from the global South, and hence those most affected by supply-chain abuses.[22] After eight months of contentious and largely unsuccessful negotiations (and perhaps prompted by yet another embarrassing revelation of abuses in Nike factories by Vietnam Labor Watch), in April 2007 the AIP reached agreement on a common code of conduct, clearly stated as something that companies should "voluntarily adopt," and a monitoring scheme for assuring compliance (Bobrowsky 1999).[23] The code prohibited child labor (defined as under age fifteen, unless local laws defined it as fourteen) and worker discrimination, abuse, and harassment. It required the paying of the local minimum or prevailing worker wage (whichever was higher), a "safe and healthy working environment," a workweek not to exceed forty-eight hours (with a limit of twelve hours of overtime, payable at no less than the normal wage, and one day off each week). Significantly, it also called for "recognition and respect for workers' rights of freedom of association and collective bargaining." Compliance was to be achieved by "independent external monitors who will conduct independent reviews" (US Department of Labor 1997).

Finally, the AIP agreement called for the creation of a new nonprofit organization to oversee the implementation of the agreed-on code and certify auditors. This step—which eventually resulted in the FLA—proved to be more difficult: the devil of implementation was truly in the details. Disagreements—between labor and NGOS on the one side, and the firms on the other—had previously troubled AIP negotiations; they resurfaced when the time came for implementation. Principle among these were the question of requiring a minimum wage versus a living wage, the right to freedom of association, how independently should "independent monitoring" be conducted (for example, should companies hire the monitors?), and whether monitoring reports should be made public. When negotiations stalled, the National Labor Committee, labor unions, and other organizations launched anti-sweatshop campaigns to keep public attention focused on the issue. Nike in particular was the subject of several campaigns, including the second annual Nike Day of Protest in October 1997.

The emergence of a student anti-sweatshop movement provided further impetus for the AIP to reach an agreement. The student movement began at

Duke University in 1998 and rapidly spread to campuses across the country. United Students against Sweatshops (USAS), a union-funded student organization with chapters on a growing number of campuses, was raising demands far stronger than those that were likely to be adopted by the industry-dominated AIP. USAS's model university code of conduct would have applied to all brands making logoed sweatshirts, T-shirts, and other apparel under university trademark licensing agreements. The $3 billion collegiate licensing sector included major brands such as Nike and Reebok, companies that not only produced logoed apparel to sell in college bookstores but also enjoyed lucrative contracts with athletic departments. The USAS code required full disclosure of the names and addresses of all contract factories engaged in production, the payment of a living wage, comprehensive, independent, and transparent factory monitoring, and full freedom of association for workers.[24]

Eventually a subgroup of the firms (Liz Claiborne, Nike, Phillips-Van Heusen, and Reebok) began to move forward, working with several NGOs to come up with a final agreement, and the FLA was formally created in October 1999. Four other companies signed on (Kathie Lee, Nicole Miller, Patagonia, and L.L. Bean), but the two unions withdrew. UNITE (the Union of Needletrades, Industrial and Textile Employees) and the AFL-CIO's Retail, Wholesale, and Department Store Union balked on the eventual resolution of the key issues that had plagued the AIP discussions throughout, which they felt had been railroaded into the final agreement by the subgroup of firms and NGOs that had produced it. The FLA charter, though calling for a living-wage study, did not commit to the eventual adoption of a living wage. Although the charter called for encouraging countries (such as China) to take steps toward respecting the right of freedom of association, it stopped short of requiring such a right in its members' codes. And, in terms of monitoring, the FLA requirement (that 10 percent of a brand's factories be monitored each year) was felt to be too minimal: an entire brand could claim to be compliant even though a small fraction of its factories had been monitored. Ultimately, only the International Labor Rights Fund remained in the FLA, on the grounds that at least one pro-labor voice should be present.

The FLA charter currently has a board of directors comprised of six business representatives chosen by the FLA's Business Caucus, six "labor/NGO" (civil society) representatives chosen by a majority of the then-serving civil society board members, and six university affiliate representatives chosen by a University Advisory Council.[25] Some two hundred colleges and universities currently belong to the FLA. The FLA's chair is selected by a supermajority vote of the board (FLA 2014).

The FLA's funding comes almost entirely from business members, which has led its critics to charge that it is captive to the firms it is supposed to be overseeing.

Although its charter calls for six "labor/NGO" board members (FLA 2014),[26] as of fall 2014 there were no representatives of labor on the board. Lynda Yantz, the head of Maquila Solidarity Network, a pro-labor/women's rights Canadian NGO, had served on the board between 2009 and 2013, but resigned in early 2013. Yantz had pressed the FLA to strength its code of conduct (in particular its complaints procedures) as well as include more labor representation on the board. In this effort she was unsuccessful. "When it turned out that FLA did not wish to implement structural changes on the latter two points, MSN stepped out. We felt like a voice crying in the wilderness . . . FLA operates more as an industry organization than as a multi-stakeholder initiative" (Good Electronics 2013).[27]

The Failures of Self-Regulation

Since virtually all major firms today profess socially responsible business practices, have adopted codes of conduct, and employ auditing firms to monitor compliance, it should be possible to see some beneficial results of CSR in terms of working conditions. Yet this has not been the case, as the example of Bangladesh clearly shows (see especially chapters 1, 3, and 4, although the challenges faced by CSR are discussed throughout this book). How could factory disasters claiming thousands of lives, and injuring thousands of others, have occurred in recently audited factories producing apparel for some of the world's largest brands and retailers, all of whom profess socially responsible practices and claim to routinely monitor their contract factories to assure compliance? Although there is a strong public-relations aspect to CSR programs, it is important to recognize that CSR has in fact created an increasingly elaborate set of mechanisms involving the definition of acceptable labor standards, outside inspections, and various penalties and rewards that the brands and retailers at the apex of the supply chain have imposed on the vendors and manufactures at the bottom. Why have these failed to be effective, and with such a significant cost in human lives?

One reason is the failure of inspections and audits. Given the global dispersion of factories, it is difficult for brands and retailers to audit all the factories in their supply chains with any regularity. When audits are conducted, they are often conducted superficially—brief visits that fail to detect significant health, safety, and wage violations. Auditors may lack adequate training to detect hazardous chemicals or electrical violations. Audits are typically announced well in advance, giving factories ample time to unlock their fire exits and remove any obstacles to safe exits, doctor their books, and warn workers that reporting violations could result in cancellation of orders and loss of jobs. Interviews with workers are often conducted on site, leading to fear of reprisals if complaints are made. Prior to the

Rana Plaza collapse, auditors in Bangladesh had little or no training in assessing structural issues, and so ignored them completely.[28]

Firms often blame second- and third-tier subcontractors for the problem, claiming to be unaware that their contract factories have outsourced orders to other, less-regulated factories. This, in fact, was the conclusion of a major study that focused on the fires and building collapses in Bangladesh (Labowitz and Baumann-Pauly 2014). Yet the major disasters that have occurred in Bangladesh's garment factories in recent years occurred at facilities that were known by major brands to have produced their goods and had been repeatedly subjected to labor rights audits conducted for these same buyers. The problem lies not with indirect manufacturing but with the structure of an industry in which contract factories must be price-takers if they wish to compete. The brands and retailers ultimately determine the terms under which their supply chains operate. If they squeeze their contract factories, the factories will respond by cutting costs in various ways: cutting wages, engaging in forced or unpaid overtime, avoiding safety measures that add to cost, outsourcing production to lower-wage factories. "Seasonal" orders add to the problem, resulting in an around-the-clock production surge when the latest "fast fashion" (or iPhone) is announced.

Significantly, factory audits almost always lack transparency: they are internal reports to the brand or retailer, not public documents. Workers have no knowledge of the results of audits, even when the findings have clear implications for their health and safety. Nor do consumers have access to potentially embarrassing information that might spur the firms to action. Ultimately, whatever ameliorative impulse the firm might have is systematically subverted by the economic imperatives embedded within the structure of the global supply chains. When business interests trump social concerns, CSR takes a back seat.

CSR represents a key shift in economic governance: from public to private regulation and enforcement. As is argued throughout this book, such a shift has proven highly profitable for business. Although it has provided millions of workers around the globe with paid work, it has done so at the cost of decent wages, safe workplaces, and—most important—any meaningful system of governance in which the workers themselves have an active and effective voice in determining the conditions of their employment.

To the extent that the "soulful corporation" of the mid-twentieth century was concerned with industrial stability—adopting labor-friendly policies at least in part to avoid strikes and labor turnover—CSR of the twenty-first century arose in large part to preserve brand value in the face of embarrassing revelations while avoiding government regulation. The result of this shift has been a parallel shift in the nature of economic governance. The tripartite model, enshrined in the ILO approach, involved three key players: labor, business, and the state. Workers acted collectively through labor unions; the state created and enforced regulations designed to protect workers' rights. Unionization and worker's rights were the result of decades of labor struggles. This arrangement, frequently referred to as the American social contract, has given way in the twenty-first century to a new arrangement in which two of the three key players, workers and the state, are replaced by other actors: independently owned contract factories and monitoring firms.

The result is a new tripartite model: brands and retailers produce their goods through contract factories, then hire firms to monitor their factories and privately report back their findings. This new arrangement, sometimes termed a "social accountability contract,"[29] effectively makes corporations responsible for governing themselves. This outcome had long been preferred by business, but was reluctantly conceded during the course of the twentieth century in response to growing labor power. But as the power of labor weakened, businesses—long opposed to state regulation—returned to a nineteenth-century approach to economic governance, this time on a global scale. The current prevailing belief in unfettered markets, the power of firms over states, the WTO prohibition of including social clauses in trade agreements, the intentional weakness of the ILO and its nonbinding conventions—all of these have created a space in which companies could effectively argue that a "trust me" approach was the only workable solution to the problem of sweatshops.

CORPORATE SOCIAL RESPONSIBILITY

Moving from Checklist Monitoring to
Contractual Obligation?

Jill Esbenshade

Codes of conduct and monitoring are the most prevalent form of corporate social responsibility (CSR) in global supply chains. According to the *New York Times*, more than fifty thousand factories employing millions of workers go through "social audits" each year (Clifford and Greenhouse 2013). There is evidence that to some degree codes and monitoring systems have changed the landscape in which brands and factories operate: there is now acceptance of public disclosure of factory names and locations, which was once held to be an unbreachable trade secret; recently there have been incidents of brands taking responsibility for unpaid back wages and severance, a still rare but previously unknown occurrence in the global supply chains constructed in part to avoid such liability; and there are indications that brands may be consolidating their far-flung production networks that have become unmanageable in the age of disclosure and monitoring (Gereffi 2013).

However, academic researchers, and more recently the popular press, have found that codes and monitoring are not equal to the task of significantly raising standards in the industry. Researchers point to some measure of improvements but emphasize that violations continue, in some areas unabated. Mark Anner's comprehensive study of the Fair Labor Association (2012a) and Patricia Barrientos and Sally Smith's (2007) study of the Ethical Trading Initiative (ETI) find that even in Multi-Stakeholder Initiatives (MSIs), which involve governance by a combination of companies and NGOs, and where there are mutually agreed-on standards for codes and monitoring, effectiveness of monitoring is restricted to certain code provisions. Whereas Anner analyzes detection by violation type in over eight hundred audit reports, Barrientos and Smith evaluate improvements in twelve in-depth garment factory cases through actually reauditing monitored factories. These disparate studies find significant attention in some "outcome standards" (health and safety, payment of required wages, and hours), little to no detection or improvement in others (living wage, permanent employment, harsh treatment, discrimination), and no progress in "process rights" (freedom of association, collective bargaining). Richard Locke's book, based on a decade of research, including hundreds of interviews, factory visits, and audit reviews of company monitoring, finds that in the areas where there have been improvements, most notably health and safety, compliance levels have plateaued and that on issues such as freedom of association and excessive working hours there have been no improvements (Locke 2013).

Overall codes have failed to measurably alter the egregious conditions for workers on the shop floor: with few exceptions workers are not paid living wages and are not able to organize, and they are *regularly* cheated out of mandatory pay, benefits, and severance. In fact, workers are owed tens of millions of dollars, and worse yet they are dying by the score in fires and building collapses. And this is happening in factories that are monitored and that often pass inspections (Claeson 2012). After almost two decades of codes of conduct and monitoring, violations are still the norm, not the exception.

This does not mean that codes and monitoring are completely misguided, rather, that they are limited; they are a salve, not a cure. I will argue below that the challenge is for codes and monitoring to change the structure of the industry, which is the only real way to address violations, and in order to create such change codes and monitoring must involve binding—not simply voluntary—agreements to which workers are a party.

Literature Evaluating Codes and Monitoring

What follows is a review of the literature on the successes, failures, and challenges of codes and monitoring covering fifty studies from the last decade on the topic. In its totality the literature emphasizes the following factors as having a positive effect on reducing (although in no way eliminating) violations. First, specific monitoring practices have been found to have a greater effect on reducing violations, and worker participation in monitoring is central to building a sustainable program from identifying problems to ensuring remediation. Second, the independence of monitors and the transparency of their reporting are crucial to ensuring that results have validity and can be effectively used to correct violations. Although the specifics of monitoring are crucial to its effectiveness, monitoring exists within a constellation of power relationships that determine not only the thoroughness of monitoring practices but also how results are implemented and acted on. The following sections deal with the role of consumers, local governments, and brands, all of whom set the context for and ultimately determine the likelihood of compliance. The final area explored in much of the literature is the inability of current monitoring to affect the structure of sourcing, which is the ultimate cause of violations. After the literature review I will add a largely overlooked factor to eliminating violations: to what extent monitoring is contractual and if it includes workers as party to the contract. I end this chapter with a variety of examples of the emergence of contractual obligations in monitoring; many of these examples also have a direct impact on the structure of sourcing.

Monitoring Practices and Worker Participation

Although monitoring is often referred to as social auditing, in fact there are no standardized practices as there are in accounting audits. Monitoring is conducted by a mishmash of internal, commercial, and independent auditors. It lacks uniformly accepted standards in terms of both what is monitored and how inspections are conducted. Broadly speaking, monitoring includes: self-assessment, brand compliance visits, "third-party" auditing by an entity hired by the brand (or sometimes contractor), "fourth-party" monitoring paid for by an oversight organization to which the brand belongs (like the FLA), and independent monitoring conducted by a group (like the Worker Rights Consortium, WRC) in which companies have no role. There is no uniform code and codes vary on such points as minimum age (Kolk and van Tulder 2002), inclusion of freedom of association and collective bargaining, and aspirations of a living wage (Jenkins 2002). Some important areas, such as building safety, have not historically been included at all. There is also variance as to whether monitoring is a checklist operation that simply captures the day of the inspection or includes a review of policies and implementation procedures on such issues as age documentation, fire drills, or antidiscrimination.

Richard Locke, a political scientist and business professor who works with leading global corporations to implement sustainable business practices, has analyzed the largest set of private audits. He finds that not only is the checklist method the base model for private and third-party monitoring but also that the checklist is not usually completed, as many auditors face such time constraints that once they find their quota of violations they move on to the next factory, not even finishing the checklist much less delving deeper into the violations they find. In *The Promise and Limits of Private Power*, Locke laments that whereas he believed in the "promise" of the enterprise of private monitoring before his research, he had to conclude that "in reality, the information collected through the audits is biased, incomplete and often inaccurate" (Locke 2013, 38).

To the extent that monitoring can be effective, researchers have identified two specific practices as being important in more accurate verification protocols: unannounced visits and confidential off-site worker interviews. The labor sociologist Jill Esbenshade (2004a), the environmental policy professor and cofounder of GoodGuide, Dara O'Rourke (2000), and Locke (2013) all reveal weaknesses in the private monitoring system through ethnographic research, which includes observing monitors at work. Off-site interviews are necessary, as O'Rourke (2006) documents that in interviews conducted in factories, management knows who is being interviewed, the questions being asked, and the length of time each interview lasts. Esbenshade (2004a) concurs, describing cases in Los Angeles where interviews are conducted on the shop floor and supervisors are even asked to translate. Locke (2013) reports that often employee interviews are not conducted at all. As a counterexample, the labor relations professor and director of the Center for Global Workers' Rights, Mark Anner (2012a), argues that in the Better Work Vietnam program, monitors from the UN's International Labour Organization (ILO), whose standards require them to take worker testimony seriously, actually find much higher rates of process violations.

Researchers have found that unannounced visits are crucial not only for the integrity of the physical inspection of the factory but also for the validity of the record checks, which constitute the basis of most audits. The professor of economics and management David Weil, who is the author of *The Fissured Workplace* (2014) and was Obama's head of the Wage and Hour Division of the Department of Labor (DOL), analyzed ninety-eight DOL surveys of Los Angeles apparel contractors from inspections conducted in 2000. He found that the two most effective of the seven evaluated monitoring components (which did not include off-site interviews), were the combination of payroll review and unannounced visits. Weil concludes that record checks must be coupled with unannounced visits in order to ensure that written documentation reflects reality. Record checks on announced visits are much less effective because keeping two sets of books is a common practice, one set in which workers' actual hours and pay are recorded, and a second set that is doctored to reflect compliance with labor standards (Weil 2005; 2010). Looking at the program in Los Angeles, Esbenshade finds that surveillance outside the factory was often counted as an unannounced visit, even when the actual appointment to check books and interview employees was made in advance. Because books were not on kept on site, one monitoring company that did conduct truly unannounced visits allowed the books to be sent over within three days, undermining the value of the unannounced inspection (Esbenshade 2004, 71–75). British researchers Barrientos and Smith (2007) consistently find violations in reauditing suppliers who had been giving passing audits through the United Kingdom's multistakeholder ETI program. They find that auditors catch primarily visible problems. They conclude that the inaccuracy of auditing results is due largely to the widespread use of double books and of coaching workers before interviews. Locke's review of hundreds of audits also found that false results are a consequence of the common use of double books, and he notes that factory owners learn over time to doctor records. He asserts that inaccurate results are partially due to the fact that auditors use a financial audit model, which privileges written documentation over worker testimony (Locke 2013, 35–37).

Although unannounced visits and off-site interviews may seem like obvious steps, they are not accepted practice. For private monitors and company sponsored CSR programs, these practices are *not* the norm. In 2006, the three largest retailers in the world, Walmart, Tesco, and Carrefour, joined a number of other firms in founding the Global Social Compliance Program (GSCP) to improve working and environmental conditions by harmonizing efforts and identifying best practices in codes and monitoring. In its "Audit Process and Methodology Reference Tools," GSCP warns that semi-announced and unannounced audits should be used only in high-risk circumstances and even then only after considering business relationships. GSCP cautions: "Note: Whilst unannounced audits are extremely effective at identifying an accurate picture of working conditions at the employment site, and may help uncover high risk issues, their use can undermine the relationships along the supply chain, reducing the ability of the buying company to remediate. The experience of many companies indicates that unannounced audits should be reserved for due diligence checks or to investigate specific issues (critical issues suspected, lack of commitment/involvement of the suppliers, suspicion of fraud)" (GSCP 2009, 6). In other words, monitors should operate on an assumption of compliance unless there are specific indications to the contrary. In terms of worker interviews, the GSCP protocol "Interviews" section begins: "Interviews with managers, trade union representatives (and/or other workers' representatives) and workers will take place on-site. However, it may be appropriate to carry out additional worker interviews off-site" (GSCP 2009, 14). But no guidance is given about when off-site interviews should be used.

Even for the ILO, which has set international standards for the importance of giving weight to confidential worker interviews, the practices of off-site interviews and unannounced visits seem nonstandard. There has been a lot of criticism in the anti-sweatshop movement about the Better Factories Cambodia (BFC) program (Ballinger 2009), which gave US trade privileges to Cambodian garment manufacturers. Shea, Nakayama, and Heymann (2010), although finding that the model developed under the ILO's monitoring in the BFC program was largely successful in improving working conditions, admonish that future monitoring ventures should include off-site worker interviews and unannounced visits, the lack of which they say brings the ILO program's integrity into question. A study by Stanford University Law School (2013) indicates that the ILO has only partially rectified these weaknesses. The report finds that the usual procedure is still to interview workers in groups in the factory and to supplement this informally with worker interviews at food stalls and such places just outside the factory gates. The Stanford study also says that although the ILO conducts unannounced visits, they sometimes wait for up to 45 minutes outside the factory, allowing management time to prepare. Furthermore, "Since 2005, factory workers have lost almost all of the access they once had into the black box of BFC's reporting . . . BFC no longer convenes meetings at monitored factories to report on its findings to workers and their representatives." Not only are workers no longer apprised of monitoring results, but those results are also no longer publicly available. The program halted its original practice of releasing public summary reports with some individual factory information, although actual factory reports were never made public (see chapter 5 of this volume). Workers have no ability, therefore, to act as any kind of check on remediation since they do not, and cannot, know what violations have been found.

The lack of worker participation in the monitoring and remediation processes profoundly undermines monitoring as a viable regulatory system. Most workers in the Barrientos and Smith study (2007) were only partially or not at all aware of the codes. Many NGOs have reported a similar lack of dissemination of information. Esbenshade (2004a) found that many workers she interviewed had no idea who the auditors were. Moreover, those who were aware had been told by management that if they revealed problems to the auditor, work would be pulled and they would lose their jobs. Seidman (2007) finds that workers in Lesotho were also silenced by a fear of ruining the reputation, and therefore market share, of their employer and their country.

Auditors not only need to elicit truthful information from workers in order to produce accurate results, but workers' participation in ongoing vigilance at the factory is also key to moving beyond the "checklist" model. We know that factory owners coach workers for interviews, falsify records, and unlock doors for the day of inspection. Only workers who are protected from retaliation and empowered by their own organizations can know and report whether the doors are unlocked and they are paid properly day in and day out. This point was painfully emphasized in a report on death by factory fires written by Bjorn Claeson (senior policy analyst at the International Labor Rights Forum). Claeson documents that many of the factories in which hundreds of workers have died in Bangladesh and Pakistan were actually monitored by brand-name companies. However, because workers are not empowered to report on the daily conditions within their facto-ries or apprised of the results of audits, which remain secret, monitoring fails to uncover dangerous and illegal conditions and fails to facilitate addressing those conditions when they are discovered, resulting in at best inaccurate reports and at worst a wave of factory fatalities like none seen in the garment sector previously (Claeson 2012). Moreover, O'Rourke (2006) also asserts that worker participa-tion is necessary not only to identify problems but also to verify compliance with remediation efforts. He gives examples of workers' committees in China that have helped improve health and safety compliance.

However, the vast majority of monitoring efforts does not protect workers, much less involve them on any equal footing in the process. Monitoring usually happens through an agreement between brands and contractors, and sometimes an agreement is signed between the brand and an oversight organization; with few exceptions workers have not been party to these agreements (Esbenshade 2004a). César Rodríguez-Garavito (2005) argues that what workers need is "empowered participatory regulation," that would focus on guaranteeing enabling rights, edu-cation, training and direct worker complaint mechanisms in the monitoring pro-cess. Rainer Braun and Judy Gearhart (2004) and Esbenshade (2001, 2004b) claim that Northern NGOs have assisted in developing a regulatory model not account-able to workers. Such regulation stands in contrast to a union-based participatory model, which is accountable to workers themselves (Compa 2001, 2004).

Independence and Transparency

Researchers also point to the level of independence of the monitors as crucial to monitoring's effectiveness, generally having more praise for independent monitors who are neither selected nor paid by the contractors or the brands. Both Anner (Anner et al. 2008) and Esbenshade (2004a, 2004b) contrast commercial monitors who are paid by the brands with independent monitors who are not. They find that the latter not only have fewer conflicts of interest but also more access to workers and a much better chance of uncovering violations of the key issue: workers' rights to organize and thereby gain the security to monitor their own factory.

The vast majority of factory inspections are conducted by auditors hired either directly or indirectly by brands and contractors themselves. Many large brands, like Nike and Gap, employ their own compliance staff. For these internal auditors, the central aspect of their employers' business, to acquire or produce clothes at a low price in a timely manner, often conflicts with the goal of assuring compliance with workers' rights. Locke quotes an auditor who expresses a typical dynamic: if an order has already been placed "before I set foot in the factory, I know we will give them the business no matter what" (2013, 38). There are also dozens of commercial firms who offer social compliance auditing services, some of the largest being the Swiss firm SGS SA (Société Générale de Surveillance), the British Intertek, the French Bureau Veritas, and the American UL (Underwriters Laboratories). These external auditors, whose services are purchased either by the brand or the contractor, have an incentive to please the client by keeping prices low with quick (and consequently less thorough) investigations. Moreover, such firms are rewarded with more business when they issue passing reports to contractors who hire them directly and when they refrain from causing problems with business relations between the brand and contractor. For instance, a *New York Times* article entitled "Fast and Flawed Inspections of Factories Abroad" reported that an SGS spokesperson, in defending a stellar inspection report of Rosita Knitwear in Bangladesh, which later erupted in protests over a plethora of code violations, "said the protocol for Rosita did not require interviewing workers outside the factory, a practice that she cautioned could undermine a relationship between a Western company and its suppliers" (Clifford and Greenhouse 2013). Moreover, as social auditing firms expand business in response to growing demand in new locations, they sometimes contract out work, resulting in the same problems of control of standards that they are monitoring for.

Independent monitoring is seen as more effective, although it is not a cure-all. "Independent monitoring" is a term used to refer to both the structure of the relationships, where companies do not directly hire auditors, and a purer form of independence where the monitoring organizations themselves are actually free from corporate influence in their governance and funding (such as the WRC). Kolk and van Tulder (2002) found in their survey of six major garment manufacturers that internal monitoring was *not* considered credible. External monitoring was deemed necessary by social auditors or NGOs, although the preferred method was to hire an external monitor through a foundation, to which the companies paid dues (such as the FLA). Frundt (2004) and Wetterberg (2010) concur that the degree of independence of monitoring is a central criteria by which the stringency of monitoring can be judged. However, Gay Seidman (2007) and Wells (2007) warn that independent monitoring also has its flaws: it depends on the brands for access to factories, it requires the trust of workers, and, perhaps most significant, it has limited capacity to cover even a tiny fraction of the hundreds of thousands of factories.

Noted individual cases of real progress brought about by monitoring have been in the context of truly independent monitors and processes that were both transparent and put workers concerns and voice front and center. For example, the WRC played a crucial role in the establishment of the first independent apparel union in Mexico at Kukdong/Mexmode (Ross 2006) and in the Mombosa Free Trade Zone of Kenya at Sinolink. The WRC was also instrumental in guaranteeing

workers' rights in the struggle at the BJ&B factory, which resulted in the first collective bargaining agreement to require higher than the minimum wage in any
export-processing zone of the Dominican Republic (Ross 2006; Esbenshade 2008).
Workers at Jerzees Nuevo Día, a Russell factory in Honduras, won a number of
concessions through the monitoring of the WRC, in conjunction with actions
by universities and a well-coordinated campaign between unionists in Honduras
and student protestors in the United States. The Honduran workers were rehired,
signed a collective bargaining agreement, received 35 percent above the local standard in benefits and wages, and won a guarantee of broader rights to freedom of
association than previously experienced in the industry, not only for themselves
but also for all workers at other Honduran Russell factories (Esbenshade 2012).
These gains, though extremely important, are generally in individual factories and
sometimes are ephemeral. Unfortunately, they are not indicative of a progressive
trend in either independence of monitoring or transparency. In fact, one sign that
transparency may have plateaued is the deterioration of the ILO's BFC program
into a "black box" system as described above.

There is consensus in the literature that transparency of monitoring procedures and results is a necessary facet of an effective system, although this finding
is largely based in theoretical argument rather than evaluation, since no major
system beyond the WRC makes reports with factory names public. O'Rourke
(2006) argues that "increased transparency is the first, and perhaps most critical,
element in advancing more accountable non-governmental governance" (909).
Hemphill (2004) supports the monitoring model but warns that strong accountability and transparency mechanisms are needed to insure effectiveness. Crinis
(2010) reports that for Malaysia, her case study, WRAP and SAI reports contain
only numbers for factories, not names, which was also noted by O'Rourke (2006)
and Hemphill (2004) in regard to FLA reports. As discussed above, the lack of
transparency of the audits coming out of Bangladesh, Pakistan, and elsewhere
has contributed to workers dying en masse (Claeson 2012; and Ross in chapter 4
of this volume). This secrecy not only endangers workers but also makes evaluation of the system and accountability almost impossible. Lack of transparency
thereby also hinders consumer action. Bartley (2007) and Robinson (Anner et al.
2008) explain that the lack of a consistent consumer demand for ethically produced goods is at least partly a result of the lack of reliable certification system.

Consumer Leverage over Brands

In terms of the role of the consumer, researchers argue that the more leverage
over brands those requiring monitoring have, the more effective the consumer
can be in affecting brand behavior. Wetterberg (2010) differentiates between the

buyer-regulated markets where the individual consumers hold sway and socially regulated markets such as college logoed goods or uniforms for city or state workers. Socially regulated markets are more conducive to improving workers' conditions because: (1) they are in an area where market access is limited (licenses for college logoed goods or procurement for public employee uniforms), (2) there are "interested intermediaries" who can provide market access in exchange for higher levels of compliance (universities or government agencies), (3) these intermediaries have engaged some independent monitoring entity (the WRC or FLA), and (4) there is on-going activism (by students, workers, or citizens) to ensure that the intermediary continues to require compliance.

Others have also pointed to the fact that institutional consumers have more leverage and reliability in their influence over brands than do a large number of individuals with similar preferences. Seidman (2007), Armbruster-Sandoval (2005), and Wells (2007) assert that the nature of individual consumer and activist action is somewhat mercurial. Institutional consumers, on the other hand, have a specific role that creates more influence (granting licenses or making large purchases). Such institutional buyers often have long-standing relationships with specific brands and can thus exert more influence on their practices. Moreover, the purchases by or licenses with universities, bookstores, cities, and states can be a stable demand that is controlled by longer-term policy decisions rather than immediate shopping choices. In a few instances, such as the Sweat-Free Communities consortium, governments act as responsible consumers in procurement, but more often governments are involved with monitoring through the intersection of their enforcement capacity with private monitoring.

Relationship to Government Enforcement

Where monitoring is actually part of government enforcement, it is more effective. Weil (2005) shows that where private monitoring is part of a government oversight program, as in Los Angeles, it can raise compliance. He finds that putting government pressure on actors further up in the industry (at the level of retailers, for example) can force monitoring further down the chain of production. Esbenshade (2004a), while focusing on the deficiencies of the DOL-supervised monitoring program in Los Angeles (most notably the myriad conflicts of interest), also acknowledges that monitoring in the context of government enforcement and the threat of embargoing goods or complaints reaching retailers provides some improvements. As Brayden King and Nicholas Pearce (2010) point out, the threat of state regulation strengthens the potential of private regulation, since companies prefer self-regulation to submitting to the state.

However, as Gereffi, Garcia-Johnson, and Sasser (2001) warn, monitoring should not be seen as a substitute for state enforcement. Although monitoring and certification are an opportunity to highlight disparities in state enforcement, since they look at laws across governments in the process of evaluating compliance, state enforcement has a breadth and potential system of consequences that cannot be replicated by private alternatives. In terms of which has a greater effect on compliance, research has shown that government enforcement clearly outweighs monitoring. Locke, Qin, and Brause (2007) find that whether factories operate in a country with a stronger rule of law and more active labor inspectorate makes more of a difference in compliance than does monitoring. Locke suggests that if companies are concerned with compliance they locate production in countries with stronger labor-law enforcement mechanisms. However, companies often choose production locations precisely to *avoid* countries with strong labor-rights enforcement because the costs of compliance drive up wages, benefits, and infrastructure costs, as argued by Nova and Wegemer in chapter 1 of this volume. Not considering the context of labor-rights compliance in sourcing location belies the notion that monitoring is a sincere effort to ensure workers' rights are respected.

Moreover, even at its most effective, monitoring does not challenge practices that fall *within* the law but are clearly undermining workers' rights. For example, in Crinis's case study in Malaysia, contractors legally hire short-term foreign workers with few labor rights in terms of overtime pay, unionization, suitability of housing, and withholding of travel documents. These foreign workers are often hired by an outsourcing company that deducts a fee from workers' wages so that workers are paid far less than nationals and far less than they were promised when recruited. Although some of these practices would violate company codes, Crinis concludes that "auditors who monitor factory compliance are not in a position to question national labour standards" (2010, 590). Looking at case studies in China and Vietnam, where half of FLA company production occurs, Anner (2012a) demonstrates the complicated and unproductive exercise of monitoring for code provisions such as freedom of association and collective bargaining rights in a context where these provisions are illegal.

If indeed government enforcement is much more significant than monitoring in achieving compliance, is there any way in which monitoring can spur more government enforcement? Kolk and van Tulder (2002) argue that as part of code implementation companies can assert pressure on local governments to enforce national laws, and the literature shows that there are instances where independent monitoring has done this. O'Rourke (2006), Anner et al. (2008), Seidman (2007), and Knight and Wells (2007) document examples from Mexico, Indonesia, El Salvador, and Guatemala where independent monitors advocated for the state to enforce laws. However, reviewing the reports from the WRC (which was responsible for the Mexican Kukdong/Mexmode and Indonesian cases), it is clear that these are fairly isolated incidents and not indicative of any general trend in independent monitoring, much less private monitoring. It seems that pressuring for government reform is a more likely outcome of a *local* independent monitor (e.g., in Coverco in Guatemala and GMIES in El Salvador) that is continuously engaged in the civil society movements within the country and for which government engagement is part of its long-term work. The recent tragedy in Bangladesh saw a push for legal reform supported by brands; however, that was in the context of the worst possible publicity for both the country and the brands that produce there.

There is, however, a debate over to what extent private regulation is a distraction from the task of shoring up national labor-law enforcement rather than complementary to or supportive of government enforcement. According to Robert Ross (2004), codes and monitoring are the weakest point in a continuum of possible labor-rights protections; unions and government enforcement are at the strong end and international law and trade sanctions are in between. Jill Murray (2003) argues that primary responsibility for regulation lies with the state. The enforcement of labor law actually fulfills two major tasks of the government: providing companies with a "level playing field" and balancing the power of companies and workers. Ronnie Lipschutz and James Rowe (2005) agree that it is in the government's interest to make sure that everyone abides by the same rules, both within their countries and between countries. Voluntary private regulation cannot play this role since it is not uniform, nor enforced, nor enforceable given the global and mobile nature of supply chains. Although some companies may sincerely want to regulate their contractors, they cannot count on others to do the same. Thus monitoring, rather than giving a company or even a country a market advantage, may actually put them at a competitive disadvantage. The same could, of course, be said for enforcing labor laws: although certainly a supposed obligation of the state, enforcement puts the country at a competitive disadvantage in attracting manufacturers and brands to locate production there.

Relationship of Brand and Supplier

The relationship between the brand and the contractor is actually a more important factor in compliance than the monitoring itself; in fact, some researchers argue that the contours of this relationship are the most important factors. Crucial aspects in this relationship include how often the brand visits the facility, the length of the relationship, and most important the ability of the contractor to renegotiate price when circumstances (like delivery schedule) are altered. Locke,

Qin, and Brause (2007), analyze eight hundred Nike audits from fifty-one countries and find that monitoring alone has little effect on compliance. Rather, factory-
level compliance is most tied to the relationships with brands that allow for
negotiation over scheduling and support for higher productivity. These researchers find that it is visits not by brand CSR staff but by brand quality control and
production staff that correlates with code compliance, indicating that it is the
intimacy of the business relationship—not the worker rights efforts—that creates space for improved labor conditions. Locke reiterates this point in his 2013
book on the subject, hailing "strategic partnerships," which are long term and
marked by frequent interaction, as more important than monitoring.[1]

All four studies that address the question find that a strong and/or more
equitable relationship between brands and contractors outweighs monitoring in
terms of the effect on compliance. Barrientos and Smith concur with Locke that
brands "had greater influence" (2007, 78) when they have longer-term relationships with the contractors, account for a higher percentage of output, and order
more regularly from the supplier. Where there is a critical mass of brands insisting on similar codes, the effect is greater. Weil (2005) and Esbenshade (2004a)
analyzed data from DOL surveys of almost one hundred garment shops in Los
Angeles in 2000 and both find that the ability of contractors to renegotiate price
when there is a change in schedule has a stronger effect on compliance than does
the comprehensiveness of monitoring.

With a growing realization that monitoring is not an antidote to widespread
labor rights violations, many brands are now turning to capability- or capacity-
building approaches. As the Global Social Compliance Program claims,
"The GSCP is ultimately working towards remediation of root causes to non-
compliances, aiming at supplier ownership of solutions and their implementation.
That is why we support the development of collaborative models to build to
capacity at supplier site" (http://www.theconsumergoodsforum.com/gscp-our-
work/capacity-building). Here root causes are understood to be not the practices
of buyers but the organizational and technical capacity of suppliers. Locke offers
a description of this model: "By providing suppliers with the technical know-
how and management systems required to run more efficient businesses, this
approach aims to improve these firms' financial situation, thus allowing them
to invest in higher wages and better working conditions" (2013, 8). However,
he says the model is built on a number of faulty assumptions. First, the model
assumes that technical upgrades lead to better wages and conditions and not
more deskilled jobs. Second, the model operates on the premise that different
parties in the supply chain have common rather than divergent interests. Third,
the program is presented as one that can be reproduced across countries regardless of social, legal, and cultural environments. Locke finds very mixed results and

concludes that gains come from longer-term committed and close relationships between brand and factory rather than the program itself. He observes that, as with monitoring, brand practices in terms of pricing, schedules, and ordering small batches all continue to undermine any improvements brought about by the supplier improvement programs that brands sponsor (Locke 2013, 101–4).

Impacting the Structure of the Industry

There is agreement among many researchers that monitoring's greatest flaw is that it does not alter the structure of the industry, which is the real root cause of violations. In his analysis of NGO monitoring, Wells (2007) points to larger problems that cannot be tackled by even the best monitoring. Monitoring is necessarily limited by the mobility and volatility of global production, which is sourced from an ever-changing list of factories in a multitude of countries, so that monitors cannot even cover the factories currently used by a given brand. Moreover, global production chains were created in large measure to avoid the kind of responsibility monitoring purports to establish (Bonacich and Appelbaum 2000). Barrientos and Smith state that "purchasing practices are being seen by many as the Achilles heel of corporate codes." They "conclude that corporate codes have a role to play in improving labour standards, but are currently doing little to challenge commercial practices . . . that underpin poor labour standards." Barrientos and Smith find that where commercial demands conflict with code compliance, commercial demands win out (2007, 713). For instance, companies place repeated small orders, with short lead times for each, in order to keep inventory at a minimum. This lean approach puts strain on factory-level production in terms of planning, with suppliers having to work in bursts. This fluctuation in workload requires factory owners to either increase overtime above code limitations and/or not pay overtime properly or hire temporary workers. Locke (2013) concurs, also emphasizing the negative effects of lean production.

Not only has monitoring failed to address pricing and sourcing, so that its effect is limited in scope and depth, but also some aspects of the industry, like wages, have deteriorated despite monitoring (Worker Rights Consortium 2013). The shift to temporary, short-term, and contract work is another example of a negative practice that actually became more widespread at the same time as the monitoring regime proliferated. Barrientos and Smith (2007), in their study of factories that received satisfactory audits through ETI, point to the fact that migrant and temporary labor are extremely common, and undermine even basic protections. Even as Cambodian manufacturers participated in the ILO's Better Factories monitoring program, they shifted most of their workforce to temporary contracts, greatly undermining workers' rights (Allard K. Lowenstein

Rise in Enforcement of Contractual Obligation

It is in the university, through contracts between the university and licensees or sponsors, where there has been significant and escalating establishment of contractual obligation, and most important an obligation that involves workers' active participation. I will present the increasing use of binding contracts by discussing three recent cases. I want to emphasize that the use of contractual obligation to effect changes has only succeeded in the context of worker struggles to assert their rights and call for enforcement *and* student activism to encourage universities to cut contracts in response to breaches of the codes.

Russell Athletic was the first major instance in which universities cut their licenses en masse to enforce the licensing contracts. It should be noted that Russell is an unusual licensing brand in that its parent company, Fruit of the Loom, owns some of its own factories, making it more obviously responsible for violations in factories wholly dedicated to its production and more able to exercise control over the factory in remediation. In October 2008 after a successful unionization campaign, Fruit of the Loom decided to close its Jerzees de Honduras factory in violation of the university codes of conduct. Over the next year over one hundred universities cut contracts with Russell for breaching the licensing agreement. As a result, Fruit of the Loom agreed to open a new unionized factory (Jerzees Nuevo Día), to rehire the fired employees, and to remain neutral over unionization at its other Honduran facilities (see chapter 14 of this volume for more details). The agreement was signed with workers' representatives and proved that universities could use the weight of contract to enforce the most violated code of conduct—the right to unionize.

Soon after, universities used the power of the contract to force a licensee to set a precedent for brands assuming the monetary obligation to its contractor's workers. In January 2009, 1,800 workers found themselves out of work and owed over $2 million when two Nike contractors in Honduras, Hugger and Vision Tex, closed without paying the legally required severance and back wages.[2] Nike went through the usual denials of (1) not having work, or significant work, in the factory, and (2) not being responsible for money owed workers by a contractor.[3] Nike then proceeded to offer to pay for training and not owed compensation—emphasizing its "goodwill" rather than its obligation. As stated by the workers in a February 2010 letter to Nike rejecting the offer: "We want to be very clear that while our stomachs are empty and we have a lot of debts, we don't need training. We are trained workers with many years of experience making high-quality products. What we need is to receive payment for the work that we have done, which is an obligation established by Nike's own code of conduct."[4] Dozens of universities threatened to cut contracts and the University of Wisconsin did so.

Given what had just happened months before with Russell, the mass termination of contracts was a very real threat. In July 2010, Nike agreed to sign an agreement with the main workers' federation that committed to pay workers' severance and to find jobs for the laid-off workers at its other contracting facilities in Honduras.

In a case of violations at the Indonesian factory PT Kizone, the University of Wisconsin sued adidas for breach of contract and the workers joined in the contractual dispute directly. PT Kizone closed in April 2011, owing workers $3.4 million in severance (see chapter 14). Other buyers in the factory, most notably Nike, made partial payment. Adidas, however, gave a half million dollars in what its own communications called "humanitarian aid"[5] rather than pay the remaining $1.8 million in owed severance. This aid largely consisted of food vouchers that workers had to spend at expensive convenience stores. These vouchers were in large denominations and no change would be issued, forcing workers to either sell them at a lower price outside the store or try to collect food that would add up to the exact amount of the voucher. As one worker testified, "I reject [the food vouchers] because for us, it is an insult, because it is nothing compared to our sweat from all the time we spent working with adidas."[6] At the same time that adidas was distributing its vouchers, the University of Wisconsin filed suit against it for breach of contract. Since adidas and UW had a sponsorship agreement, UW was required to go through a legal process to end the relationship, first arbitration and then court. When the Indonesian union representing the workers filed a motion in January 2013 to intervene in the lawsuit, Judge John Albert granted the motion, finding that the workers had a valid and legally binding interest in the contract between adidas and the UW. The judge's decision led to a remediation agreement that, unlike the sponsorship or licensing contracts, workers are a signatory to.

Both the Nike and adidas cases show how companies are struggling to maintain their position that CSR is an act of charity not a legal obligation to make workers whole. Adidas actually titled the announcement on its website that came after the remediation agreement "Adidas Group extends *help* to Indonesian workers."[7] However, it should be noted that other severance cases have been settled in the wake of the adidas case, indicating that companies are being forced to take the contractual obligation established in licensing and sponsorship agreements more seriously.

A Binding Contract Signed Directly with Workers: The Accord versus the Alliance

Finally, the Accord on Fire and Building Safety in Bangladesh, following the Rana Plaza collapse, is a legally binding agreement between brands and workers representatives. Significantly, the Accord sets a precedent in being the first CSR monitoring agreement to address the structural causes of violations through two provisions concerning pricing and stability.[8] The first states: "An agreement by signatory companies not to offer prices to, or accept prices from, factories such that the factories would be without the financial wherewithal to maintain safe workplaces and comply with upgrade and remediation requirements instituted by the Safety Inspector."[9] Another provision of the Accord requires companies to maintain production for at least two years in the factories where they have significant production (which must apply to at least 65 percent of their production in Bangladesh). Combined with the requirement to help finance building upgrades and repairs, which creates an investment of the brands in the factories, this provision aims to stabilize production in such a way that factories have an incentive to raise compliance.

Of course, this trajectory toward obligation is not without strong opposition. Many companies have rejected the Accord based on what they see as increased liability and because they object to the role in negotiations played by unions, or what the head of the National Retail Federation called a "narrow agenda driven by special interests."[10] It is precisely the elements of contractual obligation and workers being party to the agreement that makes the Accord a major departure from voluntary monitoring—and therefore anathema to many companies. The competing Alliance for Bangladesh Worker Safety, initiated by Walmart and The Gap, replicates the major flaws of CSR monitoring (for a full discussion of the Accord and the Alliance see chapter 1 of this volume). We can only hope that the Accord and not the Alliance is indicative of the future.

Neither private nor independent monitoring can replace government enforcement, and neither can effectively function without a guarantee of workers' rights to organize on their own behalf. But private regulation, through monitoring agreements, can play a significant role within this context. The strongest contribution of codes and monitoring will be the extent to which it requires changes in the sourcing structure of the industry and is tied to contractually binding agreements in which workers are a recognized party.

THE TWILIGHT OF CSR

Life and Death Illuminated by Fire

Robert J. S. Ross

In the years since the Interfaith Center on Corporate Responsibility (ICCR) was founded (1971–1973, see ICCR 2011) most of the corporate world has adopted nominal policies that project individual firms as ethical citizens, compliant with environmental and social standards and concerned about the well-being of employees—including those it indirectly engages through contracting arrangements. Corporate codes of conduct have become common and multiparty codes are proliferating. This is especially so in the global apparel business, where sweatshop, child labor, and forced labor abuses have proved extremely embarrassing and potentially harmful to reputation-sensitive brands and retailers (Esbenshade 2012 and in chapter 3 of this volume; Anner, Bair, and Blasi 2012). This paper places the issue of labor standards in the strategic context of a global "race to the bottom" in the apparel business, using US trade data as evidence for worldwide cheapening of garments and the labor of the people who make them.

In this context, researchers concerned about global labor standards and the activist anti-sweatshop movements have been skeptical about voluntary codes of conduct and self-policing, internally held social compliance audits. This paper examines factory fires and building collapses in Bangladesh as a serial case study in CSR efficacy. It uses quantitative data jointly developed by the author and staff members of the International Labor Rights Forum and the Clean Clothes Campaign and briefly reported in the ILRF document "Deadly Secrets." From that data are gleaned six high-mortality incidents for further study. For each of these fires (including two building collapses), the brands and retailers who were supplied from the factory are examined in terms of CSR policies. Very high proportions of the traceable customers of the fire-damaged and collapsed factories have had outwardly clear CSR policies that seem to hold them and their business partners to high standards of health and safety in the workplaces with which they are engaged. The conclusion is that CSR policies have neither prevented nor could they in themselves prevent the death and injury of thousands of workers in this particular place and era. Alternative policies and strategies are discussed at the end.

The Dawn of CSR

In a pathbreaking 1957 article in the *American Economic Review*, the economist Carl Kaysen called the modern corporation "soulful" (Kaysen 1957, 314). Kaysen's much-commented-on essay argued that the modern corporation was:

> No longer the agent of proprietorship seeking to maximize return on investment, management sees itself as responsible to stockholders, employees, customers, the general public, and, perhaps most important, the firm itself as an institution. To the customers, management owes an improving product, good service, and fair dealing. Where customers are themselves firms, not households, the emphasis on fair dealing is especially strong. To the employees, management owes high wages, pensions and insurance systems, medical care programs, stable employment, agreeable working conditions, a human personnel policy. Its responsibilities to the general public are widespread: leadership in local charitable enterprises, concern with factory architecture and landscaping, provision of support for higher education, and even research in pure science, to name a few. To the firm itself, as an institution, the management owes the primary responsibility of insuring the maintenance and, if possible, the expansion of its long-run position; in other words, sustained and rapid growth. (Kaysen 1957, 313)

Kaysen's perspective on the evolving global political-economic process proved largely parochial. Bounded by an American economy that was then more or less autarchic, and an American state that was thoroughly hegemonic in the world political economy, Kaysen did not anticipate the emerging era of global capitalism and the price competition that would supplant the "monopoly capital" era of which he was one of the high priests.[1] The high-price, high-wage economy of the Keynesian era was not sustained under the withering fire of global competition.

Despite the structural limits of the "soulful corporation" conception, its cultural projection was spot-on. When the low-income areas of US cities occupied by African American residents were the scene of repeated civil disturbances in the 1960s, many US firms—some with headquarters or other facilities at risk—began to deploy some resources to acknowledge "responsibility" to local communities. By 1973 the ICCR had taken the "radical" campaign for disinvestment from firms invested in apartheid South Africa into shareholder activism led by church-held pension funds.

Vernon Jordan, the Washington, DC, political and corporate insider who headed the Urban League, captured the CSR concept in a speech quoted by the *Washington Post* (1989):

> The philosophy of corporate social responsibility, as it has evolved in America, is rooted in the belief that such behavior is an essential precondition for the continued existence of the free enterprise system. It was also recognized that in a free society, *image is important—and that a good corporate image is both a defense against attacks on corporations and a policy supportive of business success* . . . Those beliefs were supported by surveys that showed that companies with strong social responsibility programs enjoyed greater financial success than others. *Put bluntly, in America, corporate social responsibility is good business.* (*Washington Post*, January 24, 1989. Emphasis added)

By the middle of the 1990s a quarter-century of deindustrialization and outsourcing had already provoked both journalistic and academic attention to labor conditions in the factories abroad producing for the US market (Buck 1979; Flannery 1978; Ross and Trachte 1983). In 1995 California and federal authorities raided El Monte, an apartment complex near Los Angeles, where seventy slave laborers had been held captive while producing clothing for name brands. The next year, the investigator Charles Kernaghan revealed that clothing branded by a major daytime television personality, Kathie Lee Gifford (who had pledged some profits to children's causes), and which was retailed by Walmart, had been implicated in child labor in Honduras and sweatshop labor in New York (Su 1997; Ross 2004, 223–27). These, among many specific and general exposés, subjected major brands and retailers to significant reputation damage by association with sordid labor conditions.

The 1990–2000 period was called by one group of researchers a "momentum building" phase in the evolution of CSR. The period saw a rise in concern from citizens, consumers, public authorities, and investors, which can be attributed to an increase in media attention to business practices and the modern communication technology that made the spread of this information possible. Membership organizations were founded and social auditing began (Katsoulakos et al. 2004, 15–17; chapter 3 of this volume).

Codes of Conduct

The typical embodiment of a firm's commitment to social responsibility is its adoption of a code of conduct. Eighty-six percent of the Fortune Global 200 had codes of conduct as of 2007. This was double the rate of a decade ago (KPMG 2007). Of those with codes, 88 percent monitor compliance in some way and 40 percent use external auditing. Sixty percent of code users, that is, about 103 of the top 200 firms, screen "business partners" against their code criteria. All of the code users have some form of reporting to the company board (KPMG 2007, 18–19).

In our studies of Bangladesh fires we did not come across a single prominent Western brand or retail buyer that did not have a code of conduct, and they all contained references to worker safety. Although codes of conduct are the basic statements of firms' CSR commitments, they are implemented in a variety of ways. Self-auditing, hired auditors, and membership in and use of third-party auditors are among these. Esbenshade discusses implementation in detail (2012; and in chapter 3 of this volume). Subscribing to industry-wide codes and monitoring initiatives often entails inspection of a firm's contractor factories and in one way or another certification of them as satisfying the code.

The evolution of CSR initiatives has taken on more importance as the form of global capitalism becomes more complete, more dominant, and more institutionally embedded (see Ross and Trachte 1990). The most recent and most elaborated ideology in the era of globalized capital is economic neoliberalism. That is, the perception and the prescription that international markets and trade are best left to operate freely without government intervention. As the prevailing ideology (but not the necessary condition) of global capitalism, neoliberalism is also the ideology that dominates the global policymaking process (Rosen 2002, 13).[2]

Absent effective legal regulatory mechanisms that operate at global scale—or governments willing to use them—social actors attempt to pressure directly the multinational corporations and firms of global capitalism. These, in turn, adopt various CSR policies, like the codes and attendant auditing, as protection from criticism, brand damage, and legal liability. Taken together—activist movements and corporate response—there emerges a reified theory of dubious validity: consumer sovereignty. Derived from neoclassical economists, the proposition has been put in equally naïve terms by both consumer activists and libertarian zealots.

With entirely different intent, F.A. Hayek's American acolyte, former representative Ron Paul, told the US House of Representatives: "The consumer is king, not the businessman . . . we should crown the consumers king and let them vote with their money on who should succeed and who should fail . . . Consumer sovereignty simply means consumers decide who succeeds or fails in the market. Businesses that best satisfy consumer demand will be the most successful. Consumer sovereignty is the means by which the free market maximizes human happiness" (Paul 1999, H11683–H1168).

The size of the sales effort including advertising stands as the simple refutation of the proposition regarding consumer sovereignty. As of 2009 the combined marketing and advertising expenditures were an estimated $778 billion (Myers 2007), and advertising agencies alone employed 411,000 persons; we may surmise that products are not selling themselves.[3] There is some evidence such expenditures are growing faster than the GDP.

Lack of Effectiveness

At its heart CSR is based on an aspiration: that maximum profitability can simultaneously be maintained with internationally acceptable labor standards. Although rarely committing firms to paying workers a living wage, these codes universally commit firms to obeying the local legal minimum wage and overtime laws (see chapter 3).

What is the likely outcome, however, if profit maximization or lowest price supply comes in conflict with maintaining high standards? Below I will show why this is apt to be the case, but in principle the problem with a nonbinding, self-imposed, self-monitoring system is that the incentives are not aligned so as to produce good behavior when good behavior is challenged by cost considerations. Should an audit show a contractor is out of compliance with this or that item on a checklist, the firm may ignore it, give its business partner some time to correct it, remind itself to look at the situation again at some later date, *or do nothing*—a firm may turn to another factory entirely. The factory owners have only the last option to fear; the former responses can all be "worked out." The firm's interest in finding another factory that will cost more to produce the same or future items hinges only on discovery by external agents, in particular retail consumers, that some embarrassing lapse has been found. In almost all cases the compliance audit report has been held closely; it is either entirely confidential or aggregated among others in a way that holds no one accountable (see chapter 3).

The empirical reality is that the global apparel context is one of ruthless competition and descending prices: the firms have not been willing to sacrifice low cost for worker safety or decent wages. Data gleaned from US government and World Trade Organization sources document the global context and Bangladesh's place within it.

The Race to the Bottom

The context of CSR and the Bangladeshi fires is set by global clothing prices and costs. The United States Office of Textiles and Apparel (OTEXA 2012), a division of the Commerce Department, maintains an online database of imports by item, country, volume, and dollar value. The volume measure is a notional unit—SME (square-meter equivalent). By dividing an annual dollar volume by the annual unit volume, the result is the per-unit cost of an imported item for any year from 1989 to the present (see Ross 2009; and Anner, Bair, and Blasi 2012 for prior uses of this method). Having done this for 1989–2012 we then used the Bureau of Economic Analysis GDP deflator index (BEA 2015) to convert all values to 2005 dollars. The result is figure 4.1.

The real, inflation corrected, world cost per unit of imports has declined steadily. Not shown is that after 2005, that is, the end of the Multi-Fiber Arrangement, there was an abrupt shift of suppliers from the Western Hemisphere to Asia (see Ross 2009). For example, Mexico's share of imports has

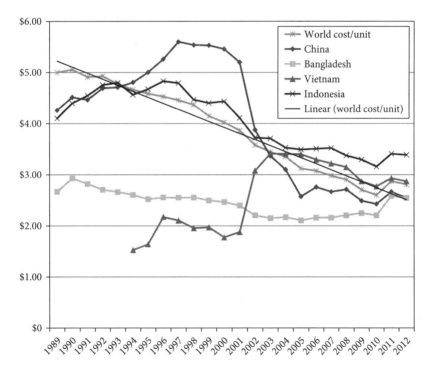

FIGURE 4.1 Real per-unit cost of imported clothing, US, 1989–2012 (2005 dollars), author's calculations

Source: Office of Textiles and Apparel, US Department of Commerce

dropped from about 15 percent to under 5 percent; there was a high correlation between source shift and GDP/capita: the work flowed away from the better paid to worse paid.

Bangladesh consistently has been the world's low-price supplier. Surprisingly, these data show that China—despite widespread reports of wage increases in the export sector (Fung 2011)—is still a low-price supplier. World per-unit cost has dropped 44 percent since 1989, 30 percent since 2000, and 16 percent since 2004.[4] In the meantime, import penetration has risen to over 97 percent (AAFA 2012). It is in the face of this global regime of price cutting that pious declarations become aspirational, not operational. The result is that a declining fraction of American expenditure is devoted to clothing. In 1984, 6.2 percent of the average household's expenditure was on clothing; in 2011 it was 2.8 percent.[5] Household average incomes rose 34 percent from 1984 to 2011, but apparel costs increased only 22 percent (US Bureau of Labor Statistics 2012).

Although it is arguably the case that firms have some control over their prices—they are highly concentrated, with but a handful of chain department stores controlling most sales—the aggressive discounters, led by Walmart, put a downward pressure on all of them. In the meantime, the tens of thousands of contractor factories in the global export business are price takers: they scramble for bids with differences at pennies per garment. The iron discipline of the race to the bottom is not a friendly context for piety. In what follows we will show how declarations of corporate social responsibility become epitaphs.

Fires and Collapses in Bangladesh

Bangladesh has a singular history of factory fires in its apparel industry. A mixed-method study that included the years 1990–2012 produced an estimate of over one thousand deaths in factory incidents (through 2011, prior to the Rana Plaza collapse in April 2013), almost all of these from fires in apparel factories (Claeson 2012).[6]

The total of 1,071 deaths, of which 982 were from fires, is no doubt an underestimate. Some of the data were generated through searches in the English-language sources of the news database LexisNexis. For the period 2006–2009, the database searches on factory fires in Bangladesh produced a mortality figure of 128 persons. However, Bangladesh's Fire Service and Civil Defense Department reported 414 factory fire deaths for the 2006–2009 period. For the years before and after 2006–2009, our estimates are based largely on LexisNexis searches.

Despite this apparent underestimation by our source, the question arises as to whether Bangladesh has a distinctive history of factory fires. A LexisNexis search

TABLE 4.1   Deaths from factory fires, Bangladesh 1990–2012

YEARS	DEATHS	DEATHS FROM FIRE
1990–2012	1,071	982
2006–2009	414	414
2010–2012	206	198

Data from NGO and LexisNexis sources, as compiled by the author and reported in Claeson 2012.

TABLE 4.2   Relative story counts, factory fires, selected countries

COUNTRY	NO. OF STORIES	DATELINE YEARS OF STORIES
Bangladesh	595	1995–2013
Pakistan	332	1993–2013
China	219	1992–2013
India	65	1995–2013
Thailand	52	1993–2013
Vietnam	9	1994–2011
Mexico	3	2000–2001
Philippines	2	2007–2010
Indonesia	1	2004

Source: LexisNexis.

of "all available dates" and "all news" (English) was performed with the following protocol. The search term was "Bangladesh w/10 factory fire AND LEAD (Bangladesh AND fire)," with Bangladesh, Philippines, Thailand, etc. successively inserted. "W/10" means the words occur within ten words of the first term. "LEAD" means the words were found in the lead paragraph. The search returns, in big events, many stories. It is clear that recent events also are covered more than they were in the past. Further, not all stories are reports of current fire incidents; some refer, for example, to an anniversary of a fire or reportage of fires in other countries. The earliest years of coverage in each country may be uneven. Nevertheless, it seems appropriate to judge that the volume of stories is an *indicator of the relative volume* of fire incidents. The comparisons were performed on April 25, 2013. The results are in table 4.2.

These data are not corrected for population or number of factories, they do not include reports of collapses, but they do provide evidence about some contentions. First, the distinctively higher number of press mentions in Bangladesh cannot be attributed to its relatively free press having more political leeway to report catastrophes. India, Indonesia, and Thailand all rank higher on a Press Freedom Index and lower on fire stories (Reporters Without Borders 2013).

Similarly, the use of English as a language of commerce is at least as common in India, so using English-language sources is not apt to distort that comparison. Additionally, given that Pakistan's manufacturing sector is much smaller than Bangladesh's (Pakistan Bureau of Statistics 2013), the large number of stories is a reminder that before the Rana Plaza collapse of April 24, 2013, the largest industrial loss of life had occurred in a fire in Pakistan on September 12, 2012 when almost three hundred persons died. It begs further scrutiny, but the conclusion remains. Bangladesh has a distinctively high profile for fires and factory disasters.

Deadly working conditions have not prevented a rising tide of orders from Western brands. Bangladesh's share of the world garment export market has steadily increased, reaching 4.8 percent in 2011 (see figure 4.2). This is an over 90 percent increase since 2005—the year twenty-three workers were killed in the Shan knitting factory and sixty-four were killed in the Spectrum building collapse.[7] The rising tide of death, it seems, was balanced by the continuation of Bangladesh as the world's low-cost provider.

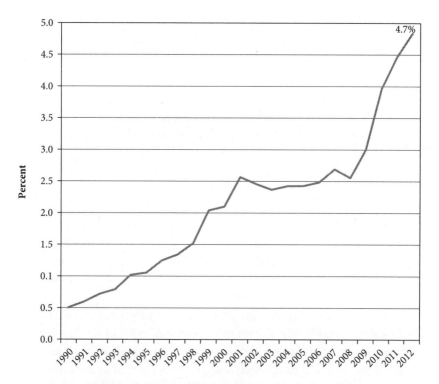

FIGURE 4.2   Bangladesh share of world clothing exports, 1990–2012

Source: World Trade Organization statistical database, online

Codes of Conduct and Factory Fires

Although many writers (for example Anner, Bair, and Blasi 2012; and Esben-shade in chapter 3 of this volume) report their perception of near-universal consensus that CSR policies have been ineffective in maintaining labor standards, there is reason to doubt that consensus is universal and thus there is cause to revisit the matter. Knowledge about such matters does not travel well across disciplines or political subcultures. Observers and commentators nested in fashion institutes do not seem to share sociologists' skepticism about codes of conduct—courses on CSR are plentiful in these settings. Business and management journals with CSR themes continue to proliferate even as the number of academic and other articles concerning labor issues multiply. In the JSTOR electronic database of over fifteen hundred academic journals in 2000, six articles had "corporate social responsibility" in the title or the abstract; in 2012, sixty-five did.

As Scott Nova and Chris Wegemer show in chapter 1 of this volume, the vol-untaristic version of CSR maintains a firm grip on the higher reaches of the corporate world in the United States. Whereas the loss of 1,138 lives in the spec-tacular Rana Plaza building collapse has become the apparent pivot of historical change in Bangladesh, only a handful of US-based firms have joined 190 mainly European firms in signing a binding agreement on factory safety and worker empowerment (Accord on Fire and Building Safety in Bangladesh 2015a). Amer-ican firms represent 22 percent of Bangladesh's apparel export market, but the big American firms (prominently Walmart and The Gap) have refused to join the Accord, saying they will fund their own factory safety efforts (the "Alliance") and balking at the binding nature of the commitments (see Brudney and Fisk 2013; Greenhouse 2013).[8]

Case Studies

We have assembled information on six high-mortality incidents in Bangladesh since 2000. For each of these we investigated to the extent possible the retail brands or retailers that had purchased material from the factories involved. For each of the firms that we found, we investigated their codes of conduct concern-ing worker health and safety. We also attempted to find out if the factories in question had been audited or otherwise certified by a third party. The sources for these investigations were the LexisNexis database and NGO reports as published on their websites. These prominently included the Clean Clothes Campaign, the Worker Rights Consortium, and others.[9] There is at least one notable exclusion from these cases.

The Choudhury (sometimes Chowdury) Knitwear fire in Narsingdi in 2000 killed fifty-three people. In the Choudhury case, "The factory building did not have a proper fire exit and the staircase was narrower than is required. The fire exits were locked and the workers were trapped inside the factory building . . . They did not have a fire hose . . . There were no trained workers who could help the unfortunate to escape" (Ahmed and Hossain 2012, 8). We exclude the case because we could find no information about buyers from the factory. The case studies below are examples of the hundreds of fires and collapses in the Bangladesh apparel industry over the last two decades. In what follows, we trace the firms that bought from the factories and their statements on relevant labor standards.

Mirpur (2001)

On August 8, 2001, a fire broke out at the Mirpur factory in Dhaka, Bangladesh. Twenty-four garment workers died as a result of the fire. Many workers were trampled to death in the building's staircase by others stampeding out of the fire zone. Of the four factories in the building, only one had fire drills. Emergency exists were locked. The Dutch retailer C&A was confirmed to have conducted an audit of the factory. C&A's audit company, SOCAM, visited the Mirpur facility two weeks before the fire and reported that although both exits were open, the staircases were partially blocked by boxes. In response to this report, C&A contacted its Taiwanese supplier who subcontracts to MAICO Sweaters—a shop housed in the fifth through seventh floors of the Mirpur factory. No other known measures were taken by C&A. The company's code of conduct for the supply of merchandise stated the following: "Suppliers must ensure that all manufacturing processes are carried out under conditions which have proper and adequate regard for the health and safety of those involved . . . Where we believe that a supplier has breached the requirements set out in this code either for C&A production or for any other third party, we will not hesitate to end our business relationship including the cancellation of outstanding orders. We also reserve the right to take whatever other actions are appropriate and possible" (C&A Buying 1998; CCC 2001).[10]

The Swedish retailer H&M also had its clothing produced in the Mirpur factory, and although the company did not conduct an audit of the facility it does have a code of conduct for its suppliers. H&M's products from Mirpur were made by Four Wings, a supplier located on the second floor of the building. After the fire, Ingrid Schullstrom, H&M's code of conduct manager, claimed that Four Wings regularly performed fire drills. Four Wings' execution of regular fire drills was in compliance with one clause of H&M's code of conduct, which states: "Everyone working on the premises, including managers and guards, must be regularly trained in how to act in case of fire or other emergency. Regular evacuation drills for all employees are required; evacuation plans and fire fighting equipment must be in place" (H&M 2010).

Despite allegedly being in compliance with this one clause, the fact that Four Wings was located in the unsafe Mirpur facility is in direct violation of another clause in H&M's code of conduct: "We require our suppliers and other business partners to make employees' safety a priority at all times. No hazardous equipment or unsafe buildings are accepted" (CCC 2001; H&M 2010).

Spectrum-Shahriyar (2005)

Although not a factory fire, the Spectrum-Shahriyar facility located in Savar, an industrial town some 30 kilometers northwest of Dhaka, collapsed on April 11, 2005 shortly before 1 a.m.[11] The building's collapse killed sixty-four workers, wounded seventy-four, and left hundreds of others without jobs. Yet the structural instability of the Spectrum facility was not unknown. On several occasions before the collapse workers tried to report their concerns regarding the safety of the building, including one worker who noticed cracks in the factory wall five days before the building crumbled to the ground. This worker was told to keep his mouth shut and work. Other structural problems that workers knew about at Spectrum were: (1) the equipment was too heavy for the factory floor, (2) exposed wiring, and (3) only bricks and sand composed the foundation of the building. Prior to its collapse, Spectrum was violating not only its construction permit but also the minimum wage and one day off per week laws (CCC 2005a, 2006).

Most of the brands who sourced from the Spectrum factory stated that they did not commission any audits at the factory. However, one of the largest retailers in the world, the French corporation Carrefour, did have an audit commissioned but did not make the results of the audit public (CCC 2005a). In addition to Carrefour, other brands with codes of conduct that had their clothing produced at the Spectrum factory were: Inditex from Spain, Solo Invest from France, Cotton Group from Belgium, Karstadt Quelle and Bluhmod from Germany, Scapino from the Netherlands, and New Wave Group from Sweden (CCC 2006).

Spectrum's poor construction conditions, as well as its minimum wage and one day off per week violations, illustrate a clear lack of compliance with the codes of conduct of the brands who produced at the facility. Carrefour's code of conduct states that the company joined the United Nations Global Compact in 2001 to comply with and promote its principles regarding human rights and labor standards in Carrefour's supply chain (Carrefour 2011, 7). Solo Invest, the other French company that had suppliers in the Spectrum factory, also applies the rules of the UN's Global Compact in its CSR charter (SOL's Europe 2013).

The Spanish corporation Inditex was named one of the "100 Most Sustainable Corporations in the World" in 2007, two years after the Spectrum building collapse (Corporate Knights 2007). The company's code of conduct for manufacturers and suppliers in regard to working conditions states: "Manufacturers and suppliers shall provide a safe and healthy workplace to their employees, ensuring minimum conditions of light, ventilation, hygiene, fire prevention, safety measures and access to a drinking water supply . . . Manufacturers and suppliers shall take the required steps to prevent accidents and injuries to health of their workers, by minimizing as much as possible the risks inherent to work" (Inditex 2001).

Additionally, Inditex has this to say about wages: "Manufacturers and suppliers shall ensure that wages paid meet at least the minimum legal or collective bargain agreement, should this latter be higher. In any event, wages should always be enough to meet at least the basic needs of workers and their families and any other which might be considered as reasonable additional needs. Manufacturers and suppliers shall not make any withholdings and/or deductions from wages for disciplinary purposes, nor for any reasons other than those provided in the applicable regulations, without the express authorization of workers." Finally, regarding days off for workers, Inditex's code of conduct for manufacturers and suppliers had stated: "Manufacturers and suppliers shall not require their employees to work, as a rule of thumb, in excess of 48 hours a week and workers shall be granted at least one day off for every 7 calendar day period on average" (Inditex 2001).

The Belgian retailer Cotton Group bases its code of conduct on the Fair Wear Foundation's (FWF) Code of Labour Practices, which is in turn based on the Conventions of the International Labour Organization (ILO) and the Universal Declaration of Human Rights. Among the standards laid out in FWF's code, the ones of relevance to Spectrum state: "safe and healthy working conditions . . . payment of a living wage . . . no excessive hours of work" (Fair Wear Foundation/ Cotton Group 2009).

Spectrum's four remaining buyers, Karstadt Quelle and Bluhmod from Germany, Scapino from the Netherlands, and the Swedish New Wave Group, all participate in the Business Social Compliance Initiative's (BSCI) code of conduct for their suppliers (New Wave Group 2012; Bluhmod 2013; Macintosh Retail Group 2013; Miller 2013, 35–36). Karstadt Quelle additionally had a quality audit conducted, reportedly using the firm Societé Générale de Surveillance (SGS) (CCC 2005b). BSCI is an initiative of the Foreign Trade Association (FTA) and states that its code of conduct is: "Based on the most important international labour standards protecting the workers' rights such as the International

Labour Organization (ILO) Conventions and other important Declarations of the United Nations, the OECD guidelines for multinational enterprises and the UN Global Compact" (FTA 2013).

Among the provisions laid out in BSCI's code of conduct are that: "legal minimum and/or industry standards wages are paid," "the workplace is safe and healthy," and "working hours are compliant with national laws and do not exceed 48 hours regular + 12 hours overtime" (FTA 2013). Spectrum violated all these provisions. Later, after the Rana Plaza catastrophe, a BSCI spokesperson said "BSCI considers its work a social audit and doesn't examine the structural soundness of the building . . . Social auditors are not technical engineers or architects. What they usually will look at is whether there is a building permit. That's pretty much where it stops" (Ensign 2013).

Garib & Garib and That's It Sportswear (2010)

The beginning of the 2010s marked a deadly start to a deadly decade for Bangladesh. In particular, among twenty-six factory fires, two had large fatalities: one at the Garib & Garib Sweater Ltd.'s factory in February, and another at a factory called That's It Sportswear in December (Claeson 2012, 22).

GARIB & GARIB

The Garib & Garib factory in Gazipur caught fire on February 25, 2010 and caused the deaths of twenty-one apparel workers. According the International Labor Rights Forum:

> A government-authorized probe into the cause of the fire said the fire was started by an electric short-circuit on the second floor of the factory. It quickly spread to the other floors filled with inflammable materials such as wool threads and other goods. Lasting nearly two hours, the fire created a thick black smoke and consumed the oxygen in the air, suffocating the workers. The smoke could not escape because of poor ventilation and the presence of unauthorized sheet metal structures that were being used for storage of highly inflammable materials on the roof of the building. Workers could not escape because exits were locked and materials blocked the stairways. The factory's fire-fighting equipment was "virtually useless", according to the Dhaka Fire Service and Civil Defence, and reportedly none of the security guards on duty knew how to operate fire extinguishers and hydrants. (ILRF 2012)

Garib & Garib was found to have produced sweaters for both the Swedish brand H&M (whose code we have discussed previously) and Mark's Work

Wearhouse, a Canadian retailer. Mark's Work Wearhouse explained that it conducted "social compliance audits, mainly with our partner Bureau Veritas (BV), based on BV's audit standards, which follow the ILO's base standards" (Claeson 2010).

According to the Mark's Work Wearhouse website, the brand has implemented a Supplier Code of Business Conduct, called the Code, through Canadian Tire Corporation, Ltd. (CTC), its parent organization. The employment standards section of the Code's Expectations Of Suppliers states: "Suppliers will employ employees who are, in all cases . . . not put at risk of physical harm due to their work environment." The workplace environment section affirms: "Suppliers will provide workers with a safe and healthy working environment consistent with all applicable laws and regulations" (CTC 2008). Mark's then, as stated above, conducts social compliance audits with their partner BV, whose audit standards mirror the ILO's base standards. Article 4, Section 2 of the ILO's 1981 Occupational Safety and Health Convention decrees the following regarding safety of the workplace: "The aim of the policy shall be to prevent accidents and injury to health arising out of, linked with or occurring in the course of work, by minimizing, so far as is reasonably practicable, the causes of hazards inherent in the working environment" (ILO 2012).

The audits conducted by BV on behalf of Mark's and its code of conduct either were not made public or communicated to the workers or did not register the safety violations in the factory. H&M was confirmed to have had an audit of the Garib & Garib Sweater factory conducted on its behalf just four months prior to the fire. The company reported that it found nothing remarkable in its audit. Garib & Garib's inadequate firefighting equipment, lack of emergency exits, and absence of smoke detectors were not mentioned (Claeson 2012). On the contrary, H&M's audit stated that there were clearly marked escape routes and emergency exits, as well as fire extinguishers (ILRF 2012).

The reality of the poor fire-safety conditions found in Garib & Garib are all violations of H&M's code of conduct, as previously quoted. In addition to being audited by H&M, and by BV on behalf of Mark's Work Wearhouse, Garib & Garib was also certified by Worldwide Responsible Accredited Production (WRAP), an industry monitoring organization. WRAP found Garib & Garib to be compliant with WRAP 12 Principles (Claeson 2012, 22). The principle that covers the conditions of the workplace states: "Facilities will provide a safe and healthy work environment" (WRAP 2015).

THAT'S IT SPORTSWEAR

Ten months after the Garib & Garib fire, on December 14, 2010, twenty-nine workers were killed in a fire at the That's It Sportswear factory in Dhaka. Owned by the HaMeem Group,[12] That's It Sportswear produced clothing for The Gap Inc., the owner of Gap, Old Navy, and Banana Republic brands, and PVH, the owner of the Tommy Hilfiger, Calvin Klein, Izod, Van Heusen, Bass, and Arrow brands. JC Penney, VF Corporation, Abercrombie & Fitch, Carter's, Kohl's, and Target also were buyers from the factory. Each of them, with the exception of Carter's, has a publicly available statement requiring suppliers to protect the health and safety of their workers.

Survivors of the fire reported that the building's emergency exits were closed, thus trapping the workers on the ninth floor. Desperate to escape the smoke and heat, workers jumped out of the windows and fell to their deaths. "The fire, which broke out in what was considered a modern building, was, like so many others, caused by an electrical short-circuit and substandard wiring. It was reported that proper fire drills were not carried out, that the exits were blocked, that the workplace was not properly supervised and that the company only had a permit for the lower floors" (CCC 2011).

A Gap spokesperson confirmed they were sourcing from the factory at the time, and that they had performed audits both in April and August prior to the fire (Hammadi and Taylor 2010). That The Gap sourced from the HaMeem factory is interesting given GAP's highly detailed Code of Vendor Conduct (COVC). Part 4, Working Conditions, Section A, Occupational Health and Safety, contains the following provisions that are related to the fire at That's It Sportswear:

> 1. The factory complies with all applicable laws regarding working conditions, including worker health and safety, sanitation, fire safety, risk protection, and electrical, mechanical and structural safety . . . 4. There are sufficient, clearly marked exits allowing for the orderly evacuation of workers in case of fire or other emergencies. Emergency exit routes are posted and clearly marked in all sections of the factory. 5. Aisles, exits and stairwells are kept clear at all times of work in process, finished garments, bolts of fabric, boxes and all other objects that could obstruct the orderly evacuation of workers in case of fire or other emergencies. The factory indicates with a "yellow box" or other markings that the areas in front of exits, fire-fighting equipment, control panels and potential fire sources are to be kept clear. 6. Doors and other exits are kept accessible and unlocked during all working hours for orderly evacuation in case of fire or other emergencies. All main exit doors open to the outside. 7. Fire extinguishers are appropriate to the types of possible fires in the various areas of the factory, are regularly maintained and charged, display the date of their last inspection, and are mounted on walls and columns throughout the factory so they are visible and accessible to workers in

all areas. 8. Fire alarms are on each floor and emergency lights are placed above exits and on stairwells." (Gap Inc. 2007)

PVH's code of conduct, which the company calls "A Shared Commitment—Requirements for Suppliers, Contractors and Business Partners," states: "Our business partners must provide a safe and healthy workplace designed and maintained to prevent accidents, illness and injury attributable to the work performed or the operation of the facility and machinery. In doing so, our business partners must comply with all national laws, regulations and best practices concerning health and safety in the workplace, as well as provide all required and appropriate workers compensation coverage in the event of injury or fatality" (PVH 2011).

Tazreen Fashions (2012)

On November 24, 2012, fire broke out at the Tazreen Fashions apparel factory in Dhaka, taking the lives of 112 workers. The origin of this fire is obscure. Fatalities were exacerbated by the factory's lack of open and secure fire exits, the extra floors added to the building, fire extinguishers that were not used (and perhaps not functional), and the refusal of floor managers to let workers leave their sewing machines even after fire alarms had begun sounding (Manik and Taylor 2012; Maquila Solidarity Network 2012b).

Owned by the Tuba Group, Tazreen produced clothing for a large number of brands and retailers. Walmart, Sears, Kik, Dickies, Disney, C&A, and Li & Fung were all buyers at Tazreen and all had CSR codes of conduct (Maquila Solidarity Network 2012b). Delowar Hossain, the owner of the Tuba Group facility, stated in an interview that a team from Walmart's local office conducted a compliance audit in 2011. He then said that the audit faulted the factory for excessive overtime, but made no mention of fire safety or other issues. In contrast to Mr. Hossain's statement, Kevin Gardner, a Walmart spokesman, has said that the company stopped authorizing production at Tazreen "many months before the fire." He did not say why the company made that decision, however. Mr. Gardner then went on to explain that accredited outside auditors inspected the factory on Walmart's behalf at least twice in 2011. That May, auditors gave Tazreen an "orange" rating, meaning there were "higher-risk violations." Three months later, the factory's grade improved to "yellow," meaning there were "medium-risk violations" (Yardley 2012).

Walmart's inspections were conducted on May 16, 2011 and in December 2011; the December audit conducted by Underwriters Laboratories (UL). A third monitoring report was carried out by Walmart in April 2012 (Bustillo, Wright, and Mattioli 2012; Greenhouse and Yardley 2012; CCC and Center for Research on Multinational Corporations 2013).

The work for Walmart was a subcontract. "The order for Walmart's Faded Glory shorts, documents show, was subcontracted from Simco Bangladesh Ltd., a local garment maker. 'It is an open secret to allow factories to do that,'" David Hasanat, "the chairman of the Viyellatex Group, one of the country's most highly regarded garment manufacturers," said. "End of the day, for them it is the price that matters" (Yardley 2012).

Walmart's Standards for Suppliers repeats familiar language: "3. Labor Hours: Suppliers must provide workers with rest days and must ensure that working hours are consistent with the law and not excessive . . . 7. Health and Safety: Suppliers must provide workers with a safe and healthy work environment. Suppliers must take proactive measures to prevent workplace hazards" (Walmart 2012).

Given the spectacular failure of the self-regulated code of conduct in November at Tazreen and then the horrific failure in April 2013 at Rana Plaza, one notes with interest that Walmart has—along with The GAP—refused to join forty European retailers in a binding safety agreement.

Walmart's failure (and refusal) is not unique, only uniquely large. Sears, Dickies (of the Williamson-Dickie Manufacturing Co.), and Disney all have similar standards statements. In Disney's case, after the Rana Plaza disaster it stated it would withdraw from Bangladesh. Not so the others. They remain in Bangladesh as buyers, and remain committed to the voluntaristic strategy and self-monitoring strategy for securing worker rights and safety.

Also implicated as buyers from Tazreen were the German firm Kik and the Dutch firm C&A. C&A had performed an audit of Tazreen in December 2011 (CCC and Center for Research on Multinational Corporations 2013).

Walmart, Sears, and Disney refused to pay compensation to the victims. Li & Fung Ltd., the Hong Kong-headquartered multinational intermediary, had brokered some production at Tazreen and agreed to pay families the equivalent of $980 for the death of a family member who worked in the factory.

The Rana Plaza Collapse (2013)

On April 24 2013, in what may have been "the worst industrial disaster in history," according to the Worker Rights Consortium's Scott Nova (see chapter 1 in this volume), a building collapse killed 1,138 garment workers in Savar. The factory building housed five firms and had retail stores and a bank on the ground floor. It had been built without full permits and floors had been added on top beyond original permissions. Workers and inspectors had found large cracks in the walls on April 23, and on the morning of the 24th the retail stores and bank did not open. As workers gathered at the building entrance that morning fearing to go in, they were ordered in and threatened with firing if they did not. Shortly after the beginning of the workday the building collapsed, killing 1,138 and hospitalizing 1,800 workers. A list of brands that sourced from the factories in Rana Plaza includes: Bon Marché, Camaieu, El Corte Ingles, Kik, Loblaw, Mascot, Matalan, Primark, Store Twenty One, Adler, Auchan, Benetton, C&A, Carrefour, Cato Corp, The Children's Place, Dressbarn, Essenza, FTA International, Gueldenpfennig, Iconix Brand, Inditex, JC Penney, Kids Fashion Group, LPP, Mango, Manifattura Corona, NKD, Premier Clothing, PWT Group, Texman, and Walmart. As discussed, almost all of these firms had codes of conduct, elements of which the factory building grossly violated.

The Rana Plaza disaster may be the crucible of historic change in Bangladesh and beyond (CCC 2013a). Spurred by outcry from campaigners in the West and tens of thousands of demonstrators in Bangladesh, a safety accord was negotiated that, for the first time, requires the firms to pay for remediation of the factories and requires worker participation in safety measures. An appeals procedure was built into the accord and also allows legal action in the home countries of the firms. The agreement has been signed by 190 firms, though only 5 of them are from the United States. Walmart and The GAP have formed their own Alliance with about 31 members, all from the United States, which does not have the same compulsory features.

Summary of Cases

In these 6 cases, distinguished from the 250 others since 1990 (Claeson 2012, 19) only by their high mortality numbers and the detail we were able to glean about purchasers, 1,300 workers were killed and hundreds of others injured. In each case of fire, exits were blocked, fire-fighting equipment was deficient or absent, and training was nonexistent or minimal. Including the Spectrum and Rana Plaza collapse, in all 6 factories illegal construction was part of the hazard story.

In each case major European and North American brands were big buyers from the factories (since virtually all of Bangladesh's clothing exports go to these two markets). In each case these major brands had codes of conduct with specific reference to labor standards and health and safety standards and expectations of compliance among their contractors. In each case the disaster occurred in a factory that had recently been audited for compliance, either by one of the firms or one of their agents, or by an industry-oriented certification scheme. None of these audits were of public record or available to workers.

Discussion

Although the empirical critiques of CSR policies have been widely broadcast, they are usually at a macro level and take the general form: "with few exceptions workers toil in what can only be considered sweatshops—where pay is low and hours long, where workers are driven by quotas and powerless to complain" (Esbenshade 2012, 562; and see chapter 3 of this volume for a review of the literature). Let us now home in on the micro: despite production for firms with explicit health and safety codes and in factories that have been audited, mortally dangerous conditions continue (see Finnegan 2013 for cases outside of Bangladesh). Analyzing the reasons for failure can lead to improved strategy.

The context of failure is the global competition among factory owners and managers to produce clothing more cheaply than a potential competitor. Circa 2007 there may have been two hundred thousand to three hundred thousand factories in the global export apparel sector, with small workshops potentially bringing the total closer to a million (Wells 2007, 63).

This dispersed supply faces relatively concentrated buying power in Western chains (see Bonacich and Appelbaum 2000; Ross 2004). Pricing power flows downward and forces prices down. In this context higher levels of labor-standard compliance would require factory owners to spend more, but the chains seem unwilling to pay more in the existing competitive context. There are few durable incentives for firms to weigh CSR policies more heavily than price considerations.

One demonstration of the nature of the incentive structure came in the latter part of 2012, after the Tazreen fire disaster. Fifteen firms, including Gap and eventually Walmart, pressed the Bangladeshi government to raise the minimum wage. This was a frank admission of the failure of the voluntaristic CSR strategy. They were not willing to pay more for products in order to improve workers' conditions unless there was a level playing field among them; a legal requirement would force a level playing field (Claeson 2012, 22).

After the 2010 fires at Garib & Garib and That's It Sportswear, lengthy negotiations began on fire safety. The large Western brands included Walmart, Gap, and PVH. Bangladeshi and global labor organizations were assisted in these talks by Bangladeshi and Western NGOs. Walmart left the talks early on. Various news outlets including the *New York Times* and the Associated Press obtained minutes of the discussion after the Tazreen disaster in 2012. *The Times* reported that "Sridevi Kalavakolanu, a Wal-Mart director of ethical sourcing, along with an official from another major apparel retailer, noted that the proposed improvements in electrical and fire safety would involve as many as 4,500 factories and would be 'in most cases' a 'very extensive and costly modification.' 'It is not financially feasible for the brands to make such investments,' the minutes said" (Greenhouse 2012).

Although the "hard law" of state enforcement contrasts with the "soft law" of civil society pressures and the "no law" of ethical intentions, even the strictest laws are only as good as their enforcement. That is a problem in Bangladesh (and elsewhere). In the instance of building safety, our cases show that Bangladesh is effectively lawless. The standards in Bangladeshi building and electrical utility codes are effectively ignored; Walmart's spokesperson's guess as to the number of factories that require remediation is effectively all of the garment export sector.

Any effective address to safety in Bangladesh would require both a short-term and long-term approach to endemic corruption and governmental ineffectiveness. Transparency International rates Bangladesh as perceived to be the most corrupt among the large clothing exporters (Transparency International 2013). No doubt related to this is the chronic lack of resources devoted to factory safety (Parvez 2013). The Dhaka *Daily Star* noted that the "Department of Inspection for Factories and Establishment is pathetically understaffed. 51 inspectors for so many factories spread all over the country is nothing but a farce" (Daily Star 2013). Human Rights Watch observed that "the Ministry of Labour's Inspection Department, responsible for monitoring employers' adherence to Bangladesh's Labour Act, is chronically under-resourced. In June 2012, the Inspection Department had just 18 inspectors and assistant inspectors to monitor an estimated 100,000 factories in Dhaka district" (Human Rights Watch 2013). In some finite period of time, then, part of the solution to worker safety in Bangladesh is the creation of a competent inspectorate with integrity.

No bureaucracy or monitoring program, however, can substitute for informed and empowered workers who are, after all, on the job all the time. Informed in this context means they have undergone safety training and know how to recognize issues and defend their own lives. Empowered means they are protected from retaliation when reporting hazards and are full participants in safety planning. The same is true of adequate compensation. Minimum-wage laws may or may not be enforced, but workers' best hope of obtaining a living wage is their ability to counter the pressures experienced by their employers from buyers who attempt to set very low prices.

The Strategic Situation and a Historical Solution

The problem of worker protection has a familiar strategic context. A dispersed number of suppliers face a concentrated number of buyers in the context of a weak state. This was exactly the situation faced by apparel workers at the time of the Triangle factory fire in 1911 in the United States. Among the assets workers had was the male franchise (which would soon be expanded to include women) and relative freedom of speech. Associational rights at work were contested in politics and in law; the state (especially the local inspectorate) had a tradition of neglect and corruption. The sweatshop then and there had a structural similarity to contemporary sweatshops. The differences are obvious—globalization and different levels of development and wealth, even with a time lag. Nevertheless it is worth observing that the aftereffect of the Triangle Fire may be similar to that of the Rana Plaza collapse: it galvanized reform efforts from responsive politicians and emboldened workers who had already begun organizing. In time (incrementally for the first twenty years and then qualitatively during the 1930s), state policy supported workers' associational rights, the social minima, and the reform of local government. There remained one large obstacle: the structure of the industry itself.

Among the foundations of what Ross (2004) called the era of decency for US apparel workers was the jobbers agreement. "Lower and lower prices to contractors meant lower and lower wages to workers," wrote Emil Schlesinger. "The contractor who survived was the one who could sweat his labor most effectively. However much he might have desired to deal fairly and squarely with labor, the competitive stress drove him inexorably to a hard bargain. His income fluctuated so directly with what he had to pay to the workers in his shop that he was tempted to resort to almost every kind of petty extortion to maintain himself in business. It is for this reason that the sweatshop and the contracting system became practically synonymous terms" (Schlesinger1951, 39).

As Anner, Bair, and Blasi show in detail in chapter 13 of this volume, jobbers agreements were negotiated between the equivalents of today's brands (or their confederations) and the union and—for a time—were successful in protecting garment workers against the fragmentation of supply chains. They have detailed here and elsewhere (Anner, Bair, and Blasi 2012) the political and legal circumstances and the nature of bargaining power in those agreements and argued persuasively that the considerations are relevant to today's global commodity chains.

The much-discussed Accord on Fire and Building Safety in Bangladesh is basically, despite important differences, a jobbers agreement. The reluctance of American firms to sign on (Ross 2013), as contrasted to the European brands, is consistent with US employers' generally more resistant attitude to labor organization. What is striking in the current agreement, however, is the large market share the current signers now represent—about 1,600 factories, which probably means upward of one-third of Bangladesh's export flow.

The American retailers were—for a short time in the spring of 2013—strongly encouraged by the US government to make concessions. In a somewhat surprising turn, the Republican-dominated US House of Representatives voted to require its military-base stores to sign the Accord and to favor sourcing from firms that have signed it (Dhaka Tribune 2013; ILRF 2013). Even in the absence of the North American giants, the firms that have signed the Accord may represent as much or more of Bangladeshi production than the American firms. Nevertheless, there remain two gigantic steps before things can markedly change in Bangladesh and elsewhere: support by the Bangladeshi state and the global spread of the template for labor reform.

In a world where CSR is ineffective and the (Bangladesh) state is corrupt and weak, interim solutions lie in a legal reconceptualization of supply chains that give workers and/or international bodies effective capacities to monitor and reshape conditions. Scott Nova (2014) has shown that the Accord on Fire and Building Safety in Bangladesh is a first step in this direction, and Anner, Bair, and Blasi (2013) have shown jobbers' agreements provide a historical precedent to build on. What is clear, however, is that the sun is setting on societies' dependence on the voluntarism of corporate social responsibility polices to improve labor standards. One hopes the twilight is brief.

Part II

GOVERNANCE OF GLOBAL PRODUCTION NETWORKS

THE DEMISE OF TRIPARTITE GOVERNANCE AND THE RISE OF THE CORPORATE SOCIAL RESPONSIBILITY REGIME

Nelson Lichtenstein

A century and more ago when war, revolution, and imperial hegemony seemed the most obvious fruits of the first era of capitalist globalization, a generation of reformers and social democrats constructed a set of political and economic arrangements, both domestic and international, designed to ameliorate class conflict and limit the tensions that arose between states that had long competed with each other for trade, markets, and labor. "We are running a race with bolshevism, and the world is on fire," asserted President Woodrow Wilson in the chaotic era following the Russian Revolution. Led by Social Democrats in Europe and the somewhat more conservative trade unionists who had bested the Socialists in the United States, representatives of the working class sought to find capitalist partners willing to make a deal in the interests of long-term social stability as well as social justice. Most state managers encouraged the effort, if only to displace and defeat the radicalism born of war and economic collapse with a more reformist statecraft (Maier 1975; Fraser 1991; McCartin 1998).

The resultant system was often denominated as "corporatism" in Europe, "tripartism" in the United States. Although exceedingly fragile during most of the interwar period, this scheme of industrial-relations governance would achieve more solid institutional stability in the immediate post–World War II decades, if largely in the capitalist nation-states of the global North. The three elements of this industrial-governance schema were a strong state, a business community firmly rooted in a single country, and a well-organized working class. Bolstering national unity and class harmony, especially during the Second World War and the Cold War that followed, representatives from each of these

entities negotiated the terms of many of the key economic and social arrangements that characterized the mixed economies of the postwar world: wages,
often on an industry-wide basis, and also government pensions, unemployment
benefits, price controls, health policy, and even the location of new industries.

Founded in 1919, the International Labour Organization (ILO) embraced
this representational and juridical process. ILO tripartism mandated that each
national delegation be composed of a set of delegates representing the government (two votes), employers (one vote) and workers (one vote). The ILO
sought to establish a set of "international labor standards" that would, in turn, be
accepted and incorporated into the national laws of affiliated governments. Such
standards normally took the form of a convention—an international treaty ratified by member states and considered legally binding on signatories—covering
a particular industry or set of workers. In addition, the ILO itself became a large
international bureaucracy with regional offices that provided technical advice,
training, and guidance in host counties (ILO 2014).

The ILO predicated much of its work on the stability of a world political economy that gave to tripartitism a functionality that coincided with how power was
actually distributed and deployed. First, of course, was the existence of an international system of strong states, almost all bordering the North Atlantic, that had the
capacity to ratify conventions and enforce the regulations and arrangements inherent in ILO-sponsored agreements, as well as other instances of social and economic
regulation. These were the kind of "thick" states that were most prevalent, for good
or evil, during the middle years of the twentieth century, an era when the relative
importance of global trade reached a nadir in comparison not only with our own
century but with nineteenth-century commerce as well (Seidman 2007).

Such powerful states, which promised to double in number with decoloniza-
tion in Africa and Asia and the rise of nationalist regimes in Latin America and
the Middle East, presumed the existence of a business sector that was sustained
by and regulated through a clearly bounded national polity. Although most
employers were not large, the most politically and economically potent enterprises during the middle decades of the twentieth century were the vertically
integrated manufacturing and transport corporations. They seemed the template
for the most sophisticated multinational business organizations and the direct
employer of thousands of workers, many well-organized and politically active.
With its own rubber plantations, glass plants, and steel mills, the Ford Motor
Company took vertical integration to an organizational extreme after World War I;
likewise United Fruit, which owned directly Central American banana plantations, railroads, and a shipping fleet, came to define the imperial corporation. US
Steel, with its captive coal and iron mines, seemed an industrial autocracy suddenly democratized with the coming of collective bargaining after 1937. For these

companies and all those which sought to emulate their vertical structure, supply chains and labor markets gravitated toward an internalization and bureaucratization during these decades. Even retailers like Sears and A&P took ownership control of some heretofore independent supply firms that were key links in their respective supply chains (May 1958; Tedlow 2003; McCraw 2009).

Although big corporations and a strong state might well generate an authoritarian polity that eviscerated working-class power, as in Nazi Germany, Imperial Japan, and the Soviet Union—where state-industrial combines were part of the state apparatus—this linkage between a set of vertically integrated industrial and commercial enterprises and a state capable of effective social and economic regulation more often provided the basis for a resurgence of trade-union influence and working-class well-being. Despite a rhetorical commitment to internationalism, labor movements that were bounded by and dependent on the citizenship rights its members held in a particular country exercised real political and economic leverage during the mid-twentieth-century decades. In the world envisioned by those who led or identified with the ILO at midcentury, a stable rights-bearing workforce confronted a set of employers who were themselves clearly rooted within the nation-state itself.

The ILO was therefore structured around a tripartite corporatism in which labor, management, and the state functioned as essential pillars, not only in terms of debate and promulgation of periodic conventions but even more important in terms of implementation of those labor standards, either through state action or some species of firm or industry-centered collective bargaining. Of course, this was just a schematic blueprint: the ILO devoted a huge amount of energy to the promulgation of conventions designed to protect those whose work lives hardly conformed to this vision: sailors and agricultural workers, women engaged in domestic labor or handicrafts, migrants and those without citizenship. But whatever its actual relationship to economic and political reality, the tripartite model was the twentieth-century template, even more so in times of war and economic crisis (Shotwell 1934; Kettunen 2013).

This system is collapsing because in recent years tripartitism has seemed such an ineffectual schema on which to stake a practical reform of the new global economic order. First, as a locus for working-class demands, protections, and civic participation, the modern state is undergoing a dramatic "thinning" process as transnational corporations become increasingly detached from and subversive of the traditional exercise of state regulatory power. Although institutions like the World Trade Organization are hardly world governments, the effort to insure a free and secure flow of private capital, international trade, and intellectual property necessarily circumscribes the power of the traditional nation-state, especially among those economies heavily dependent on export-led growth (Seidman 2007; Klabbers 2014).

Indeed, the rise of a system of buyer-driven global supply chains, with their multilayered set of factories, vendors, and transport links, has created a world system in which legal ownership of the forces of production has been divorced from operational control. Neither Walmart, Nike, Gap, nor Apple own any factories in China, Vietnam, or Bangladesh, but their vendors in those Asian nations are kept on an exceedingly short leash in which the brands and retailers based in Bentonville, Beaverton, San Francisco, and Cupertino play a decisive role in determining the design, price, production schedule, and labor regime under which their products are manufactured. Thus the global economy has been transformed during the past several years from one in which large manufacturers were dominant to one in which transnational retailers, brands, and other service-sector enterprises prevail (Gereffi, Spender, and Bair 2002; Lichtenstein 2009).

This shift has generated a system in which accountability for labor conditions is legally diffused and knowledge of the actual producers is far from transparent. The economist and US Labor Department official David Weil calls this the "fissured workplace." He references the dramatic proliferation of new forms of employment in the United States, including franchising, subcontracting, temp agencies, and the new "sharing economy" made possible by the apps that flow out of Silicon Valley. From the workers' point of view this disappearance and distancing of the boss makes negotiation or even protest over the conditions of work exceedingly difficult (Weil 2014). The globally dispersed and opaque system of production that exists today means that if workers fight for their rights in one factory or even one country, the brand that buys and controls the output might well shift its production to a friendlier or cheaper factory, sometimes in another country. Production is readily moved around the globe, from Taiwan to the mainland, from coastal China to inland provinces, from East Asia to Bangladesh. Thus does this global system devalue, constrain, and "thin" the nation-state and render institutions like the ILO marginal to the new world of supply chains, subcontracting, and hypermobile capital (Abernathy et al. 1999; Gereffi, Humphrey, and Sturgeon 2005; Bair 2006; Petrovic and Hamilton 2006; Lichtenstein 2012).

In place of the tripartite negotiations leading to new or enhanced labor standards, normally encoded in the labor laws and social provisions of a nation-state, this new system of retail-driven supply chains has generated a highly privatized, business-oriented regime that has generated a series of corporate codes that are usually denominated "corporate social responsibility." As Richard Appelbaum and Jill Esbenshade discuss in chapters 2 and 3 of this volume, these CSR initiatives proliferated in the early 1990s when scandals involving child labor, miserable working conditions, and industrial accidents in supply factories embarrassed companies like Nike, Walmart, Kmart, and Walt Disney. In response an increasing number of corporations formulated their own codes of conduct or joined business associations that had promulgated a code covering an entire industry, such as the Fair Labor Association, which focused on the garment industry. By the second decade of the twenty-first century there were hundreds of such codes of conduct. Virtually every major company contained a CSR department, sometimes relabeled "corporate sustainability," in recognition of the large emphasis CSR also put on the minimization of the carbon footprint and the reduction of other kinds of damage to the environment in the corporate supply chain (Bennett and Williams 2011).

Although these CSR initiatives were not formally negotiated, they were the product of a new kind of tripartite negotiation, but with stakeholders far different from those envisioned by the ILO in the years after 1919. The most powerful partner by far was the brand or retailer that stood at the apogee of the supply chain, which was the object of the CSR standards and reforms. Companies like Nike, Apple, Gap, and Target wrote the codes, paid for their administration, used them to rate, reward, and punish vendors and transport companies, and revised them when they failed or proved inadequate. The codes were designed to protect the reputation of the brand and thus many of the first CSR offices were housed within the public-relations departments of these corporations. Later they were often upgraded to independent status, but they remained functionally distinct and organizationally apart from the direct management of the corporate supply chain (Anner 2012b; Esbenshade 2012; Ngai and Xiaomin 2012).

The second stakeholder, whose visibility and voice probably overshadowed its actual power, came out of the burgeoning universe of nongovernmental organizations (NGOs) that have become such important players in the construction and monitoring of the CSR regime. NGOs have a long history as institutions that prick the conscience of the world and in the process ameliorate key features of modern capitalism. The first was probably the British Anti-Slavery Society, founded in 1823, which proved instrumental in the abolition of slavery throughout the world's greatest nineteenth-century empire. Influential also was the US Consumers League, which in the early twentieth century campaigned to end child labor and sweatshop conditions in the garment trades. Today there are literally thousands of NGOs, whose concerns and campaigns range from protecting whales in the Pacific to the eradication of tropical diseases in Africa (Reimann 2006). Others, like United Students Against Sweatshops, Worker Rights Consortium, and the Hong Kong-based Students and Scholars Against Corporate Misbehaviour (SACOM), seek to end abuses in the Asian and Central American factories that put inexpensive garments and athletic shoes on discount-store shelves and consumer electronics on the desk of every student and white-collar worker. NGO leverage arises from the very phenomenon that has so greatly strengthened the power of the twenty-first-century retailers: the brand identity so vital to companies that have outsourced their manufacturing capability and turned themselves into little more than design and marketing houses (Bartley and Child 2014).[1]

Thus when in the mid-1990s Vietnam Labor Watch, United Students Against Sweatshops, and other NGOs accused Nike of violating minimum wage, child labor, and overtime laws in its Chinese, Indonesian, and Vietnamese factories, the company initially disclaimed responsibility for working conditions in these vendor facilities to which it had but an episodic, contractual relationship. However, it soon became apparent that Nike was highly vulnerable to the sentiment of consumers, especially the millions of students and young people who were becoming aware of and influenced by campaigns to tarnish the footwear company's image and erode brand loyalty. Protests took place at store openings, sports media questioned the Nike spokesperson Michael Jordan, and, most significantly, sales softened to the extent that the company began a round of layoffs. CEO Phil Knight finally conceded the point in a 1998 speech, saying: "The Nike product has become synonymous with slave wages, forced overtime, and arbitrary abuse. I truly believe the American consumer doesn't want to buy products made under abusive conditions." To restore consumer confidence, Knight ordered Nike to raise the minimum wage of all its workers, sometimes above that legally mandated in host countries, limited hours to sixty per week, revealed for the first time the names and addresses of every vendor in its worldwide supply chain, and established a system of monitoring to be conducted by a third party, the Fair Labor Association, which it helped found and fund (Nisen 2013). Although Nike's CSR effort could not resolve all or even the most important workplace issues—in April 2014 at least ten thousand workers struck Yue Yuen Industrial, one of Nike's giant vendors in South China[2]—many observers agreed that by the twenty-first century Nike was probably one of the better companies when it came to implementation of an effective CSR program (Nisen 2013; Banjo 2014).

The third element in this new tripartite ensemble are the contract manufacturers themselves, sometimes including the local business associations representing the firms in a particular county engaged in the same industry. While in some cases an association of these firms can be politically powerful—the Bangladesh Garment Manufacturers Association is a notable example—they generally exist in a structurally weak context when it comes to a negotiation with the brand or retailer who contracts with them for product. Their "negotiating" posture is therefore often one of prevarication, subterfuge, and dissimulation when it comes to adherence to the codes of conduct promulgated by the firms to which they maintain a commercial relationship. Inspectors and monitors are often bribed or fed false information, workers are threatened if they expose violations of the code, and subcontracting to workshops not covered by the CSR codes is rife and often in violation of their legal obligation to the brand or retailer that has contracted for the work (Ngai 2005).

Such pathologies have many sources: a culture of corruption and lawlessness among the entrepreneurial class in many developing nations, contempt for an unskilled, nonunion workforce often rural in character, and a failure of good governance within many nations that lack democratic accountability. But even more important are the endemic, systemic pressures generated by the rationality of the global supply chains in which these contract manufacturers have such little organizational or market power. The retailers and brands that command the supply chains of the world seek the lowest price, the most rapid fulfillment of the production schedule, and the highest quality possible at the contract price. All this puts enormous pressure on the manufacturers, who squeeze their workers and subcontractors to fulfill the demands generated by the logic of the supply-chain production and distribution regime. Should rising labor cost engender prices higher than their rivals, across town or across the continent, the entrepreneur managers will soon find their workrooms silent as contracts are diverted to the lower-price producer. To these contractors, CSR is therefore a mandate that is imposed from without, and normally without proper compensation. Hence the endemic resistance to and subversion of the corporate codes of conduct and those on-site inspectors and monitors who are tasked with its enforcement (Raworth and Kidder 2009).

Two pillars of the ILO's twentieth-century governing regime are notably missing from the new tripartism outlined above. The first is the state. In those Pacific Rim countries where contract manufacturing is so prevalent, government, both on a national and local level, can still play an important role. The ILO, as well as virtually all corporate codes of conduct, require that factory managers adhere to existing labor laws and wage and hour regulations. Moreover, all of these nations are ILO members and participate in the ILO discussions that formulate those conventions and operating procedures that have a bearing on labor standards in these polities. The problem is that enforcement of such labor standards, either national or international, is extraordinarily weak because many of these states are either one-party regimes, highly decentralized, or simply lack the administrative capacity to enforce a uniform set of standards. The Chinese state is certainly a strong one when infrastructure and development issues are at stake, but in this vast country local authorities, who are often joint partners with export-oriented industries, are reluctant to enforce such labor laws and thereby put their province, company, or industry at a competitive disadvantage.

The second missing pillar is the labor movement. In East Asia, Bangladesh, and in parts of Latin America a volatile working class is emerging. In China there are thousands of strikes, demonstrations, and other protests each month, most centered in the coastal industrial districts where millions of newly proletarianized peasants have created a combustible social mix not unlike that of Lancashire during the Chartist era or Lowell and the Lower East Side during the decades when turn-of-the-twentieth-century socialists and Wobblies were active. But in most cases these workers have few institutions that can effectively represent them, certainly not in terms of the kind of trade unionism that the founders of the ILO saw as both an alternative to bolshevism and as a potent and responsible negotiating partner with management and the state in the mid-twentieth-century years. As Katie Quan and Anita Chan argue in chapters 10 and 11 of this volume, the massive working-class impulse now making itself felt in China is but imperfectly represented by the All-China Federation of Trade Unions, whose first loyalty lies with the party-state. Many other nations, like Mexico and Vietnam, also have state- or party- sponsored trade-union federations that have been hostile to a genuine voice for workers in the contract manufacturing sector. Equally prevalent is outright repression, now or in the past, which has weakened the trade unions and emasculated their capacity to function as a tripartite stakeholder (Chan 2011; Estlund and Gurgel 2014).

In 2001 Jill Esbenshade was one of the first scholarly observers to argue that with the collapse of a presumptive twentieth-century "social contract" involving unions, business, and the state, a new "social accountability contract" seemed to be coming into existence, one which posited a tripartitism consisting of the branded retailers, the contract manufacturers, and the proliferating set of NGOs who leverage the reputational vulnerability of the brands to advance worker and environmental interests (Esbenshade 2001). Esbenshade and other social scientists have had few illusions that such a new social contract might actually substitute itself for what an earlier generation of policy intellectuals called, in the United States, a "labor-management accord," or in Western Europe, a "social market economy." To some degree the labor-oriented NGOs have sought to strengthen independent trade unions, or in some instances substitute themselves for a workers' voice that has not yet been effectively organized. But laudable as those efforts might be, there can be no substitute for independent and authentic unionism when new legislation is written, implemented, or enforced. The failure of the monitoring and inspection regime under CSR is largely a function of the absence of a union presence on the shop floor because only when workers are protected by such an institution can they feel free enough to speak up and point out CSR transgressions without fear of reprisal. And finally, of course, neither of the two most important industrial nations on the planet have adopted those ILO conventions, numbers 87 and 98, insuring freedom of association. The fact that neither China or the United States has made this commitment weakens fatally the prospects for a revival of trade unionism in the twenty-first century or the effective re-creation of a new social accountability contract (Worker Rights Consortium 2013).

Not unexpectedly, the ILO has had an ambiguous relationship to the new tripartism as embodied in the CSR regime. A 1977 "Tripartite Declaration of Principles concerning Multinational Enterprises and Social Policy," amended in 2000 and 2006, calls on global corporations themselves to take the initiative in their adherence to the most far-reaching ILO labor standards, but it is notably silent on the most important way in which the key multinational companies exert their social and economic influence, through the set of buyer-driven supply chains that squeeze both contract vendors and their workers (ILO 2014). Early in the twenty-first century the ILO began an internal discussion of the posture it should take toward CSR. An ILO subcommittee on multinational enterprises expressed skepticism in 2006, arguing that "CSR cannot substitute for the role of government," indeed, that "CSR commitments represent little more than declaratory statements of intent . . . introducing a multiplicity of demands and unnecessary costs in supply chains with little return to suppliers in terms of market expansion, or to workers in terms of an improvement in working conditions" (ILO 2006a).

Nevertheless, the ILO could hardly ignore the CSR phenomenon, which in many industries and countries seemed the only game in town. In 2009, the ILO therefore established a "Helpdesk for Business on International Labour Standards" designed to advise companies seeking information on how to make their supply chains and CSR operations conform more closely to the international labor standards promulgated by the ILO. Although the Helpdesk has no operational responsibilities, hundreds of companies and other organizations have made use of its technical expertise and accumulated understanding of international labor laws and standards. That background has generated an institutional skepticism when it comes to the corporate social responsibility idea. Because workers themselves are but third-party beneficiaries of the CSR process, with no standing to bring a legal claim against the company for any failure to live up to its commitments, the CSR approach is "paternalistic," averred the Helpdesk director Emily Sims in a 2013 consideration of the ILO's work in this corporate-centered universe. "Workers must depend on management's goodwill for their rights to be respected," she asserted. The ILO concluded that CSR audits and inspections were often corrupt and unreliable, that corporate commitment too often generated but a "distorted picture of what is really going on in a company's operations," indeed, that it "is basically non-existent beyond the first-tier supplier" (Sims 2013). Still, Sims and other ILO officials recognized that "workers' rights cannot wait for better legal protections and adequate labour inspection." Inadequate and self-serving as they might be, all CSR codes of conduct call on supply firms to actually obey existing national laws, even when routinely unenforced. Thus for Sims, "CSR can help build a business culture of respect for the rule of law." This would lead to "a shift in national practice through demonstrating the feasibility of companies operating in a more responsible manner which can then be reflected in national law, leading to advances in the legal protections provided by hard law" (Sims 2013).

ILO efforts to align the CSR regime with the historic mission of the international organization can be found in two high-profile Asian initiatives. The first emerged early in the twenty-first century in Cambodia, where the ILO was heavily engaged with the Better Factories Cambodia initiative; the second began in 2013 in the wake of the tragedy at the Rana Plaza garment factory in Bangladesh, where some 1,138 souls perished when the eight-story building collapsed. Immediately afterward, an unprecedented set of true negotiations—perhaps even tripartite in character—began between key global retailers, sophisticated NGOs, and the Bangladesh garment industry.

Few nations had a more tumultuous or devastating experience than Cambodia in the decades of war, mass murder, occupation, and economic catastrophe endured by the kingdom during the 1960s, 1970s, and 1980s. By the time a semblance of authoritarian stability returned toward the end of the twentieth century, the country was one of the poorest in the world, with few resources other than cheap labor and the goodwill—perhaps derived from equal measures of guilt and humanitarian sympathy—of the United States and other Western nations. This was the context for the American decision to link preferable textile quotas to the enhancement of Cambodian labor standards as negotiated in a three-year compact, the US-Cambodia Textile and Apparel Trade Agreement (UCTA), signed late in 1999 (Kolben 2004).

Because of the weakness of the Cambodian government and that nation's desperate need for export markets, the United States had enormous leverage when prodded by reformist NGOs to make of Cambodia and its nascent garment industry a showcase for modernization and social reform. Indeed, as controversy swirled about the creation of a new and powerful World Trade Organization, exemplified by the demonstrations and clashes that disrupted the 1999 Seattle meeting of that group, a reform of Cambodian apparel industry labor conditions provided an opportunity for the Clinton administration to prove that a well-constructed set of trade agreements could reduce poverty abroad and play a beneficial role in the development process.[3] Under UCTA, the US Department of State, assisted by Commerce and Labor, would determine each year if working conditions in the Cambodian textile and garment sector "substantially comply" with a set of labor standards based on ILO criteria. If the Cambodian apparel industry did in fact measure up, then that nation's annual textile quota for the US market would increase from 14 to 18 percent, a considerable incentive to good behavior since three-quarters of Cambodia's textile and garment exports were destined for the US market in the first decade of the twentieth century. Not unexpectedly, the European Union reached a similar agreement with the Cambodian government, with firms like the Swedish-based H&M sourcing much new product there (Arnold and Shih 2010).

This trade initiative seemed an enormous success in its first few years of operation. To determine conditions in Cambodian factories, an ILO staff in 2001 began to monitor working conditions in scores of workplaces through a program that became know as Better Factories Cambodia. These surveys were more probing and accurate than those generated by the usual sort of CSR inspection. Based on the survey, BFC generated a "synthesis report" that identified and made public specific problems at named factories and firms, assessed progress in ameliorating those shortcomings, and then summarized for an international audience wage and working conditions data for the entire Cambodian textile and garment industry. This represented a clear break from the usual corporate social responsibility regime because the dozen or so BFC inspectors were paid by an independent entity and because of the initial transparency characteristic of the synthesis reports. For six years, the US government relied on BFC's monitoring and reporting to decide semiannually whether to increase the import quota for Cambodian apparel. And at the same time, apparel brands used BFC's reporting as a primary tool for monitoring their Cambodian vendors' compliance with their own codes of conduct. The Royal Cambodian Government, which retained the responsibility to enforce Cambodian labor laws and standards, restricted the availability of export licenses to factories that registered with the program, and on occasion, it actually denied a company an export license for product manufactured under substandard conditions.

Results were impressive. Employment in the garment industry tripled from 79,000 in 1998 to about 270,000 in 2004. Although wages remained among the lowest in the industrial world—in part because of the labor-intensive, cut-and-sew character of the Cambodian apparel industry—labor unions were registered in nearly five hundred factories, and the synthesis reports showed improved working conditions in key areas, including the eradication of child labor and an end to extreme overtime work. Backed and prodded by the ILO and the United States, a tripartite governance structure, composed of Cambodian unions, the Garment Manufacturers Association of Cambodia (GMAC), and the government, seemed in sight. The BFC itself was guided by a Project Advisory Committee, comprised of representatives from the government, the garment manufacturers, and elements of the trade union movement (International Human Rights and Conflict Resolution Clinic 2013). Thus Cambodia's reputation as a nation striving to advance labor standards in a world in which globalization often meant a frantic quest for cheap and exploitable labor gave apparel manufactured there a distinct competitive advantage. Nike and Disney decided to resume sourcing from Cambodian factories monitored by the BFC, despite having pulled out of the country in the 1990s when they cited labor-rights concerns as one reason for their departure. As the World Bank president Robert Zoellick put it on a 2007 visit to Phnom Penh, "Cambodia can develop an international brand for socially responsible production, resource development and tourism. That reputation would help Cambodia to sustain high growth and overcome poverty in the face of tough global completion" (ILO 2007).

Unfortunately, this industrial governance structure was built on a trade pact that was about to collapse. UCTA ended in 2005 along with the world Multi-Fiber Arrangement (MFA), of which the US-Cambodian trade agreement had been a de facto part. From this point on the ILO's Better Factories Cambodia project would be deprived of crucial leverage because the end of the MFA meant the end of the US garment and textile quotas behind which Cambodian industry had been so effectively, if briefly, sheltered. The impact on BFC and on working conditions in Cambodian factories would take a few years to become evident, but this abdication of state regulatory power proved largely subversive of what the ILO had sought to engender. When the US government ended its direct financial support to BFC, upward of 80 percent of all its funding at its peak, the ILO was forced to sustain its inspection and reporting regime by relying to a far greater degree on both GMAC as well as those global buyers, including Gap, Levi Strauss, Nike, Walmart, and Disney, which alone contributed more than a million dollars to the program. Not unexpectedly, the monitoring regime became less efficacious and transparent: it began to take on some of the characteristics of the firm-sponsored CSR inspections (Wrinkle 2011). For example, the ILO stopped reporting on and publicly identifying those individual garment factories it found noncompliant in the years after 2005, a practice that was resumed only nine years later after Stanford University researchers issued a scathing report faulting the erosion of the ILO inspection regime (International Human Rights and Conflict Resolution Clinic 2013; Meyn 2014).

Indeed, since 2010 ILO synthesis reports have tracked a deterioration of working conditions in Cambodian garment factories. A 2013 report said that its assessment of 152 garment and 3 footwear factories "demonstrates that improvements are not being made in many areas including fire safety, child labor, and worker safety and health" (International Human Rights and Conflict Resolution Clinic 2013; Radio Free Asia 2013). Both the ILO and the Stanford researchers found that in scores of factories overtime was increasingly involuntary, governmental wage standards had been violated, heat prostration was a growing problem, and that factory owners penalized those workers who sought to form unions and press grievances. Employment has grown more precarious, in part because many firms have shifted most of their workforce to temporary status or "fixed duration contracts," thereby offering employers greater leverage to demand nonvoluntary overtime or discourage union organizing. Subcontracting to smaller factories that are outside of the BFC monitoring program has also become rife (International Human Rights and Conflict Resolution Clinic 2013).

Not unexpectedly, labor militancy and governmental repression have dramatically eroded the nation's reputation as a stable and progressive site for apparel manufacture. In January 2014 hundreds of factories were shut down in a violent, disruptive mass strike, during which the military and security forces opened fire, killing four workers and injuring many more. Twenty-one union leaders were jailed for weeks without trial (Bahree 2014; Worker Rights Consortium 2014). The idea that Cambodia's once-unique path toward export industrialization might have rendered that nation exempt from the downward wage-and-working-condition pressures generated throughout the global apparel industry seems to have ended. As Ken Loo, the secretary-general of GMAC, put it shortly after the wage strikes of 2014, "We've been saying all along . . . the higher the wage is set, the more factories will have to close" (Chen 2015).[4]

The ILO experiment in Cambodia fell far short of expectations for two reasons. First, the tripartitism embodied in Better Factories Cambodia was always a tenuous arrangement, far too dependent on the carrot and stick implicit in US manipulation of its import quota from that small nation. Once this leverage dissipated, the overwhelming power of GMAC became manifest, often in tandem with a government that had grown increasingly authoritarian by the second decade of the twenty-first century. Meanwhile the power of the workers was far more apparent than real. The Cambodian trade union movement appeared more vigorous than in other East Asian nations. It was not controlled by the government and it often enrolled a majority of workers in key manufacturing facilities. But with more than a dozen trade union federations claiming to represent Cambodian textile and garment workers, the labor movement rarely spoke with one voice, nor did it have the organizational strength to actually engage in what Western observers would recognize as collective bargaining (Community Legal Education Centre and Clean Clothes Campaign 2012). This governance structure, and the weak position of worker representatives therein, helps explain BFC's reluctance to take a public position on key labor rights issues, lest it lead to a showdown with its own governance body (International Human Rights and Conflict Resolution Clinic 2013).

But even more important, the BFC project was never designed to enlist the big multinational brands and retailers as full-fledged partners in a tripartite system of governance. Instead, BFC directed its energies inward, toward resolution of conflicts and amelioration of working conditions in the vendor factories without putting pressure on those North Atlantic entities that actually controlled the supply chains that placed the orders with Cambodian manufacturers and determined the prices, and hence the wages and working conditions, under which hundreds of thousands would labor. Buyers engaged in but two activities: First, since the phaseout of the import quota system in 2005, the BFC's role changed to resemble more closely that of most other factory auditing bodies: providing confidential factory monitoring reports to factory owners and, on a for-pay basis, to international buyers. The reports cost $750, a real bargain compared with a proprietary CSR inspection of such a factory (International Human Rights and Conflict Resolution Clinic 2013). And second, the brands and retailers participated in an annual buyers forum where they met with BFC staff and trade union representatives. But this was not the kind of tripartite engagement long advocated by the ILO. The Cambodian government was not present in any formal sense, nor were the local manufacturers, and for the brands participation was entirely voluntary (Community Legal Education Centre and Clean Clothes Campaign 2012). Thus, even at the height of BFC effectiveness in the early twenty-first century, no venue or mechanism existed whereby supply-chain power and financial resources might be enlisted to raise labor standards and ameliorate working conditions within the Cambodian textile and apparel industry.

Bangladesh was just as poor and nearly as dependent on apparel exports as Cambodia. During the first decade of the twenty-first century, apparel industry wages were little more than half those of India, Pakistan, Cambodia, and Vietnam. Such rock-bottom wages lured many of the largest buyers to source product in the country, making Bangladesh the second largest garment exporter after China (ILO 2013a). But Bangladesh had also achieved dubious recognition for a series of workplace calamities reminiscent of the most satanic nineteenth-century factories and mills. Illegal and shoddy construction, corrupt and inadequate government oversight, and state repression of a weakly organized labor movement proved a deadly combination. As Robert Ross shows in chapter 4 of this volume, the death toll from Bangladesh factory fires had risen to more than seven hundred in the decade before the collapse of the Rana Plaza garment factory complex near Dhaka (*The Economist* 2012).

Rana Plaza shocked the world, generating the moral and political will that finally propelled scores of North American and European brands and retailers to agree to a new sort of tripartite governance body. The May 2013 Bangladesh Accord on Fire and Building Safety, now signed by 190 global firms, by the powerful Bangladesh Garment Manufacturers Association, and by two international union federations, IndustriALL and UNI, as well as the ILO, put a measure of legal and administrative backbone into the reform effort that sought to make those who controlled the retail-dominated supply chains responsible parties in any effort designed to mitigate unsafe factories in Bangladesh (Smith 2013). As Nova and Wegemer detail in chapter 1 of this volume, the Accord was not merely the product of one disastrous industrial accident but was pushed forward through a multiyear series of negotiations by NGOs like the college- and university-based Worker Rights Consortium and the European Clean Clothes Campaign. The Rana Plaza tragedy merely proved a dramatic occasion for final negotiations. Like Better Factories Cambodia in its early twenty-first-century heyday, the Accord did away with individual CSR codes of conduct: in Bangladesh they had proven utterly ineffective, little more than public relations. Indeed, as Ross and Nova make clear in chapters 4 and 1 of this volume, the vast majority of fires, as well as the Rana Plaza collapse, had taken place in a factory recently inspected and approved under a CSR code of conduct. In the place of these proprietary CSR programs, the Accord created a well-funded inspection regime that hired dozens of international experts and hundreds of local inspectors to determine the building integrity and safety procedures at some 1,800 factories that sourced export apparel for the brands and retailers that signed onto the Accord (Nova 2013, 2014).

The Accord has broken new ground in two ways. First, it regulates the buying practices of apparel bands and retailers, requiring them to make a multiyear commitment to supplier factories, a major deviation from the industry's footloose norm, and it requires that factories continue to pay workers their normal wages during any period when they are idled owing to safety repairs (Nova 2014). Meanwhile, the brands and retailers who have signed on to the Accord are also required to help pay for factory safety upgrades if the Bangladesh factories cannot cover the costs themselves. Article 22 of the Accord includes such options as joint investments, loans, accessing donor or government support, offering business incentives, and paying for renovations directly.[5] This generates something close to an "investment" by the top of the supply chain in the bottom.

Second, and quite unique in recent supply-chain history, the Accord mandates that all signatories sign legally binding contracts creating a potential financial liability on the part of both the Bangladesh contract manufacturers and the global buyers when reconstruction or mitigation of a factory plant becomes warranted (Appelbaum 2013; Anner, Bair, and Blasi 2013). Unlike CSR programs, which can be altered or abolished at any time, the Accord has created a set of legally binding contractual obligations whose enforcement, should consultation and ILO arbitration fail, can take place in the court of the home country of the signatory party against whom enforcement is sought (Robbins 2013).

Significantly, these new legal obligations generated resistance from those American retailers, including Gap, Walmart, and at least fifteen other companies, that source product in Bangladesh. They refused to sign the Accord and instead established a rival, the Alliance for Bangladesh Worker Safety (Anner, Bair, and Blasi 2013). Unlike the Accord, the Alliance does not require its signatories to cover the costs of factory remediation should other alternatives prove unworkable. Nor does the Alliance provide any role for Bangladesh unions or international labor bodies in its governance structure: it is composed of signatory brands and retailers on the one hand and local factory managers and owners on the other. This is consistent with the inadequate CSR approach, which marginalizes workers' voices in favor of a corporate funded and controlled partnership between brands and retailers on the one hand and factory owners on the other. The most important difference between the Accord and the Alliance, however, is that the American-dominated group, which accounts for about a quarter of all Bangladesh apparel exports, resists legal accountability and tripartite governance. To Walmart the Accord "introduces requirements, including governance and dispute resolution mechanisms, on supply chain matters that are appropriated left to retailers, suppliers and government" (Walmart 2013). An official for the National Retail Federation put it even more pointedly: "The liability issue is of great concern, at least on this side of the Atlantic. For U.S. corporations, there is a fear that someone will try to impose liability and responsibility if something goes awry in the global supply chain" (Greenhouse 2013). Precisely. "The Accord has teeth that the Alliance simply does not have," argued Rob Wayss, the first head of Accord operations in Bangladesh. "The Alliance is a modified version of the monitoring and auditing and corporate social responsibility that have been employer-led and executed and not rigorous enough" (Short 2013).

But the Accord may also have a fatal weakness, one endemic to the inadequacies inherent in social accountability tripartitism. The Accord calls for workers' representatives to be empowered participants, with a steering committee chaired by an ILO official and composed equally of union representatives and officials from participating companies. Unions are to receive inspection reports at the same time as factory managers and are empowered to share results with employed workers. And at every factory where unions have any membership, at least one of the Accord's signatory unions is authorized to participate in the development of the remediation plan (Nova 2014). As in Cambodia, where outside economic leverage was designed to strengthen the trade-union role, the Accord is also designed to strengthen the role of organized labor, not just by offering it a formal role in tripartite governance but by insuring that employment will be more continuous in Accord factories and that the cost of remediation will not fall on the workers alone.

Unfortunately, such a social democratic initiative faces enormous obstacles in Bangladesh. In contrast to Cambodia, where a reformist government, at least in the early 2000s, eagerly sought to curry favor with the United States and the ILO, the current Bangladesh governing regime is considered one of the most corrupt—or perhaps *the* most corrupt country on the planet—according to Transparency International, which by 2005 had awarded the South Asian nation this dubious honor for five years in a row (Rahman 2005). Human Rights Watch reconfirmed this doleful assessment a decade later, concluding in its 2015 *World Report* that in Bangladesh "the trend toward increasing restrictions on civil society continued," with hundreds killed or injured during the course of elections in January 2015, extrajudicial executions by the security forces, and new restrictions imposed on the press and NGOs (Human Rights Watch 2015b).

Under such conditions the growth of independent trade unionism has faced much resistance. The ruling Awami League is backed by factory owners and has many members of parliament who own factories. In the wake of the Rana Plaza tragedy, working-class strikes and demonstrations proliferated across the country, but despite a slight liberalization of the labor law promulgated in the summer of 2013 and the official registration of scores of new trade unions, government and employer resistance to labor activism began to stiffen within months following the Rana Plaza collapse. When in the fall of that year garment workers were interviewed by both Human Rights Watch and reporters for the *Wall Street Journal*, these Western institutions found "fierce opposition" and much intimidation on the part of factory managers resisting the formation of even legally sanctioned trade unions. In some instances factory owners used "local gangsters to threaten or attack workers," reported Human Rights Watch (Barta and al-Mahmood 2014).

Under such conditions it seems unlikely that a new sort of tripartitism, involving Western brands, local factory owners, and a coalition of NGOs and in-country trade unions, can provide a stable basis for an amelioration of wages and working conditions in Bangladesh. The legal responsibility that those brands and retailers associated with the Accord have assumed does represent a step forward. But unless an even more thoroughgoing reintegration, both operational and legal, of Western supply chains takes place, it will be exceedingly difficult to enforce the social responsibility provisions inherent in the new Accord. As the comparative histories of Cambodia and Bangladesh make clear, there can be no substitute for a strong regulatory state in which an independent trade union movement represents worker interests both at the worksite and on the terrain of policy and politics.

DEEPENING COMPLIANCE?

Potential for Multistakeholder Interaction
in Monitoring Labor Standards in the Value
Chains of Brazil's Apparel Industry

Anne Caroline Posthuma and Renato Bignami

This chapter examines a private-sector initiative designed to monitor and promote the upgrading of working conditions in value chains of leading apparel retailers operating in São Paulo city, Brazil. This corporate social responsibility (CSR) initiative, introduced by the Brazilian Association of Apparel Retailers (ABVTEX), is of interest because it offers the potential in several aspects to bridge regulatory gaps in ensuring compliance with national labor legislation that may exist between private monitoring programs, the public labor inspection, and trade unions. First of all, communication is being fostered gradually between this CSR initiative and the public labor inspection, raising the possibility that private and public regulatory action can interact and play complementary roles to promote labor standards in the same value chain. Second, the CSR initiative was designed to monitor working conditions among first-tier suppliers and to identify vulnerable workers in subcontracted firms at lower tiers of value chains, seeking to implement a comprehensive approach to compliance throughout the value chain of retailer members. Third, the CSR initiative emerged in response to a public commission report which recommended that retailers cannot outsource responsibility for labor standards in their value chains through clauses in their supplier contracts, thereby bringing about a state-induced shift in the behavior of private sector actors toward their responsibility for labor dimensions of their value-chain practices. Finally, the sectoral trade union was included in the CSR initiative's Consultative Council, permitting contact with the union representing workers in this sector, thereby creating the potential to overcome the rift between CSR efforts to improve working conditions and trade union strengthening of workers' voice and representation.

The expansion of global production has created a large number of jobs for workers in developing countries. However, increased concern about the quality of the jobs created in its wake has raised a number of questions concerning the most effective forms of governance that should be in place to ensure quality working conditions and compliance with labor legislation and international labor standards among firms in global value chains (GVCs). The proliferation of private-sector CSR programs in recent decades has generated a substantial body of literature and valuable expertise among various private, public, and trade-union stakeholders involved in this issue, as well as debate concerning the ability of corporate codes of conduct to sustainably improve working conditions in supplier factories in developing countries (Elliott and Freeman 2003; Prieto-Carron et al. 2006; Toffel and Ouellet 2012; Locke 2013).

The extensive literature and experience surrounding the regulation of working conditions in GVCs have underscored a number of key challenges for effective and sustainable governance of labor standards in production chains. First, the complex and interlinked patterns of production, trade, and labor use in global and national value chains create difficulties for stand-alone governance approaches by either governments, corporations, trade unions, or civil-society organizations to have adequate scope and sustainability of impact (Mayer and Gereffi 2010; Mayer and Pickles 2014). Thus a major governance challenge involves the possibility of promoting forms of collaboration between different governance stakeholders. Second, the proliferation of private-sector CSR initiatives over more than two decades has often emerged as a response to a perceived deficit of public enforcement (Vogel 2010). Hence, there are more limited cases in which private CSR initiatives and public regulation interrelate or communicate with each other. Third, codes of conduct and private monitoring programs typically focus on identifying and correcting poor labor conditions in first-tier suppliers, but have greater difficulty including approaches that are able to improve working conditions and ensure labor rights of workers at lower tiers of value chains (Barrientos, Kothari, and Phillips 2013), despite the fact that labor-standards violations are prevalent in smaller firms, workshops, and household-based enterprises embedded in value chains where subcontracting relationships can be diffuse or disguised (Weil 2012). As a result, there exists a clear need for more comprehensive governance approaches that involve communication and collaboration between different stakeholders, and that operate in line with the logic of value chains, in order to foster compliance among first-tier and also lower-tier suppliers and subcontractors (UNCTAD 2013).

This chapter examines a nascent CSR initiative being implemented in the Brazilian apparel industry based around São Paulo city from the perspective of its design, operation, and implementation. Although this CSR initiative is driven by the apparel retailers' association ABVTEX, lines of communication have been established with the public labor inspectorate and the garment workers' trade union. Consequently, the CSR initiative is of interest for its potential to involve interaction of private sector actors with representatives of the state and with workers' representative organizations. Furthermore, this CSR initiative aims to achieve a comprehensive impact on first-tier and lower-tier suppliers and subcontractors in order to create a pool of certified compliant suppliers and subcontractors, thereby eliminating the risk of noncompliant firms in the value chains of the association's members. The chapter ends by considering how far the potential of this CSR initiative has been realized and what challenges lie ahead.

In contrast to conventional approaches (which generally assume CSR initiatives are designed by lead firms in the industrialized countries and transferred to producers in developing countries), the present case study examines an endogenous CSR initiative that has been designed and implemented by a Brazilian association of apparel retailers (involving domestic and foreign subsidiary members) and introduced in the context of an active public labor inspection and trade-union movement. Furthermore, the key catalyst behind the formulation of this CSR initiative was the regulatory action of the public labor inspectorate and recommendations issued by a commission of inquiry created by the São Paulo City Council in response to evidence of forced and trafficked labor in the lower tiers of value chains of large apparel retailers in São Paulo city. The expansion and deepening of this locally embedded initiative may face new challenges as the national apparel industry undergoes a rapid and more extensive process of internationalization and insertion into the global apparel value chain and as international brands include the Brazilian market within their global market strategies.

Research Methodology

The research methodology involves a case study of the ABVTEX CSR initiative and its interface with the public labor inspection, also taking into account the role of the representative trade union of apparel workers. The research draws on three sets of data. The first datasets are sectoral figures published by the apparel and textile industry association in Brazil (ABIT) and the market intelligence company (IEMI), which are relevant sources of data on the structure and performance of the domestic and international apparel and textile industry and the evolution of production, employment, imports, and exports, among other indicators.

Second, this research makes use of datasets from the Brazilian labor inspectorate, which registers inspection results in the Federal Labor Inspection System

(FLIS) database, disaggregating for São Paulo state (which accounts for roughly one-third of total Brazilian output of textiles and ready-made garments) in order to assess the results of public labor inspection and the most common labor standards violations. The data analysis in this chapter included quantitative and qualitative indicators from FLIS, divided into two groups of firms as measured by number of employees (zero–ten and more than ten) over a ten-year period.

Third, firsthand qualitative information was used, based on the interaction between the public labor inspection in São Paulo state and the private-sector association ABVTEX. In addition, the president of ABVTEX was interviewed in person and through a written questionnaire, both conducted in February 2014, as was the president of both the Seamstresses Union of São Paulo and the National Confederation of Workers in the Textiles, Apparel, Leather, and Footwear Industries (CONACCOVEST), in March 2015.

The authors used these multiple data sources and cross-checked information to make an initial account of this case study. Although it is not within the scope of the study to evaluate the impact of this embryonic regulatory initiative (for which reliable, detailed data are still difficult to obtain), our initial analysis leads us to hypothesize that this CSR model, which involves interface between private, public, and trade union actors, has the demonstrated potential to impact positively on labor standards compliance, including below the first-tier suppliers, in the value chains of major apparel retailers in Brazil.

Conceptual Framework

In recent years, the GVC literature has increasingly begun to look into issues related to working conditions and labor standards (Cumbers, Nativel, and Routledge 2008; Quan 2008a; Anner et al. 2010; Barrientos et al. 2011; Barrientos 2013). The interfirm linkages of suppliers and subcontractors in value chains and the commercial dynamics which can involve cost-cutting and tight delivery schedules create a diversity of employment relations including "adverse incorporation" of vulnerable workers (Phillips 2013; Barrientos, Kothati, and Phillips 2013). Addressing these governance deficits in global production (Esbenshade 2004a; Mayer and Pickles 2010) requires a multilayered, cross-border and multiactor system of rules, institutions, and norms to regulate the economic and social dimensions and impacts of globalization (United Nations General Assembly and Human Rights Council 2008).

The global production network (GPN) framework provides a broad analytical context in which to discuss economic and social governance challenges and responses, given its emphasis on conceptual categories such as societal, territorial, and institutional embeddedness of production and strategic coupling in development (Henderson et al. 2002; Coe, Dicken, and Hess 2008; Coe and Hess 2013). Using GPN terminology, Neilson and Pritchard (2009) distinguish between two dimensions of governance: the vertical dimension (i.e., linear value chain relationships) and the horizontal dimension (i.e., networks or clusters of national and local actors and institutions). In discussing territorially embedded institutional systems, the authors provide a dual definition of institutions that includes (1) formal organizations and public entities, and (2) the wider set of informal social norms and practices that shape behavior, including private-sector mechanisms and codes. Thus the GVC and particularly the broader GPN frameworks provide appropriate analytical tools to conceptualize the interface between private, public, and societal governance institutions at the global, national, and local levels, particularly as concerns labor standards governance, which is the core focus of this chapter.

Perspectives on CSR policies are varied and sometimes conflicting, as explored in other chapters in this book. Most controversies rest on differing views concerning the objectives that inspire these policies and their implications for public, private, and societal spaces of regulation. Scholars have emphasized CSR's role in filling the governance gap created by the decline of the state (Vogel 2010) or as a shield against corporate risk of liability for labor-standards violations in their value chain (Maryanov 2010). Some highlight a potential displacement effect of the regulatory authority of the state and legal accountability (Cutler, Haufler, and Porter 1999; Esbenshade 2004a; Tajgman 2011). Others emphasize the positive role of CSR in global value chains as they have the potential to surpass the regulatory reach of the national labor inspectorate, although the full potential is limited by insistence on its voluntary nature (Shamir 2004).

A more nuanced approach views private labor governance as contested terrain (rather than a static, predetermined mechanism) whose configuration is forged through the balance of power between the private sector, public regulation, and societal pressure in the local context (Bartley 2005). Adopting this latter perspective, CSR can be viewed as a form of corporate governance that is shaped in a dynamic process via the interaction and relative strength (as well as the conflictive or collaborative character) of private corporations, public institutions, and societal actors in a given value chain or territorially embedded GPN.

Rather than relying on private initiatives in isolation to bridge the governance gap, recent empirical evidence highlights the crucial interface between private, public, and trade-union governance systems to promote economic and social upgrading (Kolben 2007; Locke, Qin, and Brause 2007; Amengual 2010; Locke 2013; Neilson, Pritchard, and Yeung 2014). Set in the emerging literature that explores private-public societal dynamics in the governance of labor standards in global production, the present case study raises two main implications for the CSR literature. First of all, that CSR can take on a different structure and role in a context where the public labor inspectorate has been resourced and empowered, with targeted enforcement toward the protection of vulnerable workers in lower tiers of value chains, and where a tradition of strong trade union participation exists and tripartite dialogue in the promotion of improved working conditions is currently promoted. Second, whereas CSR studies commonly assume a North-to-South transfer of CSR practices to suppliers in developing countries, this chapter describes a case in which endogenous historical and sociopolitical processes have played a decisive role in shaping a home-grown CSR initiative, showing that socially responsible value-chain governance can also emerge, with its own distinct features, among lead firms in the global South (Knorringa 2010).

Brazilian Apparel Production and Labor: A Domestic Industry Adjusts to Global Competition

The origin of Brazil's apparel industry dates back to the 1850s (Teixeira 2007). By 2013, the industry had grown to comprise 26,688 registered companies. Official employment statistics indicate that textile and apparel together comprise the second-largest source of manufacturing employment in Brazil. In apparel alone, formal employment totaled 1.13 million in 2013 (RAIS 2014). Brazil ranked as the world's fourth-largest apparel producer (in volume) in 2011, with output in 2012 measured at 1.2 million tons and an estimated value of US$55 billion (IEMI 2015). The heart of textile and apparel production is located in the state of São Paulo, comprising 28 percent of all textile and apparel firms in Brazil in 2014 and over 30 percent of the labor force in this industry. Similarly, São Paulo state accounted for 35 percent of total apparel exports and 43 percent of apparel imports in 2013 (IEMI 2015). This national industry is undergoing rapid transformations as global apparel producers have targeted Brazil's robust domestic market via rising imports, foreign direct investment (FDI), and establishing subsidiaries.

As seen in table 6.1, the period of 2005–2006 saw the start of a period of rising employment, increased number of factories, growing output, and value of output, linked to the strong surge in domestic growth and consumption. But this growth leveled out in 2011–2012 as GDP started to slow. Of interest, although employment tapered off starting in 2010, both output and the number of apparel firms continued to rise, suggesting several possible explanations—increases in labor productivity or a rise in the number of smaller enterprises and increasing use of unregistered labor in the value chains of apparel production.

TABLE 6.1 Trends in formal employment, number of firms, output, and value of output in the Brazilian apparel industry, 1990–2013

YEAR	WORKERS (FORMA)	NUMBER OF APPAREL FACTORIES	OUTPUT (IN 1,000 PIECES)	VALUE OF OUTPUT (IN US$1000)
1990	1,510,902	13,283	2,253,866	23,053,914
1995	1,209,152	13,908	3,788,123	23,419,305
2000	1,039,928	15,634	5,379,582	21,475,690
2001	1,006,559	15,367	5,135,780	16,146,434
2002	953,715	14,767	4,907,567	12,799,280
2003	966,209	15,156	4,827,731	13,078,577
2004	996,355	16,531	4,947,942	15,320,496
2005	1,009,188	18,096	4,271,296	19,355,841
2006	1,008,121	18,884	4,410,291	22,878,579
2007	1,034,332	20,070	4,807,491	29,673,389
2008	1,140,618	22,681	5,142,013	35,635,898
2009	1,300,348	24,044	5,201,081	34,891,511
2010	1,137,454	24,672	5,627,657	45,358,907
2011	1,130,114	26,264	5,515,444	50,946,234
2012	1,116,668	26,703	5,302,109	43,817,286
2013	1,130,325	26,668	5,355,374	42,336,042

Source: IEMI 2015

TABLE 6.2 World apparel commerce by top exporters and importers, 2014

TOP APPAREL EXPORTERS		TOP APPAREL IMPORTERS	
COUNTRIES	US$ MILLION	COUNTRIES	US$ MILLION
(1) China	165.082	(1) United States	83.809
(2) Bangladesh	26.108	(2) Germany	35.502
(3) Italy	21.635	(3) Japan	31.783
(4) Germany	18.320	(4) United Kingdom	24.840
(5) Vietnam	18.306	(5) France	21.756
(6) India	15.703	(6) Italy	14.834
(7) Turkey	14.974	(7) Spain	14.305
(8) Spain	11.066	(8) Hong Kong	12.606
(9) France	10.080	(9) Netherlands	12.273
(10) Netherlands	8.951	(10) Belgium	9.131
(11) Belgium	8.679	(11) Canada	9.055
(12) United Kingdom	7.480	(12) Russia	8.488
(81) Brazil	**150**	**(29) Brazil**	**2.376**
Total	428.023	Total	403.116

Source: IEMI 2015, 90

As seen in Table 6.2, whereas Brazil quickly rose to become twenty-ninth largest apparel importer globally in 2014, exports notably lagged far behind in eighty-first place (IEMI 2015). This surge of imports has placed pressure on local producers to improve their price competitiveness and production flexibility while reducing final price on the domestic market.

It is important to highlight several distinctive characteristics of the apparel industry in Brazil that contrast with many other producing nations. First, until recently, the Brazilian apparel industry remained a largely self-contained, producer-consumer country dominated by national retailers (such as Marisa, Lojas Riachuelo, and Lojas Renner), with major global brands accounting for a smaller proportion of apparel sales in Brazil. Using the framework from Gereffi and Memedovic (2003), the national value chain in the Brazilian apparel industry encompasses the full range of economic activities spanning from locally grown cotton and the production of cotton and synthetic fabric through the manufacturing stages of cut, make, and trim (CMT), full package production, full package with design (otherwise known as original design manufacturing, ODM), and original brand manufacturing (OBM) to the final sale of the ready-made garment.

Second, whereas international demand for apparel weakened in the aftermath of the global economic crisis, domestic consumption of apparel and other consumer goods in Brazil surged during the early 2000s, attracting global apparel retailers to the vibrant Brazilian market as part of their global market strategy. However, slowed rates of economic growth and rising inflationary pressures started to dampen consumer demand as of 2012 and may reverse this trend.

A third crucial characteristic involves the shifting balance between domestic and international producers in the local market and—a related phenomenon—the growing differentiation of product lines and company strategies. Apparel imports have risen rapidly and new-entrant global players have opened stores or franchises and invested in local production. Lower-end and middle-market products have been supplied mainly by large domestic retailers and imports from China. On the higher end, various domestic retailers have invested in partnerships with renowned fashion designers while others have created their own stores to raise visibility of their brands (such as Lupo and Hering). In addition, global luxury brands have entered the market and new domestic designer brands have been emerging. Large international players have tapped the Brazilian market by opening their own stores such as Gap, Topshop, Forever 21, H&M, and Zara.[1]

A fourth characteristic is the declining competitiveness of the domestic apparel industry. As seen in figure 6.1, textile and apparel imports first overtook exports in 2006 and surged rapidly thereafter, leading to a sharp decline in the trade balance for both these goods. More specifically for apparel, imports shot up by 218 percent between 2008 and 2012, whereas exports fell by 54 percent, leading to a trade-balance deficit of $2.3 billion in 2012 (a collapse of 639 percent between 2008 and 2012). Apparel imports from Asia alone surpassed $1.45 billion in 2012 (an increase of over 500 percent between 2006 and 2012), of which 60 percent came from China. In the 1990s and the beginning of the 2000s the figures

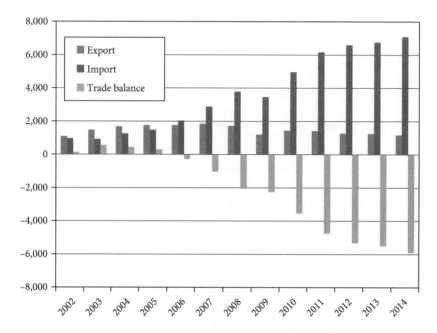

FIGURE 6.1 Trade balance in the textile and apparel industry in Brazil, 2002–2014 (textile and apparel without cotton thread), in US$ million

Source: ABIT (compiled from data by Aliceweb and Brazilian Central Bank), 2015

show a period of transition, from a very protected industry, which was the pattern in the 1980s, to a current globalized sector.

The strong valuation of the Brazilian currency to the US dollar until 2014 was a major factor fueling the surge of apparel imports. A sharp reversal in 2015, with the subsequent devaluation of the Brazilian currency to the US dollar, changed the cost of sourcing locally. Other salient cost factors have included taxes, bureaucratic procedures for imports and exports, and electricity rates.[2] These conditions compelled domestic producers to respond in diverse ways— some have sought competitive advantage through innovation, whereas others have pursued defensive strategies such as outsourcing to small-scale workshops to reduce costs and gain flexibility, which could be associated with conditions conducive to precarious labor practices.

A fifth feature has involved the fragmented structure of apparel production, in which numerous small-scale units produce and assemble outsourced products for large and medium-sized producers and retailers. Figure 6.2 illustrates the pyramid structure of Brazilian apparel production, in which nearly three-fourths of registered firms involve small enterprises that hire fewer than ten formally registered employees.

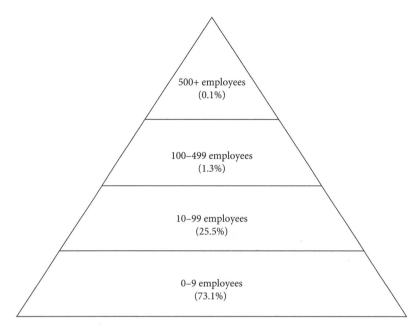

FIGURE 6.2   Structure of the Brazilian apparel industry (by firm size and number of formal employees), 2011

Source: RAIS 2012

Finally, our data show rising output (64 percent), investment (59 percent), and number of companies (18 percent) among domestic apparel producers between 2008 and 2012. At the same time, total employment registered a modest rise of 2.6 percent and the average number of employees per firm declined from fifty in 2008 to forty-four in 2012. The estimated increase of 20 percent in labor productivity over this period may account for this limited impact of growth and investment on formal job creation. Alternatively, these figures may also reveal a growing number of firms that rely on subcontracting practices through the value chain (Sousa Lima 2009)—similar to the commercial practices that are widespread in the global apparel industry. Many irregular migrant workers (particularly from Bolivia and neighboring Latin American countries) have been found working as informal laborers in small-scale workshops in the lower tiers of outsourced apparel production (Gomes de Azevedo 2005; Leite, et al. 2015).

The Seamstresses Union of São Paulo estimated 140,000 formal workers were employed in the city's apparel industry in 1998, whereas this number was halved to around 70,000 workers in 2005. Eunice Cabral, the union's president, considered that many workers dismissed at that time may have entered the industry again, but working in the informal workshops of the apparel industry (testimony to the São Paulo City Council Commission 2013, 29). Workers in small, informal workshops face multiple difficulties to organize themselves. Many workshops prevail in domestic premises, making it very difficult for unions or other representative worker organizations to assist these informal workers; thus union density is very low among such workers.

Strengthening Public Labor Inspection in Brazil

Over the past twenty-five years, public institutions for the enforcement of labor legislation have been strengthened in various countries in Latin America (Piore and Schrank 2008; Schrank 2009). In Brazil, this strengthening at the levels of judiciary, labor inspection, and the labor prosecution service has taken place within the broader process of transition to democracy that also has included opened space for expression by civil-society organizations and an emphasis on the defense of human rights. The 1988 constitution formally recognized the key role of public labor inspection to enforce compliance and established the Federal System of Labor Inspection, which introduced changes such as: (1) greater planning and focus of labor inspection activities, (2) incentives to raise effectiveness of labor inspections (with goals set to increase the quantity and intensity of inspections and number of fines issued (Pires 2008), (3) adopting educational approaches as well as more traditional punitive approaches toward promoting compliance,[3] and (4) investments in upgrading offices, equipment, and capacity development and strict standards for staff recruitment (Almeida and Carneiro 2011; Corseuil, Almeida, and Carneiro 2012). As the International Labour Organization's (ILO) Committee of Experts on the Application of Conventions and Recommendations has noted, "the functions of enforcement and advice are inseparable in practice," thereby requiring that labor inspectors distinguish cases of deliberate noncompliance that should be penalized and fined from other cases of involuntary or minor violations (ILO 2006b).

Table 6.3 shows the number of public inspections in the São Paulo apparel industry rose between 2003 and 2014 and then tapered off thereafter. This trend may be partly attributed to the declining number of labor inspectors (as retiring staff were not fully replaced with new recruitment at the time of writing this chapter). Nevertheless, the number of violations identified in some areas remained high, reflecting the effectiveness and efficiency of new inspection techniques and strategies. It is interesting to note that whereas small firms with fewer than ten employees had the largest number of undeclared workers (i.e., unregistered workers, including those without a formal work contract, the *carteira*

TABLE 6.3 Labor inspection in the apparel sector in the state of São Paulo: Most common violations, 2003–2014

YEAR	NUMBER OF INSPECTIONS IN THE APPAREL INDUSTRY	0–10 EMPLOYEES, WORKPLACES' TOP VIOLATIONS							+10 EMPLOYEES, WORKPLACES' TOP VIOLATIONS						
		UNDECLARED	WAGES	HOURS OF WORK	CHILD LABOR	DISCRIMINATION	OSH	OTHERS	UNDECLARED	WAGES	HOURS OF WORK	CHILD LABOR	DISCRIMINATION	OSH	OTHERS
2003	1.945	68	18	15	0	0	15	143	29	37	103	0	0	66	248
2004	2.885	86	22	6	2	0	7	141	34	17	80	1	0	74	167
2005	2.420	86	21	9	3	0	19	166	38	33	57	2	0	67	188
2006	2.052	78	17	10	0	0	32	180	41	43	95	2	0	78	220
2007	1.998	72	19	13	2	0	30	214	36	38	74	4	0	157	214
2008	1.834	70	19	17	0	0	33	156	25	29	54	2	0	86	207
2009	1.548	45	10	2	0	1	12	146	47	31	67	2	0	151	196
2010	1.423	87	17	5	1	0	34	135	43	45	76	1	1	162	287
2011	1.539	75	12	12	0	1	31	174	28	35	63	0	0	194	285
2012	1.170	60	17	15	4	1	55	176	24	36	56	3	0	192	238
2013	1.213	46	33	8	0	2	43	179	23	44	82	1	2	218	308
2014	841	18	22	3	3	0	76	151		72	77	2	1	149	156
Total	20.868	791	227	115	15	4	387	1.961	458	460	884	20	4	1.594	2.714

Source: Labor Inspection Federal System (Sistema Federal de Inspeção do Trabalho—SFIT) 2003–2014.

assinada that must be signed by the employer in order to entitle the worker to the range of labor rights and legally ensured entitlements),[4] the larger firms with over ten employees had a greater incidence of unpaid wages, excessive hours of work, and child labor.

Brazil underwent a series of transitions that changed its economic and political landscape in the late 1980s and again in the 2000s. The liberal market reforms of the Collor presidency were followed by fiscal and monetary policies that curbed inflation and achieved a stable macroeconomic environment under Fernando Henrique Cardoso. This stability laid the foundation for a period of strong economic growth, spurred by high commodity prices on the international market, during which the Workers' Party government under Luiz Inácio Lula da Silva and Dilma Roussef achieved significant social reforms through policies that strengthened and extended social protection coverage, implemented conditional cash transfer policies (including the *Bolsa Família* program), and revitalized labor market policies and institutions in favor of workers' rights, increased income, and formal job creation.

During this period, the federal system of labor inspection was strengthened through the development of new tools, resources, and methods of work (Coslovsky, Pires, and Bignami, forthcoming). Important expertise was developed by the labor inspectorate in areas such as the eradication of child labor and forced labor in rural sectors including cattle farming, soya production, and sugarcane harvesting. Inspectors have further enhanced their techniques for auditing local value chains by developing new tools to collect and analyze different data sources on companies and working conditions, in addition to collecting evidence of the most common labor violations, thereby raising their capacity to strategically identify and inspect workplaces with a greater likelihood of noncompliance.

New approaches to inspection have also been adopted, combining hard and soft tactics, thereby joining the strength of conventional enforcement with technical support, awareness raising, and education to enable willing firms to come into compliance (Pires 2008). Procedural innovations such as the formation of specific interministerial teams, such as the Special Mobile Inspection Group, and the creation of the so-called dirty list have focused detection, inspection, fines, and criminal procedures by the federal police in areas of grave labor violations including child labor and forced labor (Nocchi, Velloso, and Fava 2011). The Special Mobile Inspection Group was created to target cases of forced labor reported in rural areas.

Under this specific and successful experience, a multistakeholder National Pact for the Eradication of Slave Labor was formed in 2005, requiring signatory companies to sever commercial ties with businesses in their value chain that use forced labor.[5] To support the National Pact and place commercial pressure on offending enterprises, a new instrument was created (popularly called the "dirty list," or *Lista Suja*) and is maintained by the Secretary of Labor Inspection of the Ministry of Labor and Employment, making public the names of productive units and farms where conditions analogous to slave labor have been identified. By law, the labor inspector has the duty to evaluate if there are conditions analogous to slave labor in locations being inspected. The dirty list is considered one of the principal instruments to combat slave labor in Brazil. Based on the list, companies and public banks can deny credit, loans, and contracts to landowners and business people who are found using workers in conditions analogous to slave labor. By 2014, around 450 companies (accounting for nearly 30 percent of GDP) were signatories of the National Pact, although a new methodology has been adopted that aims to require effective commitment to its aims.

Other innovative programs include territorial approaches, such as programs for the eradication of contemporary forms of conditions analogous to slave labor in urban manufacturing areas, and sectoral approaches, such as a team focused on sugarcane cutting or on the value chain of the apparel industry (Costa 2010; Bignami 2011). The promotion of interaction between public and private compliance models, although not common in Brazil, is a part of new approaches being developed in order to raise labor regulation effectiveness. The labor inspectorate branch in São Paulo, the most developed state of Brazil, is leading the development of this new approach that blends public enforcement and private compliance of labor laws.

Public Inspection of Labor Standards in Apparel Value Chains in São Paulo City

When the public labor inspection uncovered forced and trafficked labor in 2006 in small workshops embedded in the value chains of large apparel retailers in São Paulo, the City Council reacted by creating an official Commission to Investigate Conditions Analogous to Slave Labor in the Apparel Industry. During the commission's work, the testimonies of many different stakeholders directly involved with the struggle against slavelike conditions in the apparel industry were heard, among them labor inspectors, judges, policemen, trade unionists, employers' representatives, and civil-society activists. The commission produced a report that same year which concluded that apparel retailers, through the Brazilian Association of Textile Retailers (ABVTEX), should develop a system to monitor labor conditions through on-site visits among their suppliers and subcontractors.[6]

Significantly, the commission report issued a recommendation that apparel retailers should be legally liable for working conditions throughout their entire value chain, representing an important evolution in the concept of CSR. Prior to the commission report, when slavelike conditions (as defined in Brazilian legislation) had been identified in firms within the apparel value chain, some involved retailers had responded by referring to a clause in their sourcing contracts specifying that supplier firms must comply with national labor legislation. However, the commission report rejected this argument, stating that a clause in supplier contracts does not absolve buyers of their legal responsibility to ensure legislated labor rights are respected for workers producing goods and services in their value chains: "it is insufficient to merely place a labor clause in a signed contract and outsource responsibility for labor standards" (São Paulo City Council 2006, 31–32, translation by the authors). Reinforcing this point, the commission report clearly stated that buyers must act to ensure responsible purchasing practices and enforce compliance with labor standards among their supplier firms. The report set some regulatory proposals that were later broadly adopted. Following the commission report, most ABVTEX members started to introduce codes of conduct and social audits within their value chains, which were conducted either by internal or external auditors, or sometimes both.

The state labor inspectorate played a supportive role in 2006 by working with the commission's investigation and the elaboration of the CSR recommendations that were submitted to ABVTEX members. Meanwhile, the labor inspectorate continued its regular inspections in the apparel sector, parallel to the new CSR measures implemented by ABVTEX members. As the number of cases of human trafficking and forced labor identified in the apparel value chain grew, the number of public inspections increased. In 2010, the branch office of the Superintendent for Labor and Employment in the State of São Paulo initiated a new program to inspect workshops that were allegedly in violation of basic labor rights regarding migrant workers.

The continuous process of public inspections, conducted concomitantly with private-sector CSR auditing, has led to the formulation of new agreements that contribute toward forging a bridge between private and public regulatory practices and thereby strengthening governance effectiveness. Each case of public inspection that has identified serious labor violations has given rise to either a legally binding agreement or a class action suit, together with the action of the Public Labor Prosecution Service, thereby creating more robust public-sector interinstitutional collaboration within the public sector in the promotion of labor standards. In most cases, a legally binding commitment to conduct adjustment, or compliance commitment, has been reached between public and private sector actors, reaffirming the requirement for a firm to conduct due diligence (which is a concept central to the corporate responsibility to respect human rights as elaborated in the United Nations Guiding Principles on Business and Human

Rights) and to monitor the entire value chain through deep private audits. This commitment (Termo de compromisso de ajustamento de conduta, TAC) is based on Articles 5 and 6 of Brazilian class-action law number 7,347/85. It makes a firm legally liable for a specific obligation (such as monitoring the entire value chain) and is legally binding; hence, it ceases to be a voluntary action. If the firm fails to comply with the terms of the commitment, then public bodies such as the Public Attorney (Ministério Público do Trabalho) or the Labor Prosecution Service can sue the firm in order to enforce its terms.

When such legal agreements are reached, the labor inspectorate is responsible for oversight to guarantee that the CSR monitoring process is carried out with expertise, adequate technical capacity, and sufficient depth, in order to reach all the tiers of the retailer's value chain.[7] For instance, in 2011 the multinational Spanish fashion retailer Zara became involved in one of these cases. After a complaint was made in the countryside of São Paulo state, the labor inspectorate started to investigate; after crosschecking data, the labor inspection identified the location and was able to inspect the premises and rescued fifteen migrant workers from a sweatshop that was sourcing inputs to the retail apparel value chain. This investigation led to a legally binding agreement settled between Zara, the Public Labor Prosecution Service, and the local branch of the Ministry of Labor and Employment. The agreement established that Zara should organize a system of private auditing while recognizing its own legal liability to ensure legally compliant working conditions in its value chain. The labor inspectorate was responsible for ensuring compliance with the obligations specified in the agreement. After auditing the entire value chain to verify compliance with the agreement, the labor inspectorate concluded that private social audits were not sufficiently effective in identifying labor violations, including those associated with violations of the fundamental principles and rights at work including forced labor, human trafficking, child labor, freedom of association, collective bargaining, and discrimination. A subsequent query was raised concerning whether the audits were being used to identify critical areas and support implementation of improvements among suppliers and subcontractors, or were enabling the company to avoid and exclude more problematic suppliers and subcontractors in its value chain.

At the same time, the Brazilian judicial system has also started to issue important decisions in those few cases where a legally binding commitment has not been achieved. A recent case in this regard involved one of the largest national retailers (*Casas Pernambucanas v. the Public Labor Prosecution Service*), which began as a class-action suit after one of the labor inspection task forces had found and released workers from slavelike conditions in a sweatshop that supplied the retailer. The initial labor inspection operation took place in 2010 and the judicial conviction was issued in December 2014. This was a landmark case, as it was the first ruling in a Brazilian court that fully recognized that brands are coresponsible for working conditions throughout their value chains. The judge added that "one cannot disregard the responsibility of those at the vertex of the production chain. The responsibility belongs to those retailers that create, define, quantify, design, model, determine the price, and pay for these inputs. Because in that case, intermediaries will only follow the standards set by the one who dictates the production needs" (Ministério Público do Trabalho 2012).

In addition, in January 2013, the state of São Paulo legislature approved legislation (law number 14,946) that established procedures to suspend a firm's license to operate in the municipality for ten years if slavelike conditions are identified in any tier of the company's value chain. This law establishes one of the toughest existing regulations against human trafficking and forced labor in Brazil and internationally.[8] As can be seen, in terms of public regulation of labor standards in apparel value chains in São Paulo city, a set of laws and legal rulings implemented over the past decade has contributed to the gradual construction of a governance system designed to address the challenge of ensuring labor standards in value chains. We now turn to the private-sector efforts to introduce a governance system to monitor labor standards in the apparel value chain.

Aiming below the First-Tier: Brazilian Apparel Retailers Adopt a Comprehensive CSR Approach to Value Chain Monitoring

The initial CSR efforts among retailer members of ABVTEX were introduced individually without a common framework. However, the key impetus to create a collective CSR initiative emerged in 2006 from the final report of the São Paulo Commission of Investigation on slave and irregular migrant labor in the apparel industry as discussed earlier. The commission report put forward policy recommendations—which included inputs from the public labor inspectorate—concerning the need for strict value chain management to upgrade labor conditions in the domestic apparel industry, including the recommendation that responsibility for labor conditions extends to workers in subcontracted firms within the same retailers' value chain. From these recommendations, ABVTEX's CSR program took shape, deriving guidelines and goals from the commission's final report and updating its approach in light of findings from private audits as well as public labor inspections.

ABVTEX was formed in 1999 and its membership includes some of the largest national and global retailers in Brazil. Members have demonstrated sufficient similarity of motivations and commitment to design and adhere to this joint CSR initiative that aims to promote compliance with labor standards in their value chains. Of particular interest, between 2006 and mid-2014, the number of members of ABVTEX had increased from six founding members (C&A, Marisa, GEP, Pão de Açúcar, Renner, and Riachuelo) to seventeen total members. The eleven new members included leading national retailers (Companhia Hering, Leader, M5, Pernambucanas, Restoque S.A., Seller and Zelo) and global lead firms (Calvin Klein Jeans, Carrefour, Walmart Brasil, and Zara), showing that membership in this domestic association grew, even among multinational subsidiaries, during the period in which private monitoring and public labor inspection were strengthened and the domestic market for apparel was increasingly liberalized.

As seen earlier, new-entrant apparel lead firms in Brazil have acted as market seekers (i.e., seeking to tap domestic demand) rather than resource takers (i.e., in search of cheap labor for export production). ABVTEX, via the design of its CSR strategy and working together with the strengthened public labor inspection, attempts to create a blended approach that offers a carrot (i.e., positive brand image and reduced corporate risk) and wields a stick (stricter public regulation and sanctions for noncompliance) to encourage compliance among existing members and new-entrant retailers (Interview with the president of ABVTEX, February 2014).

Scope of the Supplier Qualification Program (SQP)

Retailer members of ABVTEX jointly launched the Supplier Qualification Program (SQP) in 2010. The goal of the SQP is to identify and audit all suppliers of ABVTEX members by 2015, so that no uncertified supplier will exist in any member's value chain. The SQP covers the following labor standards: child labor, forced labor or work conducted in conditions analogous to slavery, irregular migrant labor, discrimination, abuse and harassment, health and safety at work, working hours, workers' benefits, and freedom of association, including the right to collective bargaining.[9] These labor standards include, and go beyond, the four fundamental principals and rights at work enshrined in the 1998 declaration of the ILO that covers: effective abolition of child labor, elimination of all forms of compulsory or forced labor, elimination of discrimination respecting employment and occupation, and freedom of association and the effective recognition of the right to collective bargaining.

The SQP has claimed to be more comprehensive than standard CSR approaches, as it targets both suppliers and subcontractors in the value chain. The president of ABVTEX identified one of the greatest challenges in the implementation of the SQP program to be the prevalence of micro and small firms in the value chains of most apparel manufacturers in Brazil, making the monitoring of these value chains complex and expensive (Interview, February 2014). In the view of the president of CONACCOVEST the SQP model could foster improvement of work conditions and labor rights in the industry (Interview, March 2015). Nevertheless, she affirms that the model should be reshaped in order to revise the imbalance between small suppliers and large retail brands. In her view, the main problem resides in the fact that ABVTEX certification charges a fixed price to provide the private audit, regardless of the size of the firm that is going to be audited. She suggests that the retailers, not their supplier firms, should bear the costs of the audits because the brands benefit directly from any improvement in working conditions at these workplaces.

Suppliers and their subcontractors are required to abide by SQP rules, hire authorized institutions to audit the workplace at their own expense, and invest the resources necessary to receive SQP qualification. In addition, first-tier suppliers must share a list of their subcontractors with their ABVTEX clients; they may maintain commercial ties solely with SQP-certified subcontractors and must report the results of certification audits to their retailer clients. In turn, retailers are obliged to ensure that their suppliers and also their subcontractors adhere to the terms of the SQP. The final goal of this approach is to create a pool of certified suppliers and subcontractors that will guarantee labor standards **and** compliant value chains for all ABVTEX members.

Auditing Procedures in the SQP

Enrollment in the SQP involves at least three types of workplace audits: when a supplier or subcontractor first enters the SQP, twelve months after certification is issued, and twenty-four months after the initial certification is issued in order to confirm compliance with basic SQP requirements. Failure to comply with any SQP standard requires the implementation of an action plan followed by a second audit; evidence of critical noncompliance means rejection of a supplier for six months followed by a second audit.

SQP audit results are confidential and disclosed only to the relevant ABVTEX members and firms in its value chain. This approach aims to strengthen good practices of companies that upgrade labor-standards compliance in their value chain.[10] The labor inspectorate conducts its own inspections in parallel to the SQP audits. According to the president of CONACCOVEST this is one of the crucial existing problems in the SQP (Interview, March 2015). She argues that the process should be carried out in a tripartite way—involving not only the apparel supplier firms but also the union that she presides over and the labor inspectorate—to supervise the overall findings as concerns labor conditions identified by the SQP.

Not all ABVTEX members have joined exclusively under the single auditing framework of the SQP. Instead, the SQP audits, which are conducted by Brazilian-based accredited accounting firms,[11] cover all ABVTEX members and coexist with other internal audits done by individual firms. For example, Zara and C&A maintain their own separate monitoring systems in addition to participation in the SQP. According to the president of CONACCOVEST, this is another point of tension between workers, small enterprise owners, and retailers because conflicting conclusions may arise, depending on which accounting firm and methodology was applied to the audit (Interview, March 2015). Each month, SQP signatories meet to discuss good practices, identify areas of risk within the value chain, and plan future activities. A steering committee has been formed to coordinate the SQP certification process; it includes representatives of ABVTEX members (although it was unclear if public sector or trade union representatives have been invited to participate).

SQP auditors use checklists covering the basic issues related to fundamental rights at work. Some research reports have suggested that checklists fail to gather sufficient depth of information on labor violations to be considered a complete assessment of any workplace (AFL-CIO 2013). However, if used together with other audit tools then checklists can become a useful instrument to determine basic remedial measures to correct labor-standards violations.

The growing use of international outsourcing by Brazilian retailers has led some ABVTEX members to consider ways to certify labor-standards compliance among overseas suppliers via international auditing companies such as WRAP, BSCI, and SMETA,[12] as well as retailer audits by ABVTEX's international members. The stated goal of this process (yet to be confirmed among ABVTEX members at the time of writing) is to achieve complete value chain monitoring of national as well as imported inputs starting in 2015 (Interview with the president of ABVTEX, February 2014).

Scope for Increased Participation by Workers' Representatives

The traditional role of trade union organization and worker representation remains a crucial force for defending labor rights in the framework of global production and value chains (Seidman 2007), even among workers in the informal economy. The representative trade union was invited by ABVTEX to be included in the SQP Consultative Council of the SQP, which it accepted. However, participation by the apparel workers' union is limited. The president of CONACCOVEST reported that, at the time of finalizing this chapter in early 2015, the union had been invited to one meeting of the Consultative Council of ABVTEX and the union representative could not speak up during the meeting. In her view, the discussion mainly addressed bureaucratic issues. The president of CONACCOVEST reported tense relations with the company representatives. Moreover, the trade union does not have access to the databank of information gathered during the private audits, thereby impeding the possibility of playing a meaningful role in constructing a new model of value-chain management that could ensure labor standards for workers are respected throughout the value chain of ABVTEX members, thus ensuring risk-free sourcing for retail brands.

Initial Steps Taken under the SQP

By the end of 2013, the SQP had registered and audited 5,811 suppliers and sub-contractors, of which 73 percent had been approved, as seen in table 6.4. Meanwhile, 1,292 orders for workplace improvements had been issued and only 6.6% of audited firms were rejected.

Despite CSR auditing, concomitant public labor inspections in 2013 identified three cases of forced labor in a subcontractor workplace of a SQP-certified supplier firm.[13] This event illustrates the genuine challenges that exist in the promotion of labor standards in the complex tiered structure of value chains that increasingly characterize global and national production (UNCTAD, 2013), as seen in the apparel industry. In such contexts where the institutional capacity exists, it may be desirable to identify sound practices for improving coordinated efforts and interaction between private monitoring and public labor inspections where they have joint goals concerning the improvement of working conditions (ILO 2013b).

TABLE 6.4 Certification of suppliers and subcontractors under the ABVTEX program (from September 2010 to December 31, 2013)

ITEM	NUMBER
Number of registered and audited suppliers and subcontractors	5,811
Number of registered suppliers and subcontractors that have been certified	4,222
Number of registered suppliers and subcontractors involved in an action plan (in the process toward certification)	1,292
Number of registered suppliers and subcontractors whose certification was rejected	386
Total number of audits conducted	6,938

Sources: See http://www.abvtex.org.br/en/information/certification-status; and interview with the president of ABVTEX, February 2014

Considerations on "Soft Law" versus "Hard Law"

Private voluntary initiatives, or soft law, have the advantage of exerting economic pressure from buyers to ensure implementation among supplier firms down the value chain and across borders (something that the labor inspection cannot do beyond its national border). Limitations of soft law include the incoherence between labor standards included in multiple voluntary standards established by different lead firms and across different sectors, the limited promotion of standards that involve enabling rights of workers (Anner 2012a), and implementation primarily among first-tier suppliers, thereby creating "regulatory enclaves" that have limited impact on improving compliance with overlook labor standards at lower layers of the value chain (Posthuma 2010).

Public regulation of labor legislation, or hard law, is based on the promotion of binding national and international labor norms by the public labor inspectorate and other relevant public authorities. Certain prerogatives are granted to public enforcement officials, such as the right of free entry in premises and workplaces. An active public labor inspectorate that is adequately resourced can reduce private-sector expenditures on auditing. However, the structure of value chains in global production poses a new set of challenges, starting with the lack of a legal definition of value chain, its cross-border nature which makes it difficult to enforce national labor legislation and no normative guidelines by which to establish legal liability for enforcement of labor standards in the entire value chain. Similarly, legal norms regulate formal employment relations, leaving a normative gap for inspections in the informal economy (ILO 2011, 2013b). Finally, labor law is based on the classic bilateral employer-employee relationship, rarely considering triangular contractual relationships that commonly arise in outsourcing relationships (Clifford and Greenhouse 2013).

Possibilities exist to bridge soft and hard law. Some forms of soft law can become legally binding regulation (Pastore 2003). For example, in the case of a commitment to conduct adjustment, when the labor inspectorate in São Paulo agrees with the Labor Prosecution Office that a given retailer will monitor its entire value chain, then this agreement becomes mandatory and legally binding, even in cases where private auditing will be used. Hence, examples of correct balance and interaction between hard and soft law can help to produce a hybrid strategy for improving value chain governance. Moreover, it must be remembered that, given the impossibility for private auditors and public inspectors to monitor labor conditions in firms at all moments, workers themselves clearly are key actors in identifying when company practices are not compliant with labor rights (Anner 2012a; Anner, Bair, and Blasi 2013). The president of CONACCOVEST attributes to the retail firms the coresponsibility for work conditions in the garment producers and supplier factories (Interview, March 2015).

Concluding Considerations

This chapter has examined an emerging CSR initiative introduced by the association of leading apparel retailers in Brazil (ABVTEX). In contrast to views that CSR must fill the governance gap owing to weak public capacity, this case study has described an incipient experience in which communication exists between a strengthened public labor inspectorate and the leading association of apparel retailers. As this experience unfolds over time and actors learn to work together, the initiative offers the possibility to bridge the public/private/societal and first-tier/lower-tier regulatory gaps that commonly exist in the promotion of labor standards in global and national value chains. In doing so, the case study described in this chapter points toward the potential for interaction between private monitoring and public labor inspection. As data become available, future research on this case study would be able to explore additional questions concerning efficiency, impact, and the effectiveness of linked-up governance, from which policy implications could be derived.

Several aspects of this incipient CSR experience stand out as key factors in shaping its future possibilities. First of all, institutional strengthening has been crucial; consistent public governance of labor standards compliance has relied on the enhanced capacity, expertise, and new approaches developed by the labor inspectorate, especially at the local and territorial level where GPNs operate. Second, greater legal coherence has been attained by inclusion of internationally adopted labor and human rights standards in SQP codes of conduct. A third and decisive element has been recognition by the leading apparel retailers of their legal liability for labor conditions throughout the entire value chain, based on the principle (set forth in recommendations from a public city-level commission report) that buyers cannot outsource responsibility for labor standards to suppliers and subcontractors in the value chain. This acceptance of liability has fostered the start of an intravalue chain auditing approach between apparel buyers, first-tier suppliers, and subcontractors under SQP.

However, important challenges remain. First of all, by early 2014, the results from SQP audits were disclosed only among the directly involved buyers, suppliers, and subcontractors (and some information could be accessed by retailer members of ABVTEX). Greater disclosure of value-chain information obtained under the SQP monitoring system could further enhance the scope for interaction between private and public actors and create the opportunity for establishing a two-way public-private exchange of information on the outcomes of labor audits and inspection. Another step forward could include making public such information to a broader set of concerned stakeholders in trade unions and civil society to promote labor standards in apparel value chains.[14] Second, the elements between private-sector audits that are conducted separately within the same sector could be further harmonized. Third, if interaction and trust continues to be fostered over time, then the complementarities between private-sector audits and public labor inspection could be enhanced, with benefits in terms of greater cost efficiency, frequency, number of workers covered, and impact on compliance. Fourth, the possibility could be explored for labor inspectors to play an oversight role, such as by setting guidelines for certification and licensing under CSR initiatives or through more informal consultative mechanisms (ILO 2013b).[15] A fifth challenge involves whether the SQP process can be expanded to apparel retailers, suppliers, and subcontractors outside of ABVTEX value chains, and whether the cost of auditing can be borne by smaller producers. Sixth, the reportedly limited involvement of representative labor organizations makes it difficult to consider this a tripartite initiative and constrains the possibility to promote labor rights such as freedom of association and collective bargaining, or to implement any type of independent workplace monitoring by workers and their legitimate representatives.

Finally, as the apparel industry in Brazil restructures in the context of global competition, a new set of challenges arises, including whether new-entrant retailers from overseas will participate in SQP for their share of domestic production or will retain their own independent CSR initiatives (thereby sustaining a parallel CSR system that could either weaken or, alternatively, be designed to reinforce the impact of SQP). Moreover, the new wave of competitively priced imports by global brands involves apparel for which the sourcing arrangements and labor conditions of workers in overseas value chains are unknown and untraced. Another pending issue concerns the extent to which the attractiveness of the vibrant domestic market could be harnessed as a positive catalyst to stimulate labor-standards compliance among new-entrant retailers and how a slow-down of economic growth and consumer demand would impact on the industry in the future.

Although solid evidence of gains for workers under the ongoing construction of the SQP approach is not yet available, and although we cannot ascribe causality, there are nevertheless initial signs that some improvements may be underway, such as rising formalization of the employment contract and a decrease in the number of existing tiers in the apparel value chain in São Paulo, setting an agenda for future research as this CSR approach unfolds.

Assuming that the continued evolution and growth of this initiative will produce solid evidence that conditions of workers have improved in São Paulo's apparel value chains, then the question arises whether these experiences are context dependent or can be generalized and transferred to other parts of Brazil or even to other countries and economic sectors. Based on the findings of this case study, the possibility for generalization would likely rely on several prereq-uisites: that the state has put in place a legally recognized and empowered public labor inspectorate with the necessary financial, human, and physical resources to conduct its work effectively; that the relevant international labor standards have been ratified and integrated into national labor law and are understood and implemented at the local level by the appropriate authorities; and that CSR initiatives of lead firms involve interaction or communication with the relevant public authorities, reinforced by the presence of active trade union and civil-society organizations to provide continued pressure for recognition of workers' rights and compliance with labor standards.

LAW AND THE GLOBAL SWEATSHOP PROBLEM

Brishen Rogers

The global sweatshop problem is in part a creature of law. National and international legal regimes encourage sweatshop production in two ways: by weaving investors' and brands' interests into the basic structure of economic globalization and by limiting workers' powers of concerted action both within and across national borders. As a result, solving the global sweatshop problem will likely require legal reforms—in particular, reforms to promote and instantiate a new form of collective bargaining that I call "transnational triangular collective bargaining," or TTCB. In TTCB, workers' organizations would link together across national borders and negotiate binding agreements both with workers' immediate employers and with the multinational brands that purchase their products. Crucially, TTCB would often benefit brands as well as workers by reducing brands' reputational risk, stabilizing their sourcing relationships, and enabling high-performance production strategies. In other words, TTCB could be the foundation of a new, more stable, and more fair global production system. Although workers' organizations can draw from existing public and private legal regimes to build TTCB, they will also need to press beyond what is required or sometimes even permitted under those regimes. In other words, law reforms will likely *follow* disruptive organizing rather than precede it, and will ideally ease the way for future organizing by institutionalizing labor conflict at the global level. This pattern of political-economic disruption followed by reform is of course common in labor law.

Part 1 of this chapter, on the new sweatshop problem, first summarizes the relationship between contemporary production strategies and the legal regimes that undergird contemporary globalization. Those regimes have effectively "constitutionalized" a set of rights for investors and brands, in the sense that states in both the global North and global South are constrained from interfering with those rights. Yet those regimes have not constitutionalized many rights for workers. As a result, brands bear little or no legal responsibility for working conditions within their value chains, even as they exert substantial power over their suppliers, and public authorities find it quite difficult to regulate labor practices. Sweatshops are one result. Part 2 outlines TTCB and argues that it can help resolve the sweatshop problem. It then summarizes various ongoing campaigns that represent promising steps toward TTCB and suggests legal reforms that would begin to enable TTCB.

The New Sweatshop Problem

Contemporary globalization is often understood as a process of removing legal impediments to the development of a global free market. It is more accurate, however, to view globalization as a project to *create* a particular sort of market through the design of international and transnational legal regimes. What has been built is something akin to a global market for goods and for the purchase of labor, but not for the sale of labor or the collective organization of labor. Indeed, various legal regimes have begun to "constitutionalize" a particular global political economy by limiting nations' freedom to regulate in particular fields. Sometimes global regimes subject national rulemaking to higher-level constraints in treaties and other regimes, and sometimes they simply deter national regulation (Schneiderman 2008; Tucker 2012, 356–58). The net result is a set of global production and investment patterns that have increased living standards for tens or even hundreds of millions around the world, but have also encouraged the reemergence of sweatshops. This part first summarizes the legal regimes underpinning globalization and traces how contemporary production strategies have coevolved with those legal regimes, giving rise to the current sweatshop problem. It then assesses existing regulatory responses—increased private monitoring by brands, and increased public regulation—and argues that such efforts are not sufficient to eradicate sweatshops.

Law and Global Political Economy

To understand the relationship between global legal regimes and contemporary production strategies it is useful to disaggregate three aspects of legal regimes: their "hardness," their "thickness," and their geographic scope or "flatness."

(Tucker 2012, 358–59). Legal regimes are "harder" or "softer" depending on the extent to which they give rise to discrete sanctions levied and enforced by a neutral third party. Hard regimes are more law-like in the classic sense, whereas soft regimes are more norm-like. Regimes are "thick" or "thin" depending on whether they weave particular groups' concerns into higher lawmaking practices. For example, a thin constitutionalization of labor rights might simply protect workers' freedom of association as an exercise of individual will, whereas a thicker conception would constitute a charter of economic democracy (Dukes 2011, 58–61). The geographical scope of legal regimes is self-explanatory: some extend only nationally, others transnationally, still others globally. The import of geographic scope is that some actors may experience the world as relatively flat in the sense that they encounter substantially similar legal entitlements across jurisdictions, whereas others' entitlements change dramatically when they cross borders.

Global legal regimes governing investment and trade on the one hand, and labor on the other, differ along all three axes. The legal entitlements of investors and purchasers of goods are relatively thick and hard, and are often transnationally or globally constituted. The legal entitlements of workers are relatively thin, soft, and nationally bounded. The relative hardness, thickness, and flatness of investors' and producers' rights is clear in the laws governing foreign direct investment and trade. A dense web of bilateral investment treaties have created favorable conditions for foreign direct investment in much of the world, in large part by ensuring investors' contractual and property rights and subjecting disputes with host countries to binding investor-state dispute resolution mechanisms. Similarly, the global trade regime, constituted through the General Agreement on Tariffs and Trade/World Trade Organization (GATT/WTO) system and a myriad of bilateral and multilateral treaties, requires individual nations to eliminate most tariffs and many nontariff barriers to trade. That system also includes dispute-resolution processes including adjudication and sanctions; decisions of the WTO's appellate body, for example, are final and binding on member states and are generally followed. These hard aspects of trade and investment regimes deter member-state defection, ensuring the stability of the system.

Laws governing trade and investment are also fairly thick in the sense that they weave investors' and producers' entitlements into the legal basic structure of globalization. Less developed nations have powerful incentives to join the WTO and to enter bilateral or multilateral trade or investment agreements in order to attract investment from wealthier nations. Finally, the global scope of trade and investment rules renders the world relatively flat for investors, since the basic logic of trade and investment regimes is to remove successive barriers to the free movement of capital and goods. Indeed, the project of removing trade barriers has been sufficiently successful that current trade negotiations, such as the proposed Trans-Atlantic and Trans-Pacific Partnerships, are focused in part on regulatory coherence among member nations to further ease the cross-border movement of goods.

To the extent that workers' rights have been constitutionalized at the global level, in contrast, they are relatively soft and thin. Public international labor law is dominated by the International Labour Organization's Core Labour Standards (ILO standards), which seek to ensure that all nations comply with ILO conventions around freedom of association, antidiscrimination, and the elimination of child labor and forced labor. The ILO standards have diffused into other global regimes at a remarkable clip, and are today increasingly incorporated into other human rights regimes, corporations' private codes of conduct, and other governance mechanisms (see, e.g., OECD 2011; OHCHR 2011; Brudney 2012). But the ILO's follow-up process is clearly soft and widely viewed as ineffective. Member states must report on their progress in implementing and enforcing the core standards but face no sanctions for failing to do so.

Labor rights in global governance are thin in that many interpret the ILO's standards on freedom of association and collective bargaining as a side constraint on investment rather than a foundational aspect of democratic capitalism. For example, the United States frequently presses trade partners to bring their labor laws into compliance with ILO standards. But that often means legalizing unions in the first instance and prohibiting violent suppression of trade union activity (ILO 2013c, 36–43). A range of thicker interpretations of labor rights is plausible. For example, a moderately thick interpretation might require nations to actively promote unionization by enacting strong remedies for antiunion behavior and by switching the default rule to one of unionization rather than individual contracting. A very thick interpretation might weave workers' concerns into the basic structure of national governance. In this reading, the ILO standards might require default unionization, sectoral or national bargaining and extension laws, and codetermination, works councils, or even generalized democratic control of investment policies. In other words, the ILO standards on collective bargaining could be the backbone of a coordinated market economy or of a corporatist or social democratic welfare state. The United States, in contrast, requires trading partners to implement only forms of collective bargaining based on individual worker choice, which are characteristic of liberal market economies and welfare states (Esping-Andersen 1990, 26–29; Hall and Soskice 2001, 8–12, 14–17).

Of course, global legal regimes do not prohibit nation-states from implementing worker protections, though they do deter egalitarian national welfare strategies. When nations do regulate labor rights, moreover, the ILO standards and various trade-labor linkages remain nationally bounded in the sense that they do little to incorporate workers' concerns into *global* governance. As argued in detail below, workers need to unite across borders to protect themselves today, and nothing in the ILO standards explicitly enables such action. The ILO standards also leave some critical issues off the table. For example, they do not touch migrant worker protections. A thicker and flatter global labor constitution would surely protect workers' citizenship rights as they move among nations seeking work. Such a constitution would likely also require member states to hold transnational corporations to some transnational duties, or to grant overseas workers some duties vis-à-vis local firms.

Of course, several labor standards are now relatively thick and flat in scope, and surely set a floor beneath labor rights. The ILO's standards on child labor and forced labor fall into this category: although soft law, they exert such normative force that no nation or brand openly flouts them today. Perhaps the gross suppression of trade unionism or absolute prohibitions on workers' freedom of association enjoy the same general acceptance. But the same cannot be said for garden-variety interference with freedom of association—that is, resistance to unionization that does not violate workers' civil rights. In fact, it seems that global labor regimes protect workers' rights only insofar as doing so perfects rather than disrupts "free" markets. Discrimination and forced labor are economically irrational. They prevent individuals from commodifying their own labor. Hiring children is economically irrational since it encourages the wrong workers to do so. Casting unionization as an exercise of freedom of association rather than as a basic entitlement of citizenship reflects this same market rationality: workers have the formal tools to limit the commodification of their own labor, but only if they collectively "purchase" representation (Bodie 2008). In this regard, contemporary globalization is a neoliberal project, one in which the state is legitimate only insofar as it "governs *for* the market and . . . molds society to the market economy's competitive rationality" (Foucault 2010; Tomlins 2015, 13).

Global Value Chains, Labor Commodification, and Sweatshops

Global production strategies have coevolved with this new set of legal regimes. In the postwar period major economies were dominated by vertically integrated industrial firms protected against international competition by Keynesian macroeconomic policies (Ruggie 1982, 393). As globalization has forced brands to compete in global product markets, they have come to focus only on core competencies such as design, branding, and strategy, and to contract for other functions, especially manufacturing, whenever possible. As a result, rather than the firm, contemporary production occurs largely through what sociologists and political economists call "global value chains," or GVCs (Gereffi, Humphrey, and Sturgeon 2005).

Sweatshops have been one result, for reasons that are not difficult to discern. The constitutionalization projects outlined above, and the resulting growth of GVCs, shattered the basic twentieth-century labor-capital accord that held employers to certain core social duties toward workers. Because GVCs involve contractual relationships rather than vertical integration, brands today bear little or no legal responsibility for working conditions among their suppliers.[1] This reflects long-standing limitations on liability in both common law and civil law, limitations rooted in the rule that an employer or enterprise is liable for the torts of its employees but not its independent contractors (American Law Institute 1958; Holmes 1891). Moreover, brands and production workers today typically fall under different nations' jurisdictions, with production often taking place in poor nations with a large supply of labor that compete against other nations for production jobs. Particularly in sectors characterized by low capital costs and low barriers to entry, such as garment and some other production work, the result can be economic chaos. Suppliers struggling to make ends meet often have no choice but to outsource work, even when doing so is prohibited by brands. Workers face long hours, forced overtime, low pay, and manifestly unsafe working conditions. Recent factory disasters in China and Bangladesh are only the most recent and visible example of the problem.

Recognizing this legal and political-economic context helps illustrate the insufficiency of existing regulatory responses. The dominant response today relies on brands' private initiatives. Given the relative lack of governance capacity in many producer nations, most brands today have adopted codes of conduct under which they pledge to monitor suppliers' compliance with a set of labor and other social standards (Brudney 2012, 563–64). Such codes have become increasingly rigorous and sophisticated in recent years, and many have been developed in conjunction with NGOs in an effort to ensure both legitimacy and effectiveness. Yet labor advocates have long suspected, with reason, that brands adopt them primarily out of public-relations purposes.

Regardless of brands' motivations, it increasingly appears that such private efforts simply cannot resolve the sweatshop problem. In a recent book based on over a decade of empirical research within factories, the political economist Richard Locke argues that such private efforts fail because they do not address the root cause of noncompliance: brands' sourcing strategies. Brands place relentless pressure on suppliers to limit costs and to turn around orders quickly. In the face of such pressures, suppliers have little choice but to use mandatory overtime, to subcontract work even where prohibited, and to hire temporary workers at very low wages (Locke 2013, 126–30). Locke instead endorses an alternative regulatory response: public enhancement of labor standards, especially around workers' freedom of association and wage rates (Locke 2013, 169–73). Such regulation is essential, he argues, because it can end ruinous competition among suppliers and encourage more collaborative brand-supplier and supplier-worker relationships centered around lean production. This is a high-performance production strategy in which employees work in teams, rotate through a variety of tasks, and collaborate with management in production planning and error correction. Lean production, Locke documents, can sustainably improve working conditions because, once implemented, worker satisfaction is higher and per-unit labor costs are lower (Locke 2013, 118–19). Locke's book is a potential breakthrough in eradicating sweatshops since it charts a path toward better work that is consistent with market dictates.

The challenge with Locke's analysis, in my view, is that the root cause of sweatshops is not brand sourcing practices per se, but rather the legal regimes and liberal political economy that encourage such sourcing. Those regimes have created powerful collective action problems among brands, suppliers, and states. Even large brands are constrained by product markets and financial markets, and since multiple brands often source from the same factories, individual brands will often lack incentives to encourage particular factories to change their practices. Regarding suppliers, the transition to lean production is costly, so unless suppliers have clear assurances that brands will give them business after they implement lean production, and financial and technical assistance in making the transition, they will generally be unable to take that step on their own (Sabel 2014, 232–33).

States that house suppliers, finally, often lack either the means or the will to regulate them. Elites often benefit handsomely from current production strategies, particularly in nations where the business and political class are closely intertwined, and can be expected to resist reforms. Even when they do not, poor nations cannot push labor costs too high without encouraging capital flight, raising both prudential and distributive concerns for those concerned with worker welfare. And public regulation is an incomplete solution in any event, since even in wealthy nations regulators can't hope to locate and sanction more than a fraction of legal violations. Without another prime mover, or basic changes to the rules of globalization, highly competitive and low-margin sectors seem trapped in an inefficient and morally troubling low-road equilibrium.

Toward Transnational Triangular Collective Bargaining

Ultimately, solving the sweatshop problem likely requires more than state and brand-based initiatives. It likely requires a different set of global initiatives that instantiate a different political economy. The question is how to get there from here. Workers' organizations engaged in TTCB may be the missing link. Such organizations could coordinate among suppliers and brands, could encourage brands to alter sourcing practices, and could push states to reform and better enforce labor laws. Doing so will not be easy, since the legal regimes summarized above erect substantial barriers to unionization, to cross-border collaboration among unions, and to state efforts aimed at enabling easier unionization. But if such barriers can be overcome, robust unions may encourage movement away from the low-trust equilibrium Locke blames for the sweatshop problem. This part first outlines some of the salutary governance effects of unionization at the national level and outlines how unions could perform similar functions globally through TTCB. It then summarizes various historical precedents for TTCB and notes some contemporary campaigns that are taking steps toward it. Finally, it discusses key logistical and legal impediments to TTCB and sketches some ways in which national and international laws could be reformed to better enable its emergence.

TTCB and Its Potential Benefits

In TTCB, workers' organizations would link together across national borders and negotiate agreements both with workers' primary employers and with the brands that purchase their products. Agreements with workers' primary employers would be standard collective bargaining agreements, the terms of which might vary from nation to nation and region to region. Agreements with brands would ideally involve specific price commitments, commitments to source only from factories that respect workers' rights, and commitments to source from those factories for the duration of the agreement. This model builds on the jobbers' agreements that effectively eliminated sweatshops in the United States for much of the twentieth century. If established, TTCB could deliver significant benefits for brands and suppliers as well as workers by solving trust problems within GVCs that prevent more stable sourcing and working relationships. In that sense, this proposal and analysis builds on Alan Hyde's insight that norms of transnational labor law tend to emerge and persist when they solve collective action problems faced by states (Hyde 2006).

TTCB could resolve trust problems within GVCs in three interrelated ways. First, by creating a counterweight to brand power within GVCs, it could encourage the move to lean production. The reason is straightforward: higher per-unit labor costs, if enforced, will lead brands to seek efficiencies, and lean production seems one of the few means of doing so. Workers' organizations can also provide a bridge among suppliers and brands that otherwise cannot coordinate. Within nation-states, unions can push all suppliers to raise standards together, helping resolve some of the collective action problems inherent in such extremely competitive and dynamic sectors. Unions could also work across national borders to raise standards while preventing capital flight, insofar as they can calibrate wage demands to national circumstances. As sociologists have documented, more encompassing unions have incentives to moderate their wage demands in order to distribute benefits among their constituencies (Rogers 1990; Streeck 2005, 271–72). Transnational bargaining structures may therefore help manage global labor competition by setting both a floor below wages and a ceiling above them.

Second, TTCB could enhance individual states' powers to enforce labor standards. This is one aspect of the "voice" function of unions famously described by Freeman and Medoff: unions can aggregate and channel workers' knowledge of workplace practices, enabling workers to discuss code violations and other problems with management (Freeman and Medhoff 1984). Nonunionized workers, in contrast, have incentives to "exit" the workplace rather than complain. For this reason, labor scholars often classify freedom of association and other citizenship rights as "enabling rights" whose protection allows workers to protect their own interests without immediate recourse to the state (Kolben 2010, 473–74). The "voice" function of workers' organizations engaged in TTCB would also make them a ready partner for employee participation and input in lean production systems.

Third, TTCB could encourage democratic transformation of governance regimes. This has often happened in states where industrialization preceded democratization and the extension of the franchise. Again, as explored in more detail below, this process may need to take place both at the national level and transnationally today. At the national level, TTCB could encourage a stronger regulatory state and encourage new egalitarian lawmaking. Moreover, although states' jurisdiction is limited to their geographic territory, unions could work across jurisdictions, helping to solve states' regulatory collective action problems. Ideally this could spark a virtuous cycle whereby worker organizations' gains lead to enhanced national and international legal protections for transnational organizing and bargaining.

Precedents for TTCB

TTCB has various partial precedents in transnational bargaining and triangular bargaining efforts. The most prominent examples of transnational bargaining have arisen in Europe and have led to "global framework agreements," or GFAs, under which brands commit to respect the ILO's standards and other workers' rights throughout their operations (Be 2008; Anner, Bair, and Blasi 2013). But GFAs are only a partial precedent for TTCB. Most have been negotiated in heavy industrial or construction sectors where workers are employed by subsidiaries or relatively well-capitalized suppliers, and they tend not to impact the sourcing decisions of brands or the price structure of their contracts. In other words, they are transnational but not triangular. As a result, they have had limited purchase so far in very low-wage sectors like garment manufacturing (Anner, Bair, and Blasi 2013). Indeed, transnational organizing and bargaining is rare today, likely because labor movements emerged within particular nation-states and, in the case of industrial unions, have relied heavily on the nation-state for stability and security (Streeck 2005, 267–69).

Examples of triangular (but not transnational) bargaining are easier to identify, particularly in the United States. The most obvious and well developed were the jobbers' agreements negotiated between workers, garment manufacturers, and purchasers in the US garment sector in the early and mid-twentieth century (Anner, Bair, and Blasi 2013; see also chapter 13). Jobbers' agreements involved three-party negotiations and binding commitments from lead firms to utilize union labor, to pay enough to enable suppliers to pay union-scale wages and benefits, and to continue to use particular suppliers for the duration of the agreement. But of course jobbers' agreements were negotiated in a very different geographic and legal context in which capital flight was less of an immediate threat and state capacity fairly well established (Anner, Bair, and Blasi 2013).

But jobbers' agreements are not unique. More recently, janitors in the United States—many of whom are irregular immigrants without basic citizenship rights, and virtually all of whom work for third-party contractors—have won union certification and substantially higher wages and benefits through similar triangular campaigns. Janitors did so by organizing across-the-board within a particular jurisdiction rather than one worksite at a time, utilizing the media to press building owners and other real estate companies to act responsibly toward outsourced janitors for whom they owe no legal duties, and reaching informal agreements with building owners to use only unionized contractors and to provide sufficient funding in contracts to enable union-scale wages (Waldinger et al. 1998). Those efforts often required a delicate legal dance around US labor-law rules concerning secondary boycotts and other rules concerning subjects of bargaining. Farmworkers, meanwhile, have long turned their exclusion from the National Labor Relations Act (NLRA) regime into an opportunity of sorts, organizing consumer boycotts against agricultural brands that would be unlawful for covered workers (Gordon 2005, 15–16, 24–26). The United Farm Workers of

America (UFW) used such tactics for years, and more recently they have been picked up by the Coalition of Immokalee Workers—which organizes workers but is not a union—in a campaign that has successfully pressed major restaurant and grocery chains to pay a penny more per pound of tomatoes, with all proceeds going directly to workers despite numerous contractual intermediaries.

Such campaigns demonstrate the potential of TTCB. For example, they succeeded in part because of workers' credible threats to disrupt lead firms' sourcing through industrial action, as well as their moral arguments that lead firms needed to take responsibility for contractors' behavior. Tactically, organizers in such campaigns have united workers both around immediate workplace grievances and around holding lead firms accountable, given the power that such firms hold over workers' immediate employers. Moreover, in each case, the resulting agreements solve collective-action problems and stabilize their respective industries, halting price competition and enabling suppliers to raise wages without risking loss of business—exactly the sorts of collective-action problems that lead to sweatshops today. It is important to note that outside the garment sector such agreements are not formally enforceable and lead firms have no duty to bargain with third-party workers. That lack of rights has surely deterred some such organizing but has not prevented it.

Given the imprint of Anglo-American law on global economic law, it is unsurprising that similar tactics are now being utilized in global organizing efforts, often led by US-based NGOs. Two recent victories in the garment sector are exemplary. One came at Russell factories in Honduras, the other at the PT Kizone factory in Indonesia. The Honduran workers obtained binding commitments from Russell: to ensure reinstatement and fund backpay for workers terminated when their factories shut down, including immediate payments of $2.5 million to recently displaced workers; to ensure that suppliers respect workers' freedom of association by dissolving company-dominated unions and refraining from interfering with organizing efforts; and to source from particular factories for a period into the future (Ben Hensler e-mail to author 2009). Whereas the workers at Russell were direct employees of the company, workers at PT Kizone were not. Adidas and Nike both sourced from the plant, which closed suddenly without paying workers nearly $3.3 million in severance pay. Although the terms of the settlement are confidential, it clearly requires adidas to execute specific financial commitments to make those workers whole (Brettman 2013).

Several other ongoing campaigns are also taking steps toward TTCB. The Asia Floor Wage campaign seeks to unite worker organizations in most garment-producing Asian nations and asks brands to commit to establish a basic wage floor in the sector. Although that campaign is not yet engaging in collective bargaining, it usefully brings together worker organizations from multiple countries and presses for third-party commitments that would change brands' sourcing behavior (Musoliek 2011). Similarly, the International Union League for Brand Responsibility is pushing for a form of TTCB that would link garment workers in a number of nations into agreements with their immediate employers and brands (see chapter 14 for a detailed discussion).

Finally, the recent Accord on Fire and Building Safety in Bangladesh, a binding contract among global unions, Bangladeshi unions, and brands, has both established binding triangular commitments and established a supervisory process that could evolve into a transnational bargaining platform (see chapter 1). Several aspects of the Accord are essential: it requires brands to source from factories that are compliant with safety codes, to continue sourcing from Bangladesh for a period of five years, and "to negotiate commercial terms with their suppliers which ensure that it is financially feasible for the factories to maintain safe workplaces." Most important, disputes arising under the Accord are subjected to arbitration and awards are enforceable in the brands' state of domicile (Accord on Fire and Building Safety in Bangladesh 2013). An alternative agreement developed by Walmart, The Gap, and other US brands, the Alliance for Bangladesh Worker Safety, also commits brands to source only from compliant factories, but does not involve unions or the ILO and does not include specific financial commitments. If the Accord succeeds both in stabilizing the industry and establishing a beachhead for unions in Bangladesh, a natural next step may be to expand the Accord beyond Bangladesh to cover the garment industries in other nations, and perhaps to other sectors as well.

With the exception of the Alliance, which is effectively a "gentlemen's agreement" with no bilateral commitments, all these efforts represent steps toward solving the sweatshop problem. That being said, none of the agreements addresses all three pieces of the puzzle: triangular commitments, between brands and workers in multiple nations, that are memorialized in collective bargaining agreements. GFAs are an incipient form of transnational bargaining, but they are not really triangular. The Accord and the Russell and PT Kizone victories are all binding and triangular but not transnational, whereas the Asia Wage Floor campaign and the International Union League efforts are transnational and triangular, but so far not binding. The subject matter of agreement also varies: Asia Floor Wage covers only wages, and Russell only backpay. Although the Accord implements a supervisory process that empowers workers, the agreement itself does not cover collective bargaining rights. A mature TTCB regime would need to be more encompassing than any of these structures, enabling unions to play the coordinating, wage-setting, and democratizing roles outlined above.

Law Reforms to Enable TTCB

Although lead firms' increasingly powerful and visible role at the top of value chains and the reduced costs of communications make this sort of organizing increasingly possible today, important legal and structural barriers remain. Structurally, most labor solidarity is local, since individual workers must trust one another to take collective action (Fantasia 1988; Rogers 2012). This helps explain why so many unions over the years have organized along ethnic or religious lines: it is far easier to build solidarity among workers who already share social ties. Although it may be possible to build a collective identity among Apple workers or adidas workers, those workers may be separated by thousands of miles and may produce for any number of brands over the course of a year. Workers' organizations engaged in TTCB would also need to overcome their own collective-action problems, rooted in conflicting national interests. This may be possible over time as those organizations engage in trust building through successful cross-border campaigns—particularly insofar as those organizations have a common interest in holding brands accountable.

Various legal regimes will also complicate efforts to build TTCB. Although transnational collective bargaining is not unlawful in most states, some of the tactics that would be involved in building transnational bargaining units are. In the United States, for example, strikes to support overseas workers are classified as unlawful secondary boycotts. European nations have varying degrees of protection for such efforts, and producer nations such as Bangladesh, Colombia, Indonesia, Thailand, Turkey, and other nations will as well (Atleson 2000, 385–96). Of course, concerted activity often leads to retaliation or even violence in many nations. Without any transnational legal regime governing labor relations, workers will have difficulty holding brands to any sort of a duty to bargain, though they have often overcome this problem in the domestic context.[2]

Since they are the home jurisdictions of the most important global brands, the United States and European nations could help unions overcome such barriers. Most important, they could hold brands to some legal duties toward workers in their supply chains. Third-party liability is not unheard of in labor and employment law. For example, the United States Fair Labor Standards Act[3] often extends liability for wage and hour violations to those who do business with labor contractors, particularly when the purchaser exerts substantial economic power over its contractors (Rogers 2010). The state of California now also holds companies in the garment, janitorial, farm labor, security, and warehouse sectors liable for employment law violations by their contractors, if they knew or should have known that the contract did not include sufficient funds to ensure compliance.[4] Although no nation or state that I am aware of extends such duties to overseas suppliers, proposed legislation in France would do just that, requiring domestic firms to take reasonable care to prevent human rights violations within their value chains.[5] The United States Congress could do the same in theory, if not under current political conditions. If France and other European nations do begin to hold domestic corporations to a duty of care vis-à-vis production workers, moreover, they could push the United States to adopt the same as a means of ensuring regulatory coherence under the Trans-Atlantic Partnership.

Short of such a direct statutory duty, Congress or the states could also require reporting on labor conditions. Again, California is a leader. Large companies doing business in the state must report on their efforts to eliminate slavery and human trafficking from their supply chains.[6] Unfortunately, given federalism concerns, it is not clear whether such efforts could be expanded to cover core labor standards compliance (Borchers 2013, 54–55). But Congress could certainly require publicly listed companies to audit their supply chains and report labor standards violations, just as they now must do with regard to conflict minerals and some other issues (Brudney 2012, 588–89). Congress could nudge brands further toward TTCB by exempting brands from reporting requirements if they have signed TTCB-style agreements.

Finally, the ILO might take various steps to encourage TTCB. Some advances could be accomplished through the ILO's monitoring bodies. For example, the ILO Committee of Experts could take the position that industrial action in support of foreign workers within the same industry should not constitute an illegal secondary boycott, or even that multinationals have some duties toward workers in their GVCs since those workers are the functional equivalent of their employees. More ambitiously, the ILO could adopt a convention or declaration detailing steps that member states should take to enable effective TTCB. The ILO's Tripartite Declaration of Principles concerning Multinational Enterprises and Social Policy provides a template of sorts, though that declaration is limited to multinationals' employees and says nothing at all about value-chain workers or value-chain responsibility (Hyde 2012, 98; ILO 2014). A new convention on work in GVCs might require member states to recognize TTCB contracts as collective bargaining agreements and to alter the rights and duties of workers, employers, and brands so as to encourage TTCB. The ILO might even establish a transnational agency empowered to serve some of the functions of classic national labor agencies.

As is typically the case in labor law, such law reforms will likely follow organizing and disruptive action by unions rather than preceding such efforts. But once in place, such new rules could enable an iterative process through which workers' organizations build more power, win victories, alter political-economic dynamics within nations and across nations, and create incentives for states to institutionalize transnational labor conflict. In other words, building TTCB structures could help workers' organizations alter the basic terms of global economic governance.

Although politically impossible now, one can imagine various alternative globalizations that draw lessons from twentieth-century welfare states. A future global basic structure could be neocorporatist, for example, with global workers' organizations, multinationals, and states collectively setting rules of the game. Alternatively, it could enact a sort of global "embedded liberalism," in which global rules creating free markets coexist with global rules ensuring equity and distributive justice in production. Or perhaps global justice requires weakening the link between employment and welfare by ensuring a global basic income together with substantially liberalized citizenship regimes. These examples are illustrative, simply intended to show the possibility of alternatives to our current global liberal market economy. Altering that basic structure will surely be a long process, especially since there is no state at the global level and both labor and capital are dispersed. But by having a new sort of stable global political economic regime clearly in sight, policymakers and worker advocates can begin taking steps toward creating that regime.

With such alternative visions in mind, the normative and structural differences between TTCB and existing private governance efforts come into sharper focus. Unilateral initiatives by brands seem far less likely to encourage a more just globalization, since brands have no incentive to encourage robust collective bargaining. Initiatives such as the Alliance for Bangladesh Worker Safety, which do not give workers a structural role in implementation, instead make workers' welfare a function of brands' desires rather than a baseline democratic right. TTCB therefore represents a far more democratically legitimate and fair approach to global governance. It is not a complete solution, and is certainly costly to design and implement. But in an era in which governance by managerial fiat masquerades as justice, simply enabling workers to represent their own needs and interests seems a radical proposition.

ASSESSING THE RISKS AND OPPORTUNITIES OF PARTICIPATION IN GLOBAL VALUE CHAINS

Gary Gereffi and Xubei Luo

Risk is inherent to the pursuit of opportunity. This paper draws on recent literature and looks at the risks and opportunities firms and their workers face in the global value chains (GVCs). For millennia, the ancient agrarian cycle, based on crops and livestock, controlled the fortunes of the world. Then came the Industrial Revolution in the mid-nineteenth century. "For the first time in history, the living standards of the masses of ordinary people have begun to undergo sustained growth," noted the Nobel Laureate and economist Robert E. Lucas, Jr. "Nothing remotely like this economic behavior has happened before" (Lucas 2002, 109–10). More recently, in the context of integration and modernization, waves of technology improvement since the first Industrial Revolution have been changing the boundaries of production and redefining the spectrum of the role of state.

Participation in GVCs, which highlight the ways in which new patterns of international trade, production, and employment shape prospects for development and competitiveness, creates opportunities and risks for enterprises. On the one hand, it generates new opportunities for profits and expands the market horizon, and on the other hand, it exposes the enterprise sector to risks previously shielded from market boundaries and geographic distance and increases the degree of potential information asymmetry. Various forces interact in different directions, exacerbating or mitigating the dynamics of risks.

Enterprises are facing a wide range of risks on a day-to-day basis. Owing to continual changes in technology, production frontiers are pushing outward and higher efficiency becomes the norm for survival (for example, personal computers).

Demand changes as new tastes and preferences create niches for new products. The higher profit markup from innovation becomes an engine of growth (for example, the iPad). One recent study suggests that in developing countries, every ten extra mobile phones per hundred people increase the rate of growth of GDP per capita by more than one percentage point by drawing people into the banking system with smartphone use (The Economist 2015). However, there are also catastrophic risks from unexpected events, such as global economic crises and natural disasters.

The information and communication technology revolution has not only sharply increased productivity but has also reinterpreted the function of time and distance: billions of activities are linked with "one click" and new demands become effective with "just-in-time" delivery. Using data transmitted from a mobile phone call, doctors thousands of miles away can analyze ultrasound results at low cost and prescribe treatment in real time. In India, for example, this innovation has shown the great potential that technology has in helping people manage risks, starting with day-to-day health issues. The world is increasingly interconnected. The largely unforeseen changes in the global arena—from the collapse of the dot.com boom in the early 2000s, to the burst of housing bubbles in 2008 and the ongoing Euro zone turmoil—have had systemic implications on the survival and growth of firms in different corners of the world, even before reactions were taken to try to disentangle the links. Shocks in access to financing and to commodities were magnified at an unprecedented scale.

To a considerable extent, participating and competing in GVCs has become inevitable. Even if a firm is not export oriented, it will be competing against imports made in the global economy unless there are protectionist barriers against imports. This paper looks at the risks and opportunities that firms and their workers face in GVCs. First, it examines the risk-sharing mechanisms that firms provide from the national and global perspectives; second, it takes a closer look at the new opportunities and challenges for firms and individuals in the global arena; third, it discusses the role of economic upgrading and social upgrading; and finally, it sheds light on how the government can help people manage risks and reap benefits through participation in GVCs.

Firms as a Vehicle of Risk Sharing

The Nobel Laureate Ronald Coase has argued that firms emerged as a social institution to overcome the constraint of transaction costs inherent in direct exchanges—that is, the costs associated with searching for, communicating, and bargaining with possible trading partners (Coase 1937). Under conditions of uncertainty, the allocation of resources is not carried out by the price mechanism. Some individuals take a fixed income, whereas others (the entrepreneurs) make the decision to seek volatile profits as a preferred but riskier choice. This reflects the fact that different economic actors have different utility functions. However, there is a natural limit to what firms can produce internally, which is why all production is not done by one firm. Through efficient resource allocation, firms are capable of generating higher income than households or individuals alone, but this requires finding an optimal balance between the decreasing returns to the entrepreneur function when firms get too large and the transaction costs of using the market.

Multiperson firms provide the mechanism of risk sharing among workers and firm owners, and between workers and firm owners:

- When risk is shared among workers, if a worker falls sick, others can share the workload to keep the firm going. Also, the risk-sharing mechanism that multiperson firms make possible allows workers to specialize and increase productivity together. Investing in specialized skills is a risky undertaking. By absorbing the costs of initial training, or by providing incentives to acquire such skills by raising wages, enterprises can tilt worker skill profiles toward specialization. By sharing the costs of training or increasing the expected returns of acquiring skills, the enterprise sector can shift the skill distribution in the workforce toward specialization (Lam and Liu 1986; Acemoglu and Pischke 1999).
- When risk is shared among owners of capital, for example through limited liability, investors can take on more creative risk with a given level of expected risk through diversifying their portfolio. As the *Economist* magazine noted in its millennium issue, "The modern world is built on two centuries of industrialization. Much of that was built by equity finance which is built on limited liability" (The Economist 1999). With the required legal and institutional frameworks, the contractual arrangements of limited liability lowers the downside risk of investments, allowing investors to separate personal liability from the debt of the production unit. It also enables them to own small pieces of many firms and diversify their investment portfolio, which reduces risk if some of their investments drop in value. Limited liability also led to the development of the stock market, facilitated corporate capital accumulation, and enabled the exploitation of economies of scale.
- When risk is shared between workers and owners of capital, for example through labor contracts, firms can provide insurance to workers who accept a lower wage in exchange for stable income. Firms can provide a steadier stream of wage income to labor owners by isolating some risks related to production. Through labor contracts, workers can relocate risks in the production process to firms and limit excessive fluctuations in employment and income to maximize welfare. To maximize profit, firms try to minimize

the cost of labor as well as the cost of other inputs. To maximize welfare, workers prefer jobs with not only higher but also more stable income. Firms, which are less risk averse than workers, care more about the average labor cost than its volatility, and thus can offer labor contracts with less volatility in pay (for example, a fixed wage) to compete for workers in exchange for a lower average level of remuneration. By leveraging the two aspects explicitly or implicitly contained in labor contracts—the level and the volatility of the remuneration—both firms and workers could be better off through risk sharing. On the other hand, workers can offer a form of insurance to firms in which they agree to reductions in wage or cutback in work hours during temporary shocks in exchange for higher wages in normal times.

Risk sharing and diversification have encouraged risk taking and have increased productivity at a massive scale. Higher income allows individuals to increase savings, purchase market insurance, improve access to finance, invest in nutrition and health, and obtain more knowledge from educational investment. Take savings, for example. If individuals are struggling to meet their current needs, saving for the future will be a slow process. Around the world, as income levels rise, savings rates also rise (Schmidt-Hebbel et al. 1992). In developing countries, a doubling of income per capita is estimated to raise the long-run private savings rate by ten percentage points of disposable income (Loayza, Schmidt-Hebbel, and Serven 2000).

However, with the division of labor and diversification of ownership of firms, new risks also emerge. The ways the enterprise sector functions and manages risk affect the risks people face and the risk management measures they employ. Firms may take risk irresponsibly at the brink of bankruptcy, creating negative externalities for society. The management of the firm, which is often in the hands of professionals who have special managerial skills, may have different interests than its owners.

If the enterprise sector fails to function smoothly or if it shifts its own risks to people, it can be a source of risks to households, communities, and even the financial sector and national government. When business shrinks or technology becomes obsolete, the enterprise sector may generate income-related risks (channeled through loss of jobs and loss of capital returns) and asset-related risks (channeled through loss of investments). Both can further translate into risks related to social inclusion, ranging from loss of insurance and other benefits provided through employment (such as health insurance and pension), to loss of connection with the professional community, as well as loss of social status and involuntary changes in lifestyles. Regulation and incentive systems need to be in place to ensure that the interests of various stakeholders are protected.

In a globalized world, characterized by lower transport and transaction costs, the interconnections across firms or sectors linked through supply networks or financial linkages multiply and intensify. Global value chains include two main types of firms: lead firms, which are typically transnational corporations (TNCs) headquartered in the advanced industrial countries that control and define the main activities in terms of price, delivery, and performance in both producer-driven and buyer-driven GVCs; and the supplier companies that produce the goods and services in GVCs, generally located in developing countries. Thus, the GVC enterprise sector links both developed and developing countries into a common global supply chain.

The GVC framework focuses on globally expanding supply chains and how value is created and captured within them (Gereffi and Lee 2012). The concept of "governance" is the centerpiece of GVC analysis. It examines the ways in which corporate power can actively shape the distribution of profits and risk in an industry and the actors that exercise such power through their activities. Power in GVCs is exerted by lead firms. These lead firms form different kinds of relationships with suppliers that result in distinct GVC governance typologies. The original typology is the distinction between producer-driven and buyer-driven chains (Gereffi 1994). More recently, a fivefold typology has been elaborated that highlights the importance of enduring forms of network governance (modular, relational, and captive) between the market and hierarchy poles of the GVC governance continuum, which are driven by price or ownership in vertically integrated firms, respectively (Gereffi, Humphrey, and Sturgeon 2005).

From the GVC point of view, enterprise sectors in national economies are part of the supply base for lead firms in GVCs. This has two concrete implications: (1) external actors (specifically, GVC lead firms) are a potentially significant form of "external risk" in national enterprise sectors, and (2) national enterprise sectors are nested within larger regional and global enterprise sectors, which are connected to GVCs. The global enterprise sector, as a series or set of industry-specific GVCs, has the potential to affect people's risk management through the same risk-sharing mechanisms that are operating at a larger scale. It can be advantageous or detrimental to national enterprise sectors and affect firms differently according to their size and industries.

Opportunities and Challenges in the Global Arena

Firms face new opportunities and challenges in the global market. They have the opportunity of supplying much larger global demand, which eliminates the scale and purchasing power limitations of the domestic market in developing economies. There also are many upgrading opportunities because the quality and price parameters have wider variation, allowing for more extensive product and process upgrading options. There is also higher risk because international standards for price, quality, standards and delivery schedules are much less forgiving. Firms typically need to have a relatively large scale of production to participate in global markets, or have a special technological edge to enter global market niches. There is also a risk from intensified competitive pressures, as everyone can compete with exporters in terms of lower prices or higher quality, so only the best can succeed in GVCs.

The presence of scale economies favors the concentration of production, which tends to minimize costs, leading to higher profits for enterprises and possibly lower prices for consumers. The higher concentration of production yields benefits of large-scale clustering and agglomeration, but also generates new risks for the economy. Shocks in one location can easily spread to the rest of the network, generating cascade effects. If the supply network is highly interconnected, low productivity in one sector can potentially affect the entire economy, as downstream sectors will also suffer (Acemoglu, Ozdaglar, and Tahbaz-Salehi 2010).

Greater openness to international trade and capital can have a large impact on macroeconomic volatility. When an economy is highly concentrated in certain productive activities, such as Nokia (whose worldwide sales in 2003 represented over one-quarter of Finland's GDP) and Samsung (which accounted for 23 percent of the Republic of Korea's exports and some 14 percent of GDP), firm-specific idiosyncratic shocks can generate significant shocks that affect GDP (Di Giovanni and Levchenko 2009).

Foreign direct investment can affect the volatility of enterprise performance in times of crisis in different ways. The ability of multinationals to shift production across countries can increase volatility, and market diversification can lend stronger stability to local subsidiaries. For instance, after the recent global financial crisis, multinational subsidiaries linked with parent firms with strong vertical production and financial linkages fared better on average than local counterparts. The demand from parent firms can help absorb the negative demand shock in the host country, while the performance of subsidiaries linked horizontally with parent firms might become more volatile as the multinationals shift more production back home (Alfaro and Chen 2011).

Multinational companies' internal capital markets and investment flows from parent firms to subsidiaries can lower subsidiaries' dependence on host-country credit conditions and hence lower their performance volatility when host countries experience credit crunches (Antras, Desai, and Foley 2009). In Poland, for example, during the recent global economic crisis, foreign ownership appears to provide a higher degree of resilience to affiliates facing external credit constraints through intragroup lending mechanisms (Kolasa, Rubaszek, and Taglioni 2010).

Supply chain management, backed by tight vertical connections among enterprises, has resulted in a high level of competitiveness for the automobile industry. Car makers at the top of a chain can procure meticulously customized, high-quality components from firms further down the chain (resulting in differentiated, high-quality cars), collect information to continuously predict the appropriate amount of outputs, and minimize inventory and associated costs. The high degree of customization and just-in-time production practice, two key drivers of success, also expose the automobile industry to worldwide shocks (Canis 2011).

The 2011 earthquake in Japan rattled the auto industry worldwide, leading to one shock after another. The disruption of production of automotive parts generated immediate impacts. Since automotive parts are highly customized, replacement from other suppliers is almost impossible. In April 2011, Nissan closed plants in Mexico for five days and plants in the United States for six days. Output at eight of Honda's Canadian, Indian, UK, and US plants was cut by half.[1] The US carmaker General Motors closed its assembly plant in Louisiana because of a shortage of vehicle parts, which in turn led to short layoffs at its New York plant, where the engines are made. Ford closed assembly plants in Belgium and the United States for one week, and plants in China, the Philippines, Taiwan, China, and South Africa for two weeks.[2]

Although firms are exposed to new challenges in an increasingly integrated world, international trade and financial linkages, remittances, and diaspora communities have the potential to serve as safety nets for individuals, families, and communities to absorb and cope with risks and shocks that are not global in nature. For individuals, communities, and national economies, remittances of foreign earnings tend to be stable and often countercyclical. Migrants are likely to send home more resources to help their families when the home country has experienced an economic downturn or crisis. For example, during the financial crisis in Mexico in 1995 and in Indonesia and Thailand in 1998, remittances increased sharply, which not only helped household consumption but also provided the needed resources to overcome credit constraints for local entrepreneurs, alleviating their risks (The World Bank 2005). Beyond remittances, diasporas can provide assistance in normal times by assisting in philanthropic activities, fostering the exchange of knowledge, and increasing trade links; in time of stress, they are more likely than average investors to finance infrastructure, housing, health, and education projects in their countries of origin. Diaspora bonds have raised over $35 billion in India and Israel, including during periods when the home country was suffering a liquidity crisis (Ratha 2010).

In terms of GVCs, the supply chain rationalization that has thinned out the number of firms in GVCs was accelerated as a result of the 2008–2009 global economic recession. As consumption declined as a result of the recession in most advanced industrial countries, which were the main markets for GVCs, the size of GVC supply chains sharply contracted. Recent studies have highlighted significant new trends in how GVCs are organized in the current period, which alter the nature of risks that national enterprise sectors will confront (see Gereffi 2014 for a summary of these changes):

- GVCs are becoming geographically more consolidated, which reflects the rise of large emerging economies after 1989. Known initially as BRICs (Brazil, Russia, India, and China), the emerging economies now include a diverse array of "growth economies" such as Mexico, South Korea, Turkey, Indonesia, the Philippines, and Vietnam, which offer seemingly inexhaustible pools of relatively low-wage workers, highly capable export-oriented manufacturers, abundant raw materials, and sizeable domestic markets (O'Neill 2011). Emerging economies are now major production centers worldwide, although their specific roles in GVCs vary according to their openness to trade and foreign investment, and other strategic considerations.
- GVCs are also becoming organizationally more concentrated, as lead firms in GVCs are streamlining their supply chains from hundreds or even thousands of suppliers spread across dozens of countries in every continent of the world[3] to a much smaller number (perhaps just twenty to thirty) of larger, more capable and strategically located manufacturers. As noted above, there is also considerable geographic concentration in which a few countries are controlling larger shares of global output in each industry (Gereffi 2014). Together, these shifts imply a much greater concentration of industrial production within the global South, higher levels of South-South trade, and the rise of emerging economy TNCs that play a far more significant role in GVCs.

The global economic recession of 2008–2009 reinforced some of the preexisting trends in GVCs, but also introduced new patterns in the global economy that affect the distribution of risk and vulnerability in national enterprise sectors. A study by the World Bank concludes that GVCs have proven resilient in the face of the recent economic crisis, which has accelerated two structural trends in the global economy: the aforementioned consolidation of GVCs and the growing salience of markets in the South (Cattaneo, Gereffi, and Staritz 2010, 6). As world trade is bouncing back from the 2008–2009 global recession, emerging economies are becoming a main engine of world economic recovery. Given stagnant consumer demand in the global North, GVCs are shifting to supply new end markets in the South, which include a renewed emphasis on the domestic markets of large emerging economies and the regionalization of what were previously global supply chains (Staritz, Gereffi, and Cattaneo 2011).

In the case of the global apparel industry, between 2000 and 2013, China's share of global apparel exports increased from 25 percent to 40 percent, and export sales increased from US$48.5 billion to $148.7 billion (see table 8.1). Countries whose market shares declined most abruptly during this period, which included

TABLE 8.1 Top 15 apparel exporters by year, 2000, 2005, 2009, 2012, and 2013

COUNTRY/REGION	VALUE ($, BILLIONS)					WORLD SHARE (%)				
	2000	2005	2009	2012	2013	2000	2005	2009	2012	2013
World	**195.8**	**271.9**	**304.2**	**355.2**	**375.9**					
China	48.5	91.4	126.2	145.5	148.7	25	34	41	41	40
EU-15	33.8	47.8	51.8	52.0	56.6	17	18	17	15	15
Bangladesh	5.0	8.2	14.5	22.8	26.4	3	3	5	6	7
Vietnam	—	4.8	9.5	15.2	18.5	—	2	3	4	5
Turkey	6.8	13.1	13.4	16.4	17.3	3	5	4	5	5
India	5.2	9.6	12.3	12.5	13.5	3	4	4	4	4
Indonesia	4.8	5.8	7.3	9.6	10.0	2	2	2	3	3
Cambodia	—	—	3.5	6.2	7.4	—	—	1	2	2
Sri Lanka	2.7	3.4	4.0	4.4	4.7	1	1	1	1	1
Pakistan	—	—	3.3	4.2	4.5	—	—	1	1	1
Mexico	8.9	6.7	3.9	4.4	4.4	5	2	1	1	1
Romania	2.7	5.2	3.2	4.1	4.3	1	2	1	1	1
Morocco	—	3.4	3.7	3.9	4.3	—	1	1	1	1
Tunisia	2.7	3.5	3.8	3.6	3.7	1	1	1	1	1
Thailand	3.7	3.9	3.6	3.5	3.3	2	1	1	1	1
China, Hong Kong SAR	10.6	8.8	—	—	—	5	3	—	—	—
USA	5.2	3.7	—	—	—	3	1	—	—	—
Rep. of Korea	4.7	—	—	—	—	2	—	—	—	—
Other Asia	3.1	—	—	—	—	2	—	—	—	—
Top 15	**148.5**	**219.2**	**263.9**	**308.2**	**327.6**	**76**	**81**	**87**	**87**	**87**

Source: UNCOMTRADE; exports based on world (aggregate) apparel imports (HS92 61+62); data for 2000–2012 retrieved by Stacey Frederick on 3/3/14, and 2013 data retrieved on 1/14/15.

"—" indicates country not in the top 15 in given year.

the phase out of the Multi-Fiber Arrangement (MFA) in 2005 that guaranteed export quotas for many smaller countries in the US and European Union markets, were Mexico, Central America and the Dominican Republic, Thailand, the Philippines, Romania, and Poland (Frederick and Gereffi 2011). Bangladesh replaced Mexico as the world's second-largest apparel exporter, jumping from $5 billion of exports in 2000 to $26.4 billion in 2013 (an increase from 3 percent to 7 percent of the world total, respectively). However, even in China, a clear winner in aggregate terms, thousands of apparel factories were shuttered and millions of workers in apparel plants lost their jobs as the industry was streamlined in the late 1990s and early 2000s (when many state-owned apparel firms were closed), and then again in the late 2000s as the recession further reduced export-oriented sales.

In short, the economic crisis has not reversed globalization; international production and consumption have remained central features of the global economy. The role of the South has grown, but inequalities among developing countries in terms of how they are positioned in GVCs are rising as well. This could generate additional sources of inequality and potential crises in the future.

Economic Upgrading and Social Upgrading

The distribution of risks and opportunities is closely related to the positioning of an enterprise within a value chain and to the nature of this value chain. Figure 8.1 illustrates this proposition for value chains associated, respectively, with five different industry groups. Economic and social upgrading (or downgrading) of firms and workers can take place in multiple trajectories (Barrientos, Gereffi, and Rossi 2011).

"Economic upgrading" is defined as the process by which economic actors— firms and workers—move from low-value to relatively high-value activities in GVCs (Gereffi 2005, 171). The challenge of economic upgrading in GVCs is to identify the conditions under which developing and developed countries and firms can "climb the value chain" from basic assembly activities using low-cost and unskilled labor to more advanced forms of "full package" supply and integrated manufacturing. It is also important to forestall the competitive pressures that can create reversals for firms and lead to economic and social downgrading (Bernhardt 2013).

"Social upgrading" refers to improvements within a specific enterprise (or associated group of enterprises) in terms of employment, remuneration, worker rights, and workplace safety and employee insurance arrangements (Barrientos, Gereffi, and Rossi 2011). This concept is central to the examination of household risks and enterprises within value chains. Social upgrading by enterprises helps reduce risks for worker households and removes some of the volatility that they would otherwise face. The extent and type of social upgrading that is possible are usually related to (but not wholly determined by) the economic upgrading in place. Other institutional factors and actors, including the extent and nature of worker organization, civil society actions, government legislation and its enforcement, can also make a difference.

Each GVC in figure 8.1 is represented as a vertical silo, with lower segments approximating the share of less-skilled types of work carried out within the value chain. All value chains include economic activities that span a broad range of skill levels. Consider agriculture, for instance. At the lowest level—the farm, typically—this value chain involves a relatively large proportion of small-scale and low-skill labor. Higher in the value chain, particularly at the points of processing and marketing, the skill level of workers rises progressively. The same is

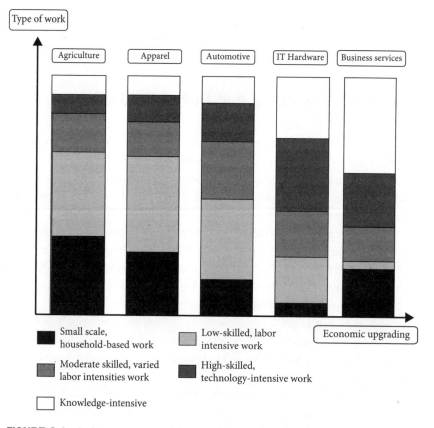

FIGURE 8.1   Industry groups, GVCs, and economic upgrading

Source: Adapted from Barrientos, Gereffi, and Rossi 2011

true for each of the other four GVCs. Skill levels rise as one moves from lower- to higher-value activities in the chain; the proportion of highly skilled workers at the top of each value chain, who carry out knowledge-intensive activities, varies according to the type of GVC we are examining. In agriculture, for example, this segment tends to be relatively small, whereas in business services, the proportion of knowledge workers is quite large.

The likelihood of enforceable standards also rises as one moves up value chains toward more formal and skill-intensive work. It is not enough merely to specify decent work standards; they must be capable of enforcement at low cost, in the ideal situation being self-enforcing. The prospects of having measurable and enforceable standards typically rise as skill levels and technology increase within value chains.

Social upgrading can be achieved through various means, involving different combinations of: (a) economic upgrading—as enterprises move up value chains, the share of skilled workers typically increases, and (b) deliberate actions to introduce enforceable standards—minimum wages, paid time off, workplace safety, insurance, and so on—for those workers whose skill levels remain low, who are more easily replaced, and who for these reasons may be badly treated. The scope for such actions widens considerably as the array of actors is expanded in GVCs. Using illustrative examples of successful social upgrading, we will develop an analytical framework to assess possibilities for action.

Alternative pathways for social upgrading are available, as figure 8.2 shows with the help of three examples. The first example, Pathway A, depicts a situation in which no significant economic upgrading has occurred. Instead, risks to workers were reduced because of deliberate actions that introduced enforceable standards. This could be the situation, for instance, of an enterprise that produced T-shirts branded with the logo of some US university. Actions by concerned student groups resulted in a slew of reforms: doing away with child labor, reducing the length of the work day, improved lighting and other work conditions, and so on.

Alternatively, social upgrading can occur along Pathway C, where almost the entire burden is borne by economic upgrading. In this case, risks for workers are reduced as small-scale household work gets turned into high-tech and knowledge-intensive work, for instance, as in the case when a weaver of traditional rugs takes to computerized design and manufacturing. In the intermediate case of Pathway B, social upgrading within labor-intensive industries like apparel can be achieved with lower risks to workers if outside institutions like the Better Work Program run by the International Labour Organization are involved to help certify standards (Rossi, Luinstra, and Pickles 2014).

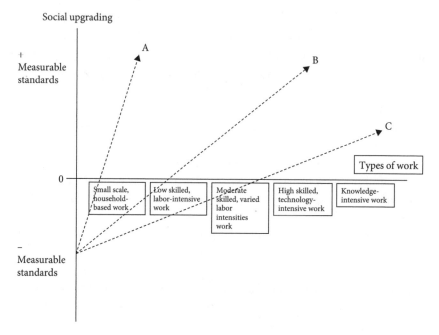

FIGURE 8.2   Different pathways to social upgrading

Source: Adapted from Barrientos, Gereffi, and Rossi 2011

When the enterprise sector gravitates toward more technology or knowledge-intensive industries—for example, from agriculture to apparel, and to business services—the share of skilled workers typically increases. As a result, labor productivity grows and more jobs of higher quality are created. However, economic upgrading does not always lead to social upgrading in the form of better wage and working conditions. On the one hand, unskilled workers in many developing countries can be excluded from the desirable job opportunities provided by technology-intensive or knowledge-intensive work, which tends to concentrate in more developed countries. On the other hand, workers in the same enterprises can face very different opportunities for social upgrading; regular workers can have better statutory employment protection and benefit from labor standards, whereas irregular workers, often overrepresented among women, youth, minority, and other vulnerable groups, may suffer discrimination.

In many enterprises in the developing world, hiring irregular workers directly or through third-party contractors to perform the most time-sensitive task in the low (unskilled) segment of the production chain is often a way for firms to reduce costs in response to last-minute orders from outsourcing companies. Although this creates new wage and employment opportunities for many low-skilled workers, it also allows firms to shift the risks of production related to fluctuations in demand to workers. Regulations need to be in place to protect workers.

To a considerable extent, reducing risk for workers and households is associated with social and economic upgrading at the enterprise (or industry) level. Since a significant proportion of international production and trade now takes place through coordinated value chains in which lead firms globally and locally play a dominant role, possibilities for upgrading are increasingly defined by where firms are located within a chain. However, in some cases we may find social upgrading without sustained economic upgrading, which can jeopardize the social gains.

This is the case in Nicaragua's apparel sector. Between 2005 and 2010, the volume of Nicaragua's apparel exports grew by 8.6 percent, but despite this increase, Nicaragua has had limited success in moving up the apparel value chain and mainly competes through low-cost apparel assembly. Nicaragua remains vulnerable in terms of economic upgrading because its apparel exports are dependent on US trade policy (specifically, the Tariff Preference Level exception offered to Nicaragua that allowed it to import textiles from East Asia). However, the country has shown advances in social upgrading, due in large part to the efforts of the tripartite National Free Trade Zones Commission to join the interests of workers, the private sector, and government. It also has become part of the Better Work Program of the International Labour Organization (Bair and Gereffi 2014).

Firms in GVCs have opportunities for economic upgrading through engaging in higher value production or repositioning themselves within value chains. However, they also face challenges meeting the commercial demands and quality standards required by foreign buyers, which smaller and less efficient producers find hard to meet (Gereffi and Lee 2012; Gereffi 2014). The GVC approach focuses heavily on this notion of interfirm networks, supply chains, and trade and production networks. Adopting a GVC approach to a considerable extent changes the focus of examination; instead of looking at a self-contained enterprise, one analyzes links within chains having different governance structures.

Adopting a GVC analytical framework opens the door, therefore, to a larger cast of economic actors and stakeholders who can act as agents of change. In addition to governments and enterprise management, national industry associations, and trade unions, positive change in working conditions can be brought about at the initiatives of buyers' associations, consumer groups, and international certification and inspection agencies, increasingly employed by buyers wary of their international human rights image (Rossi, Luinstra, and Pickles 2014).

The expansion of global production, especially in labor-intensive industries, has been an important source of employment generation. Many jobs have been filled by women and migrant workers who previously had difficulty accessing this type of waged work, and they have provided new income sources for poorer households (Barrientos, Dolan, and Tallontire 2003; Oxfam International 2004). Where this is regular employment that generates better rights and protection for workers, it can enhance social upgrading and decent work. The demand for rising standards often requires skilling of at least some workers and provision of better employment conditions.

But for many workers, this is not the outcome. Much employment is insecure and unprotected, and there are significant challenges ensuring decent work for more vulnerable workers. Irregular and low-skilled jobs—which are also low paying, thereby representing limited prospects for upward mobility—are easily eliminated when demand goes slack or regulations tighten. New risks are introduced even as some old ones abate. Along with the risk of dismissal (or work reduction) that especially lower-skilled workers (and suppliers) of enterprises face, another significant downside risk accompanying these engagements involves the enhanced probability of injury and illness. Unsafe and unsanitary work conditions are often associated with low-skilled work in the enterprise sector. Labor safety regulations may be nonexistent or they are routinely ignored when enforcement is weak.

Poorer individuals' engagements with the enterprise sector thus produce situations that can be, and often are, volatile. A simple logic for why volatility can be greatest for the worst off in these relationships is provided by Barrientos, Gereffi, and Rossi (2011, 332): "challenges . . . remain significant for irregular workers . . . New activities taken on by the factory may well . . . lead to social upgrading for regular workers—through the development of more skills and training for new capabilities—but irregular workers continue to be needed in order to respond to buyers' requirements in terms of low cost, short lead times and high flexibility; their very status impedes their social upgrading."

Not all developing countries face similar options in the context of these changes. The shift to Southern markets and the growth in South-South trade have created more possibilities for entry and upgrading in GVCs, but they also present new challenges, particularly for the least-developed countries. GVC consolidation poses opportunities as well, especially for countries and firms with rising capabilities. However, it threatens to leave many countries and firms that don't possess the required advantages on the periphery of GVCs.

In a more promising vein, the GVC literature shows that value chains oriented to different end markets entail distinct upgrading opportunities (Staritz et al. 2011; Gereffi 2014). For example, the demand in lower-income countries for less sophisticated products with regard to quality and styles may confront lower entry barriers and less stringent product and process standards in emerging markets, which can facilitate participation and make it easier for developing country firms to engage in higher value-added activities in GVCs (such as product development, design, and branding) (Kaplinsky, Terheggen, and Tijaja 2011). With more intimate knowledge of local and regional markets than multinational firms, GVCs can generate "frugal" innovations that are suitable to resource-poor environments (Clark et al. 2009). On the other hand, relying exclusively on low-income markets can lock suppliers into slimmer margins and cutthroat competition, which heighten economic risks.

Rossi's case study of garment factories in Morocco led by fast fashion buyers shows that functional upgrading in GVCs can bring about social upgrading and downgrading simultaneously for regular and irregular workers, respectively. On the one hand, factories supplying a finished product and overseeing packaging, storage, and logistics for their buyers offer stable contracts and better social protection to their high-skilled workers to ensure a continuous relationship as well as full compliance with buyers' codes of conduct. On the other hand, in order to be able to respond quickly to buyers' frequently changing orders and to operate on short lead times, they simultaneously employ irregular workers on casual contracts, especially in the final segments of the production chain (such as packaging and loading), often imposing excessive overtime as well as discriminating against them on the basis of wages and treatment (Rossi 2011).

In agrifood GVCs, private quality standards set by highly concentrated European and US supermarkets and food manufacturers have a direct impact on risks faced by consumers as well as farmers, with conflicting implications for safety and upgrading (Lee, Gereffi, and Bauvais 2012). On the one hand, stringent food safety and quality standards imposed by large food retailers and manufacturers, which generally have extensive global sourcing networks, protect consumers against social and environmental risks, but these tend to marginalize small farmers unable to comply because of high costs and a lack of required skills and facilities (e.g., cold chains to store, distribute, and ship fresh produce). On the other hand, higher standards can be a catalyst for participation in high-value-added chains, such as the role played by smallholders who successfully supply niche markets for organic or Fair Trade-certified products (Gereffi and Lee 2012, 28).

In both developed and developing countries, the economic gains of participating in GVCs do not necessarily translate into good jobs or stable employment, and, in the worst case, economic upgrading typified by a number of successful export economies, especially in low-income countries, may be linked to a significant deterioration of labor conditions and other forms of social downgrading.

A recently concluded three-year research program funded by the United Kingdom's Department for International Development, called Capturing the Gains, has a website containing many of the research findings in working papers and policy briefs (UK DFID 2013). One of the main conclusions of this project is that GVCs can be a key policy tool for sustained poverty reduction. However, facilitating the upgrading of workers and smallholders also requires public-private-civil society partnerships, as well as regional partnerships involving countries and firms that lead international production networks based in Asia, Africa, and Latin America, which are key to future upgrading of the South (Lee, Gereffi, and Barrientos 2011). These partnerships reflect novel forms of risk sharing and strategic collaboration among key value chain actors to address the challenge of promoting widespread and sustainable development.

Various examples of novel partnerships for risk sharing, innovation, and upgrading are identified in the summit briefings for the Cape Town, South Africa, meeting held in December 2012. A few of these are found in Barrientos, Gereffi, and Nathan (2012, 3–4). For example, over recent decades, the cocoa-chocolate value chain has undergone concentration in processing and manufacturing. Cocoa farmers have received limited support, often have low yields, and are poorly remunerated. Media attention has highlighted issues of child labor, and many younger innovative farmers are leaving the sector for better options elsewhere. Consumption of chocolate has grown steadily, especially in emerging economies, with predictions of future cocoa shortages. Leading chocolate manufacturers are working with civil society, donors, and governments to support farmers and their communities. Social upgrading is now recognized as critical to economic upgrading—and ensuring the future resilience of the cocoa-chocolate value chain.

One of the main challenges of globalization is to link economic and social upgrading of both material work conditions and the quantity and quality of jobs created in contemporary GVCs (Barrientos, Gereffi, and Rossi 2011). For developing countries, the trade, investment, and knowledge flows that underpin GVCs provide mechanisms for rapid learning, innovation, and industrial upgrading (Staritz, Gereffi, and Cattaneo 2011). GVCs can provide local firms with better access to information, open up new markets, and create opportunities for fast technological learning and skill acquisition. Because transactions and investments associated with GVCs typically come with quality-control systems and prevailing global business standards that exceed those in developing countries, enterprises and individuals in developing countries can acquire new competencies and skills by participating in GVCs.

Still, GVCs are not a panacea for development. Very rapid or "compressed" GVC-driven development can generate a host of new economic and social policy challenges in areas such as health care and education (Whittaker et al. 2010). GVCs can create barriers to learning and drive uneven development over time, even as they trigger rapid industrial upgrading, because of the geographic and organizational disjunctures that often exist between innovation and production. There is considerable evidence that greater profits accrue to those lead firms in the value chain that control branding and product conception (e.g., Apple) and to the platform leaders that provide core technologies and advanced components (e.g., Intel). At the same time, contract manufacturers and business-process-outsourcing service providers (e.g., call centers) tend to earn slim profits and may never gain the autonomy or capabilities needed to develop and market their own branded products. Typically, firms that provide routine assembly tasks and other simple services within GVCs earn lower profits, pay their workers less, and are more vulnerable to business cycles, not least because they are required to support large-scale employment and fixed capital (Lüthje 2002).

Overall, the government can provide a critical supportive environment in terms of infrastructure to help exporters, local communities, and small producers trying to access national and international markets, education, and training to build a skilled labor force, and sensible regulations to lower the uncertainties. Firms benefit most from participation in GVCs if they are relatively large, technologically advanced, professionally managed, and have diversified export markets (both in terms of products and countries). Suppliers also benefit from relatively close relationships with their buyers, which can facilitate learning how to upgrade to meet the standards of global markets. TNCs seek to reduce transaction costs by requiring "one-stop shops" with larger and more capable suppliers.

Workers benefit most from participation in GVCs if their conditions of work are relatively formalized (e.g., wages, length of work day and work week, defined benefits) and if they have higher skills (closely correlated with more advanced education) that allow them to carry out better-remunerated tasks. The government can play a key role to address the downside risks for workers—dismissal, debt, injury, illness—and assist in enhancing upward mobility simultaneously. Enforcing sound regulations dealing with labor conditions is crucial to protect the vulnerable segment of the labor force.

Global buyers (retailers, brands, supermarkets) typically don't pay suppliers to undertake the upgrading required to remain competitive in GVCs. Therefore, supportive government policies are an asset (e.g., helping firms to meet international standards and certification requirements, or providing loans or access to finance capital required for purchasing new or better equipment).

The policy implications for upgrading in terms of different end markets are not clear-cut. Facilitating access for export producers to multiple end markets through preferential trade agreements (multilateral or bilateral) would increase the flexibility for suppliers in developing countries to engage in upgrading. However, this will also expose them to greater competitive pressures through low-cost imports. More fundamentally, government policymakers don't know enough about the intricacies of global industries to spur specific forms of innovation in GVCs.

What government policy can do is to facilitate the development of human capital, including collaborations with universities and private firms to ensure demand-responsive forms of workforce development. In addition, government can foster global collaboration by making it easier for small and medium-sized firms to gain the information they need about global markets, and government can also sponsor local trade fairs or external trade missions to encourage global matchmaking.

Part III

PROSPECTS FOR WORKERS' RIGHTS IN CHINA

APPLE, FOXCONN, AND CHINA'S NEW WORKING CLASS

Jenny Chan, Ngai Pun, and Mark Selden

China's pivotal role in export-oriented industrialization has reshaped electronics production networks previously dominated by Japan and its former colonies Taiwan and South Korea. Central to China's export surge since the 1980s has been the role of rural migrant workers. As of early 2015, 274 million Chinese rural migrants had been drawn into the manufacturing, service, and construction sectors in booming towns and cities, an increase of 48.5 million from 2008, when the National Bureau of Statistics (NBS) began to monitor the work and employment conditions of the rural migrant labor force in the aftermath of the global financial crisis (NBS 2014, 2015). Labor unrest across China has been growing steadily for more than a decade, fuelled in part by a younger and better-educated cohort of migrant workers who are less tolerant of injustice and highly motivated to demand higher wages and better working conditions and benefits. A study of the labor conditions of one-million-strong Foxconn workers—most of them a new generation of rural migrants who were born after 1980—enable us to draw out the deep contradictions among labor, capital, and the Chinese state in the world economy.

Giant manufacturers, rather than small workshops, are better able to respond to increasing product complexity and shortening product cycles in global production. Not only the big ones, which eat the small ones, but also the fast ones, which eat the slow. Foxconn's extraordinary growth is built on its cheap, big, fast, and efficient production model. It provides advanced engineering services, component processing, and final assembly in one-stop shopping to technology firms and retailers. In a nutshell, Foxconn has risen to become the "electronics workshop of the world," with small and medium competitors squeezed out of the market.

Apple, together with other technology giants, has created global consumers with its products, and through Foxconn and other major subcontractors it has simultaneously contributed to the creation of a new Chinese working class. Not only production tasks, but also inventory management and logistics, are concentrated in strategic factories, resulting in ever-stronger interdependent relations between "big buyers" and "big suppliers" in the consumer electronics industry (Appelbaum 2008; Starosta 2010; Lee and Gereffi 2013; Chan, Pun, and Selden 2013, 2015, 2016). The mystery that our sociological investigation seeks to explore looks beyond the "inside story" of the horrific reality of life for workers who produce Apple iPhones and other electronic products emblematic of the digital age. It also seeks to address central features of contemporary global capitalism through a focus on the relationship between the richest global technology corporation (Apple) and the world's largest industrial employer (Foxconn), as well as that between Foxconn and the Chinese state. Examination of a young generation of Chinese workers' lived experience provides new light on the dialectical character of corporate domination and labor resistance in global electronics production.

The Rise of Foxconn in Greater China

Terry Tai-ming Gou (b. 1950), the founder and CEO of Foxconn Technology Group (registered as Hon Hai Precision Industry Company in Taipei in 1974), was quick to seize the new opportunities created by Taiwan's industrialization policy, the growth in international trade in the postwar geopolitical and economic order, and above all the opening to China in the 1980s (Chiang and Yan 2015). Before running his own business, he had served in the army and worked as a shipping clerk after graduating from a technical school in 1971. At that time, transnational corporations accelerated the export of capital in searching for cheap, disciplined, and productive labor, notably to East Asia, including Taiwan, Hong Kong, and South Korea. The resulting successive geographical relocations of industrial capital have been facilitated by efficient transportation and modern communications technologies, regional and international financial services, and access to immigrants and surplus labor that held down wage levels (Deyo 1989; Selden 1997; Smith, Sonnenfeld, and Pellow 2006; McKay 2006; Lüthje et al. 2013). In this context of industrial relocation, Taiwan and other emergent economies grew rapidly through global investment and subcontracting networks.

From the 1960s, IBM, the leader in business computing, shifted its labor-intensive production from the United States and Europe to East Asia to cut costs. The microelectronics components of IBM System 360 computers were assembled by workers in Japan, and then Taiwan, because "the cost of labor there was so low" that it was cheaper than automated production in New York (Ernst 1997, 40). Radio Corporation of America (RCA), the consumer electronics firm, similarly moved to take advantage of Taiwan's cheap labor and loose regulatory environment in the export-processing zones in 1970 (Cowie 2001; Ku 2006; Chen 2011). In newly industrializing East Asian countries, most factory workers were young women migrants from the countryside, whose diligence and low-cost labor was a bulwark of the "economic miracles" across the region.

During the 1980s, many of the world's technology companies abandoned low-value-added hardware production and electronics assembly to concentrate on design, R&D (research and development), marketing, and customer service in order to cut costs. In 1981, for example, Apple Computer—later Apple, Inc.—ramped up upgraded Apple II personal computers through contracting offshore facilities in Singapore (one of the original Four Asian Tigers, together with Taiwan, South Korea, and Hong Kong). Michael Scott, the first CEO of Apple Computer (1977–1981), commented: "Our business was designing, educating and marketing. I thought that Apple should do the least amount of work that it could and . . . let the subcontractors have the problems" (Moritz 2009, 208–9). In 1984, Apple launched Macintosh to compete with IBM in the fast-growing computer market. The 160,000-square-foot Fremont factory on Warm Springs Boulevard in California was opened in January: "The facility was one of the nation's most automated plants, utilizing manufacturing methods such as robotics, just-in-time materials delivery, and a linear assembly line." Two years later, the assembly of Macs was relocated to Fountain, Colorado, Cork, Ireland, and Singapore (City of Fremont, California 2012). By the end of the 1990 decade, Apple, Lucent Technologies, Nortel, Alcatel, and Ericsson, among many others, had "sold off most, if not all, of their in-house manufacturing capacity—both at home and abroad—to a cadre of large and highly capable US-based contract manufacturers, including Solectron, Flextronics, Jabil Circuit, Celestica, and Sanmina-SCI" (Sturgeon, Humphrey, and Gereffi 2011, 236). To which we may add Foxconn, which has been growing steadily to climb the global value chain.

Small and medium-sized Taiwan and Hong Kong enterprises brought in capital to China totaling US$107 billion between 1982 and 1994, more than 70 percent of the realized foreign direct investment during the period (Hsing 1998, 8). After the 1985 Plaza Accord,[1] which caused Taiwan's currency to appreciate relative to the US dollar (up about 40 percent at the peak), entrepreneurs accelerated their move to China and Southeast Asia to reduce production costs and secure big international orders (Leng 2005; Hamilton and Kao 2011). In 1988, taking advantage of China's open-door policy encouraging foreign investment, Foxconn was among the first group of Taiwanese companies to invest in coastal Guangdong, South China.

The name Foxconn alludes to the corporation's claim to produce electronic connectors at "fox-like" speed. Connectors are tiny devices that connect parts such as motherboards, memory chips, and circuits in personal computers. Like nerves sending signals around the body, a computer's connectors must be highly precise. Throughout the 1990s, the company invested heavily in the plastic and metal molding equipment to lay a solid foundation for long-term development. In 2001, it pooled 300 million yuan as a cofounder of the Tsinghua-Foxconn Nanotechnology Research Center at Tsinghua University, Beijing, the capital of China (Foxconn Technology Group 2011, 24). The joint research center leverages Tsinghua University's scientific expertise and Foxconn's large-scale electronic technology. It emphasizes nanotechnology, heat transfer, wireless networks, optical plating techniques, new materials, new energy, biotechnology, advanced surface mount technology, network chips technology, and robot technology.

An army of a thousand is easy to get; one general is tough to find. In 2003, the Foxconn leader Terry Gou acquired handset assembly plants owned by Nokia and Motorola in Finland and Mexico, respectively, enabling him to branch out from computer to mobile communications equipment manufacturing (Foxconn Technology Group 2009, 10). *CommonWealth Magazine* reported: "That year, Gou presided over successive lightning quick acquisitions across Scandinavia, South America and Asia, becoming Taiwan's first business chief to complete mergers on three different continents within a single year" (Huang 2014). By 2004, Foxconn had become the industrial leader in electronics manufacturing, surpassing Nasdaq-listed Flextronics (Pick 2006). "Terry is the most aggressive business person I've met in my life," remarked Michael Marks, the former chief executive of Flextronics (Mac 2013). To eliminate major competition, Foxconn undercuts prices and upgrades production and engineering capacity.

Foxconn's expansion across the globe is aptly summarized in a corporate slogan, "China rooted, global footprint." Operations outside China, however, for the most part provide quick turnaround on orders, reduce transportation costs, and avoid import taxes, although China remains the heart of its global corporate empire and the core of its profitability. The *Fortune* Global 500 ranked Foxconn sixtieth in 2011, forty-third in 2012, thirtieth in 2013, thirty-second in 2014, and thirty-first in 2015, demonstrating the company's rapid ascent in revenue and profit. In 2013, even in the midst of European government austerity measures and international economic uncertainty, Foxconn attained far higher annual revenues (US$133 billion) than many of its corporate customers, with the important exceptions of Apple and Samsung.[2] Although the yearly profit of Apple (US$37 billion) far exceeds that of Foxconn (US$3.5 billion) and any other company, Foxconn's growth has also been very strong (Foxconn Technology Group 2014a).

In many cities throughout China Foxconn runs multiple manufacturing facilities. But it initially centered its investment in Guangdong. In 2010, more than five hundred thousand employees worked in two Foxconn factories in Shenzhen city (Longhua and Guanlan), on the northern border of Hong Kong (Foxconn Technology Group 2010, 1). Subsequently, tens of thousands of workers were transferred to lower-wage production sites in interior China, such as Taiyuan city where the iPhone metal and electronic parts are processed, and Zhengzhou city, where iPhones are assembled (see figure 9.1). By 2015, Foxconn had thirty-plus

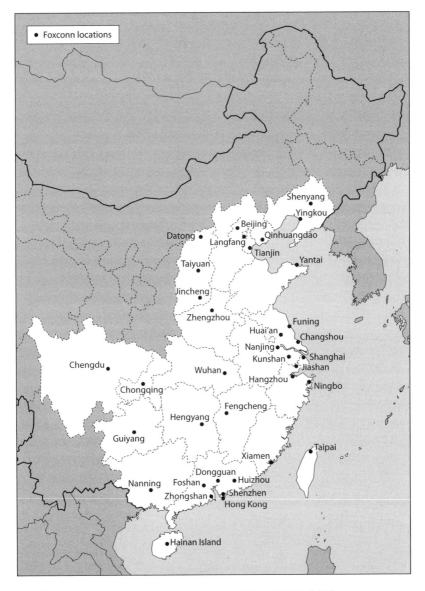

FIGURE 9.1   Foxconn locations in Greater China, 1974–2015

Source: Foxconn Technology Group websites and annual reports

manufacturing complexes in four provincial-level municipalities (Beijing, Tianjin, Shanghai, and Chongqing) and in sixteen provinces throughout China. From raw material extraction to processing to final assembly, Foxconn has built a network featuring vertical integration and flexible coordination across different facilities and twenty-four-hour continuous assembly.

"In twenty years," some business executives suggested in 2010, just two companies will dominate global markets—"everything will be made by Foxconn and sold by Walmart" (Balfour and Culpan 2010). This is, of course, a wild exaggeration that ignores the central fact of Foxconn's dependence on Apple, HP, Dell, and other international electronics firms. But it underlies Foxconn's startling rise at the expense of powerful rivals in Taiwan, China, and around the globe. As Karl Marx observed in *Capital*, "one capitalist always strikes down many others" (1990, 929). Through a close-up study of Chinese workers—the direct producers—in the world's most powerful electronics contractor, we can begin to enter Foxconn's hidden abode of global production.

Apple Meets Foxconn

Apple's commercial success is paralleled by, and based on, the scale of production in its supplying factories. As of January 2015, 334 Apple suppliers were located in China, more than were located in all other countries combined (Apple 2015a). Jeff Williams, Apple's senior vice president of operations, affirmed that "more than 1,400 talented engineers and managers were stationed in China" to manage manufacturing operations, who worked and lived "in the factories constantly" (BBC 2014). Although Apple and its largest supplier, Foxconn, are independent companies, they are inextricably linked in product development and manufacturing processes.

As Apple achieved a globally dominant position as the world's most valuable brand, followed by Samsung, Google, and Microsoft (Brand Finance 2014), the fortunes of Foxconn have been entwined with its success. "Two 'Apple business groups,' iDPBG [integrated Digital Product Business Group] and iDSBG [innovation Digital System Business Group], have become rising stars at Foxconn in the past few years," a Foxconn production manager said.[3] More than a dozen business groups compete within Foxconn on speed, quality, efficiency, engineering service, and added value to maximize profits. He elaborated: "Approximately 40 percent of Foxconn revenues are from Apple, and the remainder is divided among numerous clients. iDPBG was established at Foxconn in 2002. At the beginning, it was only a small business group handling Apple's contracts. We assembled Macs and shipped them to Apple retail stores in the United States and elsewhere. Later we had more orders for Macs and iPods."

The iPod digital music player, with a click-wheel interface and white earphones, was launched in 2001. Light, beautiful, and lovable, it changed the way music was personalized, just as the Sony Walkman had decades earlier. The iTunes Store allows consumers to instantly download and buy digital music, TV programs, and films.

Relentless consumer demand for the world's hot-selling gadgets means production lines never stop. If Apple's edge lies in technological innovation, design, and marketing, its success is inseparable from the ability of its large suppliers to produce efficiently to meet Apple's demands for high-quality new products. Jony Ive, Apple's senior vice president of design, recalled the original iPhone launch on June 29, 2007: "We were very nervous—we were concerned how people would make a transition from touching physical buttons that moved, that made a noise . . . to glass that didn't move. [But] it's terribly important that you constantly question the assumptions you've made" (Parker 2015).

Long-held assumptions about the phone user interface were shattered, giving way to a touchscreen interface. Moving fingers away from each other while keeping contact with the screen allows users to zoom into a map or a photo. We feel and touch our iPhones with the pinch-to-zoom technologies. Thousands of appealing apps, ranging from games to health care to self-learning, are downloadable to iPhones. By 2014, China had become Apple's second-largest market for app downloads, second only to the United States (Apple 2014a).

China's workers who produce the newest models of iPhones are as eager to buy them as Western consumers. One nineteen-year-old Foxconn worker dreamed about her future. "Someday," she mused, "I want to drive a brand new Honda and return home in style!" For the time being, dreaming of buying an iPhone, she is ready to work as hard as necessary to do so.

The iPhone is the biggest revenue generator for Apple. In 2010, Apple's strength was well illustrated by its ability to capture an extraordinary 58.5 percent of the sales price of the iPhone, despite (but also because of) the fact that manufacture of the product was entirely outsourced (see figure 9.2). Particularly notable is the fact that labor costs in China accounted for the smallest share, only 1.8 percent or nearly US$10, of the US$549 retail price of the iPhone. Other major component providers, mainly Japanese and South Korean firms that produce the most sophisticated components, captured slightly over 14 percent of the value of the iPhone. The cost of raw materials was just over one-fifth of the total value (21.9 percent). In short, although China has carved out a niche as a reliable assembler of the iPhone (and many other electronic products), the lion's share of the profits goes to Apple, and Japanese and Korean providers of the most sophisticated components obtain a significant share. Above all it is design, marketing, and business acumen that reap the richest rewards whereas the return

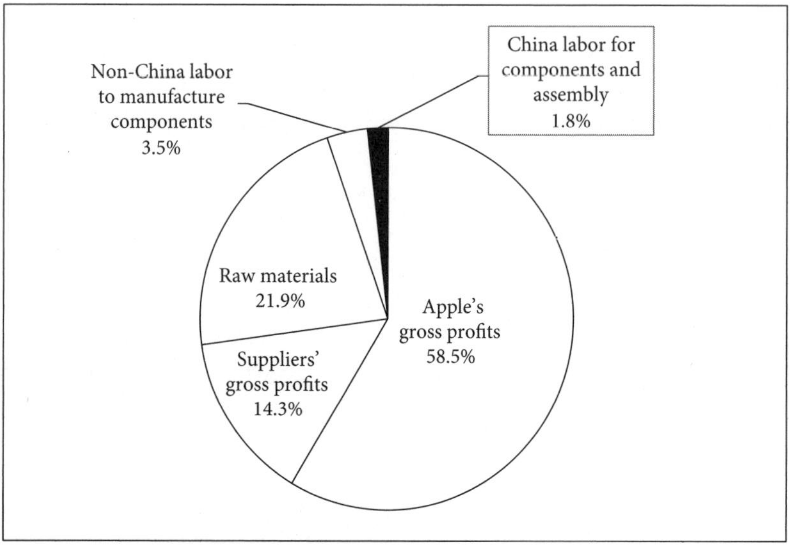

FIGURE 9.2 Distribution of value for the iPhone, 2010

Note: The percentage is calculated on the iPhone 4's retail price at US$549 in 2010. No amount for "distribution and retail" is shown because Apple is paid directly by a cellular company, such as AT&T or Verizon, which then handles the final stage of the sale.

Source: Adapted from Kraemer, Linden, and Dedrick 2011, 5

TABLE 9.1 Apple's revenues by product, 2010–2014

	2011 (ENDED SEPTEMBER 24)		2014 (ENDED SEPTEMBER 27)	
	MILLIONS (US$)	%	MILLIONS (US$)	%
iPhone	45,998	42.5	101,991	55.8
iPad	19,168	17.7	30,283	16.6
Mac	21,783	20.1	24,079	13.2
iTunes, Software, Services	9,373	8.7	18,063	9.9
Accessories	4,474	4.1	6,093	3.3
iPod	7,453	6.9	2,286	1.2
Total	108,249	100	182,795	100

Source: Apple 2013, 27; 2014b, 27

to manufacturing ranks far below, with labor, the labor of more than one million Foxconn workers in China, receiving a pittance.

Apple's revenues reached US$182.8 billion in fiscal year 2014, nearly twice as much as in fiscal year 2011. Table 9.1 shows revenues generated from sales of Apple-branded products and services: the signature Mac computer has now been far surpassed in value by the iPhone, with the iPad in second place (listed in the order of 2014 sales revenues).

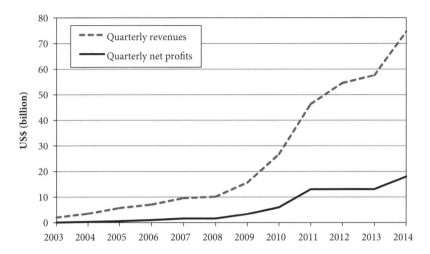

FIGURE 9.3   Apple's quarterly revenues and net profits (September–December), 2003–2014

Note: Apple's net profits grew from US$63 million in the fourth quarter of 2003 to US$18 billion in the fourth quarter of 2014—the largest quarterly earnings for any company ever. Quarterly revenues increased from US$7.1 billion to US$74.6 billion during the same period.

Sources: Apple's quarterly financial reports, various years

During September and December 2014, Apple posted record revenue of US$74.6 billion (see figure 9.3)—an increase of 30 percent over the last year—of which US$51.2 billion was from iPhone sales (Apple 2015b). Nevertheless, Apple faces aggressive competition in all products and services as Samsung, Google, Microsoft, and other giants race to upgrade personal technologies. It also faces price pressures from China's national champions. The advance of the start-up Xiaomi (meaning "small rice," founded in Beijing in 2010) and the heavy-weight Huawei (founded in 1987), for example, is indicative of China's growing technological and marketing capacity both in China and internationally.

Apple refused to disclose to us the specifics of its iPhone contracts. Jacky Haynes, senior director of Apple's Supplier Responsibility Program, responded in a February 18, 2014 e-mail concerning our question about the company's purchasing policies as they affect Chinese wages: "Over the years, we have increased the prices we pay to suppliers in order to support wage increases for workers. Confidentiality agreements prevent us from providing the data you're requesting."[4] Stated differently, Apple, the world's most profitable technology company, provided *no* evidence to substantiate its claim of increasing unit prices in order to facilitate higher wages at its independently owned suppliers.

Our interviews with Foxconn management reveal some of the ways in which Apple squeezes suppliers to provide components and products. "During the 2008–2009 global financial crisis," a midlevel production manager explained, "Foxconn cut prices on components, such as connectors and printed circuit boards, and assembly to retain high-volume orders. Margins were cut. Still, the rock-bottom line was kept, that is, Foxconn did not report a loss on the iPhone contract. Foxconn was able to stay in the black while cutting its margins by charging a premium on customized engineering services and quality assurance. The upgrading of the iPhones has in part relied on our senior product engineers' research analyses and constructive suggestions."

Until 2010, amidst the string of worker suicides,[5] Foxconn had been the exclusive contractor of the iPhone (Chan and Pun 2010; Pun and Chan 2012, 2013; Chan 2013; Pun et al. 2014). Subsequently, Apple split the orders between Foxconn and Pegatron to minimize disruption of production and maximize profits. Manufacturers, faced with buyers' ruthless demands, in turn place tremendous pressure on frontline workers and staff to retain contracts and stay profitable. Apple, although claiming to exercise corporate social responsibility in global supply chain management, never acknowledged its own culpability in squeezing suppliers and workers by imposing tight delivery schedules and high-quality demands at ever-lower prices.

iPhone Worker Protests

On the factory floor, the change in production requirements from iPhone 4 to iPhone 5 and the increase in output targets placed workers under intense stress. On September 23, 2012 a siren pierced the night at the eighty-thousand-worker Foxconn Taiyuan plant in north China as rioting erupted. By 3 a.m. on September 24, five thousand riot police officers, government officials, and medical staff had converged on the factory. Over the next two hours, the police took control of the dormitories and workshops of the Foxconn complex, detaining the most defiant workers and sending others back to their dormitory rooms. More than forty workers were beaten, handcuffed, and sent off in half a dozen police cars. In emergency mode, Foxconn announced a special day off for all workers and staff at the Taiyuan facility, where electronic components and magnesium-alloy parts for iPhones are manufactured.

On the same day, September 24, Apple CEO Tim Cook, who succeeded the late Steve Jobs in August 2011, assured the public that retail stores would "continue to receive iPhone 5 shipments regularly and customers can continue to order online and receive an estimated delivery date" (Apple 2012a). Apparently the continuous flow of product, speedy shipment, and on-time delivery were Apple's top concerns.

Following the riot, Yu Zhonghong (pseudonym), a twenty-one-year-old high-school graduate who had worked at the site for two years, wrote an open letter to Foxconn's chief executive Terry Gou.[6] The opening passage reads:

A Letter to Foxconn CEO Terry Gou

If you don't want to be loudly awakened at night from deep sleep,
If you don't want to constantly rush about again by airplane,
If you don't want to be investigated again by the Fair Labor Association,[7]
If you don't want your company to be called a sweatshop,
Please treat us with a little humanity.

Please allow us a little human self-esteem.
Don't let your hired ruffians rifle through our bodies and belongings.
Don't let your hired ruffians harass female workers.
Don't let your lackeys treat every worker like the enemy.
Don't arbitrarily berate or, worse, beat workers for the slightest mistake.

You should understand that working in your factories:
Workers live at the lowest level,
Tolerating the most intense work,
Earning the lowest pay,
Accepting the strictest regulation,
And enduring discrimination everywhere.
Even though you are my boss, and I am a worker:
I have the right to speak to you on an equal footing.

The sense in which the worker leader uses the term "right" is not narrowly confined to the realm of legal rights. On behalf of the shared interests of workers living "at the lowest level" in society, Zhonghong called for a public talk with CEO Terry Gou "on an equal footing." He also demanded that senior management and the company union act responsibly toward workers. His open letter ends with three reminders:

1. Please remember, from now on, to treat your subordinates as humans, and require that they treat their subordinates, and their subordinates, and their subordinates, as humans.
2. Please remember, from now on, those of you who are riding a rocket of fast promotions and earning wages as high as heaven compared to those on earth, to change your attitude that Taiwanese are superior.

3. Please remember, from now on, to reassess the responsibilities of the company union so that genuine trade unions can play an appropriate role.

Zhonghong recalled, "At about 11 p.m., a number of security officers severely beat two workers for failing to show their staff IDs. They kicked them until they fell to the ground. This brutality by security officers touched off the ensuing riot. Over these past two months we couldn't even get paid leave when we were sick." The ever-tightening iPhone production cycle pressured workers to speed up under staggering overtime requirements. Workers could not even take one day off a week, and the sick were compelled to continue to work.

Our collection of pay statements reveals that workers clocked in as many as 130 hours overtime a month. This was more than three times the maximum 36 hours of overtime per month limit under Chinese law. Put in other way, workers were subjected to "13-to-1" and, under extreme conditions, "30-to-1" work-to-rest schedules.

At midnight, tens of thousands of workers smashed security offices, production facilities, shuttle buses, motorbikes, cars, shops, and canteens in the factory complex. Some grabbed iPhones from a warehouse, where Zhonghong and his coworkers were on duty during the night shift. Others broke windows, demolished company fences, and pillaged factory supermarkets. Workers also overturned police cars and set them ablaze. The security chief used a patrol car public address system in an attempt to get the workers to end their "illegal activities." But more and more workers joined the roaring crowd.

Justifying the use of force, Foxconn managers blamed the workers, alleging that they were fighting among themselves. A worker retorted, "Foxconn didn't admit the daily bullying of workers by its security force but shifted all the responsibility to us. Line leaders coerced us to meet the extremely tight deadlines, generating heated conflicts." Foxconn's investigation of the mass incident concluded that it was the result of a "personal dispute," allowing the company to ignore shop-floor conditions. Workers' concerns over wage and promotion inequalities, as well as undignified treatment including sexual harassment and other forms of humiliation, were quickly suppressed. Above all, the demand for a reorganization of the company union was ignored.

With Apple pressing Foxconn to fulfill targets as demand for the new models exploded, the time was ripe for workers to display their power, although management's heavy-handed response only made worker communications more difficult. Less than two weeks after the Taiyuan workers' riot, in early October, over three thousand Foxconn workers from one production department in the Zhengzhou factory protested against management's "unreasonable demands for quality control." The Taiyuan plant manufactures iPhone casings that are sent to a larger Zhengzhou complex in adjacent Henan province for final assembly.

CEO Tim Cook announced: "We are in one of the most prolific periods of innovation and new products in Apple's history. The amazing products that we've introduced in September and October [2012], iPhone 5, iOS 6, iPad mini, iPad, iMac, MacBook Pro, iPod touch, iPod nano and many of our applications, could only have been created at Apple" (Apple 2012b). Perhaps. But what is certain, and tragic, is that the great pressure faced by the workers could only have been created at Apple. The global sale of iPhones reached an unprecedented level of 150,257,000 units in the fiscal year 2012–2013, a stunning 20 percent growth over the previous year (Apple 2013, 27).

After the iPhone 5 debut, consumers in the United States complained about scratches on the casing of a particular batch of the new iPhones, leading to product quality control investigations of final assembly at the Zhengzhou plant in central China. New quality standards contributed to workers' eye strain and headaches. A worker explained, "We had no time off during the National Day celebrations and now we're forced to fix the defective products. The precision requirement for the screens of the iPhone 5 measured in two-hundredths of a millimeter cannot be detected by human eyes. We use microscopes to check product appearance. It's impossibly strict." In the case-manufacturing process, workers were also instructed to use protective cases to prevent scratches of the ultra-thin iPhone 5 and to pay close attention to detail at a fast working pace. When several workers were penalized for not meeting the 0.02-millimeter standards, quarrels erupted between workers and quality control team leaders.

Workers understand that they stand at a strategic production point, given the tight delivery schedules for the iPhones, which are precisely timed to holiday seasons and new product launch dates. Foxconn is a key node in the Asian and global production networks, where the processing of components, final assembly, and shipment of finished products to world consumers continues around the clock, 24 hours a day, 365 days a year. This awareness potentially enhances their workplace bargaining power and empowers workers to schedule strikes and other forms of resistance at times of crisis for maximum impact and leverage. Frances Piven has succinctly examined the nature of "interdependent power," highlighting the fundamental fact that employers are dependent on workers' consent to labor, perhaps more dependent than ever before in our closely connected economy. She writes: "Distinctive features of contemporary capitalist economies make them exceptionally vulnerable to the withdrawal of cooperation; in other words, to the strike power in its many forms. These features include extended chains of production, reliance on the Internet to mesh elaborate schedules of transportation and production, and just-in-time production doing away with the inventories that once shielded corporations from the impact of the production strike" (2014, 226).

On October 5, a Friday afternoon, when production managers yelled at workers and threatened to fire them if they did not "cooperate and concentrate," workers would tolerate no more management abuse. They walked out of the workshop. The impromptu strike paralyzed dozens of production lines in Zones K and L from late afternoon to night. After the disruptions in the afternoon, senior managers imposed stringent quality standards on night-shift workers. The brief work stoppage failed to win the reasonable rest periods that workers sought.

Foxconn aims to ensure high-speed production at all times. "When work stoppages or accidents occur, we can shift orders to other facilities to minimize losses and reduce vulnerability to worker actions," a production manager explained. Meanwhile, new sources of labor anxiety and open conflicts soar.

In February 2015, on the twentieth anniversary of the passage of the national labor law, Guo Jun, the head of the legal department of the All-China Federation of Trade Unions (ACFTU), commented on the "excessive overtime" and "health and safety problems" at surveyed enterprises. He blacklisted Foxconn: "Many companies even learn from Foxconn how to make more profits" by imposing "illegal overtime work" on employees (Zhang 2015). Unfortunately, the union leader did not explain what actions would be taken to protect workers' legal rights. Without meaningful representation and organizing support from the company union, workers improvised organizing and negotiation methods. Foxconn workers have condemned and bypassed the management-controlled union to fight for their rights and interests, opting for independent collective actions including riots and strikes.

Labor Challenges to the Chinese Trade Union

The Foxconn trade union, like unions throughout China, is directly subordinate to management. The union organization mirrors the company hierarchy, from the assembly lines, business units, and business groups to the central administrative level. Chen Peng, special assistant to Foxconn CEO Terry Gou, has chaired the union since its inception. Under her leadership, Foxconn's union executive committee expanded from four representatives at its start in January 2007 to twenty-three thousand representatives in December 2012, with membership reaching 93 percent of its million-strong workforce in China (Foxconn Technology Group 2014b, 14). With this impressive growth, Foxconn has risen to become the country's biggest union—and one of the most effective in serving the corporation.

From 1988 (when it set up its offshore factory in Shenzhen) through 2006, Foxconn simply ignored its responsibility under Chinese law to set up a trade union. The Taiwanese giant established a union at Shenzhen Longhua only on the last day of 2006, submitting to municipal government requirements (IHLO 2007). In a broader sociopolitical context, the state stepped up its mobilization efforts when the total number of trade union members decreased sharply during the 1990s during the radical market reforms and layoffs, resulting in the loss of at least seventeen million union members in the state sector between 1997 and 2000 (Traub-Merz 2012, 28). In the 2000s, the ACFTU—the only official union body in China—pressed for the establishment of trade unions wherever there were workers.

The union mission statement tells workers, "when there's trouble, seek the trade union." Clearly, this government top-down action seeks to preempt the growing tide of strikes and protests across China. Enterprise-level or grassroots unions must legally register under supervision of upper-level trade unions. New union members comprise direct employees, including rural migrants but excluding student interns (whose legal status remains that of students). By December 2009, "unions had been set up in 92 percent of the Fortune 500 companies operating in China" (Liu 2011, 157). As of 2013, China had a total union membership of 280 million—in which nearly 40 percent (109 million) were rural migrant workers—by far the largest unionized workforce in the world (Xinhua 2013). This stands in sharp contrast to the United States, Europe, Australia, and many other countries, where labor unions have shrunk to a small percentage of the industrial workforce, owing to corporate restructuring, downsizing, and job export. In few countries, however, does organized labor in a bureaucratic form display a powerful presence in support of worker rights.

China's law ostensibly gives workers basic rights, including the right to elect union representatives, the right to vote union representatives out of office if they do not represent them, and protection against discrimination for participation in union activities. In the example of Foxconn, formal rights inscribed in the law are one thing, but securing the reality of those rights is another. Critically, the labor struggle is not only to get rights articulated in the trade union law, but also to translate those rights into the material reality of lived experience (Lee 2007; Chan 2009; Wang et al. 2009; Gallagher et al. 2015). Under public pressure, Foxconn has proclaimed that workers would hold genuine elections for union representation. A December 2013 Foxconn statement reiterated that "we have worked hard to enhance employee representation in the [union] leadership" and to raise employee awareness of the union's role in "promoting worker rights."[8] As of spring 2015, however, Foxconn had disclosed neither specifics of a timetable for democratic union elections nor clarified the rights and responsibilities of worker representatives. All available evidence suggests that Foxconn unions remain firmly in the grip of management.

In response to growing labor unrest, experienced officials often mediate at the site of protest to prevent labor conflict from escalating. The state seeks to channel worker grievances with bosses and/or local governments out of the streets and into court and judicial channels. Outside of the arbitration and jurisdictional procedure, as Mary Gallagher observes, "the state has struggled to maintain its labor system through more direct management of labor disputes" (2014, 87). She characterizes this as "the activist state" in which Chinese officials make extensive use of discretionary power to intervene in labor disputes, particularly when the caseloads are excessive. One frequently used strategy, analyzed in-depth by Ching Kwan Lee and Yonghong Zhang (2013), is to "buy stability" through brokering cash settlements to resolve immediate grievances, with funds directly paid by the company and by local government. Protest, if handled in this way, can provide a safety valve that preserves the authoritarian aura of the party-state (Chen 2012a, 2013). Fundamentally, the power between labor and capital remains highly imbalanced, engendering open defiance and deepening the crisis of production and social reproduction (Selden and Perry 2010; Chan and Selden 2014).

Given China's position as the "workshop of the world," victories by and defeats of its working people assume world historical significance. "If past patterns are any guide to the future," Beverly Silver concludes in her survey of world labor movements since 1870, "then we should expect major waves of industrial labor unrest . . . to occur in those regions that have been experiencing rapid industrialization and proletarianization" (2003, 169). In the twenty-first century, China's centrality in electronics manufacturing and exports opens possibilities that workers can build on their grassroots organizing experience to expand labor rights, while the iron triangle of Foxconn, the company union, and the Chinese state sustains the unequal power structures.

Analyzing the interdependent Apple-Foxconn supply chain, we examined the working lives and collective struggle of internal Chinese migrant laborers, who are living with cosmopolitan consumerism and much wider class differentiation and social inequality than the previous generation. In the course of repeated protests and strikes, Foxconn workers have exposed the high-pressure conditions under which many work extremely long hours for low wages, drawing attention from image-conscious global companies and stability obsessed government officials. Unable to turn for support to company unions, they have repeatedly chosen direct actions, resulting in uncertain outcomes.

The fragmentation of labor and the diversification of ownership in the hands of Chinese and international capital profoundly challenge proponents of expanded worker rights and democratic trade union support for those rights. Foxconn workers—some of whom have sacrificed their youthful lives as a means of desperate resistance—spoke to the disturbing truth behind China's expansive national development. "Realize the great Chinese dream, build a harmonious society," intones a government banner. The definition of that dream and the determination of who may claim it are at stake in contemporary labor struggles. Will the current period of labor insurgency in localized sites of resistance develop further to encompass alliances across class lines and across the urban-rural divide into a broadly based social movement? To a significant extent, the answer will depend on the evolving consciousness and praxis of the younger cohort of rural migrant workers who have become the mainstay of the new labor force.

LABOR TRANSFORMATION IN CHINA

Voices from the Frontlines

Katie Quan

Waves of wildcat strikes in China in recent years have forced the Chinese government and its unions to find ways to provide dispute resolution and a voice for workers, in some cases through new forms of labor relations like authentic collective bargaining and election of union leaders. These new forms of labor relations have the potential for shifting the unilateral power of management to the shared power of labor and management, so they can be viewed as a proxy for democratic practices. In the past, Chinese unions implemented a version of collective bargaining without worker representation through nonnegotiated "collective contracts," and elections through Communist Party-vetted "elections" of leaders. Therefore there is a legitimate question about whether recent developments change current practice to engage democratic worker voices. This chapter will look at writings from union leaders who are directly engaged in collective bargaining and election of union representatives, and will show that in some places in China, the rank and file is democratically electing worker leaders, and that these leaders are engaging in genuine collective bargaining. Given this situation, the chapter will further address the critical need for American workers to engage in organizing and collective bargaining with Chinese workers, and the need for union policy to facilitate these cross-border linkages.

In September 2013 the AFL-CIO president Richard Trumka made a visit to the All-China Federation of Trade Unions (ACFTU) in Beijing, becoming the first AFL-CIO president to do so. On this visit, Trumka said to his hosts in surprising candor, "American workers need to have solidarity with Chinese workers, so we can all move forward." Coming from the head of a labor movement that has led an international boycott of Chinese labor for many decades, this historic reversal of policy may have profound implications, as it opens the door for further dialogue between workers in the United States and China and sets the stage for strategic partnerships among unions in the global economy.

This breakthrough in labor diplomacy comes just as China's workers are rising up. The year 2010 saw waves of wildcat strikes across the country, during which thousands of rank-and-file workers organized work stoppages and demanded higher pay without the knowledge or participation of their unions (see chapter 11). Since then labor unrest has continued, and in 2014 a second wave of strikes took place. In April, more than 30,000 workers at the Yue Yuen factory in Dongguan that manufactures shoes for brands like Nike went on strike for more than two weeks, angry that their employer had underpaid social security contributions to their retirement funds (Qi 2014). The workers not only demanded that their benefits be restored but also that the company's union be reorganized and allowed to bargain collectively. The month before, some 1,000 workers at an IBM plant in nearby Shenzhen went on strike to protest low severance packages when their company was sold to Lenovo (Reuters 2014). During the same month, more than 140 Walmart workers in Hunan province staged a sustained street protest to get legally mandated severance pay when the store suddenly announced closure (Mitchell and Jopson 2014).

We are at a unique juncture in history when the forces of a faltering American labor movement are making connections with an ascendant Chinese movement. It poses some fundamental questions for both labor movements about new opportunities and strategic choices, such as: How can alliances be built that will strengthen labor in both countries? How can these alliances develop strategies that push back on the economic race to the bottom? How can these strategies recalibrate the global balance of power between labor and capital?

In this chapter I will offer some background for the discussion on those larger fundamental questions by providing information on two related questions: What are Chinese labor activists thinking and, given this, how can American labor activists build constructive alliances with their Chinese counterparts? To address the first question, I will select excerpts from the writings of some key Chinese labor activists that reveal their thoughts about strikes, collective bargaining, and what reforms they think should be implemented. The sources of these writings are unpublished essays and conference presentations, collected and translated by myself, from the International Center for Joint Labor Research at Sun Yat-sen University in Guangzhou, a joint project between the Sun Yat-sen University's Institute of Political Science in Guangzhou, China, and the UC Berkeley Center for Labor Research and Education.[1] To address the second question, I will draw

on existing literature about American labor engagement with China. I will conclude with implications for the future of that union engagement with China.
My perspective is shaped by having spent twenty-four years in the International
Ladies' Garment Workers' Union and its successor UNITE as a rank-and-file
seamstress, educator, organizer, lead negotiator, and international vice president.

Labor in China Today

Our image of labor in China has for many years been of one huge sweatshop at
the bottom of the race to the bottom. American workers viewed China as the
place where corporations like Walmart and Nike took our jobs to make super
profits from cheap labor that is compliant and grateful for any job. We also
watched the Chinese government turn a blind eye to many violations of its own
labor laws and jail human rights organizers. So not surprisingly we came to view
Chinese workers as hapless victims without the consciousness or ability to stand
up for themselves and fight back. The 2010 news of over a dozen suicides at the
Apple contractor Foxconn reinforced this image of powerlessness, depicting a
workforce that is so desperate that they would take their own lives.

In contrast to that image, now we are getting news of tens of thousands of
workers going on wildcat strike. Data on strikes is hard to find, as the Chinese
government does not publish those statistics, but newspaper articles report hundreds and thousands of strikes in each of the last several years, according to the
labor watchdog group China Labour Bulletin (China Labour Bulletin 2015), and
this is undoubtedly just a fraction of actual occurrences. Photos on the Internet
show strikers in defiant poses, and television interviews with strikers reveal artic-
ulate men and women who know what they want and are willing to risk political
persecution. They reflect the emergence of a workforce that is increasingly aware
of its labor rights and remarkably unafraid to exercise them. The most recent
strikes appear to be growing in size, are becoming more sophisticated in content
of demands, and are gaining increasing support from community members. Far
from the image of powerless victims, these strikers project a keen sense of self-
worth and an expectation that they be treated fairly at work.

These seemingly contradictory images of Chinese workers, the powerless
and the powerful, reflect dual, coexistent realities of labor in China today. But
within this duality, the general trend has been for workers to become more conscious of their rights and increasingly active in exercising those rights collectively.
Striker demands have progressed from minimal entitlements like payment of
back wages prior to 2010 to current demands for double-digit wage increases.
Recent demands also call for compensation other than wages, such as severance

pay at Walmart in Hunan and IBM in Shenzhen, and pension contributions at Yue Yuen in Shenzhen. At Yue Yuen the workers also demanded the right to engage in collective bargaining. Furthermore, these strikes are gaining support from coworkers in other factories and community members at large; at both Walmart and Yue Yuen, the strikes quickly spread from one workplace to affiliated workplaces where workers had the same concerns, and the strikes attracted substantial support from local community members as well as international labor rights activists. Both the Walmart and IBM strikes also featured deep community resentment against the heavy-handed intervention of the police. From these changes we can see that workers are beginning to make demands that go beyond economic demands to rights-based demands.

Remarkably, all these developments are taking place in an environment where strikes are not expressly legal and strikes are not led by unions. Chinese law is silent on the right to strike, and therefore strikes are considered as neither legal nor illegal. Union policy is to not lead strikes, so none of the hundreds, if not thousands, of strikes in the past five years were led by unions, except for the recent Walmart protest in Hunan. Notwithstanding legal ambiguity, Chinese workers have appropriated the right to strike and are using it to disrupt economic practice, legal regulations, and the social norm. Moreover, to the extent that this collective agency is gaining solidarity and support among workers and community members, what seems to be emerging is not necessarily a union-led labor movement, but a social movement for labor rights.

The role of unions in China is the subject of much debate. The law says that there can be only one official union, the ACFTU, which is under the leadership of the Chinese Communist Party. During China's Maoist period before 1978, the government owned all production and services, so theoretically there was no conflict of interest between employers and employees, and unions did not confront management. After the introduction of private capital in 1978, conflict developed between owners and workers, but the union's role did not change much—it did not openly confront capital. Today, union work is considered government work; to get a job in the union applicants must pass a civil service examination, and union and government cadre routinely rotate in and out of union work. Thus union cadre are not necessarily driven by a mission to strengthen labor.

However, the strikes staged by rank-and-file workers in the past few years have raised existential questions for the ACFTU. If workers bypass the union to go on strike, what is the usefulness of the union? If the union does not side with the workers in a strike, how could it claim to represent them? If the union does not resolve the strike, how could it claim to provide leadership? If the union fails in all of the above, what does this say about the control of the Communist Party? In the absence of national policy changes that address these questions, local union federations have chosen various responses.

In the southern province of Guangdong, union leaders have adopted a path-breaking policy of siding with strikers and promoting collective bargaining and election of grassroots union leaders. In 2010, given political sanction by the party secretary Wang Yang, they called the economic demands of the workers justified and directed their cadre to implement new forms of labor relations involving peaceful resolution of strikes, collective bargaining, and democratic election of union leaders at the factory level (Interview of W. Chen, chairman, Guangzhou Federation of Trade Unions, 2010). This policy gave union cadre a mandate to experiment with collective bargaining and election of grassroots union leaders.

However, the process of implementing these new policies has been difficult. In the next section I will present selections from writings of workers and union cadre about tension points in this transformation, or places where old ways conflict with the new. Through examining these tension points, one can understand what the problems are and how the key actors are thinking about moving forward. These excerpts happen to refer to labor relations in enterprises established by Japanese investors, but recent strikes at Taiwanese and Chinese-owned plants cited elsewhere in this article demonstrate that similar situations are occurring in those plants as well.

Nanhai Honda Strike

The Honda parts plant in the Nanhai district near Guangzhou is a Japanese-owned enterprise that was established in 2007 and produces transmission assemblies for the four Honda assembly plants in China. The workers in the plant are mostly migrant workers, and in 2010 their minimum wage was 900 yuan per month,[2] only 50 yuan higher than the town's minimum wage. In May that year, one worker pulled a switch that stopped the assembly line, and some nineteen hundred workers went on strike for higher wages without telling their union chairman, who was a management employee (as is the case with many factory-level union leaders in China). As the workers left the assembly line to gather outside the factory, management sent someone to photograph the strikers and intimidate them. Undaunted, several dozen workers surrounded the photographer and marched in place, lifted their fists over their heads, and chanted loudly, "Down with you, down with you!" This clever tactic turned the intimidation on the photographer and he beat a hasty retreat (Kong 2010).

With no one leading the workers, the situation was at a standoff. Shortly into the strike a group of men wearing union vests entered the factory grounds and confronted the strikers. Some shoving ensued that was broadcast on the Internet, and soon the violent confrontation became big news. The men with the union vests departed. Later, official union leaders would deny that these men were from the union, and instead blamed the local government. The town's union federation even issued an apology to the strikers (China Labor News Translations 2010). This was an early indication of behind-the-scenes struggle among government and union officials as to how to handle the strike.

In the heat of the battle the workers needed help, but they did not feel they could approach the union, so they reached out to someone with respected status who is known to support labor, the Renmin University labor law professor Chang Kai of Beijing. Through Chang's efforts and those of the Guangdong union deputy chairman Kong Xianghong,[3] neither of whom had actual experience with collective bargaining, the striking workers elected a bargaining committee and eventually negotiated a 500-yuan wage increase, which amounted to more than a 50 percent increase for the lowest-paid workers. Since then, with the assistance of Chairman Kong, the union at Nanhai Honda has been reconstructed, and collective bargaining has taken place every year. This success of this strike, both in the amount of the wage increase and the method of peaceful resolution, reverberated throughout the Pearl River Delta and across the nation.

Chairman Kong had been a career union cadre at the provincial level for many years and had a reputation for being committed to workers and being a powerful orator, though he was not necessarily known for innovation. He had participated in discussions about collective bargaining in Europe and observed their effects from afar, but he had never actually participated in collective bargaining, let alone led it in the heat of a strike. In a forthcoming memoir of key events in Nanhai Honda bargaining over several years, Chairman Kong, who has now retired, reflects on a number of points he has learned:

> Weren't the thirty worker representatives elected? Yes, they all made statements during bargaining, they all put forward workers' demands, and it was difficult to speak with one voice. Therefore, negotiations were difficult . . . the worker representatives found it hard to focus on responding or put forward counterproposals, some worker representatives even put forward the need to strike. Finally, with the guidance of outside advisers, the focus returned to wages and an agreement was reached. So was there a problem with [the method of] representation.
>
> The job of union or worker representatives must be in gathering and listening to workers' demands, and then afterward consolidating them. That is, they should stand firm with the majority of workers' reasonable demands, and lead the workers who have overly unrealistic demands to

give them up, so the union can concentrate on the wishes of the majority. This is the consolidated response of representation. What the thirty
bargaining representatives who had been elected on the spot lacked was
a process of "organizing and consolidation," so they had a hard time
representing a single union organization, one that truly represented the
wishes of the majority that really had power (Kong 2010).

Here Chairman Kong is trying to define democracy and apply it to union
representation. He wants diverse voices be heard, but at the same time he realizes that at the bargaining table the message has to be collectivized into a single
position, otherwise employers will not know how to respond. Union negotiators in all countries regularly face this same dilemma, but for Chairman Kong
the tension point is new because before this bargaining representatives were
not nominated and elected at large and demands were not generated from the
rank and file. He is learning by doing—the "sink or swim" method, and he is
a fast learner. He concludes that what is needed is not an absolute democracy
where everyone is represented equally, but a representative democracy where the
elected union leadership organizes and consolidates diverse demands into a single collective voice. Furthermore, Chairman Kong relates representational democracy to union power. He frames it as a practical consideration for unions,
not as an ideological or theoretical principle, as many union and party officials
often do.

Chairman Kong doesn't stop at thinking about democracy in negotiations. He
goes on to conceptualize how this representative democracy might work inside
the union as an institution:

> For the union to have power for the worker representatives, it has to
> demonstrate power that is organized and systematic. This will require
> a comprehensive organized network, and through this network there
> are operations that have effective procedures, so that the union can
> listen, gather, and consolidate the demands of the masses of workers
> from the bottom to the top. Then it can from top to bottom do out-
> reach and carry out the direction and principles of the union. Simply
> stated, through this organizing network, the union will have a broad
> mass base, and in this way representation and power will emerge . . .
>
> On this point, Nanhai Honda's union had shortcomings. The union
> was established, but there were no workshop branches or union com-
> mittees; when the union committee members left the enterprise they
> were not replaced; the union chairman was the only one who remained
> symbolically. The representatives who could protect workers' rights
> were barely there. That is, the company's union was not an organized

power, or a systematized power, therefore [it] had lost its representational power. (Kong 2010)

Chairman Kong realizes that the union may have structural and institutional power, but it lacks representational power. He takes this conclusion beyond the bargaining table to the institutional arena, to reimagine what representative democracy would look like inside the union, and argues that without bottom-up and top-down systems, unions do not have the power of the mass base. This concept is not new to China. Unions theoretically operate in the mode of "democratic centralism," which should be a bottom-up and top-down system. However, even some Chinese union leaders point out that in practice the bottom-up feature is lacking in current unions (Chen 2012b, 65–67). Some academics point out that this top-down-only feature has essentially led to a "corporatist" style of unionism (Unger and Chan 1995).

In another section of his memoir, Chairman Kong links his Nanhai Honda experience to the need for legislation concerning the right to strike:

> Although China's laws current do not have regulations regarding strikes, workers are already using (or implementing) their right to strike; this is a fact that cannot be ignored in Guangdong. Therefore, if the right to strike was legalized, it would make progress toward regularizing what are known internationally as "wildcat strikes" toward a balance between the interests of labor and capital. The Nanhai Honda strike demonstrates the lack of legality and balance: First, the workers pushed the electronic emergency button to start the strike in violation of the enterprise's right to do business and in violation of the enterprise's rules (the emergency button has a special person who is responsible for it). Second, there was no resolution of bargaining. If the workers opposed the bargaining results, they could have cast "no" votes in the Staff and Workers Congress,[4] but there are no regulations as to whether strikes or the threat of strikes can take place in the middle of negotiations. From any point of view, the strike was inappropriate and incorrect. Therefore the question of what constitutes a legal strike should be a high priority for consideration, should be researched more, and should be legislated as soon as possible. (Kong 2013)

Chairman Kong points out that, technically speaking, the Nanhai Honda strike started from the illegal act of a worker pulling the emergency switch. However, the strike happened and the union intervened. He implies that the union cannot sanction illegal activities, and says that in order to have a balanced labor relations system there needs to be a definition of "legal" strikes. The debate about whether the right to strike should be legalized has been taking place among labor activists for some time (CLNT 2011). Some opine that workers de facto have the right to strike and legislation might limit that right, whereas others say that legalization of strikes may chill the organizing momentum that workers have built up through striking. Chairman Kong was among union leaders who promoted legislation in 2013 for the right to strike; however, foreign investors (particularly from Hong Kong) voiced stiff opposition to legalizing strikes, and the final legislation that passed in 2014 not only did not provide the right to strike but also established an unprecedented restriction on striking during negotiations and mandated sanctions against workers who took part in these strikes.[5] Still, Chairman Kong's point about the need to define the legality of strikes in the context of a balanced labor relations system cannot be ignored, especially when workers do not yet have a comprehensive system of resolving disputes and getting past bargaining impasses.

In sum, the Nanhai Honda strike was a catalyst for experimentation with and a reconceptualization of new forms of labor relations. Progressive policy in Guangdong province provided an opportunity for reform-minded union leaders to step forward and create systems that would channel worker dissent into a democratic process. Implementing these new systems required labor leaders to take bold steps into the unknown, and to learn by doing. From this limited experience, some union leaders are pushing beyond the bargaining table into institutional reforms inside the union and legislative reforms that would affect all workers.

Nansha Denso Strike

Denso is a Japanese corporation that is affiliated with Toyota and is one of the largest car parts manufacturer in the world. Its plant in the Nansha district of Guangzhou is a joint venture with the Chinese government, and it manufactures fuel injection equipment and other parts. On June 19, 2010, two hundred workers who were dissatisfied with wages and supervisor treatment attended a meeting that was disguised as a dinner party, where they agreed on a strategy to strike. Two days later, the workforce refused to work and walked out, refused to elect a leadership committee, and refused to put forward demands. They knew that if they could practice these "three refusals" for three days, management could not pick out leaders to fire or intimidate, and the entire just-in-time supply chain in China would grind to a halt. Eventually the union's district officer was called in to lead the bargaining committee in negotiations, and after five days the workers won an unprecedented compensation increase of 825 RMB (68 percent), as well as a commitment to provide air conditioning in the dormitories and other provisions (Liang 2011).

The backstory to this victory reveals some tough struggle. When the government authorities found out about the strike, they wanted to call the police to arrest the strikers, but a courageous union district chairperson named Liang Jiefang held them at bay. Liang is a senior cadre who has worked in other government jobs. Though she has not worked in the union her entire career, she admitted that her relationships with other local officials allowed her to negotiate the political minefield of police and party:

> The new generation of workers born in the 80s and 90s is clearly different from the previous generation of migrant workers when it comes to pursuit of life and personal development. They feel that there is a big gap between staff wages and corporate profitability, and the right of employees to participate in the democratic management of enterprises is denied by employers who believe in [the credo] "I invest, I dictate." The longer the employees are repressed, the deeper the grievances, the higher the spirit of resistance. Once they find a vent they explode . . . In handling the relationship between the maintenance of rights and stability, the government must not, . . . use simple or rough methods to cover up increasingly acute labor-management conflicts, in particular must not in the name of so-called stability harm the spirit of the employees, sacrifice their dignity and rights, leading to greater instability in the future . . . Protection of labor rights is a prerequisite and foundation for maintaining social stability. Without effective maintenance of labor rights, it is impossible to achieve true social stability and harmony . . . when the core issue in the dispute between employers and employees was not . . . resolved through consultation, some departments, eager to seek "stability," . . . attempted to use such methods as mobilizing police power to maintain "order" in order to intimidate workers fighting for their rights, "invite" trade union cadres to have a talk at the police station to force workers to return to work, etc., which were all reasonably refused by the District Union Federation. Because the union stood with the workers from beginning to end and did not play the role of mediator, it won the trust of workers . . . those employees who were originally biased and wary of the union turned to trusting the union as the "backing" for fighting for rights and benefits. (Liang 2011, 1–2)

Chairwoman Liang premises her arguments by saying that conditions now are different than they were in the past—these workers are a new type of worker. The first generation of migrant workers to leave the countryside post-1978 was mostly young women who worked for a couple of years in urban factories and then returned to their home villages to marry and raise a family. They struggled to survive, lived on meager rations, and sent a great deal of money back to their families (Chan 2001; Pun 2005). However, the newer generation of migrant workers is comprised of both men and women who come from rural areas where the standard of living and quality of education has improved since the 1980s. Rather than sending most of their pay to their parents, they spend their earnings in buying material goods such as smartphones and computers, going to the movies, or touring other parts of China. If they quit or get fired from their jobs, they can easily migrate to other regions of China to look for work. Chairwoman Liang says that this new generation of migrant workers will not tolerate the exploitation that earlier generations suffered.

Liang also argues against the use of police repression in strikes by reframing the notion of stability and harmony, items of paramount concern to the government and party. She says that social stability will not be gained with crude police tactics to quash dissent, rather it will be gained when labor rights are protected. This is a fundamental departure from previous government/party/union policy, which regards strikes as politically destabilizing events and threats to social harmony. And though she had the backing of her Guangzhou union federation leadership in blocking police intervention, she had to battle with government and party officials in her district to prevail. Nearly a year after the strike, when she presented her case at an international conference at Sun Yat-sen University, she could not hold back tears when she recalled the "tension points" she faced in holding back the police.

Liang also stresses that unions must assume the role of worker representative rather than mediator, another fundamental departure from previous policy. Heretofore, if a labor dispute occurred the union would stand in the middle and mediate between workers and employers. Small wonder that workers did not trust that the union represented their voice. In her conference remarks, Liang said that when the strike took place she went to the factory immediately, but none of the workers would talk to her—their "three refusals" strategy included not talking to her. Only when workers saw that she fought the police and stood with them did they finally trust her.

Furthermore, in the same conference remarks Chairwoman Liang took the lessons she learned to the level of the party, and argued for reform of the party's attitudes toward unions. This stunning candor in a public setting was possible because her senior leaders, Chairman Chen Weiguang and Chairman Kong Xianghong, were present and supportive.

Transforming the role of unions depends critically on the leadership of the party and government support (bolded text in the original). With the accelerated development of [a] market economy, the party must strengthen its leadership of the trade union. [The] party's leadership of the union is its leadership over political line, direction, principles, policies, and major issues. Trade unions are mass organizations under the leadership of the party, not a party department or a subsidiary body of the executive branch . . . **The restructuring of [the] union requires a renewed recognition of its role.** In recent years, the wrong stance and role of the union [has] cause[d] the deepening of its dilemma in labor relations. Although the number of unions established surges each year, when labor rights have been violated, the percentage of cases where workers actively seek union[s] to defend employee rights stay[s] low. More embarrassing to the unions is that in most mass incidents, workers bypass the union. This is a dangerous signal. Trade unions should be a good spokesperson for the interests of workers. We must first reform our own officious, administrative, and bureaucratic tendencies, take off the "official cloak" in our ideology, eliminate the "bureaucratic tone" in our language and habits, and merge our feelings with the grassroots working people. Second, the "professional" tendency of first-line union cadres needs to be reformed. We must correct the embarrassing situations where unions are dependent on the bosses, . . . [where] without the nod or acquiescence of . . . management union presidents cannot make a move, and allow the union [to] return to being "independent" so that it can have the dignity and confidence to stand up straight for workers' interests in the contest with employers, to win the trust, support, and recognition of the majority of workers; only then can the party's class foundation and governance be continuously strengthened. (Liang 2011, 2–3)

Here Liang gives us a peek into debate inside the party regarding unions. She has heard the same positions stated from her mentors Chairman Chen and Chairman Kong, but the passion in her advocacy reveals a deep conviction of her own. She calls for the party to "strengthen" its leadership of trade unions, not as if the unions were a subsidiary department of the party but rather as a mass organization of the party. How exactly does a subsidiary department of the party differ from a mass organization of the party? Chairwoman Liang does not elaborate on the difference in roles; however, we can get some clues about her meaning from the paragraph that follows. She says that only when unions stand with workers—reform their bureaucratic tone, make decisions independent from employers, and win the trust of workers—can the "class foundation" and governance of the party be strengthened. That is, only when the unions as mass organizations stand with workers can the party exert its leadership of workers. Though argued as a strengthening of party leadership, she is in fact advocating a role that is hugely different from current practice.

Chairwoman Liang's report gives us a sense of deep tensions between the old and new at various levels. We see the external landscape changing from a compliant migrant workforce to a new one that will stand up for its rights. We begin to understand the gap between the former role of unions as mediators and the worker-allied role that progressives like Liang are advocating. And we get a window on the struggle inside the party regarding its relationship to unions. We also get a sense of the trauma involved in transforming labor relations and the struggle to frame arguments in a way that indicates reform rather than rebellion.

KRS Collective Bargaining

KRS[6] is a Japanese-owned manufacturer of auto parts like window casings. In 2010, inspired by the Nanhai Honda strike, the workers went on strike over social security insurance issues, and later that year the employer approached the union to engage in collective bargaining. In a contested election the workers democratically elected their own union representatives. A new young challenger named Qiang became the factory chairman and has led his team to bargain for wages each year since then.[7] Qiang is not a party member and does not receive much support from the union hierarchy; however, that has not stopped him from teaching himself about labor law and becoming a passionate and committed rank-and-file leader.

Bargaining has been tough each year; the employer has refused to meet worker demands for reasons ranging from the 2011 tsunami damage to corporate headquarters in Japan to lack of sales. On top of the usual difficulties, in 2013 while negotiations were taking place the employer decided to subvert the collective bargaining process by directing supervisors to circulate a petition for rank-and-file workers to sign, indicating their agreement with the employer's wage proposal. The workers were told that if they did not sign the petition, they would lose their jobs, so most of the workers felt compelled to sign. This caused a crisis for Qiang and the other union leaders sitting at the bargaining table. In a request for assistance to the next-higher-level trade union, the factory union leadership produced a report that included the following argument:

> Who is not bargaining in good faith? . . . The union did preparation, including gathering ideas about wage increases from the workers, investigating wage rates of surrounding factories, researching minimum

wages, gather[ing] financial data from the company's website, etc., and came up with negotiations proposals. And early in March we made a demand for bargaining, so that the company could provide financial data according to law, which would allow for negotiations to go forward. However, the company never responded, . . . [Our] several e-mails, verbal demands in negotiations, and written demands about finances to confirm that what the company was representing about profit forecasting was credible were never answered by the company. Even up until the last negotiations when the workers researched finances themselves, the company was not willing to comply with [the] law and bring financial information to the table.

In the course of this year's collective wage consultation,[8] the enterprise has already destroyed negotiations, and there must be a reconstruction of consultation between labor and management; management must in good faith respect the union and the collective rights of workers, and make good on the promises below. We the grassroots unions are willing to, on this basis, make best efforts to consult the union representative committee, and on the basis of passage in the union congress agree to reengage in collective consultation.

1. The four managers who pressured the workers and threatened them must make a public apology to the whole workforce.
2. Management promises that in the future it will never again use intimidating and threatening tactics to demand that the workers sign a survey.
3. Management promises that from now on in all collective consultation, it will never again violate the union's important legal rights, and will not violate the legal rights of the staff/union representatives and bargaining representatives.
4. Management promises to respect the union's important work as a part of the legal autonomy of mass organizations. (Guangzhou KRS Union Committee 2013)

American unionists will recognize that if the worker grievances as reported above are true, the employer's acts would be considered serious unfair labor practices because they did not treat the union as the sole bargaining representative and coerced the workers into signing the letter. In the United States they might file a charge at the National Labor Relations Board, but in China there is not yet any legal standard for unfair labor practices, any legal structure to adjudicate labor disputes, or any right to strike when bargaining fails to reach agreement.

When the employer breaks good faith, as in this case, there is no clear path to justice. The KRS factory union appealed to the upper-level union for assistance, but was denied assistance by a union official who did not agree with the workers' case, which is not uncommon. Thus workers who engage in collective bargaining are operating in a frustrating environment with little guidance or support from upper-level unions or the legal system.

Since workers cannot strike during an impasse in negotiations, they are left with trying to make persuasive arguments at the table. They are negotiating over wages, so they need financial data from the company; however, it is extremely common for employers to refuse to provide any financial information, and even when they do the workers are not sure if it is credible. In the United States if the employer fails to provide relevant financial information this could be the basis of an unfair labor practice, but in China, once again, there is no legal standard for what information is required and no adequate recourse for workers when it is not provided.

Besides a lack of regulations for collective bargaining, there is no mutually agreed on grievance procedure, so minor disputes become big ones, and collective mass action becomes the only way that workers can get the attention of their employers. Said Qiang about collective bargaining: "I used to think that collective wage consultation was the answer to workers' problems, and that it should even be expanded to include more subjects than just wage negotiations. But now I think collective bargaining is too limited, and there are other ways to get things done . . . for example when the employer raised the price at the cafeteria, we all boycotted the cafeteria until the prices went back down" (Qiang 2013). By 2014, after several years of tense and frustrating negotiations, he concluded: "Collective bargaining is not the answer. We will do it, but we won't count on it." And another union leader added, "From listening to all the comments on collective bargaining, it seems like we need to have a strike about every three years" (author interview with LF, 2014).

The frustrations with collective bargaining are becoming so deep that rank-and-file union leaders are saying it is not working for them and they need a strike occasionally to demonstrate to the employer that they are serious. In fact, collective bargaining may actually exacerbate labor-management tensions because there are inadequate procedures for resolving differences at the bargaining table. This frustration may be intensified by the 2014 Guangdong labor legislation that prohibits workers from striking during negotiations. The same legislation did outline some grievance procedures; however, that was only one small step taken thus far toward the need for a comprehensive national labor-relations system involving standards, regulations, education and training, implementation, adjudication of disputes, and remedies.

Given the lack of systems in this early stage of transition to new forms of labor relations, it is remarkable that a new generation of worker-leaders on the front lines is stepping forward to shoulder the responsibility of representing hundreds and thousands of coworkers and experiment with collective bargaining in many workplaces in China. From their own accounts of the process, we can see that they certainly do participate in back-and-forth collective bargaining and that they experience the same problems with employer resistance that workers face anywhere. However, what is different is the lack of a labor-relations system that will deal effectively with disputes that cannot be resolved at the collective bargaining table. The challenge for Chinese union and government officials is to construct a labor-relations system where both labor and management play by the rules, and where there is access to fair adjudication and remedy when the rules are broken.

Discussion

From just these few excerpts of the labor activists on the frontlines, we can gain a qualitatively deeper understanding of what they face and we can refine our image of who they are. Experienced trade unionists will recognize that much of what Chinese labor activists face is very similar to what all labor activists face, though there are differences. At the ground level, whether it is fighting antiunion employers, bridging the gap between rank-and-file workers and union hierarchy, or struggling with representative democracy and power, workers on the frontlines face the same fight. What is different is the government and political infrastructure—the roles of the Communist Party, union, and police, and lack of a comprehensive labor-relations system. Going forward, as dialogue and relationships are built between Chinese and American workers, it is important to be clear about what the similarities and differences are, and to choose whether to emphasize the differences or the similarities.

There are real changes in labor relations taking place in China. The insurgency among workers has forced issues to the surface, and there are genuine efforts to represent workers democratically and bargain collectively. In the past, China's attempts at electing union leaders were criticized as staged, and collective bargaining was criticized as lacking worker participation, so understandably many people doubted whether the Guangdong experience would be genuine. However these excerpts demonstrate that at least in Guangdong province there are some cases of genuine union elections and collective bargaining. As noted, there are still many problems and there is a long way to go to make these experiments universal. Nevertheless, there is some progress, and key actors like the ones quoted here are asking the right questions.

These labor activists are strong and are taking action. The excerpts reveal that they are smart—from rank-and-file workers on up, they think strategically about goals and tactics, like the three refusals and surrounding the photographer to intimidate him, and they think reflexively about how to learn from their mistakes. They are daring—they are willing to confront not just their employers but also deeply entrenched institutions like labor unions, governments, and the police. And they are forward thinking—they consider how to improve what they are doing from practical, institutional, and structural points of view. Of course not all workers and union leaders are like the three I quoted, but there are many more like these three and their numbers are growing.

Chinese workers could use support. Of course, labor relations in China will develop according to Chinese conditions, but Chinese workers would certainly benefit from the knowledge that workers in other countries have gained, both positive and negative, from more than a century of experience. Now would be an ideal time to initiate that cross-border dialogue and comparative learning because, as we have seen, in the struggle taking place between the old ways and the new, strategic choices will be made that will either give workers greater voice and participation in labor relations or will repress them.

US-China Labor Policy

Until Trumka's 2013 trip to China, the official policy of the AFL-CIO was to shun relations with Chinese unions. During the Cold War, the "free, democratic" labor movements of the world lined up against the "communist" labor movements, mirroring the political and ideological contestation taking place among nations at the time. After the collapse of the Soviet Union and the adoption of a market economy in China, animosities of the Cold War may have faded among capitalists, but it still held sway among labor movements. In 2005 the AFL-CIO was still arguing that the ACFTU's subordination to the Communist Party was a reason for not having relationships with Chinese unions (Shailor 2005), even though by that time the Communist Party has changed so much that capitalists were allowed to be members (Wolf 2001). In 2012 some labor leaders were even calling the Chinese government "fascist" (Dreyfuss 2010).

Other AFL-CIO arguments also cited human rights violations as a key reason to shun Chinese unions. For many years civil-society protest was not tolerated in China—protesters were often jailed without being charged or offered due process. After the Tiananmen Square "massacre" in 1989 where many protestors were killed, the AFL-CIO supported several labor leaders in exile who had been involved in this incident. Today Chinese society is somewhat more open than in the past, though leaders of strikes are still commonly arrested and jailed. However, as was seen in the excerpts, there is much struggle around whether or not to use police force to repress protests, and in some cases there is increasing public resentment against police intervention.

Other AFL-CIO policymakers focused their arguments on wage competition, blaming loss of American manufacturing jobs on China's low wages, trade policy, and currency manipulation (Scott 2012), as well as human rights violations noted above. Some say that the larger picture is a worldwide struggle for power, as they spread fear about Chinese ways and attempt to protect the dominance of American interests (see AFL-CIO leaders interviewed in the 2012 film by Peter Navarro, *Death By China*). Their strategy had been to isolate China by prevailing on the US government to block it from joining the World Trade Organization (Scott 1999) or receiving trade preferences unless and until it implements higher labor standards (AFL-CIO, Cardin, and Smith 2006). However, the US government has repeatedly refused to adopt labor's policy demands, both in Republican and Democratic administrations, except for a very few instances of insertion of labor clauses in bilateral and regional trade agreements.

Labor's policy of boycotting China may have been intended to punish the Chinese government, but it has not been able to change low wages or human rights violations, and indeed it may have had the perverse effect of undermining labor's power and influence even further. As multinational investment in China surged in the past thirty-five years, labor ignored and excluded Chinese workers. Today the working conditions, labor rights, and labor-relations systems of Chinese workers have a tremendous impact on the global economy, yet the global labor movement is decades behind building the kind of cross-border solidarity that is needed to defend labor standards and labor rights in the global economy.

In recent years there has been some softening of US union policy toward China. In 2009 the AFL-CIO's rival federation, Change to Win, signed a memorandum with the ACFTU that was intended to move forward with collaboration, and leaders of the Service Employees International Union, the International Brotherhood of Teamsters, and the United Food and Commercial Workers have traveled to China numerous times to meet with their Chinese union counterparts. The San Francisco Labor Council has had a sister-city labor council relationship with the Guangzhou Federation of Trade Unions for several years, as has the Los Angeles County Federation of Labor with the Shanghai Federation of Trade Unions. However, none of these visits has resulted in ongoing joint programs.

Now that both American union federations have begun to have relationships with the ACFTU, the question is no longer whether or not to engage with Chinese labor, the question is how—what will be the long- and short-range goals, and what will be the strategy and plan to meet those goals. There is no simple answer; both sides will need to engage in dialogue and feel out opportunities and interests. We learned from historical experience that people-to-people exchanges build friendships and bonds at a human level and help to break through social prejudices and political barriers. Labor organizers know that joint projects, whether based on organizing a common employer or negotiating in the same industrial sector, lead to concrete results. Modest, concrete projects will pave the way for more far-reaching programs.

From the voices of workers and union activists on the frontlines of change in China, it is clear that labor relations are in the process of transformation. In an earlier era workers may have been intimidated and compliant, but today Chinese workers have begun to stand up for themselves. The process of transformation is fraught with difficulties with employers, the police, and even inside unions. Yet as the excerpts reveal, workers and unionists on the frontlines are up to those challenges, possessing intelligence, consciousness, and agency that are worthy of our deepest respect.

American workers know very little about Chinese workers, mostly because of decades of labor policy that has kept us apart. However, now in this increasingly globalized economy, the stakes are too high for American and Chinese workers to ignore each other. Dialogue and exchange, on thoughts like those revealed in these excerpts, can lead to mutual understanding and joint action.

CSR AND TRADE UNION ELECTIONS AT FOREIGN-OWNED CHINESE FACTORIES

Anita Chan

In 2012 the Guangdong Provincial Federation of Trade Unions announced "direct" trade union elections were to be carried out in the city of Shenzhen at 163 foreign-funded enterprises.[1] The announcement brought to the fore the issue of trade union elections. Guangdong province has the largest number of foreign investors and has experienced a large number of workers' protests, and any new initiative related to changes in industrial relations there is regarded as having nationwide implications. Why was the Guangdong union federation promoting union elections in factories? To understand this, we need to take stock of a pattern of events during the 2000 decade. This chapter will analyze previous trade union elections at supplier factories of multinational corporations (MNCs), starting with the first election organized by Reebok in 2001 at a supplier factory in Shenzhen as part of its corporate social responsibility (CSR) program. It will explore whether the recent history of CSR-related factory union elections has prompted Chinese union officials to organize similar elections or whether workers have taken the initiative on their own to demand grassroots union elections.

Setting Up Factory Trade Union Branches

According to China's Trade Union Law, all enterprises regardless of ownership type and all public institutions are supposed to set up union branches (Lee 1984; Taylor, Chang, and Li 2003).[2] In state-owned companies, union branches were established at the same time as the enterprise came into existence, without going through even a formalistic election. These union branches do not represent workers vis-à-vis management but instead are extensions of enterprise management, with members of management appointed to the union posts to look after employee entertainment and to dole out minor employee welfare benefits. The union chairs enjoy the same rank and attendant privileges as the deputy manager of the factory.

Although by law the foreign-owned companies in China and domestic private enterprises are supposed to set up union branches in the first few months after the enterprise's inauguration, in reality the great majority do not, and until recently many remained without any union branch. In the past three decades, the government and the All-China Federation of Trade Unions (ACFTU) have tried repeatedly to persuade, or at times coerce, foreign managements to set up union branches. Within the past decade, the union federation began to impose quotas on lower-level union bureaus to set up new union branches in the private manufacturing sector. ACFTU has a particular incentive, since expanding union membership is an excellent revenue source for all levels of the union. Under Chinese law, workplace union revenues come from two main sources: union dues of 0.5 percent of wages deducted from the workers' monthly wage, and 2 percent of the total payroll contributed by management.[3]

Foreign-owned companies that yield to the pressure will usually work with local city district trade union officials to select who will head the factory union branch. He or she tends to come from within management, and quite often is none other than the factory's human resources manager. Within the past decade a formal election procedure has sometimes been required, and in such cases management and the district union will handpick a few employees to form a preparatory committee, which will be responsible for organizing an election. Normally the management and union will select a few candidates and then "perform" the election. Ordinary staff and workers often are not aware that there has been an election or even that there is a trade union at their workplace.[4] In ACFTU's records, though, a workplace trade union has emerged through an electoral process. ACFTU has run repeated campaigns since the 1990s to set up this type of union branches in the foreign-invested sector (Chan 2006).

This paper will examine the various forces that have driven ACFTU to go substantially further by legitimizing factory-level union elections. It will focus on foreign-owned factories because, in diverse ways, the foreign stakeholders have been key players in setting this in motion.

The Global Production Chain and Pressures to Introduce CSR

In the decades since economic reforms began in the 1980s, China has been eager to attract foreign investment and has successfully become the number one destination for the manufacturing of labor-intensive goods. The majority of the factories are owned and managed by Taiwanese, Hong Kong, and Korean companies that supply manufactured goods to foreign wholesalers or brand-name MNCs. This manufacturing sector has incorporated China into the global production chain. The chain has a number of stakeholders—the MNCs, the foreign Asian manufacturers with factories inside China who supply their products to the MNCs, the various levels of the local Chinese government/trade union, and lastly the workers—and a set of power relationships between them. Under normal circumstances, the MNCs exert pressure down through the chain (Gereffi, Humphrey, and Sturgeon 2005; Nadvi 2008). When any of them decides to initiate a trade union election, the chain's normal governance structure and power relationships become unhinged; and when the initiative comes from the workers, all other stakeholders feel threatened.

International NGOs and international union federations have played a role external to the global production chain. Most of these international NGOs are spearheaded by small groups of activists who have gathered a network of supporters. By exploiting the international media they were able to exert moral pressure on the MNCs at the head of the supply chain. The MNCs have enormous economic power but feel vulnerable to the NGOs' anti-sweatshop campaigns, whose exposés damage their brand's image. In the late 1990s, pressure from the NGOs became intense, particularly in the footwear industry. Most MNCs ultimately accepted CSR to improve working conditions in the supplier factories. They set up "human rights offices" in their corporations and inside their large supplier factories and sought to monitor and address violations of their corporate codes of conduct. The problematic character of this labor monitoring regime has been explored at length by many scholars, including those in this volume.

By 2003, the CSR initiative was at its height internationally, and the Chinese government and businesses mistakenly thought that the US government would soon impose SA8000 certification on all imports to the United States. The foundational elements of this standard are based on the UN Declaration of Human Rights, a number of ILO conventions including freedom of association, no child labor, etc. and international human rights norms and national labor laws.[5] This was taken seriously as a serious threat by China. There was a lot of debate in the Chinese press either lambasting SA8000 as a trade barrier or arguing that China should take the threat seriously and begin to raise labor standards. Not willing to submit to this foreign pressure but worried about losing its international market share, China found a solution. In 2005 it created its own CSR code of conduct, the China Social Compliance for the Textile and Apparel Industry, CSC9000T.[6] To the outside world China was also embracing CSR. From China's perspective, it showed that it could hold its own and did not have to bow to foreign standards. But after a couple of years CSC9000T disappeared from the media, and during my subsequent years of field research I have not heard about CSC9000T. One can assume that this Chinese certification has not been used much.

During this period, anti-sweatshop NGOs abroad argued that because external monitoring had failed, the only solution was to empower workers to set up elected union branches and to enable these to engage in discussions with management. In the course of the past decade and a half, various parties have attempted to take the initiative at supplier factories within China to set up democratically elected bodies. It should be noted that none of these were set up as unions independent of ACFTU. As these efforts developed over time, the workers themselves sometimes took the initiative.

Below are five types of cases that were either pilot projects, have set precedents, or are perceived as significant. These cases are divided into two broad categories: (1) trade union branch elections initiated by parties other than workers, and (2) branch elections initiated by workers. I will present these cases chronologically, as the earlier elections had an impact on some of the elections that came after. They each involved a two-stage process—first to initiate and then to hold an election. An election could be initiated by one stakeholder, but then organized and held by another stakeholder, which could lead to a different outcome. Particularly important is a case where workers initiated a demand to set up a trade union, but acceded to the official trade union taking over the organizing of the election.

Elections Initiated by Parties Other Than Workers

Elections Initiated and Organized by an MNC involving Worker Participation

In the late 1990s Nike became a main target of the international anti-sweatshop movement, but it was Reebok, one of its competitors, that first actively addressed the remedy of factory-level union elections. Jill Tucker, who was the director of Reebok's Asian regional human rights compliance office, had launched a successful program of union elections in Indonesia and then in Thailand. But she had been finding it frustratingly difficult to get its suppliers in China, which were mostly Hong Kong, Taiwanese, and South Korean footwear manufacturers, to improve labor conditions for Chinese migrant workers from the countryside. Tucker's hope was that through elected representative bodies in Reebok's Chinese supplier factories, workers would be able to channel their grievances and finally attain "sustainable compliance" with Reebok's corporate code of conduct. Tucker realized that a level playing field in the industry would be essential, and her hope was that other MNCs in the industry would learn from Reebok's experimentation and follow suit.[7]

The first supplier chosen by Reebok to try out a union election was KTS, a Hong Kong-Taiwan-owned factory in Shenzhen that employed five thousand workers.[8] It was the first democratic trade union election at any of China's foreign-funded factories. Prior to the 2001 election, groundwork had to be laid. For a year Tucker built up an infrastructure within KTS to cultivate workers' trust in Reebok and overcome their fear of management. She had the entire Chinese labor law painted on an external wall of the factory compound, set up a responsive complaint mechanism, an elected occupational safety and health committee of workers, and an ombudsman office that spread the concept of "human rights." When I visited the factory in 2002, a year after the election was held, KTS workers freely used the expression "human rights" in conversations with me, and by the time Reebok had organized the trade union election, they were attuned to the concept.

Tucker was able to insist on these provisions because Reebok was the factory's only customer, and its power to provide additional orders or withhold orders overrode the preferences of KTS's onsite management. Reebok drew up a proposal for workplace union election procedures and showed these to the district trade union. KTS management and the KTS trade union branch chair, who had been appointed to the post by the local government, looked on passively. The local government and district trade union were aware of Reebok's activities but chose not to intervene because they were eager to retain good relations with Reebok, for fear Reebok would place its orders elsewhere. Those were the days when MNCs had quite a lot of bargaining power even over local governments in China.

Tucker invited Hong Kong NGOs to observe the election at KTS and to run a weekly training course for the newly elected trade union committee. They were trained in the basic principles of how to run a union organization, on the techniques of collective bargaining, and more important, the concept that a union branch is not an administrative arm of management. The newly elected union committee members gained confidence, and in the next six months negotiated for a number of improvements. For instance, workers were now paid 80 to 90 percent of their wage during sick leave, and 75 percent when the production lines did not operate for various reasons. These were substantial gains for workers.

This golden period for workers lasted for less than a year. KTS changed ownership, and the new management stood firm against new union demands and even refused to honor some of the recent improvements. When the new management cut the home-visit transport subsidies that workers had received every year for the Chinese New Year, the newly elected union branch protested and mobilized a petition signed by 90 percent of the employees. This was an enormously successful undertaking, but in the end management refused to budge. The union was unable to pursue the issue, and workers and staff became demoralized. Soon rumors of corruption among some of the trade union committee members began to surface. Reebok no longer intervened on the grounds that the newly elected union branch needed to learn to manage on its own. Without the backing of Reebok and the Hong Kong NGOs, in a couple of years the union committee was ripped apart by in-fighting and vanished into the background.

After setting up the union branch at KTS, Tucker launched a similar program at a large Taiwanese-owned Reebok supplier factory in Fujian called Shunda, with thirteen thousand employees. The distance between Fujian and Hong Kong presented a logistics problem that affected the success of the project. Tucker and her Hong Kong staff could not monitor closely the Chinese CSR staff on site, and Shunda workers were not exposed to the concepts of "human rights" and "labor rights" to the same extent as KTS workers.

I was able to stay at the factory for two weeks in 2002 both immediately before and during the union election, and I observed the election firsthand. Although Shunda management went along with Reebok's demands, the district (a district is equivalent to a large suburb of a city) trade union tried several times to overturn Reebok's plans for the election and argued with Jill Tucker over the election procedures. However, what counted most was that the factory's management felt enormous pressure to retain Reebok's favor, and the district union was an appendage of the district government, which was eager to attract and retain foreign investors. It did not want to get into a conflict with Taiwanese factory management. Tucker was aware of this power configuration, and again and again was able to get her way.

The election operated in a decidedly democratic fashion. Candidates self-nominated or were nominated by coworkers. One hundred eighty candidates ran for thirty seats on the union committee. Each shop floor and department at the factory elected its own representatives. The candidates were each given an opportunity to deliver a five-minute speech at a large assembly of their own shop floor constituencies, attended by a thousand or more workers. I attended most of these assemblies. The majority of the candidates' speeches were brief, of little substance, and ended with a few vague promises to do their best to help their colleagues. But among them were a small number of speakers who, although they were young workers from the countryside, could intuit what trade unionism entailed and outlined concrete actions if elected. On the day of the election they attracted the largest number of votes. The incumbent trade union chair, a mid-ranking member of factory management, received few votes and was ousted.

Whereas the first stage of the election process, which I was able to observe closely, was democratic, in the second stage there was manipulation by management when the thirty elected representatives selected from among themselves the union's executive committee members, the chair, and the deputy chair. An ordinary production-line worker who had received the largest number of votes in the first round had delivered a rousing speech highly critical of management. He hoped to be elected as the union chair, but he was not informed of the time and venue of the second round of elections. The two-stage election process, as will be seen in other cases as well, presents management (and also sometimes the district union) a good opportunity to manipulate the procedures to get rid of the candidates they judged would actively work on behalf of workers.

After the election, the district union refused to let Reebok invite Hong Kong NGOs to run training sessions at Shunda. The new union was left on its own with only distant support from Reebok. Very quickly the newly elected trade union chair was co-opted by management through a salary raise and perquisites. A lot of workers with grievances individually approached the union branch in the belief that the union representatives they had just elected could help solve their problems. The few conscientious union committee members who attended to this avalanche of workers' grievances came under enormous pressure and harassment from management. In less than a year, they either quit the factory or acquiesced to management.

In 2005, adidas bought Reebok and the first thing it did was to get rid of the CSR department to make sure that no vestiges of Reebok's CSR program remained. Work conditions deteriorated and the turnover rate became so high that in a few years few workers had any knowledge of the union election organized by Reebok. In 2007, when it was time to hold another union election, the corrupt incumbent chair was "reelected"; many workers were unaware of the election.[9]

The two Reebok-organized elections led to a number of unintended developments within ACFTU. At the time of the first election at KTS in Guangdong, ACFTU had been unprepared and the district union let Reebok intrude into its turf, so to speak. A year later in Fujian at the Shunda factory, the district union began to put up a weak resistance. The following year, in 2003, when Reebok was due to organize a reelection at KTS in Guangdong, ACFTU went on the offensive.

Tucker received a letter from the district union forbidding Reebok from organizing a reelection, stating that this would be "foreign intervention" in Chinese affairs.[10] That same year, suddenly, there was a spate of media reports that several provinces were holding "direct elections" (*zhixuan*) in a number of enterprises (Howell 2008), in which workers or their representatives were able to elect the trade union committee and chairperson. The stated aim was to democratize workplace unions. By proclaiming "direct elections" ACFTU could avoid using the word "democratic," which would have contradicted Article 9 of the Trade Union Law, "Trade union organizations at various levels shall be established according to the principle of democratic centralism," which in effect means a system that ensures centralized top-down control (Trade Union Law of the People's Republic of China, Order of the President No. 62). Another unstated reason was ACFTU's eagerness to dissociate its "direct elections" from Reebok's "democratic elections."

The campaign triggered debate within the trade union structure. Two camps emerged from within ACFTU over this issue—a reform wing advocating direct elections, led by the chair of the ACFTU Department for the Construction of Grassroots Organizations, versus a conservative camp (Howell 2008). Reading between the lines in newspaper articles, the reformers seemed to have won. At that time the anti-sweatshop movement in the West was vigorously pushing MNCs to pressure suppliers to comply with their codes of conduct and to support the workers' rights. Some Chinese government and trade union officials were worried, under the erroneous belief that the CSR initiative was a trade barrier against Chinese exports and that MNCs would withdraw orders to penalize their noncompliant suppliers. ACFTU had the added worry that companies like Reebok would appropriate its own union bureaucracy's raison d'être (Ying 2003). In 2003 and 2004 various union bureaucracies competed to hold direct elections. For instance, Zhejiang province claimed that it had held "direct" elections in three hundred factories. Interestingly, the two district unions that prevented Reebok from intervening now claimed ownership of the two Reebok elections and publicized their "achievements" by showcasing the two union branches as "model branches."[11] ACFTU since then has announced that direct elections of factory union branches should be the norm for all trade union elections. One can only be skeptical about how democratic these elections are or whether workers even know they are being held. Nonetheless, proclaiming elections was a step forward.

Elections Initiated and Organized by a Foreign Union Federation and an NGO involving Worker Participation

In 2003, in part inspired by the Reebok project the International Textile, Garment and Leather Workers' Federation (ITGLWF), which had more than two hundred affiliated union organizations worldwide, together with the New York-based NGO Social Accountability International (SAI), launched a project called Promoting Worker Representation in Chinese Factories. Aware that there are legal restrictions in China on freedom of union association, the main initiator of the project, Neil Kearney, the director of ITGLWF, circumvented this problem by what is known as "parallel means." Instead of setting up workplace union branches, the project would set up workers' "representative bodies" alongside the official workplace union. The program involved training sessions with both workers and management so as to secure the latter's cooperation.[12] The local district unions were aware of the project but did not openly intervene, perhaps because the project was not about elections of trade union committees and it never proceeded far enough to present any challenge to the union status quo.

The pilot project lasted for two years. After much effort and delay SAI was able to convince three MNCs to each get one of its suppliers to participate. I was able to observe training sessions run for both workers and management. The election of workers' representation was presented to both parties as a win-win situation and the elections were organized by NGO training staff. The process was time-consuming and costly, and after two years even Kearney had doubts that the elected committees were sustainable without continuous after-project training and monitoring. More important, success of this approach, which was similar to the Reebok elections, hinged on the MNCs' and suppliers' continued willingness to cooperate. In 2005 when Kearney convened an end-of-project meeting with about a dozen Hong Kong and Chinese labor NGOs, which I attended, the consensus was that the project was a mission impossible. A year later, when I had a chance to talk to workers at one of the three suppliers, I was told the elected workers' committee had fizzled out shortly after the NGOs' postelection training ended.

Neither the Reebok elections nor the ITGLWF-SAI pilot projects could be considered successful in what they set out to do. A problem that ran through both projects was that a few "training" sessions before and after the election—about the global production chain, international labor rights, trade union rights, the Chinese labor law, and the nature of a democratic election—were not enough to transform the consciousness of the thousands of workers who had no awareness of trade unionism or experience in democratic representation. The project had a ring of artificiality. The few workers who were willing to take the lead could not survive in their jobs in a hostile environment and had to resign. When the opportunity to elect their own representatives was not born out of workers' own initiatives, but out of a culture of dependency, there was no sense of solidarity and support from coworkers. In hindsight, both of these top-down foreign interventionist pilot projects—one by an international corporation and one by an international union federation—were doomed to fail.

However, a positive development did emerge out of these failed experiments of trade union elections and CSR initiatives. They helped jolt ACFTU into launching its own factory-level elections. Realizing the positive publicity that such democratic elections could generate in the West, and at the same time still able to easily control the newly elected union branches, ACFTU was willing to embrace the rhetoric of democratic elections as a norm for union elections. This is in line with the previously unimplemented Article 9 of the Trade Union Law.

Elections Initiated and Organized by ACFTU involving Worker Participation—the Initial Walmart Unionization Effort

In 2006, the chair of the ACFTU Department for the Construction of Grassroots Organizations took a bold step that no one had expected—he launched an underground organizing campaign at a number of China's Walmart stores, persuading employees to sign up. Secretive founding ceremonies of more than a dozen store branches of the union were held late at night. At each, new union members sang the "Internationale" and held genuinely democratic union-committee elections. The district's union officials the next day announced the union branches as a fait accompli to the Walmart store management. This was a significant break from ACFTU's normal way of setting up union branches at private companies together with management without informing the workers (Chan 2011, 199–216).

This new initiative at Walmart stores was significant in a number of ways. It was the first-ever surreptitious grassroots union organizing effort by ACFTU. It was the first time ACFTU vigorously took on a foreign corporation, and what's more, the world's largest, and one that is notoriously antiunion. It was also the first time ACFTU discussed with foreign trade unions how to organize grassroots union branches.[13] But when the Walmart corporation decided to play ball with ACFTU and to recognize union branches at all its Chinese stores, ACFTU reverted to its earlier way of setting up union branches hand in hand with management and filled the stores' trade union committees with store management personnel. Often the human resources manager served as trade union chair.[14]

In 2008 ACFTU announced with much fanfare that the municipal trade union in Shenyang in northeastern China had signed a collective agreement with Chinese Walmart's head office. The agreement was to be a template for collective agreements for all Walmart stores in China. But workers gained little from the agreement, and when one of the few remaining genuinely elected Walmart store union chairs insisted on making some changes to the agreement, the city union sided with Walmart and he was forced out (Chan 2011, 213). Since then, there have been no reports that ACFTU has reintroduced anywhere in China the initial grassroots Walmart store-organizing model.

Recent reports reveal that workers at Walmart stores are usually paid no more than the minimum legal pay and often are forced to work extremely flexible work hours and do unpaid "voluntary" work. The result is a turnover rate of almost 100 percent a year at many stores. As a worker leaves, Walmart's new policy is to replace the position with two part-time workers to increase the proportion of casual staff, who have less protection under Chinese law. The majority of workers no longer are aware that there is a workplace trade union (Unger, Beaumont, and Chan 2011, 217–38).[15] But the Chinese press on occasion has continued to use Walmart as a model of direct elections.

The above three types of elections shared several features. No matter which of the stakeholders initiated and organized an election, workers' understanding of trade unionism was limited, having been exposed for the first time to new ideas of collective representation and democratic elections. Not having taken the initiative themselves, workers had difficulty sustaining any resistance when managers and union bureaucrats retook control of the union branches and workers committees. The space opened up for the new branches to operate had always been limited. For instance, Reebok would not include collective bargaining in the newly drawn-up union charter. The training program initiated by the international union federation allowed management personnel to be present at workers' training sessions and repeatedly emphasized to workers that the results should be win-win for both management and workers. In the case of Walmart, the secret organizing of union branches at some stores taught workers that their branch could operate independent of Walmart management, and indeed a small number of workers subsequently confronted Walmart to improve work conditions. But when ACFTU withdrew its support and made a cozy agreement with Walmart, these workers also soon had to capitulate.

This outcome did not deter ACFTU from continuing to uphold the grand project of holding direct elections. In June 2008, ACFTU announced that it would launch a "hundred-day focused action" to set up workplace unions in the suppliers of Fortune 500 corporations and their nebulous web of subsidiaries. Half of these China-based enterprises did not have unions. The plan's target was to organize 80 percent of them within three months, unionizing a total of ten thousand workplaces. Special task forces were to be sent to workplaces to unionize factories. This lightning speed of union organization could only be accomplished by a fallback to the traditional top-down method of setting up unions in "consultation" with management. Eight years after Reebok held the first democratic union election, ACFTU had come back full circle.

Trade Union Elections Initiated by Workers

Elections both Initiated and Organized by Workers—the Uniden and Ole Wolff Cases

Although ACFTU had not progressed much in reforming itself, the idea of workers' right to representation has emerged in the Chinese mass media and is taking root among workers. Cases of workers struggling to set up their own union branches are appearing. Two examples are discussed here to demonstrate the emergence of labor agency. Both cases set precedents, and the workers' strikes and their efforts to establish union branches were widely reported in the Chinese press.

Uniden is a Japanese MNC that manages an electronics factory in Shenzhen. The labor regime at this factory of sixteen thousand employees was reported to be harsh, and workers also encountered numerous problems with wages and excessive work hours. As early as 2000, groups of workers had demanded that a union branch be established, but were defeated (Chan 2010, 38–42). Between 2000 and 2005 five strikes erupted. Each time, the local government intervened on the side of management, ending with the firing of "troublemakers." In December 2004, workers mounted a fourth strike and presented management with fifteen demands, two of which were to set up a union branch and for management to promise not to retaliate by firing worker representatives (Feng 2004). Three days later at an open meeting, workers elected twelve representatives who went to negotiate with management. The latter promised a series of reforms including setting up a factory-level union branch by July 2005. But management almost immediately broke all of the promises and imposed harsher policies.

In April 2005, at a time when a wave of nationalist anti-Japanese rallies were sweeping across the country, almost all the factory's workers joined in a fifth strike. Security guards and the police were called in to beat up the strike leaders, provoking three days of large-scale confrontations between strikers and police. The organizers of the strike issued a number of open letters to local government bureaucracies and to management, and made good use of mobile phones and the Internet to coordinate their hourly and daily activities and to disseminate the latest developments to the public (Feng 2004). These reports and open letters provided a vivid picture of the scale and intensity of the struggle. A letter to the city mayor captured an emotional and violent strike scene:

> At 7 a.m. worker representatives were scheduled to assemble in the courtyard, but the moment they appeared security guards came to grab them and cordoned off the stage to prevent the women workers from coming close. But our women workers rushed up to protect their representatives. There was kicking and pushing . . . Screams and cries filled

the air and echoed inside and outside. Our Uniden women workers were so determined and strong. Many men workers were just standing there looking on. The women with tears in their eyes broke through the cordon and stood next to the representatives. They screamed, "running dogs, running dogs" at the security people and drove them out . . . Then everyone sat down and sang the Internationale, and when they reached the phrase "without the Communist Party there would not have been a new China," all ten thousand people sang with tears in their eyes . . . After that they signed their names to support the representatives. Four thousand seven hundred people signed it to demand a union (Shi 2008).

Management retreated by again promising to hold a union election, but soon afterward the local authorities arrested some of the leaders and their family members (Cody 2006). Left without leaders, workers became demoralized and lost control of the union election, which was controlled and manipulated from above. Nonetheless, the Uniden strikes were the longest repeated large-scale effort in China by migrant workers to organize themselves.

The second case was in October 2006 in Yantai city, Shandong province, at a small Danish-owned factory called Ole Wolff Electronics. A protest by 110 workers (mostly women) erupted over poor work conditions and the firing of local workers who were to be replaced by migrant workers. To "protect their rights," the workers signed a letter requesting that a union branch be established, and when management stonewalled they went on strike. In reaction, management drove fifty workers out of the factory dormitory and fired six activists. The incident was reported in the local newspaper. When ACFTU in Beijing learned about this, it openly declared that the workers had the right to set up a union branch. At one point the striking workers were in contact with one of ACFTU's leaders in Beijing by mobile phone who flew to the Shandong provincial capital to instruct the provincial union to support the Ole Wolff unionization effort. On the twelfth day of the strike, the workers held an election and announced the formation of the Ole Wolff union branch, which the provincial union recognized. But once the strike ended, management and the local district union did not cease harassing the union branch officials and labor activists. The district union forbade the new union from seeking collective bargaining. Management proceeded to fire fifty workers. The workers phoned ACFTU in Beijing for help, but ACFTU was no longer supportive. The fight dragged on until the remaining workers became tired, divided, and demoralized. Management intimidated them into signing documents agreeing not to go on strike again.

In early 2009, the case was reported in the Danish press, and the Ole Wolff company came under intense pressure back home. Later that year, with the help of a Danish trade union, the laid-off workers sent a representative, a factory electrician-turned-paralegal named Zhang Jun, to Denmark to negotiate with Ole Wolff, the factory owner.[16] A settlement was reached and the fired workers received some compensation. But not long after, Wolff moved his factory to Guangdong.

The above is only a brief summary of a lengthy and complicated three-year dispute between a company, working hand-in-hand with a district union against a group of poorly educated women workers. Throughout the entire struggle, Zhang Jun sought to make use of China's legal statutes when he met with local authorities. Although he did not face threats of physical harm, in the end he was fired by his factory, blacklisted, and unable to find another job as an electrician (Liu 2010).

So far as I know, the Ole Wolff Union was the first trade union branch in China set up during a strike that was directly recognized by ACFTU. It created a precedent that a workplace union branch that was formed autonomously by workers was as legitimate as one set up by the official union. It was also the first time a workplace trade union representative travelled abroad to seek justice from a foreign factory owner. It reflects how international publicity and modern transportation are shortening the physical and psychological distance between the workers at the bottom and the MNC owner at the head of the supply chain.

Elections Initiated by Workers but Organized by the Trade Union—the Nanhai Honda Case and the Ohms Case

Although Walmart store workers had not been able to take advantage of ACFTU's widely publicized unionization campaign, it changed the public discourse in China about trade union elections. ACFTU no longer openly denounced calls from below for genuine representation, as seen in the Ole Wolff case.

In that sense the groundwork was already laid for workers at the Nanhai Honda transmission auto parts plant in Guangdong province when they went on strike in May 2010. The initial demand was for a large pay raise. When Japanese management would not concede and the existing trade union chair opposed the workers and behaved obsequiously with management, the striking workers added one more demand—an election to select a new trade union committee and chair. Whereas the higher levels of ACFTU are wary about suppressing workers for making such demands, the local district union sometimes pursues different interests. The district trade union where the Honda plant is located is no more than one of the departments of the local city-district government, which had no sympathy for the striking workers. The district union hired a crowd of thugs armed with batons and unleashed them to suppress the workers. Photos and videos of the thugs in action went viral on the web in China, and the violent scenes were picked up by the international news media. The deputy chair of the provincial union stepped in and offered to assist the workers to negotiate with management. The Guangzhou city government, which owned half of the Honda joint venture, was also eager to end the strike, as the production stoppage in the parts plant had halted production in the giant Guangzhou Honda assembly plant and at three Honda assembly plants elsewhere. The CEO of the city-owned Guangzhou Automobile Group went in person to the striking auto-parts plant to negotiate with Japanese management. In the end the workers achieved a raise of 33 percent and the promise of a genuine election of the union branch committee (Chan 2014).

But the provincial trade union took a few months before setting up election procedures. By then the workers' emotional commitment had subsided, and when the provincial trade union suggested that the incumbent trade union chair should continue in his job till he served his term, the workers did not object. An election was then held, but the newly elected union committee was swept up mostly by management staff (Lau 2012; Chan and Hui 2014).

The provincial union, having publicized its initial intervention as a great success in negotiating a peaceful settlement to the strike (as opposed to ending it by suppression), intervened a second time in 2011 to engage in a scheduled round of collective bargaining. It put pressure on management to ensure workers again gained something. But in the third round in March 2013, the wage negotiations encountered problems. About a hundred workers from one department went on strike dissatisfied with management's wage-increase formula that privileged upper-level employees over frontline workers—an 18 percent increase for the top rank, but only 10 percent for the lowest rank. The strike was over in a day when the 10 percent was increased to 14 percent (Liu 2013). The strike attracted media attention because Nanhai Honda was still under public scrutiny.

Initially the Nanhai Honda strike was portrayed by both academic researchers and the mass media as a watershed in recent Chinese labor history. Labor scholars have written about it as a manifestation of heightened worker consciousness, organizational ability, and determination that enabled the workers to hold out for seventeen days and won. However, as in the other cases documented in this chapter, the Nanhai Honda workers did not break through party control to choose their own trade union chair, nor did they show a consciousness or determination to persist in this demand (Chan and Siu 2012). The collective bargaining that ensued was "party-state led" (Chan and Hui 2013). Time and time again, ACFTU's bottom line was that workers should not be allowed to select their own union branch committee, even when elections were allowed.

The Walmart campaign at its initial stage was the only time ACFTU initiated and organized genuine elections, and that was very short-lived.

Two years after the original Honda Nanhai strike, another strike that drew much attention erupted at Ohms, a Japanese-owned electronics factory in Shenzhen. In 2012 more than seven hundred out of the plant's eight hundred workers went on strike, presenting management with twelve demands to raise wages and improve work conditions and also to elect their own trade union committee. At the time, the trade union chair was the personnel department manager (Anonymous 2012). When the dispute remained unresolved, the city and district union offices descended on the factory to provide "guidance" and helped workers to organize a "direct election" (Liu Bin 2012). Two months later seventy-four newly elected worker representatives in turn elected a new ten-member union branch committee. The original union chair was voted out (as had been the case at the two Reebok elections) and was replaced by a shop-floor production leader. The mass media covered the election in detail, complete with a large number of photos, indicating that Ohms had been selected by the Shenzhen trade union to serve as a model. Indeed, the Shenzhen union soon announced that the Ohms direct election had marked a new stage in trade union elections (Li 2013). Generating favorable publicity for management as a strategy in this case is not a first by any count. But after the city union's endorsement of the Ohms election, it was announced that 163 enterprises in Shenzhen, which each has over a thousand employees, would undergo the same direct election procedure.

Unfortunately, the new Ohms trade union chair quickly showed that he leaned more on the side of management than representing the workers. At a press conference immediately after the election, he expressed gratitude to management for coming to observe the election and said that he would promote a win-win situation with management, adding that because there was a big cultural gap among the workers, as their trade union chair it was his responsibility to guide them to build a harmonious relationship in which the "enterprise loves its employees" and "employees love their enterprise" (Tao 2012). He had no qualms about expressing contempt for his union members' low social status. Less than a year after the election, 106 workers handed a "letter of suggestion" to the local district union applying for permission to recall this new factory union chair (An Ohms Worker 2013). Blogs and miniblogs claimed the city and district trade union had manipulated the election a year earlier, and that shortly after that election, strike activists had been demoted. Workers claimed that the factory union chair had been inactive since the election, that requests during and after the strike to restructure the wage system fell on deaf ears, and that the union branch let management use 20,000 RMB of union money to hold management-sponsored activities. It was claimed he also failed to act when twenty-two workers eligible to sign ongoing contracts were dismissed and were cheated out of their full sever-ance pay by management. The furious workers got the attention of mass media by mounting the roof of the factory and threatening to jump (China Labour Bulletin 2013).

The district union authorities refused the requests to recall the factory's union chair. If the union chair in this high-profile case could be dumped by the workers who elected him, it would open a floodgate to similar demands, since there are an uncountable number of pro-management trade union chairs in China.

Each of the cases described in this chapter set a precedent, though none succeeded in building an accountable workplace union branch. The cases point to two posi-tive outcomes, however. In a little over a decade, starting with scant awareness of labor rights and trade unionism as a vehicle for change, workers' consciousness of the importance of collective representation in the form of democratically elected trade unionism is emerging. The second positive development is that despite ACFTU's initial resistance to workers having any say in choosing their own union branch committees, starting with the Reebok elections in 2001 ACFTU publicly, though grudgingly, began to recognize the principle of what it calls "direct" elec-tions. "Direct," as opposed to "democratic," harmonizes with ACFTU officials' belief that workers should not be entitled to their own representation that can bargain with, rather than consult with, management. It is ACFTU's prerogative to consult with management. The way to prevent workers from choosing their own representatives is to control or to manipulate the choice of candidates running in elections. Chinese workers to date are only beginning to realize the critical nature of the election process and have yet to organize cross-workplace, cross-trade, or cross-regionally to demand their right to choose their own candidates. Apart from structural constraints, as argued by Chris Chan (2014), Chinese workers' collective consciousness is still in its infancy when placed in historical context (Chan and Siu 2012). But the legitimation of elected representation since 2001 has opened up new possibilities for workers to express demands with less fear of repression.

In elections that were not initiated by workers, labor played a passive role; in elections that were initiated by workers, labor instigated elections through strikes. In the former, since the workers were passive actors, the gains could easily and quietly be withdrawn, as in the Reebok and Walmart cases. Yet even when workers themselves seize the initiative, they have difficulty maintaining the momentum and in the end their efforts are undermined and collapse. The Ole Wolff and Uniden struggles are prime examples. What some workers do gain are experience, organizational capacity, strategic acumen, the feeling of emancipa-tion from daily drudgery, and the elation of discovering labor solidarity and a sense of empowerment. These are the building blocks of labor movements. It allowed both the Ole Wolff workers and the Uniden workers to repeatedly mount a resurgence in actions for several years before they were finally defeated.

At this stage in the development of China's labor politics, courage and persistence on the part of workers are the necessary ingredients to overcome an external environment that is still very hostile to such workers' new-found assertiveness. That is why all these cases are isolated incidents, almost one of a kind. An overall supportive environment is missing. For instance, despite all the good will of Jill Tucker to give workers a voice, the Reebok project ultimately relied on workers to continue to struggle on their own and a hope of subsequent participation by other multinational corporations to provide a level playing field among competing companies. The higher levels of the union traditionally have provided no institutional support. As Zhang Jun, the legal consultant of the Ole Wolff workers, reminisces today, ACFTU backed them initially only because in 2006 the union was engaging in a publicity campaign about the Walmart elections and could not very well simultaneously crush the Ole Wolff workers. It will take some years before both the subjective and objective environments can mature. In the meantime workers have been learning to persist, as they did at Ohms when they called for a union chair reelection.

This chapter has suggested that ACFTU is not supportive of such reelections, nor are district unions likely any time soon to cease neutering elected factory union branches. Nor have multinational corporations been successful in efforts to let workers hold democratic elections for union branches. Nonetheless, the multinational corporations' CSR initiative, which began as a public-relations exercise, started a chain reaction that forced ACFTU to recognize the validity of holding union branch elections.

Part IV
A WAY FORWARD?

THE SUSTAINABLE APPAREL COALITION AND HIGG INDEX

A New Approach for the Apparel and Footwear Industry

Jason Kibbey

In the early 1990s, broad stakeholder concern over the prevalence of sweatshops compelled apparel and footwear companies to build individual compliance programs to manage the social and labor performance of their supply chains. These programs focused primarily on auditing factories to determine if they complied with company codes of conduct and local laws. This approach has proven to be very expensive for factories and brands alike, yet the overall effectiveness at achieving workers' rights remains in question. Although there has been clear progress on issues such as child labor and overtime, recent tragedies demonstrate unacceptable failures in protecting the basic safety of workers despite the prevalence of compliance programs. Further, despite significant investment in compliance programs over the past twenty-five years, satisfaction with the effectiveness of these programs remains low for both brands and manufacturers, and there is very little academic research that documents improvements in the lives of workers from this approach.

When leading companies began working on environmental sustainability (including energy, water, waste, biodiversity, land use, and chemistry management) they recognized that the "go it alone" approach (each company developing its own system) used for social compliance would not be sufficient to achieve systemic change for environmental sustainability. They needed to work together to achieve systemic improvement in energy use, water and air quality, and waste reduction. If collaboration at scale could be demonstrated with environmental impacts, perhaps it could also be used for the elusive goal of achieving workers rights in the global apparel economy.

This chapter presents the Sustainable Apparel Coalition and its primary focus, the Higg Index, as a new mechanism for measuring and improving environmental and social conditions throughout the apparel and footwear value chain.

Early History of the Sustainable Apparel Coalition

Recognizing that individual compliance programs would not be scalable or cost effective for environmental sustainability, two unlikely collaborators—Yvon Chouinard, the owner of Patagonia, and John Fleming, the EVP of merchandising for Walmart—invited ten leading companies to work together to create a common mechanism for the measurement of sustainability throughout the apparel and footwear value chain. They wanted to use measurement as a vehicle to re-create the apparel manufacturing system. They eventually emerged with a vision of reducing negative environmental impact to a minimum and making the industry a positive force in the communities where it operated.

After an initial focus on environmental sustainability, the Sustainable Apparel Coalition expanded its scope to include social measurement. Because there were already so many social and labor assessments in use at the time the Coalition made the decision to expand its focus, the process of selecting social and labor indicators to assess performance took significantly longer than it did to develop environmental indicators. From the beginning, the Coalition imagined using holistic measurement with more depth and breadth than any industry-wide measurement initiatives in the past.

Sustainable Apparel Coalition Membership

Achieving the Sustainable Apparel Coalition's vision requires collaboration on a large scale. From the original ten companies, the Coalition now includes over one-third of the worldwide apparel turnover and leaders from throughout the industry. The membership goes beyond brands and retailers and includes leading manufacturers. The Coalition is built on the premise that collaboration must include the entire value chain—and key stakeholders as well. The hope is to rewrite the unfortunate history of telling those upstream to deal with problems while looking to absolve the downstream users of responsibility. The Coalition also includes industry partners such as associations and service providers that want to help scale this change. Finally, membership includes key stakeholders from NGOs, academic institutions, and even governments, which are crucial actors in creating improvement.

This scale of collaboration is still an experiment—but it seems a promising one. As of spring 2015 there were over 150 members (see appendix) from the entire value chain of the apparel industry and many of its stakeholders.

Theory of Change: The Higg Index

All Coalition members commit to using and developing the Higg Index, a suite of tools for measuring and managing the social and environmental impact of apparel and footwear products. The Higg Index is a holistic assessment that thoroughly measures all of the impact areas for apparel and footwear including social, labor, energy, water, waste, and chemicals management. The actors in the supply chain can thus take a long-term view of their impacts. Unfortunately the apparel industry has a history of working on only one issue at a time: focus on climate one year, chemicals the next, and worker safety the year after. Or, even worse, switching between issues before there has been progress on any one of them. These issues are too critical to simply be the focus of a year's work; they must be constantly managed for improvement. All of the impacts are interconnected and must be looked at as a whole.

Before they use the Higg Index for the first time, many companies and factories have no idea how well they manage their social or environmental impacts, let alone how well they compare with their peers. The Higg Index gives everyone—whether brand, manufacturer, or retailer—a starting point. It also gives them access to benchmarking so they can see how they rate against their peers in real time.

Origins of the Higg Index

The Sustainable Apparel Coalition believes in building on great work and not reinventing the wheel. The Higg Index came from the Outdoor Industry Association and the European Outdoor Group's Eco Index, Nike's Material Sustainability Index, the Global Compliance Program's Environmental Facilities Module, and tools from the Fair Labor Association and Social Accountability International's assessments. We started with what we thought were the best tools available and then tested, modified, and integrated them with one another to make the current Higg Index.

What the Higg Index Measures

Overall, the Higg Index seeks to measure all significant social and environmental indicators to assess how well businesses manage their social and environmental performance. For environmental impacts the Higg Index measures energy, water, waste, air emissions, chemistry, biodiversity, and land use. For social and labor impacts it measures practices around recruiting and hiring, compensation, work hours, worker involvement and communication, and worker treatment and development. Tables 12.1 and 12.2 list these indicators in greater detail for the environmental and social and labor facilities modules, respectively. The Higg Index also includes a brand module that examines business processes that have significant impacts on social and environmental performance, such as lead time and long-term commitments to vendors.

TABLE 12.1   Example assessment areas, environmental facilities module

ENERGY AND CARBON	WATER	AIR EMISSIONS	CHEMISTRY MANAGEMENT
· Energy efficiency · Energy usage · Fuel sources · Reductions · Management systems	· Water sources · Water management practices · Water quantity · Wastewater emissions (BOD, COD, toxics, ph, heavy metals, color, temperature, foam, nitrogen, oil and grease	· Particulate matter · NOx · SOx · VOCs · ODS · Toxic pollutants · Water vapor	· Restricted substances list · Chemical inventories · Regulatory awareness and management

TABLE 12.2   Example assessment areas, social and labor facilities module

RECRUITMENT AND HIRING	COMPENSATION	WORK HOURS	WORKER INVOLVEMENT AND COMMUNICATION	WORKER TREATMENT AND DEVELOPMENT
· Contracts · Labor laws · Preventing underage and forced labor · Antidiscriminatory processes · Equal opportunity practices · Training	· Payment method · Living wage · Wage calculation · Overtime · Wage information communication · Wage deductions · Benefits	· Hour limits · Voluntary overtime · Overtime limits · Days off · Management of worker hours	· Freedom of association · Collective bargaining · Workplace committees · Grievance processes · Worker participation in compliance audits · Suggestion box	· Antiharassment and antiabuse policies and practices · Disciplinary processes · Life skills · Counseling · Medical care · Diversity · Nondiscrimination

Production Phases

The Higg Index includes all stages of production when it measures brands, manufacturers, and products, including design, materials, cut and sew, packaging, transportation, use and service, and end of use. It also measures general business practices related to supplier engagement that correlate to social performance.

Focusing on just one part of production runs the risk of making very unsustainable products that give the appearance of being sustainable. This is where there is the greatest risk of greenwashing. For example, a shirt made of organic cotton may have been sewn in a facility with bonded labor. It might be dyed with chemicals that are harmful to both workers and the wearer of the shirt. It may have been flown via airfreight from South Asia to North America, thus depositing an incredibly large carbon footprint. This shirt isn't sustainable, but unless we look at all the stages of production, it could incorrectly be described as such in today's market. That is why the Higg Index includes all stages of production when it measures products.

Three Lenses for Assessing Impact: Brand, Facility, Product

The Higg Index measures social and environmental issues through the three different modules: a brand module, a facilities module, and a product module. The brand module measures all of the policies, procedures, and practices that determine the social and environmental impact of products. The facilities module measures the environmental and social management of the garment and footwear facilities, including final assembly and materials manufacturing. The product module looks primarily at the materials in apparel and footwear products and rates their sustainability performance. Social and labor issues are broadly measured in both the brand and facilities modules. Because fabric is often traded as a commodity with little traceability, there is insufficient credible information on the social conditions of fabric production to accurately measure and report the social impacts in the product module. Over the coming years as traceability significantly improves in the apparel and footwear value chain, the Sustainable Apparel Coalition expects this to change and will adjust its product module to reflect advances in access to information.

TRANSPARENCY

To be credible, scores need to be transparent and verifiable. Eventually they must be shared with all stakeholders, including consumers. The Sustainable Apparel Coalition wants everything in place so that every single product—every shirt, dress, and shoe—can be measured using the Higg Index. The information about social and environmental performance could be communicated to consumers through a hangtag on a product or by utilizing mobile or web technology.

VERIFICATION

In order to share social and environmental scores or other assessment information publicly with consumers or stakeholders, that information must be first verified by independent third parties. For self-assessments without verification, the Sustainable Apparel Coalition allows sharing only among value chain partners. Sharing such information more broadly without verification is a violation of the Higg Index's terms of use. The Coalition will begin pilot testing its verification methodology in the summer of 2015 and will finalize and scale verification in 2016. This will allow credible information to be shared throughout the value chain and with all of its stakeholders.

SCORING

Average scores on the Higg Index are set deliberately low so that they are seen as a place to move from and not an acceptable status quo. Average scores are typically in the range of 20–50 points out of 100. Even leaders do not typically score 100 on the Higg Index overall. Leadership scores typically fall in the range of 50–70 (out of 100) points. The goal of the scoring is to be aspirational and create an incentive for all players in the system to improve their performance and to incentivize the long-term investment that leads to system change. By using scores set deliberately low, the Higg Index lays out a roadmap for improvement for the entire industry.

Higg Index vs. Traditional Compliance Methodology

The Higg Index is not a classic compliance model in which companies either pass or fail an audit. The Sustainable Apparel Coalition believes that the assessment itself should be aspirational. It points the way to the future. It shows where the entire industry should go over the next ten years. The industry needs to move beyond using a successful audit as an excuse to not do anything else. Passing should be the starting point, not the finish line.

That's why assessment starts with compliance as the baseline. Performance is typically broken out into three different levels. Level one is basic compliance and understanding of key concepts. Level 2 is management and improvement of key impact areas. Level 3 is leading practices and innovation where brands and manufacturers embrace leading practices with the largest potential for positive impact and push the limits of what is currently possible. The eventual goal is for all actors in the system to reach a level of leadership that achieves significant system change.

Web Tool and Bi-Directional Information Flow

Using the Sustainable Apparel Coalition's web tool, companies fill out their assessments, see and understand their supply chains, and compare themselves against others. We believe benchmarking is a critical driver of change. People in clothing companies are competitive. The first time the Coalition announced the average scores and companies could see how they were doing compared with their peers, you could hear a pin drop in the room. The expectation is that benchmarking and transparency is most likely to bring up the bottom performers rather than increase the scores of top performers.

Decision makers up and down the value chain use information that is shared in both directions. Traditionally information flows downstream from facilities to brands and retailers. The Coalition's web platform shares the information upstream as well as downstream so that facilities receive transparency into how effective a brand is in measuring for social and environmental impact. The methodology was designed to share responsibility for improvement throughout the supply chain. Many impacts begin with decisions at the brand level and can't be solved by a factory alone. Similarly, brands must understand where problems are likely to develop with their supply chain partners in order to improve overall social and environmental responsibility.

Higg Index Is a Tool and a Starting Point

The assessment tools of the Higg Index are still an experiment. They represent the collective work of the entire value chain from manufacturers and chemical companies to brands and NGOs. These powerful players created the tools. The Sustainable Apparel Coalition facilitates the constant evolution of the tools.

The Higg Index is only a tool for change, it is not the change itself. The Coalition's value proposition is relatively simple: get the apparel and footwear industry and its stakeholders to agree on how to measure and improve the social and environmental impact of the industry, create a baseline measurement, and ensure improvements every single year. After launching the Higg Index at the end of 2013, the industry completed its baseline measurements during 2014. During the coming years, it will need to demonstrate improvement to validate the Coalition's theory of change.

Ultimately, the Coalition's work requires moving beyond building tools to *using* them and seeing improvement. For an apparel and footwear industry to be an agent of *positive* change instead of *harm*, the measurement systems must demonstrate real change on the ground.

Appendix: Sustainable Apparel Coalition Members as of May 2015

BRANDS

adidas
Asics
Brooks
Burberry
Columbia
Desigual
Disney
ECCO
EILEEN FISHER
Esprit
Fast Retailing
Fenix Outdoor Group
HanesBrands
IC Group
IKEA
KEEN

Kering
Levi Strauss & Co.
Loomstate
Lululemon Athletica
Madura Fashion & Lifestyle
Malwee
Marmot
New Balance
Nike
OHLIN/D
Patagonia
Pentland Brands
PUMA
PVH Corp.
Threads for Thought
VF Corporation

RETAILERS

ANN INC
C&A
Gap, Inc.
H&M
Inditex
Kohl's Department Stores
L. L. Bean, Inc.
Macy's

Mountain Equipment Co-op
N Brown Group
Primark
REI
Target
Walmart
Williams-Sonoma Inc.

MANUFACTURERS

1888 Mills
Advansa
Allied Feather and Down
Archroma
Artistic Milliners
Arvind Mills
Avery Dennison
Bayer Material Science
Bemis

Birla Cellulose
Charming Trim
CRAiLAR
Crystal Group
CWS-boco
Downlite
DuPont
DyStar
Esquel Group

Freudenberg Vildona
Gildan
Hanbo Enterprises Holdings Ltd
Hirdaramani Group
Hong Kong Non-Woven Fabric Ind.
 Co., Ltd
Huntsman
Indo Count
Invista
KG Denim
Lands' End
L&E International
Lenzing
Li & Fung Limited
Lubrizol
Makalot Industrial Company
MAS Holdings
Novozymes

Pinneco Research Ltd
Polygiene
Pratibha Syntex Limited
PrimaLoft
Ramatex Group
Rubia Natural Colours
The Rudholm Group
Saitex International
Sympatex
TAL Apparel
Teijin Fibers Limited
Tiong Liong Corporation
Toray Industries
Wah Fung Group
WL Gore & Associates
Yunus Textile Mills
Yu Yuang Group

INDUSTRY AFFILIATES

American Apparel & Footwear
 Association
bluesign technologies ag
Bureau Veritas
Control Union Certifications
Cotton Connect
Cotton Incorporated
Cradle to Cradle Products Innova-
 tion Institute
European Outdoor Group
FITI
FLO-CERT
GreenEarth Cleaning

Indicate
International Wool Textile
 Organisation
MGH Group
Oeko-Tex
Outdoor Industry Association
RESET Carbon
SCS Global Services
SGS
Valora
Verité
Xeros Cleaning

NONPROFIT, GOVERNMENT, AND EDUCATION

Aid by Trade Foundation
Better Cotton Initiative
C&A Foundation
Caux Round Table
Danish Fashion Institute
Deutsche Gesellschaft für
 Internationale

Duke Center for Sustainability
 and Commerce
Environmental Defense Fund
Fair Trade USA
Fairtrade International
Glasgow Caledonian University
MADE-BY

Natural Resources Defense
  Council
Solidaridad Network
Stockholm International Water
  Institute
The Sustainable Fashion
  Academy
Sustainable Fashion Business
  Consortium

The Swedish School of Textiles
Textile & Fashion Industry
  Training Centre Textile
  Exchange
University of Delaware
US Environmental Protection
  Agency
Utrecht University
World Resources Institute

LEARNING FROM THE PAST

The Relevance of Twentieth-Century New York
Jobbers' Agreements for Twenty-First-Century
Global Supply Chains

Mark Anner, Jennifer Bair,
and Jeremy Blasi

Weeks after the horrific April 24, 2013 collapse of the Rana Plaza garment factory
building in Bangladesh that killed 1,138 workers, a handful of apparel brands
and retailers signed a breakthrough factory inspection agreement with two
global union federations. By the second anniversary of the Rana Plaza tragedy,
this agreement—the Accord on Fire and Building Safety in Bangladesh (here-
after Accord)—had more than two hundred signatories. The Accord is the first
legally binding, sector-wide agreement to impose obligations on Western firms
to improve labor conditions in their overseas contract factories. Among other
duties, the Accord requires that signatory companies be inspected by an independent team of fire and building safety experts; that any threats to health and
safety identified by inspectors be remediated; and that workers be included in the
inspection and remediation process.

Marking the six-month anniversary of the Accord, Philip Jennings, the general secretary of the service-sector Union Network International (UNI Global
Union) declared: "The Accord now covers more than 1,600 factories and will
provide safety for millions of workers. This new dawn rose out of these ruins,
and we will never forget it" (IndustriALL 2013). In this chapter, we will illustrate that, although the Accord does represent a "new dawn" for Bangladeshi
garment workers in that it provides a new approach for addressing sweatshop
issues in global supply chains, the model it represents is not novel in the history of the sweated trades. Indeed, one of the reasons we believe the approach
holds so much promise is that it reflects core elements of what is, to our

knowledge, the most successful effort to systematically eradicate sweatshop conditions in any nation's apparel industry. As we describe, the negotiation of collectively bargained contracts, or jobbers' agreements, between workers, contractors, and lead firms, which ensured fair prices and stable orders in the domestic apparel supply chain, was the key force behind a dramatic decline in sweatshop conditions in the US apparel industry during the middle part of the twentieth century.

We revisit the history of jobbers' agreements in order to situate the Bangladesh Accord and other campaigns for buyer responsibility agreements with global brands and retailers in a much longer struggle against sweatshops. The downward pressure that pervasive subcontracting networks put on garment workers' wages and work conditions is not a new problem unique to the era of economic globalization. Indeed, it is as old as industrial apparel production itself. The principal root cause of sweatshop conditions, then and now, can be found in the sourcing practices of the buyers that coordinate these supply chains.

If the sourcing strategies of powerful buyers are the driving force behind poor labor conditions, then an effective solution to this problem requires the regulation of buyer practices. We develop this point by drawing out the parallels between contemporary supply chains and the emergence of domestic subcontracting networks in New York's Garment District during the early twentieth century. The centerpiece of the strategy to eradicate New York's sweatshops was jobbers' agreements—contracts negotiated by the International Ladies' Garment Workers' Union (ILGWU) and companies called "jobbers" that, much like today's brands, designed, but did not manufacture, apparel. Under the jobbers' agreements, jobbers were held contractually "jointly liable" for wages and work conditions in their contractors' shops. The history of the jobbers' agreements, we argue, holds crucial lessons about how to regulate the power of lead firms vis-à-vis their suppliers in today's global supply chains.

In the sections that follow, we begin by outlining some of the causes for persistent and pernicious sweatshop practices and by reviewing some of the scholarly debate about possible solutions to them. We then focus on the mid-twentieth-century jobbers' agreements in the United States: how they came about, how they functioned, and what they achieved. The final section explores similarities between the jobbers' agreements and current approaches to labor conditions and workers' rights, including the Accord, and suggests additional steps that might be taken to address the sweatshop practices that for too long have forced millions of workers to toil in unsafe buildings and endure low pay, excessive overtime, and inhumane production quotas.

Sweatshops: Root Causes and Proposed Solutions

Over the last two decades, competition in the global apparel industry has intensi-fied as a result of an end to World Trade Organization-mandated controlled trade in textile products, the resulting explosion of production in China and then Viet-nam, and the consolidation of major buyers and especially retailers in the apparel supply chain (Abernathy et al. 1999; Chan 2003; Gereffi and Frederick 2010; Bair and Gereffi 2011). China's share of the US import market (by volume), increased from 13.55 percent in 1989 to 42.03 percent in 2014. In 2014, Vietnam was the second-largest apparel exporter to the United States (10.73 percent), with Ban-gladesh in third place (6.28 percent).[1] Changes in the global geography of apparel production occurred alongside changes in the organization of the apparel mar-ket in importing countries such as the United States, where consolidation and growth at the retail end of the apparel supply chain over the past several decades has led to "the overwhelming domination of the market by a handful of enor-mous retailers" (Milberg 2008, 420).

Technological changes and the advent of lean retailing further facilitate the expression of buyer power among major retailers (Abernathy et al. 1999). Today's manufacturers must manage much shorter lead times because retailers, rather than stocking extra items in store inventory, prefer to use point of sale technology to track purchases and reorder replacements on a continual basis. Some buyers even expect their large suppliers to track retail sales themselves so that they know when and how many of each item to replenish. One of the most direct impacts of the shift to shorter lead times, more styles, and more volatile orders is in the area of working hours. Forced, excessive, and inadequately com-pensated overtime is an endemic problem in the global apparel industry (Locke 1992; Piore 1997).

Our research has shown that, as the real dollar price per square meter of apparel entering the United States declined by 48 percent from 1989 to 2010, there was a corresponding decline in respect for workers' rights in top apparel exporting countries.[2] In our view, the paired trends shown in figure 13.1 reflect that, as brands and retailers seek out suppliers to produce their products at the lowest price and with the quickest turnaround, suppliers experience greater pres-sure to violate the internationally recognized rights to freedom of association and collective bargaining, and the governments that regulate supplier factories and enforce labor laws experience increased pressure to ignore such violations. Because labor is the most significant production cost in apparel assembly, violat-ing these rights reduces union strength, and thus weakens a key mechanism for increasing wages and benefits and enforcing legal protections such as prohibi-tions on forced and excessive overtime.[3]

FIGURE 13.1   Unit price of US apparel imports

Source: Anner, Bair, and Blasi 2013

There is a growing consensus, at least among social scientists, that codes of conduct and auditing programs have failed to eliminate, or perhaps even substantially reduce, incidents of labor violations in global supply chains (Esbenshade 2004a; IDS 2006; Seidman 2007; Anner 2012a; Locke 2013). Yet there is considerable debate about what can be done about it. Richard Locke and his collaborators, for example, observe the failure of factory managers to utilize best practices in managing workflow and production challenges, leading to avoidable labor violations (Locke, Amengual, and Mangla 2009). Andrew Schrank and Michael Piore argue that labor inspectors, instead of acting like policemen when violations are detected, are more effective when they work with noncompliant factories in the role of "advisor or consultant," helping actors reconcile compliance with competitive pressures (Piore and Schrank 2006, 3). Locke also argues that improved work conditions and better respect for workers' rights can best be achieved by a mix of private voluntary regulation and public (national state) regulation (Locke 2013). Still others claim that the potential buying power of ethical consumers has not been leveraged in the fight against sweatshops (Robinson, Meyer, and Kimeldorf 2013). Studies of ethical consumption underscore the importance of educating shoppers about their options and creating market contexts that encourage them to make purchasing decisions that are consistent with their commitments to avoid sweated products (Hainmueller, Hiscox, and Sequeira 2011).

Although each of these prescriptions has merit, no approach can be truly effective unless it also targets the structural characteristics of the global apparel industry. In short, an effective strategy for fighting sweatshops must address the sourcing and pricing dynamics between suppliers and buyers and ensure that buyers' business practices do not undermine compliance by negatively affecting the terms and conditions of work at suppliers' factories. The question that remains is: How do we arrive at a fair pricing and stable sourcing mechanism that benefits workers? We argue that the answer lies in binding agreements negotiated between workers, suppliers, and buyers. There is a historical precedent for achieving such a mechanism. During much of the twentieth century, jobbers' agreements brought stability to subcontracting relations within the US apparel industry and went a long way toward eradicating sweatshop conditions in those regions where workers were organized.

Regulating Buyers: Jobbers' Agreements in the United States

The relationship between subcontracting and sweatshops dates back to the origins of industrial apparel production in the United States. The epicenter of the industry, New York City, was the birthplace of the so-called outside model of production, in which manufacturers contracted with small-scale independent sewing shops to produce some of the garments they designed and/or marketed. The outside model eventually surpassed the traditional "inside" system whereby manufacturers employed their own garment workers. Over time, it became so pervasive that a new term—"jobber"—was coined to refer to individuals and firms that designed or sold apparel, but did little to no manufacturing of their own. Already in 1893, a New York State Bureau of Labor inspector reported that, although "there were probably one hundred wholesale cloak houses" in the Garment District, "not over half a dozen provide their own factories and workshops" (Levine 1924, 17). As observed by Steve Fraser, jobbers "inhabited an economic underworld where chiseling, subterfuge, and tainted goods were the common currency." The outside manufacturer in early twentieth-century New York "defended his razor-thin margin of profit by means both legitimate and shady, but especially by exerting a constant downward pressure on wages and working conditions" (Fraser 1991, 26).[4] This downward pressure was exerted on independent sewing shops that the jobber contracted with, enabling him to better manage volatility and fluctuating demand, and eventually to avoid the union contracts that were becoming common in larger factories, thanks to a wave of historic strikes orchestrated by the rapidly growing ILGWU.

The ranks of the ILGWU increased in the early 1900s during a time of intense labor unrest, including a massive strike at the Triangle Shirtwaist Company in

1909. Two years later, in 1911, a fire at Triangle killed 146 workers, most of them young immigrant women. In the aftermath of the tragedy and the massive public response it provoked, the governor of New York created a commission to investigate factory safety and to make recommendations for improving worker health and welfare. One of the most active members of the factory investigating commission was its vice-chair, New York Assemblyman Alfred Smith. By 1913, sixty of the sixty-four laws recommended by the commission had been enacted.

In 1924, the now-governor Alfred Smith created another commission to investigate the apparel industry, this time in response to a period of protracted labor conflict and the looming threat of an industry-wide strike. In its final report, the members of this commission acknowledged that many of the problems in the industry were rooted in the outside system of production and the competition that pervasive subcontracting networks generated among sewing shops. They observed that the formal independence of the contractor and the jobber was belied by the former's reliance on the latter, emphasizing that the relationship should be viewed more in terms of substance than form: "By whatever name he may call himself, the jobber controls working conditions; he controls employment, and that element of control imposes upon him the responsibility that he shall so conduct his business that proper working standards may be upheld instead of undermined." The report went on to recommend changes to the structure of contracting relations as would "tend to regularize the flow of work into sub-manufacturing shops . . . cause closer relations between jobbers and manufacturers, and stabilize working conditions in the shop" (Stein 1977, 280–81). Yet these advisory recommendations were never implemented.

Changing the structural dynamics of the industry was imperative for the ILGWU. Cutthroat price competition among contractors not only created downward pressure on wages and work conditions but it also made it difficult for the union to organize workers because jobbers could easily move orders from an organized to a nonunion shop. Aware of the threat that subcontracting posed to organized labor, the ILGWU argued as early as 1923 that jobbers and contractors were part of an integrated process of production (Quan 2008b). As such, they should be jointly liable for wages and work conditions in contracting shops. The challenge confronting the union was how to institutionalize this liability. The solution it devised was the jobber's agreement: a collective bargaining agreement between the union local representing the garment workers in a factory and the buyer (i.e., jobber) whose apparel was being sewn in that shop.

Although the first jobbers' agreements were signed in the 1920s, they proved difficult to enforce, both because the process of negotiating contracts with individual buyers was time consuming and because jobbers were shifting orders out of the city to nonorganized factories, or "runaway" shops, in lower-cost regions such as northeastern Pennsylvania. This status quo persisted until 1933, when the passage of the National Industrial Recovery Act (NIRA) resulted in Codes of Fair Competition that essentially extended the logic of the jobbers' agreements to the entire industry. The Codes regulating the garment business recognized the principle of joint liability and specified that the prices paid by jobbers should be "sufficient to enable the contractor . . . to pay the employees the wage and earnings provided for in this Code, together with an allowance for the contractor's overhead" (Schlesinger 1951, 37). By the time the US Supreme Court ruled the NIRA unconstitutional in 1935, the ILGWU was strong enough to negotiate collective bargaining agreements that included some of the key provisions of the now-invalidated Codes. Organized labor's position was buttressed by other New Deal-era legislation, including the National Labor Relations (Wagner) Act of 1935 and the Fair Labor Standards Act of 1938.

Clearly, the political context created by the New Deal facilitated the ILGWU's growth during the middle third of the twentieth century and increased its ability to bring employers to the bargaining table. In this sense, the US state played an important role in the fight against domestic sweatshops. But what proved decisive was the union's strategic decision to leverage its new strength in pursuit of a specific objective—namely, negotiating collective bargaining agreements with both the apparel contractors that directly employed the union's members as well as the jobbers that, as clients of the contractors, indirectly employed garment workers.

As the ILGWU grew more powerful, both the contractors and the jobbers responded by forming associations of their own that could bargain collectively with the union. Employers' associations for jobbers and contractors were typically organized around a particular product and market niche. For example, in the dress segment of the industry, the National Dress Manufacturers represented jobbers of higher-priced dresses, the Affiliated Dress Manufacturers included midmarket jobbers, and the Popular Price Manufacturers was comprised of jobbers whose dresses were sold at lower prices. This structure was more or less reflected in the organization of the contractors; the employers' associations for dress contractors included United Popular Dress (low- to midmarket) and United Better Dress (mid- to upmarket) (Melman 1994). Agreements negotiated with these groups of employers provided more coverage than the early jobbers' agreements because they applied to all the companies that were members of the signatory association instead of just one firm.

Thus the New Deal marked a turning point in the ILGWU's battle against sweatshops. Within a decade, jobbers' agreements had become the lynchpin of an industrial-relations model described as triangular collective bargaining— so named because the goal was to regulate, via a set of paired contractors' and jobbers' agreements, relations between the three sides of the production triangle: the workers as represented by the union and the jobbers and contractors, each represented by their own employers association.

The implementation of jobbers' agreements had a significant and far-reaching impact on conditions of employment for unionized garment workers. In August 1938, *Life* magazine devoted a lengthy cover story to the transformation, noting that "thirty years ago the industry stank of the sweatshop and the cruelest kind of exploitation. Workers toiled 16 hours a day for $2 to $8 a week. Today, they get $15 to $35 for working 35 hours a week, only a few hours more than they once worked in two days."[5] Wages varied within the apparel industry, but the overall trend is clear: During the middle decades of the twentieth century, the earnings of garment workers—a heavily feminized and, at least in New York, largely immigrant workforce—kept pace with general manufacturing wages (Anner, Bair, and Blasi 2013).

Although it is true that the capacity of the federal and state departments of labor to enforce minimum wage and hour laws was much more robust during the heyday of the jobbers' agreements than it is today, such enforcement cannot explain the increase in garment worker earnings. This is evident from the fact that apparel wages during this period exceeded minimum wages by a large margin. Between 1947 and 1990, for example, annual average garment worker earnings never fell below 146 percent of the federal minimum wage, and in many years they were more than 200 percent of the minimum.[6] Indeed, somewhat remarkably for an industry that has become equated with low pay, by the late 1940s and early 1950s, apparel workers received the highest hourly rate in the nondurable goods sector, according to data compiled by the US National Compensation Survey. Thus, while national and state minimum wage laws provided a wage floor, the jobbers' agreements secured earnings for workers far beyond those guaranteed by governmental regulation.

The wage premium is one important indication of the impact of jobbers' agreements, but their achievements were even more striking in the area of benefits. For example, Joel Seidman finds that the union "used its bargaining power to achieve a comprehensive system of welfare programs, including retirement pay, severance pay, weekly supplementary benefits, and hospital, disability, and medical benefits— *all of them entirely financed by employer contributions*" (Seidman 1968, 62, emphasis added). Working hours was another area where the jobbers' agreements left their mark: in an industry notorious for chronic excessive overtime, in 1960 apparel employees were working an average of 36.3 hours a week, according to the National Compensation Survey. Indeed, apparel workers often recorded the shortest workweek of any sector in all the nondurable and durable goods sectors (Seidman 1968, 55). In sum, these data indicate that apparel workers, largely as a result of jobbers' agreements, were able to increase wages, extend benefits, and reduce hours of work well beyond what was stipulated by law.[7]

By 1959, the success of the jobbers' agreements in eradicating sweatshops was so universally recognized that no less a conservative than Senator Barry Goldwater would speak out in their defense on the Senate floor, stating: "We conferees are in the very peculiar position of every one of us agreeing that we do not intend to upset the status quo of the garment or apparel industries . . . I have been engaged in the retail end of this business all my life. I have watched what has happened in the garment section of New York and the garment section of Philadelphia and St. Louis and Chicago and on the west coast, and have seen sweatshops disappear. I have seen order come out of chaos. I have seen unions create profits for businesses which were unable to produce profits, and Mr. President, none of us wants to disturb for one second the status that the garment trade now occupies under the present law."[8] Goldwater's statements were made in the context of debate over the then-proposed Landrum-Griffin revisions to the National Labor Relations Act (NLRA). It was feared that the jobbers' agreements would be rendered illegal by a proposed amendment prohibiting "any labor organization and any employer to enter into any contract or agreement . . . to cease doing business with any other person."[9] The jobbers' agreements did just that: they required jobbers to contract only with unionized contractors.

Supporters of the jobbers' agreements insisted that the provision should not apply where the companies involved have a unity of interest through an integrated process of production. Senator Jacob Javits expressed his view that the "elimination of sweatshops" was "heavily attributable" to the system of joint liability.[10] And Senator John F. Kennedy argued that doing away with the right to negotiate jobbers' agreements would "invite chaos in the industry."[11] Ultimately, the amendment was passed, but a garment industry proviso was added to the NLRA, specifically exempting companies in the apparel industry from the hot cargo and secondary boycott prohibitions of the Act. In preserving the jobbers' agreements as an effective tool against sweatshops, Congress explicitly adopted the theory of the garment supply chain as an "integrated process of production" into federal law. Jobbers' agreements, which had already changed the way business in much of the apparel sector was conducted, had become institutionalized.

Core Elements of Jobbers' Agreements

Jobbers' agreements institutionalized the principle of buyer liability in three specific ways.[12] First, they prevented contractors from competing on labor costs by negotiating wages directly with the jobber. Second, they stabilized subcontracting relationships by requiring jobbers to register their designated contractors with the union. Third, they made jobbers directly liable for certain labor costs beyond wages. Our brief description of these policies enables an analysis of how the logic of the jobbers' agreement model might be replicable in today's globalized apparel industry.

Paying for Decent Labor Conditions

Decent work conditions in the US garment industry were not established until competition among contractors on the basis of labor price was arrested. The ILGWU accomplished this by reaching up to the top of the supply chain and negotiating the cost of labor directly with jobbers. The jobbers' agreements included numerous provisions detailing the jobbers' obligations for wages and work conditions in contracting shops. These included:

- Minimum wages by occupational category (sewer, cutter, presser, etc.), both for "week workers" (cutters, sample makers, etc.) and "piece-rate workers" (primarily sewing machine operators).
- A process for setting piece rates sufficient to yield the minimum wage for a sewer of average efficiency, as well as a process for resolving any disputes that might arise in the negotiation of these rates.
- Provisions triggering wage increases in the case of inflation or increases to the statutory minimum wage.
- Hours of work, including provisions regarding maximum permissible overtime and the compensation rules for overtime work.

To be sure, such provisions are hardly atypical of collective bargaining agreements, but it is important to emphasize that these provisions were included in the union's contracts with the jobber even though the jobber was not the direct employer of the workers.

The union also had a matching agreement with the employers' association representing apparel contractors, but this contract, which was signed after the jobber's agreement was finalized, repeated the language regarding wages and work conditions that had already been negotiated between the union and the jobbers' association. The sequencing of these negotiations reflected the fact that what the contractors were able to pay to their workers depended largely on what the contractors were, in turn, being paid by the jobber.

The jobbers' agreements also contained language regarding the price negotiation between the jobber and the contractor. Jobbers were obligated to pay prices sufficient to enable the contractor to pay workers the wages and earnings provided for in the agreement, in addition to a reasonable amount to cover the contractor's overhead and profit. Like other provisions, this requirement was subject to binding arbitration by an independent chairperson designated to resolve disputes in the industry.

In short, because all workers were required to be paid the wage levels spelled out in the contract regardless of where they worked, and because jobbers were required to pay all their contractors prices sufficient for these wages to be paid, contractors could no longer vie for a jobber's business by undercutting competitors' labor costs. Consequently, competition among contractors was based less on price than on quality and efficiency.

Regulating and Stabilizing Contracting Relations in the Supply Chain

The second central component of the system created through triangular bargaining was a regime for regulating and stabilizing relationships between jobbers and contractors. Specific provisions designed to achieve this objective included:

- Requiring jobbers to designate, at the outset of an agreement, all contractors that it intended to use during the course of the (typically three-year) agreement, and to register designated contractors with an administrative board comprised of representatives from the union and the jobbers employers' association.
- Restricting the supply of contractors that could be so designated to unionized shops.
- Permitting a jobber to register only the number of contractors actually required to manufacture its garments.
- Requiring jobbers to distribute work evenly across all designated contractors and prohibiting the use of new contractors except when additional capacity was needed.
- Prohibiting the discharge of a designated contractor for any reasons other than poor quality or late delivery.

The intent of these provisions was to promote long-term, stable relationships between jobbers and contractors. Just as the inclusion in jobbers' agreements of language regarding wages and work conditions in contracting shops was intended to arrest competition on the basis of labor costs, so too were the detailed clauses regulating the jobber-contractor relationship meant to preclude jobbers from constantly switching between contractors to secure a short-term advantage on price.

This system had a number of important consequences. First, it caused the buyer to consolidate its orders among a smaller number of contractors whose factories were then filled up with that jobber's work, or perhaps with orders from several buyers that were party to the same master jobber's agreement. The goal was to minimize dramatic fluctuations in the amount of work given to a contractor over the course of the year so that the contractor could provide steady employment and pay workers the wage levels established by the agreement. Second, it created a powerful incentive for individual contractors to accept unionization and to agree to the higher labor standards provided for in collectively bargained agreements because, by doing so, contractors gained the opportunity to become a designated supplier of one or more jobbers and consequently to gain access to steady orders at fair prices. Moreover, by stabilizing production contracts, it eliminated the need of contractors to rely on long hours, including forced overtime to meet short-term production goals. Indeed, stable contracts are what allowed the union to negotiate a 35-hour workweek for apparel workers.

Additionally, the close regulation of the contracting relationship (e.g., the requirement that orders be distributed evenly among contractors), the prohibition of discharge without cause, and the availability of a dispute resolution mechanism in the event of a disagreement between the buyer and the supplier gave all of the parties confidence in the bargain they had struck. Cheating on the part of jobbers through the placement of orders in nonregistered or nonunionized shops tended to be detected and sanctioned, including by the weapon of the so-called jobbers' strike.

Finally, because the registration period lasted for the life of the agreement (typically three years), and because designated contractors in good standing were assured steady business as long as the jobber had orders to give, the system enabled economic security for contractors and job security for workers. In short, the contractor registration system ensured that decent wages and conditions were feasible, incentivized contractors to agree to such conditions, and brought stability to interindustry relations that had been chaotic and chronically insecure.

Guaranteeing Payment to Workers

A third important aspect of the jobbers' agreements was that they held jobbers liable for direct payment of certain production costs. These provisions helped to ensure that workers received the compensation and benefits due to them in the occasion that their direct employer—the contractor—went belly up or absconded without paying them, a critical problem in the notoriously footloose garment industry.

First, the jobbers' agreements included provisions requiring jobbers to make direct contributions into benefit accounts for workers' pensions, healthcare, and accrued vacation. Under the jobbers' agreement system, employee benefits were paid not by the contractor, but rather by the jobber as the indirect employer of the contractor's workers. These funds were administered by the union, not the contractor, which made them portable—a desirable trait in an industry with high turnover among contractors and workers. Crucially, this design also ensured that significant liabilities did not accrue on poorly capitalized contractors. As a result, workers did not lose their benefits if their direct employer went under. Second, the jobbers' agreements held jobbers liable for a portion of unpaid wages in the case of abrupt contractor closure. Typically, jobbers were responsible for up to two weeks of compensation left unpaid by a bankrupting contractor.

The Decline of the Jobbers' Agreements

During the last third of the twentieth century, the globalization of textile and apparel manufacturing eroded the system of jobbers' agreements that had proved such a successful tool in the battle against sweatshops. At one level, geographical shifts in production were nothing new. Jobbers had long tried to circumvent union contracts by placing orders with unorganized contractors outside New York City and eventually outside the northeast. The union responded by launching organizing drives in these locations, and in this way, expanded its reach into new areas, including states in the mid-Atlantic and Midwest and even Puerto Rico. However, when new trade regimes encouraged US manufacturers to open factories in Mexico and the Caribbean basin, the union confronted an even greater challenge in organizing workers offshore.

Alongside the decision of traditional manufacturers to relocate or expand operations in lower-wage countries, the landscape of the industry was transformed by the emergence of "private label" (store-brand) lines by retailers and brands. Unlike traditional jobbers, most of whom started as apparel manufacturers, these new buyers had no history of garment production and have never negotiated a collective bargaining agreement with an apparel industry union. According to one long-time ILGWU organizer, the brands and retailers that dominated today's apparel industry "got into business by end-running or circumventing the jobber-contractor formula we had developed in the U.S." (Bair 2012, 14). In other words, by sourcing from overseas contractors, global buyers avoid having to pay for the kinds of labor standards that the ILGWU had, to a large degree, succeeded in imposing on the domestic industry through jobbers' agreements.

By the turn of the twenty-first century, it was clear that what began as an emergent trend toward offshore production by apparel manufacturers had morphed into the fundamentally new paradigm of global sourcing by retailers and brands. On the domestic front, this transformation is manifest in the twin trends of increasing import penetration and declining garment worker wages. Import penetration of the US apparel market rose modestly through the 1970s and then increased dramatically over the course of the next decade. Although unaffected by the initial rise in imports, real wages began a significant and protracted decline around 1980, such that by 1990 they were well below 1965 levels. Apparel employment tracked the decline in wages, particularly in New York City, where the number of garment workers plummeted from 140,000 in 1980 to about 90,000 in the mid-1990s, and to about 17,000 in the early 2000s (Ross 2002).

In addition, during the 1980s and 1990s, much of the industry relocated from New York to Los Angeles, where the workforce was largely immigrant (many undocumented) and nonunionized, and where, despite some significant victories for the union, the jobbers' agreement model had never fully taken root (Laslett and Tyler 1989; Bonacich and Appelbaum 2000).[13] The 1994 passage of NAFTA and the 2004 phaseout of the Multi-Fiber Arrangement further accelerated the decline of the domestic garment industry, leaving behind a truncated workforce that was highly vulnerable to threats of further capital flight.

By the turn of the twentieth century, the union was no longer signing new jobbers' agreements because so many jobbers had either closed or moved their business entirely offshore, essentially bringing to an end the system of joint liability that had regulated much of the domestic apparel industry for more than five decades.

A Joint Liability Model for Today's Global Supply Chains?

The jobbers' agreements of the mid-twentieth century in the United States did a remarkable job in reducing sweatshop practices. But are jobbers' agreements relevant for today's hypercompetitive, globalized apparel industry? We believe that they are. Indeed, one can see elements of jobbers' agreements in the strategies that workers, unions, anti-sweatshop activists, and states are developing in the struggle to address the persistence of pernicious sweatshop practices, such as the use of unsafe buildings that reduce production costs but increase worker deaths. These efforts include: (1) global framework agreements, (2) university codes of conduct and student corporate campaigns, (3) the Accord on Fire and Building Safety in Bangladesh, and (4) the International Union League for Brand Responsibility. We will examine each briefly.[14]

Global Framework Agreements

The most frequently cited contractual instrument to enforce labor rights are international or global framework agreements (GFAs). Negotiated between international union federations and multinational companies or global brands, these agreements outline labor rights commitments and provide a grievance structure for contesting violations of these commitments. More than fifty GFAs have been signed since 1988 in numerous sectors, including manufacturing, telecommunications, agriculture, and retail. However, to date only two of these cover apparel production workers (Stevis and Fichter 2012).

One of these was a GFA negotiated in 2007 by the International Textile, Garment and Leather Workers' Federation (ITGLWF) and Inditex, the Spanish company that designs and markets the apparel brand Zara. In their analysis of the ITGLWF-Inditex agreement, Gregoratti and Miller underscore both the promise and the limitations of GFAs as tools in the fight against sweatshops. On the one hand, they find evidence that this agreement has been used effectively to remediate violations of workers' right to freedom of association by contractors in individual cases. However, they also concluded that Inditex's failure to maintain consistent production levels or adjust its prices to accommodate increased production costs impeded factory-level bargaining and undermined the sustainability of improvements (Gregoratti and Miller 2011). GFAs do not contain any substantive provisions regulating the sourcing or pricing practices of the lead firm itself, such as the requirements included in jobbers' agreements that buyers make long-term commitments to suppliers and pay prices consistent with decent wages.

As is typical of GFAs, neither of the GFAs in the apparel industry includes binding arbitration clauses or other formal processes for resolving disputes between the signatories in the event that they cannot be resolved through dialogue. In sum, GFAs are like jobbers' agreements in that they are negotiated agreements between companies and organized labor over labor rights issues along these companies' supply chains, but they differ from jobbers' agreements in three important ways: they do not address issues of pricing and contract stability, they typically do not involve contractors in the negotiating stage, and they lack robust and binding enforcement mechanisms.

University Codes of Conduct and Student Corporate Campaigns

As a result of strong and persistent student campaigns, since 2000, most major universities in the United States and Canada have incorporated supply chain codes of conduct in their trademark licensing contracts with major athletic apparel firms such as adidas and Nike, a US$4 billion-a-year business (Feather-stone and USAS 2002). Unlike corporate codes of conduct, which do not subject the brands adopting them to any explicit legal obligations, university codes of conduct are unique in that they impose binding duties on the brands to ensure labor standards compliance by their suppliers. These duties are incorporated into business contracts between the universities and the licensees; failure to comply is a breach of contract.

Several developments emerging from the university codes of conduct effort are especially noteworthy. In 2010, Knights Apparel, following a joint campaign by union activists in the Dominican Republic and student activists in the United States, launched a new line of university-licensed apparel, Alta Gracia. Clothing sold under the Alta Gracia label is manufactured at a factory in the Dominican Republic with labor standards that far exceed the industry norm and where workers' rights to organize and bargain collectively are fully respected. To enable these conditions, Knights committed to pay prices that enable the factory to pay workers three times the prevailing wage, to maintain consistent production volumes so that these higher wages can be paid year round, and to respect the right of workers to unionize and bargain collectively (Kline and Soule 2011).

In 2013, Alta Gracia merchandise registered US$11 million in sales, and by 2015 it was anticipated that workers would receive a share in annual profits through a bonus system that was negotiated by workers with management in the firm's first collective bargaining agreement (Kline and Soule 2014).[15] As of April 2015, Alta Gracia had 170 employees, up from 135 employees previously, and the Alta Gracia line of collegiate apparel had a presence in over a thousand college and university bookstores. As an indication of its plans to move beyond a sole reliance on the collegiate market, the company also signed a contract with the National Hockey League.[16]

In another major development, the Central General de Trabajadores (CGT) of Honduras concluded a series of agreements with the apparel giant Fruit of the Loom and its subsidiary, Russell Corporation, resolving a controversy surrounding Russell's closure of a factory in which workers had attempted to organize a union.[17] In October 2009, following an investigation by the Worker Rights Consortium, an intense student campaign, and several months of negotiations with Honduran union leaders, Russell's parent company, Fruit of the Loom, agreed to open a new factory to replace the one it had shuttered and to rehire the closed plant's 1,200-plus employees, to pay each of the workers affected by the closure nine months' back pay ($2.5 million in total), to not oppose future organizing drives (a union "neutrality clause"). and to provide the Honduran union CGT with access to workers at all of its Honduran facilities.

The agreement with CGT also outlines a process of third-party mediation and arbitration that makes fulfillment of these commitments enforceable in US courts (Greenhouse 2009). The Knights Apparel and Russell agreements are similar to jobbers' agreements in that the cost of decent pay and work conditions is assumed by the lead firms. However, whereas jobbers' agreements imposed higher standards on a group of employers, thus leveling the playing field, today's lead firms must compete with other buyers whose products are being manufactured by workers in many countries who earn less and who lack proper union representation.[18]

Accord on Fire and Building Safety in Bangladesh

The most significant recent development to impose substantive, binding obligations on apparel buyers is the Accord on Fire and Building Safety in Bangladesh. The Accord is explored more fully in chapter 1 in this volume and it is not necessary to review its details here. What is relevant for our discussion is to point out that there are at least four key ways in which the Bangladesh Accord reflects core principles of the historical jobbers' agreements. First, like the jobbers' agreements of yesteryear, the Accord requires signatory brands and retailers to make multi-year commitments to their suppliers in Bangladesh, and makes the brands and retailers responsible for ensuring that these suppliers are financially capable of complying with the applicable labor standards: signatory firms may adjust prices or use various other means to ensure that factories have the financial capacity to comply with remediation requirements. (The extent to which signatory companies are complying with this requirement remains to be seen.)

Second, the Accord calls for workers' representatives to be fully equal and empowered participants in the implementation of agreements. The steering committee comprises three union representatives (one from each of the two global union federations that signed the agreement and a representative of the Bangladeshi labor movement) and three representatives of participating companies. Third, as in jobbers' agreements and collective bargaining agreements generally, these commitments are not merely general statements of intent, but rather legally enforceable obligations. Disputes that arise under the Accord may be resolved through binding arbitration; any arbitral award could then be enforced in a court of law of the home country of the party against whom enforcement is sought. Finally, like the jobbers' agreements, the Accord covers a broad portion of the industry. Its more than two hundred signatories include many of the world's leading global brands and retailers, sourcing from sixteen hundred factories in Bangladesh. A high level of density is important because it means that increased costs resulting from the agreement will not put any participating company at a competitive disadvantage relative to any other signatory, thereby easing implementation.

To be sure, the Accord is limited compared with the original jobbers' agreements, covering only one area of labor standards—namely, worker safety—and applying to facilities in only one country, Bangladesh. And, though at the time of writing the Accord had completed inspections for fire, electrical, and structural safety at all 1,700 factories supplying member brands, it remains to be seen whether all elements of the Accord will be fully implemented and proven effective in practice, The agreement is, nonetheless, a dramatic step forward and the fullest embodiment yet of the jobbers' agreement model in the modern, global era. If successful, the Accord may not only finally address the worker safety crisis in Bangladesh but also usher in a new paradigm for effectively enforcing global labor standards.

International Union League for Brand Responsibility

A final development of note is the creation of an international coalition of garment worker unions with the explicit goal of securing what would essentially be jobbers' agreements—described by proponents as "buyer responsibility agreements"—on a global scale. As described further by Jeff Hermanson in chapter 14, the International Union League for Brand Responsibility, founded in 2013, includes some of the most active garment-sector unions in Bangladesh, Cambodia, El Salvador, Honduras, India, Indonesia, Dominican Republic, Nicaragua, Sri Lanka, and Turkey. It has thus far developed regional networks of unions organizing at facilities owned or contracted by adidas, Gildan, and Fruit of the Loom and has supported union efforts at particular factories producing for these lead firms. In the long term, its organizers seek to wage campaigns to compel these and other brands to participate in triangular negotiations with representatives of the company's supplier factories and the unions representing workers at those factories, with the goal of obtaining agreements that parallel the jobbers' agreements of years past. It remains to be seen to what extent the League's vision is one that will be embraced by the international union federations that work in the apparel sector: IndustriALL and UNI Global Union.

In recent years, the sweatshop debate has become characterized by a new consensus about the failure of extant approaches to significantly improve labor compliance in global supply chains for apparel products. Although numerous approaches have been proposed, most of these fail to address what the bulk of available data suggests is the principal root cause of pervasive labor violations: the sourcing practices of global brands and retailers.

Our emphasis on jobbers' agreements is not meant to discount the role of domestic and international labor-law enforcement in the pursuit of worker rights. Indeed, jobbers' or buyers' agreements will be much more effective where they are buttressed by well-functioning domestic labor law and institutions (Locke, Qin, and Brause 2007). Because the contractual approach to joint liability that we outline here depends on worker self-organization, any program that enhances the will and capacity of governments to protect workers' right to organize and bargain collectively would complement this model.[19]

But effective domestic laws and international labor standards in and of themselves do not ensure fair pricing mechanisms and stable contracts, which were critical elements of the jobbers' agreement model at the center of the battle against sweatshops in the United States. Pursuing jobbers' or buyers' responsibility agreements is a strategic decision, one based on targeting the main sources of power and control in buyer-driven supply chains—namely, brands and retailers. It also reflects a labor strategy that opts for international solidarity over economic nationalism.

In pursuing this strategy, workers and their advocates today confront a very different economic and political landscape than the one that spawned jobbers' agreements. The ILGWU's efforts to secure joint liability for domestic garment workers were critically enabled by a federal government that supported the rights of workers to organize and bargain collectively. Garment workers in New York City also benefitted from a geographically concentrated industry susceptible to labor pressure via strikes. In contrast, today apparel production is dispersed—and easily transferred—among dozens of countries. There are, however, aspects of the constellation of forces in the current era that make something like jobbers' agreements, at least in a limited form, plausible. It is true that global garment workers are weak in terms of traditional sources of structural and associational power (Silver 2003). But workers and the organizations that represent them are central participants in transnational activist networks that include students, NGOs, and international unions (Bair and Palpacuer 2013; Anner 2013).

These labor-activist alliances have used consolidation at the top of the apparel industry to their advantage by targeting brands, institutional buyers (universities), and retail chains to bring about major agreements with powerful corporations including Nike, Fruit of the Loom/Russell, and adidas (Anner 2011). Largely in response to these activities, lead firms have attempted to protect their reputations by putting millions of dollars into CSR initiatives. Yet as the limitations of these initiatives are increasingly exposed through disasters such as the one at Rana Plaza, and with the growing capacity of the transnational anti-sweatshop movement, lead firms will be pressured to accept bigger and bolder initiatives. This might just create the perfect storm for a new approach, one that brings lead firms to the bargaining table and forces them to engage in negotiations that reflect the spirit of the jobbers' agreements.

Without question, pursuing a version of joint liability in today's global sub-contracting networks is a daunting task, but, as recent developments suggest, it is not beyond the realm of possibility. In fact, as the breakthrough Accord in Bangladesh attests, there is significant movement in this direction. Ultimately, the prospects for success depend on the extent of power wielded by apparel workers and their allies in the developed world—students, consumers, nonprofit organizations, and unions—as well as the sustained attention of journalists and the beneficence of forward-thinking industry leaders.[20] In our view, achieving modern-day jobbers' agreements and sustaining the resulting gains will require a strong labor movement at both the national and the global levels. Internation-ally, the Accord is a first step in a new direction for IndustriALL and UNI of negotiating substantive economic agreements with brands and retailers regard-ing labor conditions in global supply chains. Local labor movements also need to be strengthened, and continued reports of violence against organizers, includ-ing in Bangladesh, is a worrisome trend (Human Rights Watch 2015a). Going forward, a critical question for the Accord will be the extent to which signatory companies publicly denounce such violations and insist on workers' meaning-ful involvement in the Accord's implementation. Although recognizing that this and many other questions await answers, our view is one of guarded optimism because we see frustration with the existing CSR model giving way to innovative strategies that aim not to address the symptoms of the sweatshop scourge, but rather to address its underlying cause.

WORKERS OF THE WORLD, UNITE!

The Strategy of the International Union League for Brand Responsibility

Jeff Hermanson

The global apparel industry, like much of the global manufacturing industry, is plagued by low wages, long hours, and unsafe and unhealthy working conditions. Freedom of association and the effective right to collective bargaining, the most basic human rights of workers, are largely nonexistent and widely violated. The reality is that the global apparel industry is a sweatshop industry. This state of affairs is not an accident. Sweatshops are the result of a system of production that encourages, incentivizes and ultimately requires sweatshops (Anner, Bair, Blasi, 2012). The answer to the sweatshop problem must look to a solution that radically transforms the system of global apparel production.

The system of production that characterizes the global apparel industry is not new. Before the rapid globalization of the apparel industry, which began in the 1970s, apparel production in the United States took place in thousands of mostly small shops clustered in the northeastern United States, with smaller clusters in the southeast and in California. These shops, called "contractors," produced for Seventh Avenue brands like Calvin Klein, Ralph Lauren, and Donna Karan, and for retailers like Macy's and Kmart that had their own "private labels." The brands and retailers were called "jobbers" because they outsourced (jobbed out) their production.

The US and Canadian Experience

The system of outsourced production originated in the United States in the early twentieth century, in part as a union-avoidance strategy and in part because it enabled the brands to reduce their responsibility for fixed costs in a seasonal industry. The outsourcing system saw many competing independent producers all seeking the same limited supply of orders from the jobbers, in what was called the "auction block" system: the work went to the lowest bidder, driving down costs to the brands and putting downward pressure on the wages of the workers in the outsourced contractors. The small factory owners were forced to squeeze the workers to the limit, resulting in a proliferation of sweatshops throughout the New York City area. The labor historian John R. Commons described the outsourcing system of the early twentieth century as "the sweating system."[1]

The International Ladies' Garment Workers' Union (ILGWU) responded to this system by organizing workers in the contracting shops, primarily through the general strike. Two early examples of this approach were the dressmakers' strike of 1909, termed the "uprising of the twenty thousand," and the cloakmakers' strike of 1910, or "the Great Revolt" (ILGWU Timeline, 2011). These strikes gave the ILGWU a power base, not only in the brands' "inside shops" (directly owned manufacturing facilities) but also in the proliferating contractor factories.

As the "sweating system" grew and more brands became jobbers by outsourcing all or most of their manufacturing, the ILGWU began to use its power base to force the brands to sign jobbers' agreements—agreements that obligated the brands to use unionized contractors, to provide the contractors with steady work, and to pay a price sufficient to support the costs of union wages and benefits, as well as overhead costs for the factory, including a "reasonable profit."

As one would expect, the brands fought hard to avoid signing jobbers' agreements. The union overcame this resistance by organizing workers throughout the production network of a targeted brand, including inside shops and outside contractors, then declaring a strike against the jobber, calling on the workers to stop work on the brand's garments and picketing the factories and the brand's premises. Since some contractors would have orders from more than one brand, where possible workers would simply put the target brand's work on the side while they continued to work on the garments of other brands.

This method of organizing, combined with the occasional general strike,[2] succeeded in building the power of the ILGWU in the major apparel labor markets of the United States and Canada and established a collective bargaining structure that by the 1960s saw jobbers' agreements with most of the major US and Canadian women's apparel brands, guaranteeing stable work with union wages and benefits to over 450,000 US and Canadian garment workers. Workers in ILGWU contracting factories enjoyed wages above the median industrial wage, received paid holidays and vacations, and had family health insurance and a modest pension. The jobbers' agreement and the contractors' agreements were interlocking, with the same wages and benefits stipulated in both agreements. Jobbers were responsible for paying a percentage of the contractors' payroll into union vacation and holiday funds, and into health and pension funds as well. Contractors were responsible for paying wages, but if they failed or were unable to pay, jobbers were obligated to pay.

The employers' principal union avoidance strategy during this entire period was the "runaway shop"—nonunion jobbers encouraging their contractors to move out of the highly organized New York City Garment District, first to Brooklyn, Queens, and the Bronx, then to Connecticut, upstate New York, New Jersey, and Pennsylvania, and later to Chinatown in lower Manhattan, Puerto Rico, and the southern states. The spread of production out of the Garment District greatly increased the influence of New York's organized crime families, who had long controlled the garment trucking firms that moved work from jobber to contractor and back again, using their control of this crucial function to extort money from employers who paid them to cross union picket lines and break strikes.

The ILGWU countered these moves with a strategy known as "follow the work," sending organizers into the new production areas, organizing the workers, and declaring strikes against the jobbers. In the 1958 dressmakers' general strike, which targeted the growing dress contracting industry in Pennsylvania and their New York City jobbers, the ILGWU sent organizers from the urban jungle of the Garment District to the rural countryside of Pennsylvania. Fighting for equal pay with their New York City counterparts, the mostly female garment workers of eastern Pennsylvania confronted the mob truckers and their thugs in the streets of small towns, while their city brothers and sisters picketed the jobbers' shipping rooms and showrooms on Seventh Avenue. The Luchese and Bufalino mob bosses fought back with violence to protect what was known as the "invisible government" of the garment contracting business, but proved no match for the power of committed and organized workers. Together the workers of Pennsylvania and the New York City Garment District won a major victory, establishing Pennsylvania as "union territory" and demonstrating once again the power of coordinated mass direct action (Melman 1994).

The strategy of "follow the work" was less successful in the South, where a racially divided workforce faced a powerful and entrenched power structure all too willing to use racist violence, enabled by local law enforcement, to thwart union campaigns. In spite of this unfavorable environment, the ILGWU made important gains and conducted militant strikes in Georgia, Alabama, and Mississippi during the 1960s.

Globalization Breaks the Union's Power

The 1970s saw the beginning of the employer move to offshore production, one that the ILGWU could not easily counter by following the work, and that ultimately led to the accelerating decline of US and Canadian garment production, the breaking of the union's power, and the return of the sweatshop, this time as a global reality.

As global apparel production grew from an incidental factor in the 1960s and early 1970s to an existential threat to the unionized US and Canadian garment industries, the ILGWU's main efforts were focused on trade policy campaigns ("Stop Imports!" and "Roll Back Imports!") in support of trade legislation and appeals to the consumer to "Look for the Union Label." Some efforts were made to support unions in key garment producing countries, and these efforts showed promise and involved important experience by US and foreign trade unionists that would prove useful later on. But the international solidarity efforts were insufficient to stem the growth of the global sweatshop or to create a powerful union counter to the employers' move offshore.

Why was there not a greater effort to follow the work and build the kind of global union power needed to stabilize employment and raise conditions for workers everywhere? One reason was that after the purge of leftists during the McCarthy era and the turmoil of the antiwar movement in the 1960s, the union leadership was not internationalist in outlook and instinctively turned to a strategy of "Buy American" as the patriotic solution to the problem of competition from imports (Frank 2000). There was concern that the membership would not support a strategy of organizing foreign factories, that it would be too costly, and that it would not succeed.

One major problem that was encountered in the initial international organizing efforts by the ILGWU was the mobility of the key players—brands and their supplier factories. The brands move their production from place to place in response to trade rules, raw material availability, and labor costs. This means that union organizing in individual factories often results in plant closure, either because the supplier chooses to flee to avoid unionization and higher labor costs, or because the brand pulls its work out as costs rise, and the contractor and the workers are left without work.

This mobility has been the downfall of many organizing campaigns. In 1991 the ILGWU and the Amalgamated Clothing and Textile Workers' Union (ACTWU), under the auspices of the International Textile, Garment and Leather Workers' Federation (ITGLWF), undertook an organizer training and campaign support program with the Federación Nacional de Trabajadores de Zonas Francas (FENATRAZONAS) in the Dominican Republic. The program resulted in organizing and collective bargaining victories at ten factories employing over ten thousand workers in the free trade zones of the Dominican Republic that produced apparel for the US market. This was the first application of the ILGWU's clandestine organizing model (known in Spanish as *la pecera*, or "the fishtank") in the Third World, and it was a great success (Gordon and Jessup 2000).[3] But over the next ten years, all of the first group of organized factories were closed or moved, and the Dominican union struggled to survive.

In Honduras and Guatemala, expatriate US activists were hired by ILGWU, trained in the fishtank organizing model, and supported in efforts to encourage and assist local unions in organizing foreign-owned apparel factories producing for export. This led to successful campaigns in both countries. In Honduras, a campaign at a Korean-owned Gap contractor, Kimi de Honduras, saw workers fired and rehired through pressure on the Gap, and after a year of organizing, a successful strike led to one of the first collective bargaining agreements in the sector. At a Phillips-Van Heusen shirt factory in Guatemala, CAMOSAS, a combination of solid worker organizing and pressure on the US brand led to union recognition and a collective bargaining agreement, the first in the Guatemalan maquila industry. In both cases, the factories were closed well before the expiration of the collective bargaining agreements (Quinteros 2000).

In these cases, as in the Dominican Republic, the workers won an organizing victory, and their union successfully bargained for higher wages and better conditions, but the brand closed down the factory or withdrew production, and the supplier factory pulled up stakes and moved to another country. Finding a way to counter this employer strategy is the key to developing a successful strategy for organizing the global apparel industry.

The Race to the Bottom and the Workers' Response

One important result of the current system of production in the global apparel industry is the decline in real wages in most apparel producing countries. Such unconscionably low wages have provoked mass fainting attributable to malnutrition in Mexican maquiladoras and Cambodian sweatshops (Worker Rights Consortium 2013; Better Factories Cambodia 2014). Another result is the denial of the basic human rights of workers in most apparel producing countries, especially in the biggest exporters of apparel to the US market: China, Vietnam, and Bangladesh.

In China, where workers are forbidden from forming unions other than the official, government-controlled All-China Federation of Trade Unions (ACFTU), they have since 2010 engaged in thousands of unsanctioned strikes and have taken advantage of regional labor shortages to resign from low-wage workplaces, to the extent that the government has been forced to raise minimum wages in coastal regions and to instruct the ACFTU to take up collective bargaining in an effort to pacify labor relations. A massive 2014 strike by forty-eight thousand workers at the Yue Yuen shoe factory in Dongguan, the largest supplier of athletic footwear to all the global brands, including Nike and adidas, inspired solidarity actions in Taiwan, Hong Kong, Australia, the United States, United Kingdom, and Turkey, and an unprecedented picket of adidas, Nike, and New Balance retail stores in Guangzhou by students from Sun Yat-sen University. The strike, caused by the workers' discovery that the Taiwan-based company had been cheating them out of legally mandated social security benefits for over ten years, resulted in the Chinese government's declaration that the company had to pay the benefits, after which it sent in the riot police to herd the workers back to work with batons and police dogs (*China Labour Bulletin* 2014).

In Vietnam, where workers similarly have no option other than the government-affiliated Vietnam General Confederation of Labor (VGCL), there are many wildcat strikes in the big foreign-owned factories, often resulting in wage hikes and other concessions to worker demands (Quynh 2015). Here too the government has tried to control the periodic surges in worker militancy by a combination of repression and concessions, declaring most strikes illegal and arresting the leaders while offering periodic increases in the minimum wage.

In Bangladesh, where trade union organizing has for years been repressed by employer violence, regressive labor laws, and conscious government neglect, we have seen the most extreme consequences of the outsourcing of production and irresponsible brand and factory behavior: there have been many tragic factory fires, culminating in the 2013 Rana Plaza disaster in which over 1,100 workers lost their lives when the factory building collapsed on top of them. This tragedy may finally have awakened people around the world to the true cost of "everyday low prices" and the immense profitability of the major global brands. In response, the global anti-sweatshop movement, led by the Worker Rights Consortium (WRC), the Clean Clothes Campaign, and the global unions IndustriALL and UNI, successfully campaigned to pressure over a hundred brands to sign the legally binding Bangladesh Fire and Building Safety Accord, although still other brands have tried to blunt this campaign by forming the voluntary Bangladesh Safety Alliance. As hundreds of thousands of workers struck and demonstrated in the streets of the factory districts, a tripartite process recommended a substantial increase in the minimum wage. However, the resulting 76 percent increase only raised the monthly wage of garment workers to US$67, far below the amount necessary to lift workers and their families out of desperate poverty.

The garment workers of Bangladesh have continued to mount massive strikes and demonstrations against the unsafe conditions and poverty wages, which are often suppressed with brutal police and private "security" repression.[4] After years of inaction, the combination of economic disruption and global public opinion finally forced the Bangladesh labor authorities to accept the registration of over one hundred new factory-level garment worker unions in 2013. Newly energized independent "grassroots unions" are growing in size and capacity, and are generating new struggles. Unfortunately we also see a pattern of violent repression from powerful local employers, who act with impunity even as the Bangladesh government and employers' associations claim they are the victims of a "conspiracy to destroy the RMG industry" (*New Age* 2014).

The unsafe conditions, low wages, and unstable employment that are endemic in the garment industry have produced resistance and opposition, and national unions in a number of apparel-producing countries have developed greater organizing capacity in recent years. In Indonesia, the fourth-largest producer of apparel for export to the US market, workers have made use of relatively better labor laws to organize into several national confederations comprising millions of workers. Through mass mobilizations and general strikes, these unions have forced the Indonesian government to increase the minimum wage significantly, and they continue to press for higher wages and an end to "outsourcing" (in Indonesia this refers to the use of short-term contract workers rather than to the subcontracting of production). In 2012 the unions joined together to conduct a national strike by more than two million workers (*Jakarta Globe* 2012). But in an example of the dynamic driving the downward pressure on wages, when as a result of their militant action workers won a 44 percent increase in the minimum wage in the Jakarta industrial belt, many brands encouraged their contract factories to seek a waiver postponing the increase and refused to pay higher prices. Even after several large increases in the minimum wage, Indonesian garment workers continue to receive far less than a living wage.

In Cambodia, too, workers have organized broadly, overcoming employer violence and the murder of the national union leader Chea Vichea (*Aljazeera* 2013) to create strong national unions. However, in spite of the proliferation of unions, and in spite of the ILO's Better Factories Cambodia monitoring program, Cambodian workers have been able to achieve significant improvements in wages and conditions only by mass struggles that have been met with brutal repression. In 2014, wages set at US$100 per month meant that many workers suffered from malnutrition even though they worked long hours; and the combination of malnutrition and lack of adequate rest were the cause of the mass fainting incidents that have become common in Cambodian garment factories. In December 2013, hundreds of thousands of Cambodian workers struck in support of demands for a minimum monthly wage of US\$160, only to have the Cambodian government and military repress the strike with brutal violence, killing five workers and seriously wounding dozens more with live ammunition (*Wall Street Journal* 2014a). Finally, after the Cambodian unions regrouped, focused their organizing on key geographic areas, and courageously mounted a highly visible and disciplined demonstration involving marches through the factory districts by over one hundred thousand workers wearing orange T-shirts and stickers proclaiming "We need \$177," the government raised the monthly minimum wage to US\$128 (*Wall Street Journal* 2014b).

In Central America, organizing campaigns have resulted in some very important victories, especially in Honduras. In October 2008, Fruit of the Loom, the country's largest private-sector employer, with nine factories and 10,000 workers, closed the Jerzees de Honduras factory, which employed 1,250 workers producing collegiate licensed apparel under the Russell Athletic label. The closing occurred during an organizing campaign by Honduran Central General de Trabajadores (CGT), which sought help from WRC and United Students against Sweatshops (USAS). After an investigation by WRC found that the closing was motivated by antiunion animus, and a year-long campaign by USAS resulted in Russell Athletic losing over a hundred university licenses and being dropped by major sports apparel retailers, Fruit of the Loom came to the bargaining table and negotiated an agreement to reopen the factory, now called Jerzees Nuevo Día, pay the workers for their lost earnings, recognize the union, and negotiate a collective bargaining agreement. It also agreed to adopt a new labor-relations approach that would ensure freedom of association in all its Honduran factories and would commit to bargain with CGT whenever it established unions in other plants. In November 2009, Fruit of the Loom and CGT signed a formal, binding agreement setting forth these terms and establishing an oversight committee composed of two company and two union representatives to resolve any disputes, with ultimate recourse to binding arbitration (Adler-Milstein, Champagne, and Haas 2013). This agreement, known as the Honduras Labor Framework, has resulted in a significant advance in organizing in the maquila sector in Honduras. By this writing, Fruit of the Loom has signed collective bargaining agreements with CGT in three of its Honduran factories and is in the process of negotiating a collective bargaining agreement in a fourth factory. A second collective bargaining agreement was signed at Jerzees Nuevo Día in April 2015.

Fruit of the Loom has adopted a similar stance in El Salvador, where it is the largest private-sector employer, with nine factories and eleven thousand workers, and where there has never been a collective bargaining agreement negotiated in the maquila sector. The Salvadoran union SITRASACOSI has established a union in one of the Fruit of the Loom factories, and has begun a dialogue with the company about a labor framework agreement along the lines of the Honduran agreement.

Nike also negotiated with CGT in Honduras, agreeing to pay over a million dollars in severance and giving priority hiring to workers from two closed contract factories. In 2013, a Nike and adidas factory, Pinehurst Manufacturing, was also organized after a long struggle, and finally signed a collective bargaining agreement with CGT. In Haiti, newly organized workers protested for an implementation of the country's US$7-a-day minimum wage, resulting in negotiations with three major brands and their supplier factories and agreements on higher wages and piece rates.

Looking across the globe, we see increasingly volatile labor relations in the apparel industry as a whole, and growing experience by workers and their organizations in waging struggles for better wages and working conditions. In addition, we see greatly increased capacity for working with international partners. In the brands' home countries organizations like the Clean Clothes Campaign, United Students against Sweatshops, Maquila Solidarity Network, Asia Multinational Resource Center, Korea TNC Watch, and Globalization Monitor (to mention only a few) now regularly work with these national unions and assist on campaigns that are increasingly global in character. We have seen enough of these global campaigns and their effectiveness that we now speak of a "global anti-sweatshop movement." The formation of Industri-ALL Global Union from the merger of global union federations in the metals, chemical, and mining and textile and apparel manufacturing industries has also increased the potential capacity for international union solidarity actions. This is the baseline for considering new strategies for coordinated actions to improve conditions broadly.

A Strategy for Organizing and Transforming the Global Apparel Industry

It is in this context, and on the basis of the collective experience described above, that garment workers' unions and their allies have begun to develop a strategy that will make use of the growing strength of the national unions and the global anti-sweatshop movement to force the brands to permit the progressive organization of their supplier factories and to pay the costs of progressively better standards for workers in those factories. Many unionists and anti-sweatshop activists across the globe have concluded that it is possible, with great effort and much transnational coordination, for workers to organize unions in many factories that produce for a single global brand, and thereby gain enough power to get the brand to sign an agreement that obligates it to guarantee higher wages and to maintain its production in those unionized factories even as labor costs rise. As in the case of the ILGWU jobbers' agreements described above, the agreement with the brand would set minimum standards for wages, benefits, and working conditions, as negotiated by the unions that represent the workers in the individual factories, and would mandate freedom of association in all the brand's supplier factories, whether owned or contracted.

In April 2013, in a meeting in San Salvador, El Salvador, several unions of the global South, including CGT of Honduras, SITRASACOSI and STIT of El Salvador, FEDOTRAZONAS of the Dominican Republic, FESTMIT and FESITEX of Nicaragua, PT Kizone Workers' Committee of Indonesia, CCAWDU of Cambodia, GATWU of India, and BIGUF of Bangladesh agreed to form a new organization, the International Union League for Brand Responsibility. The League members adopted statutes and an action plan, and began carrying out a global campaign targeting dozens of factories of a single brand—adidas—for organizing. As the campaign began, the League sent a message to adidas, demanding a meeting to negotiate an agreement that would commit adidas to keep its production in the factories being organized, to use its relationship with the factories to ensure freedom of association and permit the organizing and collective bargaining process, and to pay enough to the factories to support the increased cost of labor that would result from collective bargaining.

The League strategy was to organize enough power in each country to bring the brand to the bargaining table with national- and factory-level unions, while each national- and factory-level union would be responsible for negotiating a collective bargaining agreement with the factories that it has organized. The brand agreement and the factory collective bargaining agreements would provide a stable framework for gradually improving conditions for workers in the organized factories, for gradually accumulating union strength in relation to the brand, and for going on to organize the remaining factories in the brand's production network.

Only by securing strong agreements that guarantee stable, long-term relationships with the factories producing a brand's goods, and only by requiring brands to pay for improved conditions that result from successful collective bargaining, can we begin to put an end to the "race to the bottom," a race that takes place not only between apparel production factories but also between countries. The evidence from the first two years of struggle shows that this strategy will take many more months and even years to be successful in a global supply chain as big and complex as that of a brand like adidas. However, it is also clear that important gains are being made toward this end and that the interim gains for workers in the targeted factories are significant.

The first important incremental victory of the League campaign against adidas came just one month after the formation of the League, in May 2013. The Korean-owned PT Kizone factory in Indonesia was a major producer of sports apparel for Nike and adidas. In January 2011, after months of struggle to get wage payments and benefits for the 2,800 workers, the owner of the factory simply disappeared. Green Textiles, the agent that had been placing orders at PT Kizone for the brands, continued to operate the factory and paid the workers' wages and benefits until April 2011, when the factory closed for good, leaving the workers owed $3.4 million in severance. After a pressure campaign by USAS, Nike and other smaller buyers paid $1.6 million to the workers, leaving a balance owed by adidas of $1.8 million. Adidas refused to pay, saying it had no responsibility for the debts of an independent subcontractor. USAS and the PT Kizone Workers' Committee mounted a major public campaign in which former PT Kizone workers toured US campuses with USAS support to get the universities to end their contracts with adidas. After more than a dozen universities cut their contracts, the University of Wisconsin, a major "adidas school," filed suit in Wisconsin. The university asked the court for a declaratory judgment that adidas had violated the University of Wisconsin's licensing agreement, which included a code of conduct holding each licensee responsible for the payment of all legally mandated benefits. Adidas argued that since the PT Kizone factory was not owned by adidas, but was merely a "supplier," adidas should not be held responsible (CCC 2012b).

The PT Kizone Workers' Committee, supported by the League, USAS, and the Service Employees International Union (SEIU), retained the highly respected San Francisco law firm Altshuler Berzon LLP and filed a motion to intervene in the lawsuit as a "third-party beneficiary" of the licensing agreement. In a historic and groundbreaking decision, the Wisconsin court ruled in favor of the workers' motion, permitting the Workers' Committee to be directly involved in the suit, and the stage was set for a settlement. Within a few weeks of the decision, adidas asked to meet and negotiate. The League executive coordinator and representatives of the PT Kizone Workers' Committee met in San Francisco at the offices of Altshuler Berzon with the adidas general counsel and vice president for business affairs and two other top executives, and over the course of twelve hours negotiated a settlement that was described as a "complete victory" by the PT Kizone workers. Once again, the ability of workers to hold global brands responsible for conditions and benefits in supplier factories through organizing and campaigning was demonstrated (CCC 2013).

In addition, although adidas was chosen as the first major target of the International Union League, the affiliated unions have continued organizing workers in factories producing for other brands and have assisted one another when they encountered the same brands in factories in more than one country. The Central

American and Caribbean unions of the League have formed union networks in the supply chains of the T-shirt manufacturers Hanes, Gildan Activewear, and Fruit of the Loom, bringing together factory-level and national union leaders in meetings to exchange experiences and plan common strategies. These networks have already resulted in multi-union, transnational campaigns using direct action and public exposure to prevent unionized factories from closing, to force rehiring of fired union activists, and to pay higher wages. The growing strength and combined experience of the national unions in Haiti, Honduras, and El Salvador, and the ability to conduct coordinated public exposure campaigns in the brands' major markets, has resulted in the ability to establish unions and protect them against the firing of leaders and supporters while they build toward a majority. In the Dominican Republic, the League's support for FEDOTRAZONAS and the formation of the Gildan Union Network helped improve the strategic position of the union at Dortex, Gildan's textile plant that provides fabric for the sewing plants of Haiti and the Dominican Republic, resulting in a favorable resolution of a long-simmering dispute with a company-supported rival union.

In Haiti the League worked closely with the union federation Batay Ouvriye to win payment of a 40 percent higher basic wage in factories producing for Gildan, Hanes, and Fruit of the Loom, three of the largest T-shirt brands in the world, and through their contract supplier factories, the largest employers in Haiti.

The International Union League was instrumental in supporting the Cambodian affiliate CCAWDU in its three-month strike against the six thousand worker industrial laundry and garment finishing plant SL Garment. Working with the Clean Clothes Campaign, the League successfully engaged the factory's major buyers, Gap, H&M, and Inditex, to encourage a settlement on terms favorable to the union, unfortunately not before Cambodian military police fired live ammunition to disperse a union march, killing an innocent street vendor. A month later, in December 2013, eight Cambodian unions including CCAWDU declared a general strike against four hundred garment factories, demanding an increase of the $3-per-day minimum wage to $160. After a week of protests that effectively shut down production, the unions were attacked by military police, again using live ammunition, and this time five workers were killed and dozens wounded. The Cambodian unions and their international allies continued to organize and build support for their demands, while the government banned public gatherings and even leafletting. As mentioned above, when the repression finally eased, the unions undertook a major organizing effort, focused on the biggest industrial parks and factories, to mount a one-hundred-thousand-strong worker demonstration in support of their wage demands, and won an additional 24 percent increase in the monthly minimum wage.

In India, the International Union League affiliate, GATWU, has used engagement by the League with the brands adidas, Gap, and H&M, combined with
worker organizing in the factories, to force India's largest apparel manufacturer,
Gokaldas Exports Ltd., to comply with the government-mandated cost of living
allowance ("dearness allowance"), significantly increasing the incomes of tens of
thousands of workers throughout the region as other employers followed suit.
Fired worker activists in another major producer, Shahi Group, were reinstated in
their jobs after League pressure on the buyers, Gap and H&M, giving a powerful
boost to the organizing.

Challenges and Difficulties to Be Overcome

The International Union League has faced serious challenges and setbacks as
well. In Nicaragua, the Korean multinational SAE-A Trading Co. Ltd. crushed
an organizing effort by the League-affiliated union FESTMIT, making use of the
pro-investment, pro-employer stance of the Sandinista government and its corporatist unions to foment violent interunion clashes and to directly threaten and
repress the militant leaders of FESTMIT.

Another important challenge faced by the International Union League is
the lack of support from the global union federation IndustriALL. Industri-
ALL's apparel-textile sector, formerly organized in the ITGLWF, has been the
weakest and slowest to develop of all the industrial sectors brought together
by the merger of the International Metalworkers Federation (IMF), International Federation of Chemical, Energy, Mine and General Workers' Unions
(ICEM), and ITGLWF in 2012. IndustriALL's leadership has committed to
transform IndustriALL into "an organizing and campaigning union" and to
leave behind the more moderate "social dialogue" approach of the past, but
this transformation has not yet occurred. Meanwhile, the leaders of Industri-
ALL see the International Union League as an unwanted interloper on their
turf. About half of the unions in the League are IndustriALL members and
half are not. All share the view that the League is a necessary organization for
the specific purpose of brand campaigns in the global apparel industry. First, the
League enables direct participation in the formulation and implementation
of strategy by national unions and factory-level unions, including unions
that are not IndustriALL members. This level of participation was impossible
within the structures of the ITGLWF and has not yet been shown to be possible within the structures of IndustriALL. Second, one of the principles of
the League is that negotiations with global brands will be conducted with the
direct participation of the national- and factory-level unions. This is counter

to the practice of IndustriALL, which has continued the ITGLWF strategy of negotiating and signing global framework agreements (GFAs) with global brands without the real participation of the unions that represent workers at the national and factory level. Up to now, GFAs signed in the apparel industry have all been voluntary (and hence unenforceable) statements of good intentions that have proven ineffective in promoting union organizing and collective bargaining. In fact, the existence of a GFA is often a hindrance to taking an aggressive stance against a global brand, diverting focus from the often vicious struggles taking place in the brand's supplier factories to the more civilized social dialogue in the corporate offices and IndustriALL headquarters. These criticisms of IndustriALL's approach, especially concerning GFAs, are shared by many US and some European affiliates and by many unions in the global South.

To some extent, the social-dialogue approach is a reflection of the background of the largely European officialdom of the "Global Union Federations" (GUFs), whose experience in relation to European employers is quite different from that of trade unionists in the global South or in the United States. It also reflects the influence within IndustriALL of the apparel unions in the brands' home countries, especially in Germany, Sweden, Japan, and Spain, which have for the most part merged into general manufacturing unions as the numbers of apparel workers declined, and which, if they still represent any significant number of apparel workers, represent workers in corporate headquarters and distribution centers, historically places where labor relations are stable and workers are generally better off. The social-dialogue approach does not seem as well suited to countries where unions are routinely suppressed with violence and where labor laws are repressive or dysfunctional.

In the campaign to support the Cambodian unions' struggle, for example, IndustriALL adopted a strategy of "working with the global brands" that source from Cambodian factories, joining them in sending letters to the Cambodian government, meeting with government ministers, and asking the government to stop the banning of public gatherings, ensure due process for the detained activists, and establish a tripartite mechanism for determining the minimum wage. In order to "work together with the global brands" in their approach to the government, IndustriALL had to agree to make demands that were considerably weaker than the demands of the Cambodian unions, who had issued a statement calling for the release without charges of the detainees, a restoration of all civil rights including the right to strike, and an immediate increase in the minimum wage.

When the League, including its Cambodian affiliate CCAWDU and the US apparel union Workers United-SEIU, pointed out that the brands bore a great deal of responsibility for low wages, indeed were profiting from government repression of the unions, and suggested that the brands should be pressured to force their supplier factories to raise wages, the IndustriALL leaders rejected this approach. The League argued that the Cambodian government was unlikely to cease its repression and its strategy of keeping wages low to attract foreign investment, especially because the political opposition party was allying with the unions on this issue and the government could not afford to appear weak or to make concessions to the opposition. The League argued that the IndustriALL strategy of pressuring the government in concert with the brands was unlikely to succeed, and proposed an industrial strategy to circumvent the political impasse by targeting the major brands with a campaign to force them to raise wages in their supplier factories. Using the Bangladesh Accord on Fire and Building Safety as an example of brand responsibility, the League proposed that the unions and IndustriALL seek a Cambodia accord on wages.

The challenges faced by the International Union League and its member unions are not new. Governments have often promoted low-wage strategies to encourage outside investment and have often used the police and military to repress struggles. Employers have often promoted "yellow unions," "company unions," and "sweetheart unions" to prevent workers from having legitimate representation. GUFs have long been relatively moderate institutions, emphasizing good relationships with employers based on the European "social partnership" approach. Employers have used intimidation, coercion, and even violence when necessary to repress and crush organizing efforts. And of course, capital mobility—closing and moving factories to a new location—is the typical last resort of an employer, to be implemented if a campaign cannot be defeated by other means.

The unions of the International Union League for Brand Responsibility believe that a different type of transnational organization may overcome these challenges, an organization based on equality of its member unions and bottom-up participation in all aspects of strategy development and implementation, including negotiations with the global brands. It is this approach that will bring rank-and-file factory workers face to face at the bargaining table with the top executives of some of the most powerful and wealthy corporations in the world. What is new, or not so new but newly grasped, is the determination to avail ourselves of the power that comes from the unity and conscious solidarity across national boundaries of factory workers, all working at the same crafts, all working on the same product, all working for the same ultimate employer, joining together to confront those who direct and profit from their labor, using their strategic position at the crucial point of production to exercise the ultimate power of workers, the power of stopping the process cold. As we build that power in strategic locations across the global supply chain of the brands and learn how to exercise that power in a coordinated and strategic fashion, we can win binding agreements that permit real improvements in workers' employment terms and conditions, and real power to have a voice in the global economy.

Notes

INTRODUCTION

1. See, for example, Featherstone and USAS 2002; and Ross 2004.

2. Of course, consumers' actions are not necessarily consistent with their expressed beliefs in sustainability (see, for example, Bennett and Williams 2011).

3. The former: http://www.gscpnet.com/; http://www.bureauveritas.com/; http://www.pwc.com/gx/en/sustainability/index.jhtml. The latter: http://www.workersrights.org/; http://www.fairlabor.org/fla/; http://en.maquilasolidarity.org/; http://www.laborrights.org/.

4. For a more detailed discussion of the growth of giant contractors and some implications for labor, see Appelbaum and Lichtenstein 2006; Appelbaum 2008, 2009, 2011.

5. http://nikeinc.com/pages/responsibility#.

6. For an instructive debate on the strengths and weaknesses of ethical consumption, see the November/December 2011 issue of *Boston Review*, in particular the articles by Locke 2011; Nova 2011; Schorr 2011; and Szasz 2011; and the response by O'Rourke 2011.

1. OUTSOURCING HORROR

1. The price of ready-made garments exported from Bangladesh was over $20 billion in 2012–2013; typical Free on Board (FOB) markups yield a value of more than $80 billion at retail.

2. Notably, the brands that were early pioneers of these systems of private regulation were those, such as Nike and Gap, that suffered the most reputational damage in the 1990s as a result of media exposés over sweatshop conditions.

3. Tesco is the world's third-largest general retailer. Carrefour, the second largest after Walmart, joined the Accord the next day.

2. FROM PUBLIC REGULATION TO PRIVATE ENFORCEMENT

1. Other firms using Tazreen at the time of the fire included Sears, Kik, Dickies, Disney, C&A, and Li & Fung; all had CSR codes of conduct governing their production.

2. See chapter 4, where Ross notes that this (his estimate) most likely understates the actual number of deaths, since it is based on an English-language LexisNexis search of news databases. In one comparison period (2006–2009), his search found 128 factory fire deaths, while Bangladesh's Fire Service and Civil Defense Department found 414—more than three times as many.

3. For a series of essays that examine the role of big buyers, see Hamilton, Senauer, and Petrovic 2012.

4. The notion of "countervailing power" as characterizing labor-capital relations in the United States was first advanced in 1952 by the economist John Kenneth Galbraith (2012).

5. By the mid-1950s, 35 percent of all wage and salaried workers were unionized (Meyers, 2004).

6. Sullivan was one of a group of prominent African American leaders who saw "black capitalism" as an important avenue out of poverty for the African American community.

He was the founder of Philadelphia's Opportunities Industrialization Centers (OIC), which provided skills training and job placement for those with few prospects; OIC eventually grew into a national effort. He also started a number of programs that provided investment funds for black-owned businesses.

7. A sixth principle, "Working to eliminate laws and customs that impede social, economic, and political justice," was added in 1984. See http://www.marshall.edu/revleon sullivan/principled/principles.htm.

8. See http://www.eeoc.gov/laws/statutes/titlevii.cfm.

9. For a complete chronology of Nike's labor issues, see Ballinger 2015.

10. In 2010 Su was appointed as California's labor commissioner.

11. Separate settlements were made with Millers Outpost and Tomato Inc. The workers had previously received $1.3 million—roughly $1 million confiscated from the El Monte sweatshop and $300,000 from other brands and retailers whose garments were made there. White and McDonnell 1997.

12. See Appelbaum 1999; Bonacich and Appelbaum 2000.

13. Although the United States has not seriously considered enforceable labor standards for trade agreements, some small steps have been taken at the state level. The California Transparency in Supply Chains Act (SB 657), which was signed into law by former (Republican) governor Arnold Schwarzenegger and took effect on January 1, 2012, "requires companies to report on specific actions taken to eradicate slavery and human trafficking in their supply chain" by reporting on the extent to which they engaged in third-party verification, independent (and unannounced) auditing, supplier certification, internal accountability, and training (see http://www.state.gov/documents/organization/164934.pdf). Although the act involves self-reporting and lacks an effective enforcement mechanism, it does reflect a strong concern with human trafficking, and provisions provide a possible window for assessing supply-chain compliance with labor standards (Mattos 2012). A similar bill, HR 2759, was introduced in the US House of Representatives with bipartisan support in 2011, but has not been voted on.

14. The eight core Conventions are: freedom of association and protection of the right to organize (no. 87), right to organize and collective bargaining (no. 98), forced labor (no. 29), abolition of forced labor (no. 105), minimum age (no. 138), worst forms of child labor (no. 182), equal remuneration (no. 100), and discrimination (no. 111).

15. As of September 2015, one hundred thirty-eight countries had ratified all eight core Conventions; Brunei joins the United States and the Cook Islands in ratifying only two. Nineteen countries have ratified seven; nine countries have ratified six; eight countries have ratified five; five countries have ratified four; and one country has ratified three. For a complete interactive list of ratifications, see ILO, 2015e.

16. The survey, which was conducted and administered by the Wharton School, was based on 1,712 respondents from 113 countries, representing a 25 percent response rate, which the report claims was "generally representative of the Global Compact participant base." https://www.unglobalcompact.org/docs/about_the_gc/Global_Corporate_Sustainability_Report2013.pdf.

17. An interactive comparison of the codes of conduct of thirteen leading oversight companies as of June 2014 can be found at https://docs.google.com/spreadsheet/ccc?key=0AiyymkoG0zs0dHBwYUIzelAwZDBRQXc0MXhZV05kTEE&usp=sharing#gid=0, or can be downloaded at https://secure.lsit.ucsb.edu/hist/d7_labor/sites/secure.lsit.ucsb.edu.hist.d7_labor/files/sitefiles/CSR_Research_Files/Code%20of%20Conduct%20Comparison%207-8-14.pdf.

18. The largest publicly traded monitoring companies include SGS, Intertek, and Bureau Veritas.

19. The criteria that determine schools' ratings include "the number of courses offered that contain social, environmental or ethical content," the number of courses that "specifically address the intersection of social and environmental issues in mainstream, for-profit business," "the extent to which students are actually exposed to such content," and "the number of scholarly articles written by business school faculty, published in peer-reviewed, business journals in calendar years 2009 and 2010 that contain social, environmental or ethical content." The full report, as well as an interactive website that permits a detailed analysis of results, is available at http://www.beyondgreypinstripes.org/.

20. China, which ranks seventieth, offers the MBA at China Europe International Business School, a cooperative arrangement between the European Foundation for Management and Development (an international network, based in Brussels, that "aims at influencing the European Agenda putting forward management education and development issues," EFMD 2015), and Shanghai Jiao Tong University.

21. See Reich's (1997) autobiographical account of his years as labor secretary, *Locked in the Cabinet* (NY: Knopf, 1997). Reich also tried a positive strategy, initiating a "Trendsetter List" and working with the National Consumers League and National Retail Federation to identify sweat-free firms. Of course, all such lists relied on self-reporting and are thus of doubtful reliability. For a detailed account of Reich's efforts and the emergence of the FLA, see Bobrowsky 1999.

22. Participants included "Nike, Liz Claiborne, Warnaco, Phillips-Van Heusen, L.L. Bean, Tweeds, Patagonia, Nicole Miller, Karen Kane, Kathie Lee Gifford; unions included the Union of Needletrades, Industrial and Textile Employees (UNITE) and the Retail, Wholesale, and Department Store Union of the AFL-CIO; and NGOs were represented by the National Consumers League (NCL), Lawyers Committee for Human Rights (LCHR), and the Interfaith Center on Corporate Responsibility (ICCR). Reebok, the business association Businesses for Social Responsibility (BSR), and two NGOs, the International Labor Rights Forum (ILRF) and Robert F. Kennedy Memorial Center for Human Rights (RFK Center), joined shortly afterwards and participated in the negotiations drafting the code and monitoring principles." Bobrowsky 1999, note 18.

23. This account of the emergence of the FLA draws heavily on Bobrowsky's detailed report.

24. See Bobrowsky 1999, 40–41, for a more detailed discussion of the pressure put on AIP by USAS and other organizations.

25. The original charter had only a single university representative, but the university role was expanded when it was clear that overseeing university trademark licensing codes would be a major part of its remit. See FLA 1999.

26. The FLA charter defines "labor/NGO" as "consumer, human rights, labor rights, labor union, religious and other public interest organizations (including student groups), related to fair labor standards," http://www.fairlabor.org/sites/default/files/fla_charter_2-12-14.pdf, 6.

27. As of fall 2014 the vacancy created by MSN's departure had not yet been filled.

28. Structural engineers are now involved in apparel factory inspections in Bangladesh.

29. The term "social accountability contract" was first used, although with a slightly different emphasis, in Esbenshade 2004a. See chapter 3.

3. CORPORATE SOCIAL RESPONSIBILITY

1. Whereas Richard Locke's 2007 study found that long-term relationships and percentage of production were not correlated with higher compliance, his 2013 book, which compiles many years of research, reversed this finding.

2. Workers were originally owed $2.6 million, but received nearly half a million through the liquidation of the equipment in the two facilities. So the total still owed was $2.18 million. See: http://digitalcommons.ilr.cornell.edu/cgi/viewcontent.cgi?article=134 9&context=globaldocs.

3. See "https://news.uns.purdue.edu/x/2009b/0911NikeStatement.pdf" for denial #1 and "http://nikeinc.com/news/nike-statement-regarding-vision-tex-and-hugger" for denial #2.

4. Memo from Worker Rights Consortium with translation of letter, p. 6, at: http:// digitalcommons.ilr.cornell.edu/cgi/viewcontent.cgi?article=2148&context=globaldocs.

5. See: http://www.adidas-group.com/en/sustainability/News/2013/PT_Kizone_ April_2013.aspx.

6. WRC memo, p. 3, at: http://www.workersrights.org/freports/PT%20Kizone%20 Update%2010.23.12.pdf.

7. Emphasis added. See: http://www.adidas-group.com/en/sustainability/News/2013/ PT_Kizone_April_2013.aspx.

8. It should be noted that the contracts signed over a decade earlier between the DOL and brands in Los Angeles to monitor in Los Angeles did include a fair-pricing provision. However, these are not strictly CSR since they were signed with the government under coercion of embargoing goods.

9. Clause 18, p. 4 of Accord on Fire and Building Safety in Bangladesh, at: http:// en.maquilasolidarity.org/sites/maquilasolidarity.org/files/Core-Principles-of-BFBSA.pdf.

10. See: http://www.nytimes.com/2013/05/23/business/legal-experts-debate-us-retailers-risks-of-signing-bangladesh-accord.html?pagewanted=all&_r=0.

4. THE TWILIGHT OF CSR

This chapter was written with the primary assistance of Zachary Nussbaum (Clark University 2014), and also Sarah Suprenant and Breanne Coates (Clark University, 2013).

1. See Ross and Trachte 1990 for a historical, developmental perspective on this era. Kaysen would soon after that publication be a high official in the national security apparatus of the John F. Kennedy administration.

2. The paradox is that many of the Asian newly industrialized countries, in particular China, Taiwan, Korea, and Singapore, obtained their manufacturing export prowess through more dirigiste than laissez-faire policies. See, for versions of this insight, Chang 2008, 2010.

3. Extracted from County Business patterns: Number of Firms, Number of Establishments, Employment, and Annual Payroll by Enterprise Employment Size for the United States, All Industries, 2010. http://www.census.gov//econ/susb/data/susb2010.html. For a theoretical approach see Holleman et al. 2009.

4. There is a qualifier to these findings. The spread of informal styles—the casualization of fashion—cheapens the mix of clothes people buy and that retailers import. When jeans and a checkered shirt replace suits, the price per unit imported goes down.

5. From the AAFA (2012): "On average, every American, including every man, woman, and child in the United States spent $910 on more than 62 garments in 2011."

6. This study was a headed by the International Labor Rights Forum using data (and a method) that Ross generated for various years and for NGO and official reports for others. The Clean Clothes Campaign and the Fair Wear Foundation also participated. Most of the factory fires were caused by electrical faults.

7. Mortality data from previously mentioned LexisNexis study; export data from World Trade Organization statistical database.

8. Author's calculation from US OTEXA import data and WTO export data.

9. Searches within "Bangladesh fires" results were conducted using the search terms "audit," "compliance," and "accreditation." "Audit" was used as a search term to find any mention of an audit, auditors, and/or auditing in a news article reporting on a fire in Bangladesh since 2000, as they relate to CSR. Similarly, "compliance" was used as a search term in order to see if compliance in relation to CSR was mentioned in a report on a Bangladeshi fire. "Accreditation" was chosen as a search term to find out if the locations of the fires in Bangladesh were accredited by an auditing firm hired by a corporation as part of its CSR initiative. In addition the websites of the following NGOs were searched: the International Labor Rights Forum (ILRF http://www.laborrights.org/), the Clean Clothes Campaign (CCC http://www.cleanclothes.org/), the Maquila Solidarity Network (http://en.maquilasolidarity.org/), the Institute for Global Labour and Human Rights (http://www.globallabourrights.org/), and the Business and Human Rights Resource Centre (http://business-humanrights.org/).

10. The quote from C&A was available on its website, http://www.socam.org/uploads/tx_fwdownloads/CoC_English_Master_01.pdf, through late April, 2013. As of May 7 it was not available, and C&A's code-of-conduct language had changed slightly. The quote is still available in a *Times 100* case study at http://businesscasestudies.co.uk/ca/implementing-codes-of-conduct/introduction.html#axzz2UWNSkwRA (as of May 27, 2013).

11. The tragic irony should be noticed: this is the same town where, eight years later, the latest building collapse cost 1,138 lives.

12. Also spelled in some places "Hameem" and "Hamim."

5. THE DEMISE OF TRIPARTITE GOVERNANCE AND THE RISE OF THE CORPORATE SOCIAL RESPONSIBILITY REGIME

1. A typical SACOM press release headlined, "Poisoned Workers Demand Steve Jobs Successor Live Up to CSR," August 26, 2011, http://www.sacom.hk/?p=879. The press release was then picked up by Johnson 2011.

2. "More Than Ten Thousand Workers Strike at Massive Dongguan Shoe Factory," *China Labour Bulletin*, http://www.clb.org.hk/en/ online edition, April 14, 2014. The workers were protesting the failure of Yue Yen to pay its seventy thousand workers their full social security and housing fund contributions.

3. Prodded by Labor Secretary Robert Reich, the Clinton administration sought to ameliorate sweatshop production in other countries as well. The "Apparel Industry Partnership," which soon transformed itself into the industry-dominated Fair Labor Association, was born during Reich's tenure in the cabinet.

4. But Loo may have captured the logic of global labor arbitrage correctly. With poststrike wages rising nearly 40 percent in one year, Cambodian factory production remained flat, abruptly ending the 20 percent annual growth rate characteristic of the previous decade. As GMAC's Loo put it, the garment industry "migrates from one country to another. It moves around seeking out the country with the lowest labor cost." Christina Larson, "Cambodia's Wages Rise, Orders Don't," *Bloomberg Businessweek*, February 9–15, 2015, 19–20.

5. Paragraph 22 reads in part: "Participating brands and retailers will negotiate commercial terms with their suppliers which ensure that it is financially feasible for the factories to maintain safe workplaces and comply with upgrade and remediation requirements instituted by the Safety Inspector" (www.bangladeshaccord.org/wp-content/uploads/2013/10/the_accord.pdf).

6. DEEPENING COMPLIANCE

The views expressed herein are those of the authors and do not necessarily reflect the views of the International Labour Organization or the Brazilian Ministry of Labor and Employment.

1. In cases where the parent company has signed an international framework agreement (such as Zara's parent company, Inditex), this instrument may be used to bring in trade union representation and broaden the scope for tripartite governance to regulate labor standards in GVCs (Hermstadt 2007).

2. ABIT. 2015. Press briefing ("Coletiva de imprensa"), by Rafael Cervone, president of ABIT.

3. Similar to the distinction between a so-called Latin model of flexibility and technical guidance in opposition to the Anglo-Saxon deterrence model (Piore and Shrank 2008).

4. In Brazil, a formal work contract is reflected in the signed work card (*a carteira assinada*).

5. A note of clarification is required here. The definition provided in Article no. 149 of the Brazilian Penal Code considers a worker is in conditions analogous to slave labor if found in: (1) forced labor, (2) debt bondage, and (3) exhausting workday, and (4) degrading conditions of work.

6. Available at: http://www1.camara.sp.gov.br/central_de_arquivos/vereadores/CPI-TrabalhoEscravo.pdf (last consulted November 15, 2013).

7. These activities are consistent with ILO Convention no. 81, which states that competent public authority is required to promote "effective cooperation between the inspection services and other . . . private institutions engaged in similar activities."

8. This law has been praised by the UN Special Rapporteur on Contemporary Forms of Slavery. The law has been proposed by the leading party in the state of São Paulo legislature (the Brazilian Social Democratic Party, PSDB), an opponent of the federal government (the Workers' Party, PT). Although São Paulo was the first state to enact legislation of this type, the states of Tocantins, Maranhão, and Mato Grosso do Sul have subsequently started discussing similar legislation with the National Commission for the Eradication of Slave Labor.

9. Regulations of ABVTEX's Supplier Qualification Program, p. 4, http://www.ABVTex.org.br/regulamento_1507_en.pdf (last consulted November 15, 2013).

10. General information and procedures concerning the certification process are available on the ABVTEX website (http://www.abvtex.org.br). Making the monitoring results transparent has been emphasized as an important factor supporting the drive toward achieving and sustaining compliance (Polaski, 2006).

11. In 2015, these auditing firms included: Bureau Veritas, the Brazilian Association of Technical Standards (Associação Brasileira de Normas Técnicas—ABNT), Intertek, and SGS.

12. These are major audit methodologies carried out by independent transnational firms. WRAP stands for Worldwide Responsible Accredited Production (http://www.wrapcompliance.org/), BSCI for Business Social Compliance Initiative (http://www.bsci-intl.org/), and SMETA is the Sedex Members Ethical Trade Audit (http://www.sedexglobal.com/ethical-audits/smeta/).

13. The subcontractor was embedded in the value chain of a SQP-certified supplier to a global brand and ABVTEX member. See http://www.bbc.co.uk/news/world-latin-america-14570564 (last accessed November 15, 2013).

14. For example, Nike already makes its value chain information available to the public on its website, http://manufacturingmap.nikeinc.com.

15. As noted in ILO 2013b, there are various potential ways to bridge the gap between private and public regulation of labor standards in value chains, such as cooperation, collaboration, and oversight.

7. LAW AND THE GLOBAL SWEATSHOP

1. The exception perhaps proves the rule: under the US Alien Tort Claims Act (ATCA), multinationals may bear responsibility for violations of the law of nations by their suppliers, such as genocide, slavery, and torture; but even that liability is tenuous. Some circuit courts have held that corporations can never be liable under ATCA and some require that defendant firms actually intend that their suppliers engage in such crimes rather than merely acquiescing in their commission. *Cardona v. Chiquita Brands Int'l*, 760 F.3d 1185 (11th Cir. 2014) (no corporate liability under ATCA); *Kiobel v. Royal Dutch Petroleum*, 621 F.3d 111 (2d Cir. 2010) (accord); see also *Kiobel v. Royal Dutch Petroleum* (Leval, J., concurring) (corporate liability available under ATCA, but aiding and abetting liability under ATCA requires that defendant act "with a purpose" to bring about human rights violations); but compare *Doe v. Nestle*, 766 F.3d 1013 (9th Cir. 2014) (corporate liability available under ATCA, with lower standard for aiding and abetting).

2. Another set of challenges comes from antitrust (or "competition") laws, which generally prohibit agreements to set prices for a particular good or commodity. Brands have raised the possibility of antitrust liability as a reason not to agree to union demands that they commit to source from particular factories or ensure particular prices for garments overseas. Since there is not global antitrust authority, this will be for the time being an issue of national-level or European law. Although there are few precedents on point, the US antitrust authorities have declined to take action against the Worker Rights Consortium's Designated Suppliers Program, under which universities would commit to source from particular overseas factories, on the grounds that the agreement would have few if any anticompetitive effects (US Department of Labor 2011). If TTCB leads to more explicit and more costly commitments by brands, such issues may need to be addressed through additional statutory exemptions to antitrust laws.

3. 29 U.S.C. §§ 201 et seq. (2010).

4. California Labor Code § 2810(a).

5. No. 1524, Proposition de loi relative au devoir de vigilance des sociétés mères et des entreprises donneuses d'ordre (November 6, 2013), at http://www.assemblee-nationale.fr/14/propositions/pion1524.asp.

6. California Transparency in Supply Chains Act of 2010, California Civil Code § 1714.43.

8. ASSESSING THE RISKS AND OPPORTUNITIES OF PARTICIPATION IN GLOBAL VALUE CHAINS

This chapter was originally prepared as a background paper of the *World Development Report 2014: Risk and Opportunity*. The findings, interpretations, and conclusions expressed are entirely those of the authors. They do not necessarily represent the views of their affiliated organizations. An earlier version of this chapter appeared as "Risks and Opportunities of Participation in Global Value Chains," *Journal of Banking and Financial Economics*, no. 2 (2015), published by the Faculty of Management, University of Warsaw.

1. "Quake Update," *Automotive News*, April 4, 2011.

2. "Piecing Together a Supply Chain," *New York Times*, May 12, 2011.

3. In 2011, for example, Nike's products were made in 930 factories in 50 countries, employing more than 1 million workers. However, Nike itself had just 38,000 direct employees, most of whom worked in the United States. All of the other workers in Nike's global supply chain were employed by subcontractors based in developing economies (Locke 2013, 48). Over 80 percent of Walmart's more than 60,000 suppliers are located in China alone (Gereffi and Christian 2009, 579).

9. APPLE, FOXCONN, AND CHINA'S NEW WORKING CLASS

1. On September 22, 1985, the finance ministers and central bank governors from the United States, the United Kingdom, West Germany, France, and Japan signed an accord at the Plaza Hotel in New York City to control currency markets. The United States, then running enormous deficits, devalued its currency to make exports more competitive, whereas the Japanese yen and various East Asian industrializing economies' currencies were strengthened.

2. By revenues in fiscal year 2013, Samsung Electronics (US$208.9 billion) ranked thirteenth and Apple (US$170.9 billion) ranked fifteenth on *Fortune* Global 500. In terms of profit, however, Samsung brought in US$27 billion in 2013 compared with Apple's much higher US$37 billion for the same year.

3. Unless otherwise specified, we conducted interviews with Foxconn workers and managers in major cities across China between 2010 and 2015. All transcripts, notes, and digital files are on file with the authors.

4. Apple's five-page e-mail correspondence dated February 18, 2014 is on file with the authors.

5. In 2010, eighteen rural migrant workers attempted suicide at Foxconn facilities across China, resulting in fourteen deaths and four survivors with crippling injuries. They ranged in age from seventeen to twenty-five—the prime of youth. The tragedy was dubbed the "suicide express" in local media.

6. The full letter, in the original Chinese, is on file with the authors.

7. Apple commissioned the Washington DC-based Fair Labor Association to audit major suppliers' conditions in China beginning in early 2012 after deadly aluminum-dust explosions at Foxconn (Chengdu) and Pegatron (Shanghai) in May and December 2011, respectively.

8. Foxconn Technology Group's seven-page statement to the authors dated December 31, 2013, 4–5.

10. LABOR TRANSFORMATION IN CHINA

1. This Joint Center was in operation from 2010 until 2014, when it was closed by Chinese authorities. Some documents are archived at http://laborcenter.berkeley.edu/topic/labor-in-china/.

2. In 2010 the exchange rate was 1 dollar to 6.3 yuan, so their wage was about $143 per month.

3. In China, union leaders at various levels are called "chairman" or "chairwoman." In this chapter we will meet a provincial-level chairman, a district-level chairwoman, and a factory-level chairman. They are all addressed as chairman or chairwoman.

4. In China the Staff and Workers Representative Congress is a body of employees that includes both lower-level and management employees. It is not the same as the union, but has the authority to ratify collectively bargained agreements.

5. An English translation of the final legislation can be found at http://laborcenter.berkeley.edu/pdf/2014/guangdong-regulation-collective-contracts.pdf.

6. The names of the factory and workers have been changed to protect the workers from possible reprisals.

7. Guangdong guidelines call for bargaining over wages, though in practice other subjects are also taken up. Typically this wage bargaining takes place once a year, though in some factories there are separate negotiations for annual bonuses, and in a very few other workplaces there are three-year collective bargaining agreements.

8. In China, collective bargaining is called "collective consultation." Consultation is a more deferential term implying a request with no give and take; however, in practice what takes place is actually bargaining.

11. CSR AND TRADE UNION ELECTIONS AT FOREIGN-OWNED CHINESE FACTORIES

1. *Nanfang Dushibao* (Southern Metropolis News), May 28, 2012.

2. According to the Trade Union Law of the People's Republic of China (PRC) passed in 2001, the workplace-level union branch is a voluntary organization set up by workers, but it "shall be established according to the principle of democratic centralism" (Chapter 2, Article 9).

3. See Trade Union Law, Chapter 5, Article 24, on source of trade union funds.

4. The author collected this kind of qualitative information over the course of more than two decades of field research in a number of research projects at foreign-invested factories.

5. Social Accountability International, http://www.sa-intl.org/_data/n_0001/resources/live/2001StdEnglish.pdf.

6. Attaining Sustainable Business in China, http://www.csrchina.net/page-566.html.

7. In 2000 and 2001, I was able to interview Jill Tucker a number of times in her Hong Kong office and in one of the Reebok supplier factories inside China.

8. A much more detailed account of the election can be found at Anita Chan 2009.

9. Information from a research assistant of mine who visited the factory after the election and interviewed workers outside the factory gate.

10. Jill Tucker showed me the letter from the union.

11. This information is based on my own field research in Shenzhen and by my PRC colleagues in Shunda in 2003.

12. This stirred up a strong reaction from the American trade union federation, the AFL-CIO, which saw it as an infringement of the principles of trade unionism and was skeptical that a "parallel" technique would lead anywhere. See Phil Fishman, AFL-CIO, "Testimony presented to the Congressional-Executive Committee on China," http://www.cecc.gov/pages/roundtables/070703/fishman.php?mode=print (accessed May 23, 2013).

13. There are two examples I am aware of. For several years the American union SEIU (Service Employees International Union) had been sending staff members to China to interest ACFTU in organizing Walmart stores. The Vancouver & District Labor Council and the Beijing Municipal Federation of Trade Unions also discussed how to organize Walmart stores in Beijing in August 2006 (Report of the Vancouver & District Labor Council delegation tour to China, August 14–18, 2006), on file with author.

14. Information gained from meeting with a few Walmart workers from different stores in 2014.

15. Additional information was provided by a current Walmart store worker who has been conducting research on the conditions at other stores either through Walmart workers' blogs or by visiting Walmart stores in other cities when he has a chance.

16. I was in Germany at the time, and I accompanied Zhang Jun as an interpreter in his trip to Denmark. With the help of a Danish trade union we were able to trace the whereabouts of Ole Wolff to a farmhouse in the middle of Denmark. He and his son initially tried to close the door on us, but then agreed to negotiate.

13. LEARNING FROM THE PAST

This chapter is based on the longer journal article by the authors (Anner, Bair, and Blasi 2013).

The authors thank the *Comparative Labor Law & Policy Journal* for its permission to reprint segments of that article here. The authors would also like to thank the Kheel Center for Labor-Management Documentation and Archives at Cornell University for granting us access to the ILGWU archives, Ethan Erickson for his outstanding research assistance, and Professors Marty Wells and Kate Bronfenbrenner of Cornell's School of Industrial and Labor Relations for facilitating our research. Thanks as well to Tim Bartley, Gary Blasi, Peter Evans, Jeff Hermanson, Nina Pillard, Andrew Schrank, Jodi Short, David Weil, and the participants of the Institute of Behavioral Science working group at the University of Colorado at Boulder for their helpful comments on earlier drafts of this chapter.

1. US Department of Commerce, Office of Textiles and Apparel (OTEXA), http://otexa.ita.doc.gov (last accessed March 29, 2014).

2. The Cingranelli and Richards Human Rights Dataset (CIRI), which we use for our labor rights score, contains standards-based quantitative information on government respect for internationally recognized freedom of association rights in approximately 195 countries for the years 1981 to 2010. Scores are recorded on a three-point scale, with "0" for low to no respect for core labor standards, and "2" for high levels of respect.

3. For a more detailed examination of these trends and relationships, see Anner, Bair, and Blasi 2013, 8–14. As we illustrate therein, the decline in real dollar price per square meter of apparel can be seen for specific products sourced from various suppliers and thus does not appear to be driven by a change in the mix of products entering the US market. The decline in price paid for apparel is discussed further in chapter 1 of this volume.

4. The authors thank Nelson Lichtenstein for referring them to this source and quote.

5. "A great and good union points the way for America's labor unions," *Life*, August 31, 1938, 43–44.

6. Authors' calculations based on Bureau of Labor Statistics, Average Hourly Earnings for Production Workers in Women's and Misses' Outerwear Industry, and the New York Department of Labor minimum wage records.

7. None of this is to say that conditions in the industry were excellent across the board or that the ILWGU was beyond legitimate criticism. Several activists and scholars have argued that improvements in working conditions were not enjoyed equally among all ethnic groups and, in particular, that the quality of the ILWGU's organizing and representation was poor for Puerto Rican women workers. See, e.g., Benin 2000. The overall history of the industry, nonetheless, reflects a remarkable transformation that cannot be understated. As the veteran organizer Jeff Hermanson has reflected, "There's some truth to [the radical critique of the ILGWU by Progressive Labor and other organizations], but it overlooks the amazing fact that immigrant workers in New York City, rural women in Pennsylvania, African-American workers in Alabama and Georgia and Mississippi, were making wages and enjoying benefits similar to autoworkers in Detroit, right up until those standards were smashed by the globalization of production" (e-mail to authors, March 10, 2015).

8. Cong. Rec. 8709 (1949): 95.

9. Pub. L. No. 86–257, 73 Statute 543–544, 29 U.S.C. § 158(e).

10. 105 Cong. Rec. 17381 (1959).

11. 105 Cong. Rec. 17327 (1959).

12. This section draws from our analysis of a set of thirty-two collective bargaining agreements that were negotiated by the ILGWU over the course of more than sixty years, from 1930 to 1994. This data from the ILGWU archive at Cornell was supplemented by interviews in spring 2012 with former and current officials of the ILGWU (or its successor unions) who had intimate knowledge of the jobbers' agreements.

13. There are now three times as many apparel businesses in Los Angeles as in New York (BLS 2012).

14. For a more detailed exploration of the approaches covered below and statutory and common-law approaches to joint liability, see Anner, Bair, and Blasi 2013, 25–40.

15. In April 2015, Hanesbrand Inc. purchased Knights Apparel from the private equity firm Merit Capital Partners. However, Alta Gracia, which was a subsidiary of Knights, was not part of the deal.

16. Authors' interviews with an Alta Gracia community education coordinator, April 24, 2015.

17. Fruit of the Loom is the largest private employer in Honduras, with seven major apparel and textile facilities in the country. For details surrounding the closure, see WRC 2008.

18. In the case of the Russell agreement, a further difference is that it applies to factories in Honduras that are owned and operated by Russell's parent company, Fruit of the Loom, as opposed to independent contractors with no ownership relation to the lead firm.

19. International legal mechanisms, particularly the inclusion of labor standards in free trade agreements, also have a key role to play (Polaski 2003), especially when they are linked to worker organizing (Frundt 1998).

20. Peter Dreier and Richard Appelbaum, "*New York Times* deserves a Pulitzer Prize for reporting on Bangladesh sweatshop," *Huffington Post*, May 13, 2013, http://www.huffington post.com/peter-dreier/new-york-times-bangladesh-sweatshops_b_3317561.html (accessed July 10, 2013).

14. WORKERS OF THE WORLD, UNITE!

1. "The term 'sweating,' or 'sweating system,' originally denoted a system of subcontract, wherein the work is let out to contractors to be done in small shops or homes . . . The system to be contrasted with the sweating system is the 'factory system,' wherein the manufacturer employs his own workmen, under the management of his own foreman or superintendent, in his own building" (Commons 1901, 319–20).

2. Some of the largest general strikes were in 1933, which saw the ILGWU recover over a hundred thousand members lost during the first years of the Great Depression; the dressmakers' strike of 1958, which extended the ILGWU's representation to the growing number of contractors in Pennsylvania; and the 1982 general strike of more than ten thousand Chinese garment workers in New York City's four hundred Chinatown factories to secure a collective bargaining agreement in a key area of sportswear production (ILGWU Timeline 2011).

3. The model is called "the fishtank" because it involves maintaining absolute secrecy ("staying under water") in the initial phase of leadership identification, recruitment, and training, until an organizing committee is consolidated, the workforce is analyzed, and a plan made for achieving majority status in the workplace and "coming out of the water" to campaign for recognition (Quinteros 2000; BWI 2014).

4. One chilling example is the April 2012 kidnapping, torture, and murder of the Bangladesh Garment & Industrial Workers Federation organizer Aminul Islam, with the probable involvement of Bangladesh military intelligence agents.

References

AAFA. 2012. "AAFA releases ApparelStats 2012 report." https://www.wewear.org/aafa-releases-apparelstats-2012-report. Accessed May 24, 2013.

Abernathy, Frederick, John T. Dunlop, Janice Hammon, and David Weil. 1999. *A stitch in time: Lean retailing and the transformation of manufacturing—Lessons from the apparel and textile industries.* New York: Oxford University Press.

Accord on Fire and Building Safety in Bangladesh. 2013. "Accord on fire and building safety in Bangladesh." http://bangladeshaccord.org/wp-content/uploads/2013/10/the_accord.pdf. Accessed May 13, 2015.

——. 2014. "Accord reaches important milestone by completing initial inspections of factories in Bangladesh." http://bangladeshaccord.org/2014/10/accord-reaches-important-milestone-completing-initial-inspections-factories-bangladesh/. Accessed May 13, 2015.

——. 2015a. "Signatories." http://bangladeshaccord.org/signatories/. Accessed May 13, 2015.

——. 2015b. "Inspection reports and corrective action plans." http://accord.fairfactories.org/ffcweb/Web/ManageSuppliers/InspectionReportsEnglish.aspx. Accessed May 13.

Acemoglu, D., A. Ozdaglar, and A. Tahbaz-Salehi. 2010. "Cascades in networks and aggregate volatility." No. w16516. National Bureau of Economic Research. http://citeseerx.ist.psu.edu/viewdoc/download?doi=10.1.1.362.690&rep=rep1&type=pdf. Accessed May 11, 2015.

Acemoglu, D., and J.-S. Pischke. 1999. "The structure of wages and investment in general training." *Journal of Political Economy* 107, no. 3: 539–72.

Adler-Milstein, Sarah, Jessica Champagne, and Theresa Haas. 2013. "The right to organize, living wage, and real change for garment workers." In *Lessons for social change in the global economy: Voices from the field,* edited by Shae Garwood, Sky Croeser, and Christalla Yakinthou, 13. New York: Lexington Books.

AFL-CIO. 2013. "Responsibility outsourced: Social audits, workplace certification and twenty years of failure to protect worker rights." http://www.aflcio.org/content/download/77061/1902391/CSReport.pdf. Accessed May 13, 2015.

AFL-CIO, U. Cardin, and U. Smith. 2006. "Section 301 petition." http://www.aflcio.org/content/download/722/6573/AFL-CIO's+301+Worker+Rights+Petition+on+China+from+2006.pdf. Accessed May 12, 2015.

Ahmed, Jashim Uddin, and Tamima Hossain. 2012. "Industrial safety in the readymade garment sector: A developing country perspective." *Sri Lankan Journal of Management* 14, no. 1: 1–13.

Akter, K. 2014. "Remarks by Kalpona Akter, Bangladesh Center for Worker Solidarity." Public Eye Awards, January 23. https://www.evb.ch/fileadmin/files/documents/Public_Eye_Awards/2014_Public_Eye_Kalpona_Akter_Speech-Bio.pdf. Accessed May 13, 2015.

Alam, J. 2012. "Factory owner: I didn't know fire exits needed." *Associated Press,* November 29. http://apnews.excite.com/article/20121129/DA2RJM0G0.html. Accessed May 13, 2015.

Alfaro, L., and M. Chen. 2011. "Surviving the global financial crisis: Foreign ownership and establishment performance." No. w17141. National Bureau of Economic Research. http://home.gwu.edu/~xchen/crisis_MNC.pdf. Accessed May 11, 2015.

Aljazeera. 2013. "Who killed Chea Vichea?" Last updated October 31, 2013. http://www.aljazeera.com/indepth/features/2013/10/cambodia-murder-mystery-who-killed-vichea-20131028103744329535.html.

Ali Manik, J., and V. Bajaj. 2012. "Killing of Bangladeshi labor organizer signals an escalation in violence." *The New York Times*, April 9. http://www.nytimes.com/2012/04/10/world/asia/bangladeshi-labor-organizer-is-found-killed.html. Accessed May 13, 2015.

Ali Manik, J., S. Greenhouse, and J. Yardley. 2013. "Western firms feel pressure as toll rises in Bangladesh." *The New York Times*, April 25. http://www.nytimes.com/2013/04/26/world/asia/bangladeshi-collapse-kills-many-garment-workers.html. Accessed May 13, 2015.

Allard K. Lowenstein International Human Rights Clinic. 2011. "Tearing apart at the seams: How widespread use of fixed-duration contracts threatens Cambodian garment workers and the Cambodian garment industry." http://www.law.yale.edu/documents/pdf/Intellectual_Life/Cambodia_TearingApartattheSeams.pdf. Accessed May 11, 2015.

Almeida, R., and P. Carneiro. 2011. "Enforcement of labor regulation and informality." *American Economic Journal: Applied Economics* 4, no. 3: 64–89.

Amengual, M. 2010. "Complementary labor regulation: The uncoordinated combination of state and private regulators in the Dominican Republic." *World Development* 38, no. 3: 405–14.

American Law Institute. 1958. *Restatement (second) of agency § 219.* Philadelphia: American Law Institute.

Anner, Mark. 2011. *Solidarity transformed: Labor's responses to globalization and crisis in Latin America.* Ithaca, NY: Cornell University Press.

——. 2012a. "Corporate social responsibility and freedom of association rights: The precarious quest for legitimacy and control in global supply chains." *Politics and Society* 40, no. 4: 609–44.

——. 2012b. "The limits of voluntary governance programs: Auditing labor rights in the global apparel industry." Working paper 001. Penn State Project for Global Worker Rights.

——. 2013. "Workers' power in global value chains: Fighting sweatshop practices at Russell, Nike and Knights Apparel." In *Transnational trade unionism: Building union power,* edited by Peter Fairbrother, Marc-Antonin Hennebert, and Christian Lévesque, 23–41. New York: Routledge, Taylor and Francis.

Anner, Mark, Kim Voss, Sakhela Buhlungu, Ian Robinson, and Gay W. Seidman. 2008. "Labor history symposium: Gay W. Seidman, beyond the boycott." *Labor History* 49, no. 3: 341–68.

Anner, Mark, Jennifer Bair, and Jeremy Blasi. 2012. "Buyer power, pricing practices, and labor outcomes in global supply chains." Institutions Program Working Paper Series. University of Colorado. http://www.colorado.edu/ibs/pubs/pec/inst2012-0011.pdf. Accessed May 30, 2013.

——. 2013. "Towards joint liability in global supply chains: Addressing the root causes of labor violations in international subcontracting networks." *Comparative Labor Law & Policy Journal* 35: 1–43.

An Ohms Worker. 2013. "Why we want to recall the labor union chairman" (in Chinese). *LabourWorld*, March 12. http://www.worldlabour.org/eng/node/557. Accessed May 8, 2015.

Anonymous. 2012. "Shenzhen Ohms factory workers went on strike: Capital and labor, lies and realities" (in Chinese). http://blog.sina.com.cn/s/blog_71bfdef601011738.html. Accessed May 8, 2015.

Antras, P., M. Desai, and F. Foley. 2009. "Multinational firms, FDI flows and imperfect capital markets." *Quarterly Journal of Economics* 124, no. 3: 1171–1219.

Appelbaum, Richard. 1999. *Report of the Los Angeles Jewish Commission on sweatshops.* Los Angeles, CA: Pacific Southwest Region of the American Jewish Congress.

——. 2008. "Giant transnational contractors in East Asia: Emergent trends in global supply chain." *Competition and Change* 12, no. 1: 69–87.

——. 2009. "Big suppliers in greater China: A growing counterweight to the power of giant retailers." In *China and the transformation of global capitalism*, edited by Ho-fung Hung, 65–85. Baltimore, MD: Johns Hopkins University Press.

——. 2011. "Transnational contractors in East Asia." In Hamilton, Senauer, and Petrovic, *The market makers*, 255–70. Oxford: Oxford University Press.

——. 2013. "Achieving workers' rights in the global economy." Paper presented at the American Sociological Association meeting, August 10–13, New York City.

Appelbaum, Richard P., and Nelson Lichtenstein. 2006. "A new world of retail supremacy: Supply chains and workers' chains in the age of Wal-Mart." *International Labor and Working Class History* 70: 106–25.

Apple. 2012a. "iPhone 5 first weekend sales top five million." Last updated September 24, 2012. http://www.apple.com/pr/library/2012/09/24iPhone-5-First-Weekend-Sales-Top-Five-Million.html.

——. 2012b. "Apple announces changes to increase collaboration across hardware, software and services." Last updated October 29, 2012. http://www.apple.com/pr/library/2012/10/29Apple-Announces-Changes-to-Increase-Collaboration-Across-Hardware-Software-Services.html.

——. 2013. "Annual report for the fiscal year ended September 28, 2013." http://www.sec.gov/Archives/edgar/data/320193/000119312513416534/d590790d10k.htm.

——. 2014a. "Apple adds UnionPay payment option for app store customers in China." Last updated November 17, 2014. http://www.apple.com/pr/library/2014/11/17Apple-Adds-UnionPay-Payment-Option-for-App-Store-Customers-in-China.html.

——. 2014b. "Annual report for the fiscal year ended September 27, 2014." http://files.shareholder.com/downloads/AAPL/3710236455x0x789040/ed3853da-2e3f-448d-adb4-34816c375f5d/2014_Form_10_K_As_Filed.PDF.

——. 2015a. "Supplier map." https://www.apple.com/uk/supplier-responsibility/our-suppliers/.

——. 2015b. "Apple reports record first quarter results." Last updated January 27, 2015. https://www.apple.com/pr/library/2015/01/27Apple-Reports-Record-First-Quarter-Results.html.

Armbruster-Sandoval, R. 2005. "Workers of the world unite? The contemporary anti-sweatshop movement and the struggle for social justice in the Americas." *Work and Occupations* 32, no. 4: 464–85. doi:10.1177/0730888405278990.

Arnold, Dennis, and Toh Hah Shih. 2010. "A fair model of globalisation? Labour and global production in Cambodia." *Journal of Contemporary Asia* 4, no. 3: 401–24.

Atleson, James. 2000. "The voyage of the Neptune Jade: Transnational labor solidarity and the obstacles of domestic law." In *Labour law in an era of globalization: Transformative practices and possibilities*, edited by Joanne Conaghan, Richard Michael Fischl, and Karl Klare, 379–400. Oxford: Oxford University Press.

Bahree, Megha. 2014. "Wage wars unravel stitches of Cambodia's $5B garment sector." *Forbes Asia*, August 27. http://www.forbes.com/sites/meghabahree/2014/08/27/

cambodias-garment-sector-is-getting-torn-between-poor-labor-and-unyielding-foreign-owners/. Accessed May 12, 2015.

Bair, Jennifer. 2006. "Global capitalism and commodity chains: Looking back, going forward." *Competition and Change* 9, no. 2: 129–56.

——. 2012. "The limits to embeddedness: Triangular bargaining and the institutional foundations of organizational networks." vol. 8. Working paper, Institute of Behavioral Science, University of Colorado, Boulder.

Bair, Jennifer, and Gary Gereffi. 2011. "Towards better work in Central America: The prospects for success in Nicaragua." Paper presented at the Workers, Businesses and Governments: Understanding Labor Compliance in Global Supply Chains conference, Washington, DC, October 26–28.

——. 2014. "Towards better work in Central America: Nicaragua and the CAFTA context." In Rossi, Luinstra, and Pickles, *Towards better work*, 251–75.

Bair, Jennifer, and Florence Palpacuer. 2013. "From varieties of capitalism to varieties of activism: The anti-sweatshop movement in comparative perspective." *Social Problems* 59, no. 4: 522–43.

Balfour, Frederik, and Tim Culpan. 2010. "The man who makes your iPhone." *Bloomberg*, September 9. http://www.bloomberg.com/bw/magazine/content/10_38/b4195058423479.htm.

Ballinger, Jeffrey. 2009. "'Better work' for garment workers: Which side are you on?" *Labor Notes*. http://www.labornotes.org/2009/12/%E2%80%98better-work%E2%80%99-garment-workers-which-side-are-you. Accessed May 11, 2015.

——. 2015. "Nike chronology." http://depts.washington.edu/ccce/polcommcampaigns/NikeChronology.htm. Accessed May 11, 2015.

Banjo, Shelly. 2014. "Inside Nike's struggle to balance cost and worker safety in Bangladesh." *The Wall Street Journal*, April 21. http://www.wsj.com/articles/SB10001424052702303873604579493502231397942. Accessed May 12, 2015.

Barrie, L. 2012. "Tchibo commits to factory fire safety programme." *Just-style*, September 20. http://www.just-style.com/news/tchibo-commits-to-factory-fire-safety-programme_id115615.aspx. Accessed May 13, 2015.

Barrientos, S., C. Dolan, and A. Tallontire. 2003. "A gendered value chain approach to codes of conduct in African horticulture." *World Development* 31, no. 9: 1511–26.

Barrientos, S., G. Gereffi, and A. Rossi. 2011. "Economic and social upgrading in global production networks: A new paradigm for a changing world." *International Labour Review* 150, nos. 3–4: 319–40.

Barrientos, S., G. Gereffi, and D. Nathan. 2012. "Economic and social upgrading in global value chains: Emerging trends and pressures." Capturing the Gains Summit Briefing, December. http://www.capturingthegains.org/pdf/CTG-GVC.pdf.

Barrientos, S., U. Kothari, and N. Phillips. 2013. "Dynamics of unfree labour in the contemporary global economy." *The Journal of Development Studies* 49, no. 8: 1037–41.

Barrientos, Stephanie, and Sally Smith. 2007. "Do workers benefit from ethical trade? Assessing codes of labour practice in global production systems." *Third World Quarterly* 28, no. 4: 713–29.

Barta, Patrick, and Syed Zain al-Mahmood. 2014. "Bangladesh workers face fight to form unions." *The Wall Street Journal*, September 11. http://www.wsj.com/articles/SB10001424127887323455104579012201357331012. Accessed May 12, 2015.

Bartley, Tim. 2005. "Corporate accountability and the privatization of labor standards: Struggles over codes of conduct in the apparel industry." *Research in Political Sociology* 14: 211–44.

———. 2007. "Institutional emergence in an era of globalization: The rise of transnational private regulation of labor and environmental conditions." *American Journal of Sociology* 113, no. 2: 297–351. doi:10.1086/518871.

Bartley, Tim, and Curtis Child. 2014. "Shaming the corporation: The social production of targets and the anti-sweatshop movement." *American Sociological Review* 79: 653–79.

BBC. 2014. "Apple 'deeply offended' by BBC investigation." Last updated December 19, 2014. http://www.bbc.co.uk/news/technology-30548468.

Be, Dominique. 2008. "A report on the European Commission Initiative for a European framework for transnational collective bargaining." In *Cross-border social dialogue and agreements: An emerging industrial relations framework?*, edited by Konstantinos Papadakis, 221–36. Geneva: International Labour Office.

BEA. 2015. "GDP price deflator." http://www.bea.gov/index.htm. Accessed May 13, 2015.

Benin, Leigh David. 2000. *The new labor radicalism and New York City's garment industry.* New York: Routledge.

Bennett, Graceann, and Freya Williams. 2011. *Mainstream green: Moving sustainability from niche to normal.* New York: Ogilvy & Mather. http://www.ogilvyearth.com/wp-content/uploads/2011/05/OgilvyEarth_Mainstream_Green.pdf. Accessed May 11, 2015.

Berg, A., S. Hedrich, S. Kempf, and T. Tochtermann. 2011. "Bangladesh's ready-made garments landscape: The challenge of growth." November. McKinsey & Company. http://www.mckinsey.de/sites/mck_files/files/2011_McKinsey_Bangladesh.pdf.

Bernhardt, T. 2013. "Developing countries in the global apparel value chain: A tale of upgrading and downgrading experiences." Capturing the Gains working paper no. 22, February. http://www.capturingthegains.org/pdf/ctg-wp-2013-22.pdf.

Better Factories Cambodia. 2014. "New study finds high levels of anemia, food insecurity, among Cambodian garment workers." Last updated September 29, 2014. betterfactories.org/wp-content/uploads/2014/09/2014_09_25-Press-Release-for-the-Food-Provision-Study_FINAL-ENG.pdf.

BGMEA. 2015. "Trade information." Last modified April 11, 2015. http://bgmea.com.bd/home/pages/TradeInformation#.VVGQkyHOOko.

Bignami, R. 2011. "Trabalho escravo contemporâneo: O sweating system no contexto brasileiro como expressão do trabalho escravo urbano." In *Trabalho escravo contemporâneo—O desafio de superar a negação.* 2nd ed. São Paulo: LTR.

Blanpain, Roger, Ulla Liukkunen, and Yifeng Chen, eds. 2014. *China and ILO fundamental principles and rights at work.* Alphen aan den Rijn: Kluwer.

BLS. 2012. "BLS spotlight statistics: Fashion." Washington, DC: Bureau of Labor Statistics.

Bluhmod. 2013. "BSCI-business social compliance initiative and Bluhmod." http://www.bluhmod.de/en/news/current/detail/article/bsci-business-social-compliance-initiative-1/. Accessed May 13, 2015.

Bobrowsky, David. 1999. "Creating a global public policy network in the apparel industry: The apparel industry partnership." http://old.gppi.net/fileadmin/gppi/Bobrowsky_Apparel_Industry.pdf. Accessed May 11, 2015.

Bodie, Matthew. 2008. "Information and the market for union representation." *Virginia Law Review* 94: 1–62.

Bonacich, Edna, and Richard P. Appelbaum. 2000. *Behind the label: Inequality in the Los Angeles apparel industry.* Berkeley: University of California Press.

Borchers, Patrick J. 2013. "Conflict-of-laws considerations in state court human rights action." *University of California Irvine Law Review* 3: 45–61.

Bowen, Howard R. 2013. *Social Responsibilities of the Businessman.* Iowa City: University of Iowa Press.

Brand Finance. 2014. "Brandirectory: Ranking the world's most valuable brands." http://brandirectory.com/league_tables/table/global-500-2014.

Braun, Rainer, and Judy Gearhart. 2004. "Who should code your conduct? Trade union and NGO differences in the fight for workers' rights." *Development in Practice* 14, nos. 1–2: 183–96.

Brettman, Alan. 2013. "Adidas settles with Indonesian workers over PT Kizone." *The Oregonian/OregonLive*, April 23. http://www.oregonlive.com/playbooks-profits/index.ssf/2013/04/adidas_settles_with_indonesian.html.

Brudney, James J. 2012. "Envisioning enforcement of freedom of association standards in corporate codes: A journey for Sinbad or Sisyphus?" *Comparative Labor Law & Policy Journal* 33: 555–603.

Brudney, James, and Catherine Fisk. 2013. "Wal-Mart, Gap skirt the issue." *Los Angeles Times*, May 17. http://articles.latimes.com/2013/may/17/opinion/la-oe-fisk-bangladesh-apparel-accord-20130517. Accessed May 9, 2015.

BSCI. 2013. "Statement on the Rana Plaza building collapse in Bangladesh." Last modified April 30, 2013. http://www.bsci-intl.org/news-events/statement-rana-plaza-building-collapse-bangladesh. Accessed May 13, 2015.

Buck, Rinker. 1979. "The new sweatshops: A penny for your collar." *New York* 12, no. 9: 29.

Burke, J., and S. Hammadi. 2012. "Bangladesh textile factory leaves more than 100 dead." *The Guardian*, November 25. http://www.theguardian.com/world/2012/nov/25/bangladesh-textile-factory-fire. Accessed May 13, 2015.

Bustillo, Miguel, Tom Wright, and Shelly Banjo. 2012. "For Wal-Mart, Sears, Tough Questions in Bangladesh Fire." *Wall Street Journal (online)*, November 29. http://www.wsj.com/articles/SB10001424127887323751104578148463240906892. Accessed September 14, 2015.

BWI. 2014. "La Pecera: Ideas para la construcción de una estructura de poder a favor de los trabajadores." Unpublished PowerPoint presentation.

Canis, B. 2011. "The motor vehicle supply chain: Effects of the Japanese earthquake and tsunami." Congressional Research Service (CRS) Report for Congress, R41831. https://www.fas.org/sgp/crs/misc/R41831.pdf. Accessed May 11, 2015.

C&A Buying. 1998. "The C&A code of conduct for the supply of merchandise." http://www.socam.org/uploads/tx_fwdownloads/CoC_English_Master_01.pdf.

Carrefour. 2011. "2011 sustainability expert report." http://www.carrefour.com/sites/default/files/84595_RA_EXPERT_001-117_GB_2011_V2.pdf. Accessed May 9, 2015.

Cattaneo, O., G. Gereffi, and C. Staritz, eds. 2010. *Global value chains in a postcrisis world: A development perspective.* Washington, DC: The World Bank.

CCC. 2001. "Update on Bangladesh garment factory fire that killed 24." http://digitalcommons.ilr.cornell.edu/cgi/viewcontent.cgi?article=1150&context=globaldocs. Accessed May 27, 2013.

——. 2005a. "Spectrum disaster update: Protests continue as companies still fail to help their workers." http://archive.cleanclothes.org/newslist/187. Accessed May 28, 2013.

——. 2005b. "Looking for a quick fix: How weak social auditing is keeping workers in sweatshops." http://www.cleanclothes.org/resources/publications/05-quick-fix.pdf/at_download/file%20. Accessed October 24, 2013.

——. 2006. "Spectrum disaster—one year after the collapse." http://archive.cleanclothes.org/news/spectrum-disaster-one-year-after-the-collapse. Accessed May 28, 2013.

———. 2011. "That's It Sportswear fire: One year on workers still dying in unsafe buildings." http://www.cleanclothes.org/news/2011/12/15/thats-it-sportswear-fire-one-year-on-workers-still-dying-in-unsafe-buildings. Accessed May 9, 2015.

———. 2012a. "Hazardous workplaces: Making the Bangladesh garment industry safe." http://www.cleanclothes.org/resources/publications/2012-11-hazardousworkplaces.pdf. Accessed May 13, 2015.

———. 2012b. "Background on PT Kizone, Indonesia." http://www.cleanclothes.org/news/2012/05/09/background-on-pt-kizone-indonesia. Accessed May 11, 2015.

———. 2013a. "Bangladesh workers must continue to wait for full compensation." http://www.cleanclothes.org/news/press-releases/2013/09/12/bangladesh-workers-must-continue-to-wait-for-full-compensation. Accessed October 24, 2013.

———. 2013b. "WE WON! Adidas pays Kizone workers." Last updated April 29, 2013. http://www.cleanclothes.org/news/2013/04/29/we0won0adidas-pays-kizone-workers.

———. 2015. "Who needs to pay up?" http://www.cleanclothes.org/ranaplaza/who-needs-to-pay-up. Accessed May 13.

CCC and Center for Research on Multinational Corporations. 2013. "Fatal fashion analysis of recent factory fires in Pakistan and Bangladesh: A call to protect and respect garment workers' lives." http://www.cleanclothes.org/resources/publications/fatal-fashion.pdf. Accessed October 24, 2013.

CCC and SOMO. 2013. "Fatal fashion." http://www.cleanclothes.org/resources/publications/fatal-fashion.pdf. Accessed May 13, 2015.

Center for American Progress, Just Jobs, and Worker Rights Consortium. 2013. "Global wage trends for apparel workers, 2001–2011." July. Center for American Progress. http://cdn.americanprogress.org/wp-content/uploads/2013/07/RealWageStudy-3.pdf. Accessed May 13, 2015.

Chan, Anita. 2001. *China's workers under assault: The exploitation of labor in a globalizing economy.* New York: M. E. Sharpe.

———. 2003. "A 'Race to the Bottom': Globalisation and China's labour standards." *China Perspectives* 46: 41–49.

———. 2006. "Realities and possibilities for Chinese trade unionism." In *The future of organised labor: Global perspective*, edited by Craig Phelan, 275–304. Oxford: Peter Lang.

———. 2009. "Challenges and Possibilities for Democratic Grassroots Union Elections in *China*: A Case Study of Two Factory-level Elections and Their Aftermath." *Labor Studies Journal* 34, no. 3: 293–317.

———. 2011. "Unionizing Chinese Wal-Mart stores." In Chan, *Wal-Mart in China*, 199–216.

———, ed. 2011. *Wal-Mart in China.* Ithaca, Cornell University Press.

Chan, Anita, and Kaxton Siu. 2012. "Chinese migrant workers: Factors constraining the emergence of class consciousness." In *Chinese peasants and workers: Changing class identity*, edited by Beatriz Carrillo and David S. G. Goodman, 79–101. Cheltenham, UK: Edward Elgar.

Chan, Chris King-Chi. 2010. *The challenge of labour in China: Strikes and the changing labour regime in global factories.* London: Routledge.

———. 2014. "Constrained labor agency and the changing regulatory regime in China." *Development and Change* 45, no. 4: 685–709.

Chan, Chris King-Chi, and Elaine So-Ieng Hui. 2013. "The development of collective bargaining in China: From 'collective bargaining by riot' to 'party-state-led wage bargaining.'" *The China Quarterly* 217: 221–42.

——. 2014. "The dynamics and dilemma of workplace trade union reform in China: The case of the Honda workers' strike." *Journal of Industrial Relations* 54, no. 5: 653–68.

Chan, Jenny. 2009. "Meaningful progress or illusory reform? Analyzing China's labor contract law." *New Labor Forum* 18, no. 2: 43–51.

——. 2013. "A suicide survivor: The life of a Chinese worker." *New Technology, Worker and Employment* 28, no. 2: 84–99; and *The Asia-Pacific Journal* 11, no. 31: 1–30. http://www.japanfocus.org/-Jenny-Chan/3977.

Chan, Jenny, and Mark Selden. 2014. "China's rural migrant workers, the state, and labor politics." *Critical Asian Studies* 46, no. 4: 599–620.

Chan, Jenny, and Ngai Pun. 2010. "Suicide as protest for the new generation of Chinese migrant workers: Foxconn, global capital, and the state." *The Asia-Pacific Journal* 37, no. 2: 1–50. http://japanfocus.org/-Jenny-Chan/3408.

Chan, Jenny, Ngai Pun, and Mark Selden. 2013. "The politics of global production: Apple, Foxconn, and China's new working class." *New Technology, Work and Employment* 28, no. 2: 100–115, and *The Asia-Pacific Journal* 11, no. 32: 1–32. http://www.japanfocus.org/-Jenny-Chan/3981.

——. 2015. "Apple's iPad city: Subcontracting exploitation to China." In *Handbook of the international political economy of production*, edited by Kees van der Pijl, 76–97. Cheltenham, UK: Edward Elgar.

——. 2016. "Chinese labor protest and trade unions," In *The Routledge companion to labor and media*, edited by Richard Maxwell, 290–302. New York: Routledge.

Chang, Ha-Joon. 2008. *Bad samaritans: The myth of free trade and the secret history of capitalism.* New York: Bloomsbury Publishing USA.

——. 2010. *23 things they don't tell you about capitalism.* New York: Bloomsbury Publishing USA.

Chen, Hsin-Hsing. 2011. "Professionals, students, and activists in Taiwan mobilize for an unprecedented collective-action lawsuit against a former top American electronics company." *East Asian Science, Technology and Society* 5, no. 4: 555–65.

Chen, Michelle. 2015. "Cambodia's garment workers aren't backing down." *The Nation*, January 23. http://www.thenation.com/blog/195817/cambodias-garment-workers-arent-backing-down. Accessed May 12, 2015.

Chen, W. 2012b. *You Yu Si—Reflections on 30 years of union work.* Beijing: Chinese Academy of Social Sciences Publishing House.

Chen, Xi. 2012a. *Social protest and contentious authoritarianism in China.* New York: Cambridge University Press.

——. 2013. "The rising cost of stability." *Journal of Democracy* 24, no. 1: 57–64.

Chiang, Charlie Z. W., and Ho-Don Yan. 2015. "Terry Gou and Foxconn." In *Handbook of East Asian entrepreneurship*, edited by Fu-Lai Tony Yu and Ho-Don Yan, 300–312. Abingdon, Oxon, UK: Routledge.

China Labor News Translations. "The Nanhai Honda strike and the union." *China Labor News Translations.* July 18, 2010. http://www.clntranslations.org/article/56/honda. Accessed September 27, 2015.

China Labour Bulletin. 2013. "Shenzhen workers demand ouster of trade *union* chairman after "model election." http://www.clb.org.hk/en/content/shenzhen-workers-demand-ouster-trade-union-chairman-after-%E2%80%9Cmodel-election%E2%80%9D.

——. 2014. "Defeat will only make us stronger: Workers look back at the Yue Yuen shoe factory strike." Last updated May 22, 2014. http://www.clb.org.hk/en/content/

defeat-will-only-make-us-stronger-workers-look-back-yue-yuen-shoe-factory-strike.

———. 2015. "Strike Map." http://strikemap.clb.org.hk/strikes/en. Accessed April 29, 2015.

City of Fremont, California. 2012. "Staff report 1491: Report to council on referral of former Apple Macintosh factory history." Last updated September 18, 2012. http://fremontcityca.iqm2.com/Citizens/Detail_LegiFile.aspx?ID=1491&highlightTerms=macintosh.

Claeson, Bjorn. 2010. "Twenty-one locked-in apparel workers die in another factory fire in Bangladesh." Labor Is Not a Commodity blog. http://laborrightsblog.typepad.com/international_labor_right/2010/03/twenty-one-locked-in-apparel-workers-die-in-another-factory-fire-in-bangladesh.html#more. Accessed May 28, 2013.

———. 2012. "Deadly secrets: What companies know about dangerous workplaces and why exposing the truth can save workers' lives in Bangladesh and beyond." Labor Is Not a Commodity blog. http://laborrights.org/sites/default/files/publications-and-resources/DeadlySecrets.pdf. Accessed May 23, 2013.

Clark, N., J. Chataway, R. Hanlin, D. Kale, R. Kaplinsky, L. Muraguri, T. Papaioannou, P. Robbins, and W. Wamae. 2009. "Below the radar: What does innovation in the Asian driver economies have to offer other low income economies?" INNOGEN working paper no. 69. http://oro.open.ac.uk/15241/1/. Accessed May 11, 2015.

Clifford, S., and S. Greenhouse. 2013. "Fast and flawed inspections of factories abroad." *The New York Times*, September 1. http://www.nytimes.com/2013/09/02/business/global/superficial-visits-and-trickery-undermine-foreign-factory-inspections.html. Accessed May 13, 2015.

CLNT. 2011. "Should China create a law on strike?" http://www.clntranslations.org/article/62/strike+law. Accessed May 8, 2014.

Coase, R. H. 1937. "The nature of the firm." *Economica New Series* 4, no. 6: 386–405.

Cody, Edward. 2006. "Short-lived strike reflects strength of Japan-China ties." *Washington Post*, April 25. http://www.washingtonpost.com/wp-dyn/content/article/2005/04/25/AR2005042501555.html. Accessed May 8, 2015.

Coe, N., P. Dicken, and M. Hess. 2008. "Global production networks: Realizing the potential." *Journal of Economic Geography* 8, no. 3: 271–95.

Coe, N., and M. Hess. 2013. "Global production networks, labour and development." *Geoforum* 44, no. 1: 4–9.

Commons, John. 1901. "Sweating System in the Clothing Trade," John R. Commons, Report U. S. Industrial Commission, in 1901, Vol. XV, 319–52; Washington, D.C.; US Government Printing Office.

Community Legal Education Centre and Clean Clothes Campaign. 2012. "10 Years of the Better Factories Cambodia project: A critical evaluation." http://www.cleanclothes.org/resources/publications/ccc-clec-betterfactories-29-8.pdf. Accessed May 12, 2015.

Compa, Lance. 2001. "Wary allies." *American Prospect* 12, no. 12: 8–9.

———. 2004. "Trade unions, NGOs, and corporate codes of conduct." *Development in Practice* 14, nos. 1–2: 210–15.

Corporate Knights. 2007. "2007 Global 100 List." http://www.global100.org/annual-lists/2007-global-100-list.html. Accessed May 28, 2013.

Corseuil, C. H., R. Almeida, and P. Carneiro. 2012. Inspeção do trabalho e evolução do emprego formal no Brasil. IPEA discussion paper 1688. Brasilia: Institute for Applied Economic Research.

Coslovsky, S., R. Pires, and R. Bignami. Forthcoming. "Labour relations in contemporary Brazil: Stable regulations, dynamic enforcement." In *Labour relations in developing countries*, edited by D. Fuller, H. Gospel, and H. Kwon. Oxford: Oxford University Press.

Costa, P. T. M. 2010. *Combatendo o trabalho escravo contemporâneo: O exemplo do Brasil.* http://www.ilo.org/wcmsp5/groups/public/---americas/---ro-lima/---ilo-brasilia/documents/publication/wcms_227300.pdf. Accessed May 8, 2015.

Cowie, Jefferson. 2001. *Capital move: RCA's seventy-year quest for cheap labor.* New York: The New Press.

Crinis, Vicki. 2010. "Sweat or no sweat: Foreign workers in the garment industry in Malaysia." *Journal of Contemporary Asia* 40, no. 4: 589–611.

CTC. 2008. "Canadian Tire Corporation, Limited: Supplier code of business conduct." http://www.marks.com/webapp/wcs/stores/servlet/MarksStorefrontAssetStore/wcm/documents/supplierCode.pdf. Accessed May 16, 2015.

Cumbers, A., C. Nativel, and P. Routledge. 2008. "Labour agency and union positionalities in global production networks." *Journal of Economic Geography* 8: 369–87.

Cushman, John H., Jr. 1998. "Nike pledges to end child labor and apply U.S. rules abroad." *The New York Times*, May 13. http://www.nytimes.com/1998/05/13/business/international-business-nike-pledges-to-end-child-labor-and-apply-us-rules-abroad.html.

Cutler, C. A., V. Haufler, and T. Porter, eds. 1999. *Private authority and international affairs.* Albany: State University of New York Press.

Daily Star. 2013. "'Manpower-less' department of inspection." http://www.thedailystar.net/beta2/news/manpower-less-department-of-inspection. Accessed May 30, 2013.

Deyo, Frederic C. 1989. *Beneath the miracle: Labor subordination in the new Asian industrialism.* Berkeley: University of California Press.

Dhaka Tribune. 2013. "US okays safety accord bill on Bangladeshi RMG." June 18. http://www.dhakatribune.com/labour/2013/jun/18/us-okays-bill-safety-accord-rmg-bangladesh. Accessed June 21, 2013.

Di Giovanni, J., and A. Levchenko. 2009. "International trade and aggregate fluctuations in granular economies." Working paper, University of Michigan. http://crei.cat/files/filesActivity/34/di%20giovanni.pdf.

Dreyfuss, R. 2010. "China in the driver's seat." http://www.thenation.com/article/154484/china-drivers-seat. Accessed May 9, 2014.

Drucker, P. 1951. *The New Society: The Anatomy of the Industrial Order.* New York: Harper and Brothers.

Dukes, Ruth. 2011. "Hugo Sinzheimer and the constitutional function of labour law." In *The idea of labour law*, edited by Guy Davidov and Brian Langille, 57–67. Oxford: Oxford University Press.

The Economist. 1999. "The world this millennium." Millennium issue, December 23. http://www.economist.com/node/346572. Accessed October 28, 2015.

———. 2012. "Garment factory fires: A 'Distinctly South Asian' tragedy." http://www.economist.com/blogs/banyan/2012/12/garment-factory-fires. Accessed May 12, 2015.

———. 2015. "Planet of the phones." Last updated February 28, 2015. http://www.economist.com/news/leaders/21645180-smartphone-ubiquitous-addictive-and-transformative-planet-phones.

EFMD. 2015. "EU Cooperation: An Overview." https://www.efmd.org/eu-cooperation. Accessed October 26, 2015.

Eidelson, J. 2012. "Photos show Walmart apparel at site of deadly factory fire in Bangladesh." *The Nation*, November 26. http://www.thenation.com/blog/171451/photos-show-walmart-apparel-site-deadly-factory-fire-bangladesh#. Accessed May 13, 2015.

Elliott, K., and R. Freeman. 2003. *Can labor standards improve under globalization?* Washington, DC: Institute for International Economics.

Ensign, Rachel Louise. 2013. "Fixing problems in developing world factories is challenge for auditors." *Wall Street Journal*, May 1. http://blogs.wsj.com/riskandcompliance/2013/05/01/fixing-problems-in-developing-world-factories-is-challenge-for-auditors/. Accessed May 28, 2013.

Ernst, Dieter. 1997. "From partial to systemic globalization: International production networks in the electronics industry." Berkeley Roundtable on the International Economy working paper 98. http://brie.berkeley.edu/publications/WP%2098.pdf.

Esbenshade, Jill. 2001. "The social accountability contract: Private monitoring from Los Angeles to the global apparel industry." *Labor Studies Journal* 26, no. 1: 98–120.

——. 2004a. *Monitoring sweatshops: Workers, consumers, and the global apparel industry*. Philadelphia: Temple University Press.

——. 2004b. "Codes of conduct: Challenges and opportunities for workers' rights." *Social Justice* 31, no. 3: 40–59.

——. 2008. "Going up against the global economy: New developments in the anti-sweatshop movement." *Critical Sociology* 34, no. 3: 453–70.

——. 2012. "A review of private regulation: Codes and monitoring in the apparel industry." *Sociology Compass* 6, no. 7: 541–56.

Esping-Andersen, Gosta. 1990. *The three worlds of welfare capitalism*. Princeton, NJ: Princeton University Press.

Estlund, Cynthia, and Seth Gurgel. 2014. "Will labour unrest lead to more democratic trade unions in China?" In Blanpain, Liukkunen, and Chen, *China and ILO*, 13–82.

Fair Wear Foundation/Cotton Group. 2009. "The Fair Wear code of labour practices for labour conditions in the garment sector." http://www.sonatex.de/cms/projects/sonatex/media/pdf/bc_fairwear.pdf. Accessed May 13, 2015.

Fantasia, Rick. 1988. *Cultures of solidarity: Consciousness, action, and contemporary American workers*. Berkeley: University of California Press.

Featherstone, Liza, and USAS. 2002. *Students against sweatshops: The making of a movement*. New York: Verso.

Federal Labor Inspection System (*Sistema Federal da Inspeção do Trabalho*). 2003–2014. https://sfitweb.mte.gov.br. Accessed May 12, 2015.

Feng, Xiaoxiao. 2004. "Sixteen thousand workers in the Japanese enterprise Uniden in Shenzhen are staging a big strike: Let's all go to support our compatriots" (in Chinese). ChinaUnix net, December 17. http://bbs.chinaunix.net/viewthread.php?tid=468440. Accessed May 8, 2015.

Finnegan, Brian. 2013. "Responsibility outsourced: Social audits, workplace certification and twenty years of failure to protect worker rights." http://www.aflcio.org/content/download/77061/1902391/CSReport.pdf. Accessed June 1, 2013.

FLA. 1999. "Fair Labor Association charter document: Amended agreements (June)." http://www1.umn.edu/humanrts/links/flacharter.html. Accessed May 11, 2015.

——. 2014. "Charter document, Fair Labor Association: As amended, February 12, 2014." http://www.fairlabor.org/sites/default/files/fla_charter_2-12-14.pdf. Accessed May 11, 2015.

Flannery, Michael. 1978. "America's sweatshops in the sun." *AFL-CIO Rank and File Federationist* 85, no. 5: 16–19.

The Forverts. 1911. "The morgue is full of our victims!" Last modified March 16, 2011. http://forward.com/articles/136207/the-morgue-is-full-of-our-victims/. Accessed May 13, 2015.

Fossett, K. 2013. "Few meaningful changes in wake of Dhaka factory collapse." *Inter Press* Service, May 3. http://www.ipsnews.net/2013/05/few-meaningful-changes-in-wake-of-dhaka-factory-collapse/. Accessed May 13, 2015.

Foucault, Michel. 2010. *The birth of biopolitics: Lectures at the College de France, 1978–79.* Edited by Michel Senellart. Translated by Graham Burchell. New York: Picador Palgrave MacMillan.

Foxconn Technology Group. 2009. "Corporate social and environmental responsibility annual report 2008." http://ser.foxconn.com/SelectLanguageAction. do?language=1&jump=/cser/Annual_Report.jsp.

——. 2010. "Foxconn is committed to a safe and positive working environment." Last updated October 11, 2010. http://regmedia.co.uk/2010/10/12/foxconn_media_statement.pdf.

——. 2011. "The Foxconn Bridgeworkers No. 189." (in Chinese). Last updated June 30, 2011. Company Monthly Magazine, Shenzhen city, China.

——. 2014a. "Board of directors approved financial statements of 2013." Last updated March 28, 2014. http://www.honhai.com.tw/Message_En.html?index=37.

——. 2014b. "Foxconn corporate social and environmental responsibility annual report 2013." http://ser.foxconn.com/SelectLanguageAction. do?language=1&jump=/cser/Annual_Report.jsp.

Frank, Dana. 2000. *Buy American: The untold story of economic nationalism.* Boston: Beacon Press.

Fraser, Steve. 1991. *Labor will rule: Sidney Hillman and the rise of American labor.* New York: Free Press.

Frederick, S., and G. Gereffi. 2011. "Upgrading and restructuring in the global apparel value chain: Why China and Asia are outperforming Mexico and Central America." *International Journal of Technological Learning, Innovation and Development* 4, nos. 1–3: 67–95.

Freeman, Richard, and James L. Medoff. 1984. *What do unions do?* New York: Basic Books.

Frundt, Henry J. 1998. *Trade conditions and labor rights: U.S. initiatives, Dominican and Central American responses.* Gainesville: University Press of Florida.

——. 2004. "Unions wrestle with corporate codes of conduct." *Working USA* 7, no. 4: 36–69.

FTA. 2013. "The BSCI code of conduct." http://www.bsci-intl.org/our-work/bsci-code-conduct. Accessed May 9, 2015.

Fung, Victor. 2011. "Global supply chains—past developments, emerging trends." Speech at the Century 21 Club, November 24. http://www.fungglobalinstitute. org/publications/speeches/global-supply-chains--past-developments-emerging-trends-193.html. Accessed May 23, 2013.

Galbraith, John Kenneth. 2012. *American Capitalism: The Concept of Countervailing Power.* Eastford, CT: Martino Fine Books.

Gallagher, Mary E. 2014. "China's workers movement and the end of the rapid-growth era." *Dædalus: The Journal of the American Academy of Arts and Sciences* 143, no. 2: 81–95.

Gallagher, Mary E., John Giles, Albert Park, and Meiyan Wang. 2015. "China's 2008 labor contract law: Implementation and implications for China's workers." *Human Relations* 68, no. 2: 197–235.

Gap Inc. 2007. "Code of vendor conduct." http://www.gapinc.com/content/dam/csr/documents/COVC_070909.pdf. Accessed May 28, 2013.

Gereffi, Gary. 1994. "The organization of buyer-driven global commodity chains: How US retailers shape overseas production networks." In *Commodity chains and global capitalism*, edited by G. Gereffi and M. Korzeniewicz, 95–122. Westport, CT: Praeger Publishers.

——. 1999. "International trade and industrial upgrading in the apparel commodity chain." *Journal of International Economics* 48, no. 1: 37–70.

——. 2005. "The global economy: Organization, governance, and development." In *The handbook of economic sociology*, edited by Neil J. Smelser and Richard Swedberg,160–82. 2nd ed. Princeton, NJ: Princeton University Press.

——. 2013. "Can global brands create just supply chains? Response." *Boston Review*, May 21. http://www.bostonreview.net/forum/can-global-brands-create-just-supply-chains/host-countries-can-act. Accessed May 11, 2015.

——. 2014. "Global value chains in a post-Washington consensus world." *Review of International Political Economy* 21, no. 1: 9–37.

Gereffi, Gary, and M. Christian. 2009. "The impacts of Wal-Mart: The rise and consequences of the world's dominant retailer." *Annual Review of Sociology* 35: 573–91.

Gereffi, Gary, and Stacey Frederick. 2010. "The global apparel value chain: Trade and the crisis." Washington, DC: The World Bank Development Research Group.

Gereffi, Gary, R. Garcia-Johnson, and E. Sasser. 2001. "The NGO-industrial complex." *Foreign Policy* 125: 56–65. doi:10.2307/3183327.

Gereffi, Gary, John Humphrey, and Timothy Sturgeon. 2005. "The governance of global value chains." *Review of International Political Economy* 12: 79–82.

Gereffi, G., and J. Lee. 2012. "Why the world suddenly cares about global supply chains." *Journal of Supply Chain Management* 48, no. 3: 24–32.

Gereffi, G., and O. Memodovic. 2003. "The global apparel value chain: What prospects for upgrading by developing countries?" UNIDO Sectoral Studies Series. https://www.unido.org/fileadmin/user_media/Publications/Pub_free/Global_apparel_value_chain.pdf. Accessed May 8, 2015.

Gereffi, Gary, David Spender, and Jennifer Bair, eds. 2002. *Free trade and uneven development: The North American apparel industry after NAFTA*. Philadelphia: Temple University Press.

Gomes de Azevedo, F. A. 2005. "A presença de trabalho forçado na cidade de São Paulo." Master's thesis, University of São Paulo.

Good Electronics. 2013. "With Apple the FLA is not convincing as a multi-stakeholder initiative." Last updated August 5, 2013. http://goodelectronics.org/news-en/with-apple-the-fla-is-not-convincing-as-a-multi-stakeholder-initiative.

Gordon, Jennifer. 2005. "Law, lawyers and labor: The United Farm Workers' legal strategy in the 1960s and 1970s and the role of law in union organizing today." *Pennsylvania Journal of Labor and Employment Law* 8: 1–72.

Gordon, Michael E., and David Jessup. 2000. "Organizing in the export processing zones: The bibong experience in the Dominican Republic." In *Transnational cooperation*, edited by Michael E. Gordon and Lowell Turner. Ithaca, NY: Cornell University Press.

Greenhouse, Steven. 2009. "Labor fight ends in win for students." *The New York Times*, November 17. http://www.nytimes.com/2009/11/18/business/18labor.html. Accessed May 8, 2015.

——. 2012. "Documents indicate Walmart blocked safety push in Bangladesh." *New York Times*, December 5. http://www.nytimes.com/2012/12/06/world/

asia/3-walmart-suppliers-made-goods-in-bangladeshi-factory-where-112-died-in-fire.html. Accessed May 30, 2013.

——. 2013. "U.S. retailers see big risk in safety plan for factories in Bangladesh." *New York Times*, May 22. http://www.nytimes.com/2013/05/23/business/legal-experts-debate-us-retailers-risks-of-signing-bangladesh-accord.html?pagewanted=all. Accessed May 27, 2013.

Greenhouse, S., and J. Yardley. 2012. "As Walmart makes safety vows, it's seen as obstacle to change." *The New York Times*, December 28. http://www.nytimes.com/2012/12/29/world/asia/despite-vows-for-safety-walmart-seen-as-obstacle-to-change.html?_r=0. Accessed May 13, 2015.

Gregoratti, Catia, and Doug Miller. 2011. "International framework agreements for workers' rights? Insights from River Rich Cambodia." *Global Labour Journal* 2, no. 2: 84–105.

GSCP. 2009. *Audit Process and Methodology Reference Tools*. http://www.theconsumergoodsforum.com/gscp-our-work/reference-tools.

GSCP. 2015. "Our Work on Resolving Non-Compliance and Building Capacity." http://www.theconsumergoodsforum.com/gscp-our-work/capacity-building. Accessed September 14, 2015.

Guangzhou KRS Union Committee. 2013. "Guangzhou KRS union committee complaint." Guangzhou: Unpublished.

Günter, Hans. 1981. "The tripartite declaration of principles concerning multinational enterprises and social policy (History, contents, follow-up and relationship with relevant instruments of other organisations)." http://www.ilo.org/wcmsp5/groups/public/---ed_emp/---emp_ent/---multi/documents/publication/wcms_125794.pdf. Accessed May 11, 2015.

Hall, Peter A., and David Soskice. 2001. "An introduction to varieties of capitalism." In *Varieties of capitalism: The institutional foundations of comparative advantage*, edited by Peter Hall and David Soskice, 1–68. Oxford: Oxford University Press.

H&M. 2010. "Code of conduct." http://about.hm.com/content/dam/hm/about/documents/en/CSR/codeofconduct/Code%20of%20Conduct_en.pdf. Accessed May 27, 2013.

Hainmueller, Jans, Michael J. Hiscox, and Sandra Sequeira. 2011. "Consumer demand for the fair trade label: Evidence from a field experiment." Review of Economics and Statistics: Forthcoming. Former: MIT Political Science Department Research Paper No. 2011-9B. http://papers.ssrn.com/sol3/papers.cfm?abstract_id=1801942.

Hamilton, Gary G., and Cheng-shu Kao. 2011. "The Asia miracle and the rise of demand-responsive economies." In Hamilton, Petrovic, and Senauer, *The market makers*, 181–210.

Hamilton, Gary G., Benjamin Senauer, and Misha Petrovic. 2012. *The market makers: How retailers are reshaping the global economy*. New York: Oxford University Press.

Hammadi, Saad, and Matthew Taylor. 2010. "Workers jump to their deaths as fire engulfs factory making clothes for Gap." *Guardian News and Media*, December 14. http://www.guardian.co.uk/world/2010/dec/14/bangladesh-clothes-factory-workers-jump-to-death.

Hassan, F. 2014. "RMG industry of Bangladesh: Past, present and future." *Dhaka Tribune*, September 16. http://www.dhakatribune.com/long-form/2014/sep/16/rmg-industry-bangladesh-past-present-and-future. Accessed May 13, 2015.

Hemphill, Thomas A. 2004. "Monitoring global corporate citizenship: Industry self-regulation at a crossroads." *The Journal of Corporate Citizenship* 14: 81–95.

Henderson, J., P. Dicken, M. Hess, N. Coe, and H. Yeung. 2002. "Global production networks and the analysis of economic development." *Review of International Political Economy* 9, no. 3: 436–64.

Henn, F. 2013. "Factory audits and safety don't always go hand in hand." *National Public Radio*, May 1. http://www.npr.org/2013/05/01/180103898/foreign-factory-audits-profitable-but-flawed-business. Accessed May 13, 2015.

Hermstadt, O. 2007. "Are international framework agreements a path to corporate social responsibility?" *University of Pennsylvania Journal of Business and Employment Law* 10, no. 1: 187–224.

Heuer, William H., and Ilkka A. Ronkainen. n.d. "Nike in Southeast Asia: Case study." https://www.google.com/url?sa=t&rct=j&q=&esrc=s&source=web&cd=1&cad=rja&uact=8&ved=0CB4QFjAAahUKEwjg0r_U0d7IAhUJ1CYKHcL4Cd4&url=http%3A%2F%2Fwww.swlearning.com%2Fmarketing%2Fczinkota%2Fint_mkt_7e%2Fcases%2FNikeInSEAsia.doc&usg=AFQjCNHZsP6YX7_pQfFiPaDgb8LWmly0rQ&sig2=TiyFEPyj2WeH3w6smOXvjA. Accessed October 25, 2015.

Hickman, M. 2010. "21 workers die in fire at H&M factory." *The Independent*, March 2. http://www.independent.co.uk/life-style/fashion/news/21-workers-die-in-fire-at-hm-factory-1914292.html. Accessed May 13, 2015.

Holleman, Hannah, Inger L. Stole, John Bellamy Foster, and Robert W. McChesney. 2009. "The sales effort and monopoly capital." *Monthly Review* 60, no. 11: 1–23.

Holmes, Oliver Wendall, Jr. 1891. "Agency." *Harvard Law Review* 4: 345.

Housing and Building Research Institute. 2015. "Welcome to the Bangladesh national building code." http://buildingcode.gov.bd/. Accessed May 13, 2015.

Howell, Jude. 2008. "All-China Federation of Trades Unions beyond reform? The slow march of direct elections." *The China Quarterly* 196: 845–63.

Hsing, You-Tien. 1998. *Making capitalism in China: The Taiwan connection*. New York: Oxford University Press.

Huang, Elaine. 2014. "Hon Hai precision: You are your own greatest enemy." *CommonWealth Magazine*, October 16. http://english.cw.com.tw/article.do?action=show&id=14853.

Human Rights Watch. 2013. "Bangladesh: Tragedy shows urgency of worker protections." Last updated April 25, 2013. http://www.hrw.org/news/2013/04/25/bangladesh-tragedy-shows-urgency-worker-protections.

——. 2015a. "Whoever raises their head suffers the most: Workers' rights in Bangladesh's garment factories." http://www.hrw.org/sites/default/files/reports/bangladesh0415_web.pdf. Accessed May 13, 2015.

——. 2015b. "World report 2015: Bangladesh." http://www.hrw.org/world-report/2015/country-chapters/bangladesh?page=3. Accessed May 12, 2015.

Hyde, Alan. 2006. "A game theory account and defence of transnational labour standards—A preliminary look at the problem." In *Globalization and the future of labour law*, edited by J. D. R. Craig and S. M. Lynk, 143–66. Cambridge: Cambridge University Press.

——. 2012. "Legal responsibility for labour conditions down the production chain." In *Challenging the legal boundaries of work regulation*, edited by Judy Fudge, Shae McCrystal, and Kamala Sankaran, 83–99. Oxford: Hard Publishing.

ICCR. 2011. "A faithful voice for justice: ICCR and 40 years of shareholder advocacy." http://www.iccr.org/about/FaithfulVoiceForJustic_brochure.pdf. Accessed May 13, 2013.

IDS. 2006. "The ETI code of labour practice: Do workers really benefit?" http://www.ethicaltrade.org/sites/default/files/resources/Impact%20assessment%20summary.pdf. Accessed May 8, 2015.

IEMI. 2015. "The Brazilian textile and apparel industry sectoral report 2014." Produced by IEMI with support from SINDITÊXTIL–SP and SINDIVESTUÁRIO, São Paulo.

IHLO. 2007. "ACFTU (All-China Federation of Trade Unions) established a union at Foxconn on the very last day of 2006." Last updated January 2, 2007. http://www.ihlo.org/LRC/ACFTU/030107.html.

ILGWU Timeline, ILGWU Website, The Kheel Center ILGWU Collection. 2011. Cornell University ILR School, Ithaca, NY. http://ilgwu.ilr.cornell.edu/timeline/.

ILO. 2006a. "InFocus initiative on corporate social responsibility (CSR)." http://www.ilo.org/public/english/standards/relm/gb/docs/gb295/pdf/mne-2-1.pdf. Accessed May 12, 2015.

——. 2006b. "General survey of the reports concerning the Labour Inspection Convention, 1947 (No. 81), and the protocol of 1995 to the Labour Inspection Convention, 1947, and the labour inspection recommendation, 1947 (No. 81), the labour inspection (mining and transport) recommendation, 1947 (No. 82), the Labour Inspection (agriculture) Convention, 1969 (No. 129), and the labour inspection (agriculture) recommendation, 1969 (No. 133)." http://www.ilo.org/public/english/standards/relm/ilc/ilc95/pdf/rep-iii-1b.pdf. Accessed May 8, 2015.

——. 2007. "Biennial country programme review (2006–2007): Cambodia." http://www.ilo.org/public/english/bureau/program/dwcp/download/cambodiareview.pdf. Accessed May 12, 2015.

——. 2011. "Labour administration and labour inspection." http://www.ilo.org/wcmsp5/groups/public/---ed_norm/---relconf/documents/meetingdocument/wcms_153918.pdf. Accessed May 8, 2015.

——. 2012. "C155—Occupational safety and health convention, 1981 (no. 155)." http://www.ilo.org/dyn/normlex/en/f?p=1000:12100:0::NO::P12100_ILO_CODE:C155. Accessed May 28, 2013.

——. 2013a. "Bangladesh: Seeking better employment conditions for better socioeconomic outcomes." http://www.ilo.org/global/research/publications/WCMS_229105/lang--en/index.htm. Accessed May 12, 2015.

——. 2013b. "Labour inspections and private compliance initiatives: Trends and issues: Background paper for the meeting of experts on labour inspection and the role of private compliance initiatives." http://www.ilo.org/wcmsp5/groups/public/---ed_dialogue/---lab_admin/documents/meetingdocument/wcms_230798.pdf. Accessed May 8, 2015.

——. 2013c. "The social dimensions of free trade agreements." http://www.ilo.org/global/research/publications/WCMS_228965/lang--en/index.htm. Accessed May 11, 2015.

——. 2014. "Tripartite declaration of principles concerning multinational enterprises and social policy." http://www.ilo.org/empent/Publications/WCMS_094386/lang--en/index.htm. Accessed May 12, 2015.

——. 2015a. "Origins and history." http://www.ilo.org/global/about-the-ilo/history/lang--en/index.htm. Accessed May 11, 2015.

——. 2015b. "Tripartite structure." http://ilo.org/global/about-the-ilo/who-we-are/tripartite-constituents/lang--en/index.htm. Accessed May 11, 2015.

——. 2015c. "Background." http://www.ilo.org/declaration/thedeclaration/background/lang--en/index.htm. Accessed May 11, 2015.

——. 2015d. "The text of the declaration and its follow-up." http://www.ilo.org/declaration/thedeclaration/textdeclaration/lang--en/index.htm. Accessed May 11, 2015.

———. 2015e. "Ratifications of Fundamental Protocols and Conventions by Country." http://www.ilo.org/dyn/normlex/en/f?p=1000:10011:0::NO:10011:P10011_DISPLAY_BY,P10011_CONVENTION_TYPE_CODE:2,F. Accessed October 26, 2015.

ILRF. 2012. "Garib & Garib (Bangladesh)." http://www.laborrights.org/creating-a-sweatfree-world/sweatshops/factory-profiles/garib-garib-in-bangladesh.

———. 2013. "ILRF applauds house amendment: Apparel sold at U.S. military bases must comply with Bangladesh safety accord." http://www.laborrights.org/creating-a-sweatfree-world/news/ilrf-applauds-house-amendment-apparel-sold-at-us-military-bases-must. Accessed June 21, 2013.

Inditex. 2001. "Code of conduct for manufacturers and suppliers." http://www.inditex.com/documents/10279/28230/Grupo_INDITEX_codigo-de-conducta-de-fabricantes-y-proveedores_ENG.pdf/ade5106d-f46a-487b-a269-60c2e35cdcf4. Accessed May 9, 2015.

IndustriALL Global Union. 2013. "Families hold candlelit vigil at Rana Plaza site six months on." October 24; available at http://www.industriall-union.org/families-hold-candlelit-vigil-at-rana-plaza-site-six-months-on (last accessed 9/12/2015).

International Human Rights and Conflict Resolution Clinic. 2013. "Monitoring in the dark: An evaluation of the International Labour Organization's Better Factories Cambodia Monitoring and Reporting Program." https://humanrightsclinic.law.stanford.edu/wp-content/uploads/2013/03/Monitoring-in-the-Dark-Stanford-WRC.pdf. Accessed May 12, 2015.

International Trade Union Confederation. 2014. "ICTU global rights index: The world's worst countries for workers." http://www.ituc-csi.org/IMG/pdf/survey_ra_2014_eng_v2.pdf. Accessed May 13, 2015.

IRRC Institute. 2012. "Key performance indicators for investors to assess labor & human rights risks faced by global corporations in supply chains." http://www.irrcinstitute.org/pdf/HR-Summary-Report-Jan-2012.pdf. Accessed May 11, 2015.

Jacoby, Sanford. 1997. *Modern manors: Welfare capitalism since the New Deal.* Princeton, NJ: Princeton University Press.

Jakarta Globe. 2012. "More than 2 million workers strike in Indonesia." Last updated October 3, 2012. http://www.thejakartaglobe.com/archive/more-than-2-million-workers-strike-in-indonesia/.

Jenkins, Rhys. 2002. "Political economy of codes of conduct." In *Corporate responsibility and labor rights: Codes of conduct in the global economy*, edited by Ruth Pearson, Rhys Jenkins, and Gill Seyfang, 13–30. London: Earthscan.

Johnson, K., and J. Alam. 2013. "Big brands rejected Bangladesh factory safety plan." *Yahoo News*, April 26. http://news.yahoo.com/big-brands-rejected-bangladesh-factory-safety-plan-122206229.html. Accessed May 13, 2015.

Johnson, Robert. 2011. "New sweatshop scandals for Disney, Mattel and Apple." *Business Insider*, August 29. http://www.businessinsider.com/mattel-disney-chinese-sweatshop-child-labor-2011-8. Accessed May 12, 2015.

Kaplinsky, R., A. Terheggen, and J. Tijaja. 2011. "China as a final market: The Gabon Timber and Thai Cassava value chains." *World Development* 39, no. 7: 1177–90.

Katsoulakos, P., M. Koutsodimou, A. Matraga, and L. Williams. 2004. "A historic perspective of the CSR movement." Athens University of Economics and Business in Partnership with CSRQuest, October 24. http://www.csrquest.net/uploadfiles/1D.pdf. Accessed May 9, 2015.

Kaysen, Carl. 1957. "The social significance of the modern corporation." *The American Economic Review* 47, no. 2: 311–19.

Kettunen, Pauli. 2013. "The ILO as a forum for developing and demonstrating a Nordic model." In *Globalizing social rights: The International Labour*

Organization and beyond, edited by Sandrine Kott and Joelle Drox, 210–30. New York: Palgrave Macmillan.

King, Brayden G., and Nicholas A. Pearce. 2010. "The contentiousness of markets: Politics, social movements, and institutional change in markets." *Annual Review of Sociology* 36, no. 36: 249–67. doi:10.1146/annurev.soc.012809.102606.

Klabbers, Jan. 2014. "Marginalized international organizations: Three hypotheses concerning the ILO." In Blanpain, Liukkunen, and Chen, *China and ILO*, 181–96.

Kline, John, and Edward Soule. 2011. *Alta Gracia: Work with a salario digno*. Washington, DC: Georgetown University Reflective Engagement Initiative.

——. 2014. *Alta Gracia: Four years and counting*. Washington, DC: Georgetown University, Reflective Engagement Initiative.

Knight, Graham, and Don Wells. 2007. "Bringing the local back in: Trajectory of contention and the union struggle at Kukdong/Mexmode." *Social Movement Studies* 6, no. 1: 83–103.

Knorringa, P. 2010. "Reach and depth of responsible production: Towards a research agenda." In Posthuma and Nathan, *Labour in global production networks in India*, 81–99.

Kolasa, M., M. Rubaszek, and D. Taglioni. 2010. "Firms in the great global recession: The role of foreign ownership and financial dependence." *Emerging Markets Review* 11, no. 4: 341–57.

Kolben, Kevin. 2004. "Trade, monitoring, and the ILO: Working to improve conditions in Cambodia's garment factories." *Yale Human Rights & Development Law Journal* 7: 79–107.

——. 2007. "Integrative linkage: Combining public and private regulatory approaches in the design of trade and labor regimes." *Harvard International Law Journal* 48, no. 1: 203–56.

——. 2010. "Labor rights as human rights?" *Virginia Journal of International Law* 50: 449–84.

Kolk, Ans, and Rob van Tulder. 2002. "The effectiveness of self-regulation: Corporate codes of conduct and child labour." *European Management Journal* 20, no. 3: 260–71.

Kong, X. 2010. "Moving negotiations: Memoirs of June 4, 2010 collective wage negotiations at Nanhai Honda." Guangzhou: Unpublished.

——. 2013. "Embarrassing negotiations: Memoirs of the 2013 Nanhai Honda negotiations." Guangzhou: Unpublished.

KPMG. 2007. "Business codes of conduct of the Global 200." http://www.kpmg.com/CN/en/IssuesAndInsights/ArticlesPublications/Documents/business-codes-global-200-O-0804.pdf. Accessed May 17, 2013.

——. 2008. "Business codes of the Global 200: Their prevalence, content, and embedding." https://www.kpmg.com/CN/en/IssuesAndInsights/ArticlesPublications/Documents/business-codes-global-200-O-0804.pdf. Accessed May 11, 2015.

Kraemer, Kenneth L., Greg Linden, and Jason Dedrick. 2011. "Capturing value in global networks: Apple's iPad and iPhone." http://econ.sciences-po.fr/sites/default/files/file/Value_iPad_iPhone.pdf.

Ku, Yu-ling. 2006. "Human lives valued less than dirt: Former RCA workers contaminated by pollution fighting worldwide for justice (Taiwan)." In Smith, Sonnenfeld, and Pellow, *Challenging the chip*, 181–90.

Labowitz, Sarah, and Dorothée Baumann-Pauly. 2014. "Business as usual is not an option: Supply chains and sourcing after Rana Plaza." http://www.stern.nyu.

edu/sites/default/files/assets/documents/con_047408.pdf. Accessed May 11, 2015.

Lam, K. C., and P. W. Liu. 1986. "Efficiency and sharing of investment in specific human capital under risk aversion." *Economics Letters* 20, no. 1: 83–87.

Laslett, John, and Mary Tyler. 1989. *The ILGWU in Los Angeles, 1907–1988*. Inglewood, CA: Ten Star Press.

Lau, Rena. 2012. "Restructuring of the Honda Auto Parts Union in Guongdong, China: A 2-year assessment of the 2010 strike." *Working USA: The Journal of Labor and Society* 15, no. 4: 497–515.

Lee, Ching Kwan. 2007. *Against the law: Labor protests in China's rustbelt and sunbelt.* Berkeley: University of California Press.

Lee, Ching Kwan, and Yonghong Zhang. 2013. "The power of instability: Unraveling the microfoundations of bargained authoritarianism in China." *American Journal of Sociology* 118, no. 6: 1475–1508.

Lee, Joonkoo, and Gary Gereffi. 2013. "The co-evolution of concentration in mobile phone value chains and its impact on social upgrading in developing countries." Capturing the Gains working paper 25. http://www.capturingthegains.org/pdf/ctg-wp-2013-25.pdf.

Lee, J., G. Gereffi, and S. Barrientos. 2011. "Global value chains, upgrading and poverty reduction." Capturing the Gains briefing note no. 3, November. http://www.capturingthegains.org/pdf/ctg_briefing_note_03.pdf.

Lee, J., G. Gereffi, and J. Beauvais. 2012. "Global value chains and agrifood standards: Challenges and possibilities for smallholders in developing countries." *Proceedings of the National Academy of Sciences of the United States of America* 109, no. 31: 12326–31.

Lee, Lai To. 1984. *The structure of the trade union system in China, 1949–1984.* Hong Kong: University of Hong Kong Press.

Leng, Tse-Kang. 2005. "State and business in the era of globalization: The case of cross-strait linkages in the computer industry." *The China Journal* 53: 63–79.

Leon H. Sullivan Foundation. 2013. "The Global Sullivan Principles." http://www.thesullivanfoundation.org/The-Global-Sullivan-Principles.html. Accessed May 11, 2015.

Levine, Louis. 1924. *The Women's Garment Workers.* New York: Arno.

Li, Yulin. 2013. "Recalling the trade union in Ohms: Democracy needs to be learned" (in Chinese). *Southern Metropolis News*, April 15.

Liang, J. 2011. "Report on Nansha strike." Guangzhou: Unpublished.

Lichtenstein, Nelson. 2009. *The retail revolution: How Wal-Mart created a brave new world of business.* New York: Henry Holt.

——. 2012. "The return of merchant capitalism." *International Labor and Working-Class History* 81: 8–27.

——. 2013. *State of the union: A century of American labor.* Princeton, NJ: Princeton University Press.

Lipschutz, Ronnie D., and James K. Rowe. 2005. *Globalization, governmentality and global politics: Regulation for the rest of us?* RIPE series in global political economy. New York: Routledge.

Liu, Jian. 2010. "Weile Zhongguo gongren de zunyan: Auliwei nügong weiquan jishi." (In defense of the dignity of Chinese workers: A story of how the Ole Wolff woman workers protect their rights). *Zhongguo gongren* (*Chinese Workers*), July 2010. http://www.chineseworkers.com.cn/_d270684129.htm. Accessed September 20, 2014.

Liu, Mingwei. 2011. "'Where there are workers, there should be trade unions': Union organizing in the era of growing informal employment." In *From iron rice bowl to informalization: Markets, workers, and the state in a changing China*, edited by Sarosh Kuruvilla, Ching Kwan Lee, and Mary E. Gallagher, 157–72. Ithaca, NY: Cornell University Press.

Liu, Yang. 2013. "Unable to come to an agreement on a wage increase rate, Nanhai Honda resumed strike" (in Chinese). *Southern Metropolis* net, March 20. http://epaper.oeeee.com/K/html/2013-03/20/content_1824635.htm.

Liu Bin. 2012. "Bantian gonghui jiji jieru yuanman huajie laozi jiufen." (Bantian Trade Union successfully resolves an industrial dispute). *Shenshen longgang zonggonghui (Shenzhen Longgang Federation of Trade Unions)*, April 13. http://www.lgzgh.org/detail.aspx?cid=8339. Accessed September 20, 2014.

Loayza, N., K. Schmidt-Hebbel, and L. Serven. 2000. "What drives private saving around the world?" Policy Research Working Paper Series, No. 2309. Washington, DC: The World Bank.

Locke, Richard M. 1992. "The demise of the National Union in Italy: Lessons from comparative industrial relations theory." *Industrial and Labor Relations Review* 45, no. 2: 229–49.

——. 2011. "Systemic, global change: Exploitative labor practiced in factories originate in consumer behavior. *Boston Review*. http://www.bostonreview.net/BR36.6/ndf_richard_m_locke_ethical_consumption.php. Accessed May 10, 2015.

——. 2013. *The promise and limits of private power: Promoting labor standards in a global economy*. Cambridge: Cambridge University Press.

Locke, Richard, Matthew Amengual, and Akshay Mangla. 2009. "Virtue out of necessity? Compliance, commitment, and the improvement of labor conditions in global supply chains." *Politics & Society* 37, no. 3: 319–51.

Locke, Richard, F. Qin, and A. Brause. 2007. "Does monitoring improve labor standards? Lessons from Nike." *Industrial & Labor Relations Review* 61, no. 1: 3–31.

Los Angeles Times. 1994. "Stores that sell clothes made in sweatshops face crackdown: Labor department may seek to prevent retailers from profiting from goods made under illegal conditions." Last updated September 9, 1994. http://articles.latimes.com/1994-09-09/business/fi-36618_1_federal-labor-laws.

Lucas, R. E., Jr. 2002. *Lectures on economic growth*. Cambridge: Harvard University Press.

Lüthje, B. 2002. "Electronics contract manufacturing: Global production and the international division of labor in the age of the Internet." *Industry and Innovation* 9, no. 3: 227–47.

Lüthje, Boy, Stefanie Hürtgen, Peter Pawlicki, and Martina Sproll. 2013. *From Silicon Valley to Shenzhen: Global production and work in the IT industry*. Lanham, MD: Rowman & Littlefield.

Mac, Ryan. 2013. "Foxconn CEO Terry Gou on his company's growing relationship with GoPro." *Forbes*, March 18. http://www.forbes.com/sites/ryanmac/2013/03/18/foxconn-ceo-terry-gou-on-his-companys-growing-relationship-with-gopro/.

Macintosh Retail Group. 2013. "Supplier's code of conduct." http://www.macintosh.nl/en/sustainable_business/code_of_conduct/. Accessed May 9, 2015.

Maier, Charles. 1975. *Recasting bourgeois Europe*. Princeton, NJ: Princeton University Press.

Manik, Julfikar Ali, and Jim Taylor. 2012. "Bangladesh finds gross negligence in factory fire." *New York Times*, December 17. http://www.nytimes.com/2012/12/18/world/asia/bangladesh-factory-fire-caused-by-gross-negligence.html. Accessed May 28, 2013.

Maquila Solidarity Network. 2012a. "Bangladesh: Workers still dying in unsafe buildings." http://en.maquilasolidarity.org/node/1039. Accessed May 13, 2015.

———. 2012b. "Another preventable factory fire takes the lives of Bangladeshi workers." Last updated November 26, 2012. http://en.maquilasolidarity.org/node/1111.

———. 2012c. "Gap pulls out of Bangladesh fire safety program." http://en.maquilasolidarity.org/node/1104. Accessed May 28, 2013.

Marx, Karl. [1867] 1990. *Capital: A critique of political economy.* vol. 1. Translated by Ben Fowkes. London: Penguin Classics.

Maryanov, D. C. 2010. "Sweatshop liability: Corporate codes of conduct and the governance of labour standards in the international supply chain." *Lewis & Clark Law Review* 14: 397–442.

Mattos, Ed. 2012. "New California law takes aim at forced labor." Labor Is Not a Commodity blog, March 19. http://laborrightsblog.typepad.com/international_labor_right/2012/03/new-california-law-takes-aim-at-forced-labor.html. Accessed May 16, 2015.

May, Stacy. 1958. *The United Fruit Company in Latin America.* New York: National Planning Association.

Mayer, F., and J. Pickles. 2010. "Re-embedding governance: Global apparel value chains and decent work." Capturing the Gains working paper no. 2010/1. http://www.capturingthegains.org/pdf/ctg-wp-2010-01.pdf. Accessed March 8, 2014.

McCartin, Joseph. 1998. *Labor's great war: The struggle for industrial democracy and the origins of modern American labor relations, 1912–1921.* Chapel Hill: University of North Carolina Press.

McCraw, Thomas. 2009. *American business since 1920: How it worked.* Wheeling, IL: Harlan Davidson.

McKay, Steven C. 2006. *Satanic mills or silicon islands? The politics of high-tech production in the Philippines.* Ithaca, NY: Cornell University Press.

Melman, David. 1994. "The cause and effect of the ILGWU dress industry general strike of 1985." PhD diss., Bernard M. Baruch College, The City University of New York.

Meyers, Gerald. 2004. "Union Membership Trends in the United States." http://digitalcommons.ilr.cornell.edu/cgi/viewcontent.cgi?article=1176&context=key_workplace. Accessed October26, 2015.

Meyn, Colyn. 2014. "ILO names factories with poor conditions." *The Cambodia Daily*, March 18. https://www.cambodiadaily.com/archives/ilo-names-factories-with-poor-conditions-54406/. Accessed May 12, 2015.

Milberg, William. 2008. "Shifting sources and uses of profits: Sustaining US financialization with global value chains." *Economy and Society* 37, no. 3: 420–51.

Miller, Doug. 2013. *Last nightshift in Savar: The story of Spectrum sweater factory collapse.* Alnwick: McNidder & Grace.

Ministério Público do Trabalho. 2012. "Ministério Público do Trabalho vs. Arthur Lundgren Tecidos S/A," Process number 0000108-81.2012.5.02.0081, 81ª Vara do Trabalho de São Paulo, Justiça do Trabalho -2ª Regiã.

Mitchell, T., and B. Jopson. 2014. "Official China union raises stakes in Walmart closure programme." *Financial Times.* http://www.ft.com/intl/cms/s/0/2038fd78-b262-11e3-b891-00144feabdc0.html?siteedition=intl#axzz2xGvIg5qN. Accessed May 13, 2015.

Moody, Kim. 1988. *An injury to all: The decline of American unionism.* New York, Verso.

Moritz, Michael. 2009. *Return to the little kingdom: Steve Jobs, the creation of Apple, and how it changed the world.* New York: The Overlook Press.

Murray, Jill. 2003. "The global context: Multinational enterprises, labor standards and regulation." In *Rising above sweatshops: Innovative approaches to global labor challenges*, edited by Laura Pincus Hartman, Denis Gordon Arnold, and Richard E. Wokutch, 27–48. Westport, CT: Praeger.

Musoliek, Bettina. 2011. "The Asia floor wage campaign—Decent income for garment workers in Asia." Paper documenting talk presented at the Global Labour University workshop "Precarious Work: Understanding the Challenges, Finding Union Strategies," Berlin, May 31–June 1.

Myers, Jack. 2007. "Ad spend to grow 3% in 2007, 7% in 2008, 3% in 2009." http://www.marketingcharts.com/wp/television/jack-myers-ad-spend-to-grow-3-in-2007-7-in-2008-3-in-2009-1703/. Accessed June 1, 2013.

Nadvi, Khalid. 2008. "Global standards, global governance and the organization of global value chains." *Journal of Economic Geography* 8, no. 3: 1–21.

National Bureau of Statistics of the People's Republic of China. 2014. "Investigative report on the monitoring of Chinese rural migrant workers in 2013" (in Chinese). http://www.stats.gov.cn/tjsj/zxfb/201405/t20140512_551585.html.

———. 2015. "Statistical communiqué of the People's Republic of China on the 2014 national economic and social development." http://www.stats.gov.cn/english/PressRelease/201502/t20150228_687439.html.

Neilson, J., and B. Pritchard. 2009. *Value chain struggles: Institutions and governance in plantation districts of South India.* London: Wiley-Blackwell.

Neilson, J., B. Pritchard, and H. Wai-Chung Yeung. 2014. "Global value chains and global production networks in the changing international political economy: An introduction." *Review of International Political Economy* 21, no. 1: 1–8.

New Age. 2014. "Stay alert against RMG sector conspirators: PM." Last updated December 8, 2014. http://newagebd.net/74435/stay-alert-against-rmg-sector-conspirators-pm/ - sthash.9ibiiG4j.dpbs.

New Wave Group. 2012. "Social responsibility." http://www.nwg.se/en/about-new-wave/our-responsibility/social-responsibility.html. Accessed May 9, 2015.

Ngai, Pun. 2005. "Global production, company codes of conduct, and labor conditions in China: A case study of two factories." *China Journal* 5: 101–13.

Ngai, Pun, and Yu Xiaomin. 2012. "Wal-Martinization, corporate social responsibility and the labor standards of toy factories in South China." In Chan, *Wal-Mart in China*, 34–70.

Nisen, Max. 2013. "How Nike solved its sweatshop problem." *Business Insider*, May 9. http://www.businessinsider.com/how-nike-solved-its-sweatshop-problem-2013-5. Accessed May 12, 2015.

Nocchi, A. S. P., G. N. Velloso, and M. Neves Fava. 2011. *Trabalho escravo contemporâneo: O desafio de superar a negação.* São Paulo: LTr Editora.

Nova, Scott. 2011. "PR coup." *Boston Review.* http://www.bostonreview.net/BR36.6/ndf_scott_nova_ethical_consumption.php. Accessed May 18, 2015.

———. 2013. "Bangladesh: The catastrophic failure of the apparel industry's f factory-inspection regimes and the birth of a new model." *EHS Today*, October 14. http://ehstoday.com/safety/bangladesh-catastrophic-failure-apparel-industrys-factory-inspection-regimes-and-birth-new-mo. Accessed May 12, 2015.

———. 2014. "Testimony of Scott Nova, executive director of the Worker Rights Consortium, hearing on 'Prospects for democratic reconciliation and improving workers' rights in Bangladesh,' Senate committee on foreign relations, February 11, 2014." http://www.foreign.senate.gov/imo/media/doc/Nova_Testimony.pdf. Accessed May 12, 2015.

OECD. 2011. "OECD guidelines for multinational Enterprises." http://dx.doi.org/10.1787/9789264115415-en.

OHCHR. 2011. "Guiding principles on business and human rights: Implementing the United Nations 'protect, respect and remedy' framework." http://www.ohchr.org/Documents/Issues/Business/A-HRC-17-31_AEV.pdf. Accessed May 11, 2015.

O'Neill, J. 2011. *The growth map: Economic opportunity in the BRICs and beyond.* New York: Penguin.

O'Rourke, Dara. 2000. "Monitoring the monitors: A critique of PricewaterhouseCoopers' labor monitoring." Last updated September 28, 2000. http://web.mit.edu/dourourke/www/PDF/pwc.pdf.

——. 2006. "Multi-stakeholder regulation: Privatizing or socializing global labor standards?" *World Development* 34: 899–918.

——. 2011. "Ethical consumption: A response." *Boston Review.* http://www.bostonreview.net/BR36.6/ndf_dara_orourke_response_ethical_consumption.php. Accessed May 15, 2015.

OTEXA. 2012. "U.S. imports of textiles and apparel." http://otexa.trade.gov/scripts/tqads2.exe/catpage. Accessed May 9, 2015.

Oxfam International. 2004. *Trading away our rights: Women working in global supply chains.* Oxford: Oxfam International.

Pakistan Bureau of Statistics. 2013. "Census of manufacturing industries district-wise, 2005–2006." http://www.pbs.gov.pk/sites/default/files/industry_mining_and_energy/publications/CMI_2005-06_district-wise.pdf. Accessed May 23, 2013.

Parker, Ian. 2015. "The shape of things to come: How an industrial designer became Apple's greatest product." *The New Yorker*, February 23. http://www.newyorker.com/magazine/2015/02/23/shape-things-come.

Parvez, Sohel. 2013. "Safety drives flop on scanty budgets: Allocation insufficient for monitoring, inspection of factories." *Daily Star*, February 1. http://archive.thedailystar.net/newDesign/news-details.php?nid=267350.

Pastore, B. 2003. "Soft law, gradi di normatività, teoria delle fonti." *Lavoro e diritto* 17, no. 1: 5–16.

Paul, Ron. 1999. "Congressional record, November 8, 1999 (Extensions): Good time for Congress to reassess antitrust laws, H11683-H11684." http://thomas.loc.gov/cgi-bin/query/D?r106:7:./temp/~r1063WbG98::. Accessed September 13, 2012.

PBS Newshour. 2013. "Global standards for garment industry under scrutiny after Bangladesh disaster." Last updated April 26, 2013. http://www.pbs.org/newshour/bb/world-jan-june13-bangladesh_04-26/. Accessed May 13, 2015.

Petrovic, Misha, and Gary G. Hamilton. 2006. "Making global markets: Wal-Mart and its suppliers." In *Wal-Mart: The face of twenty-first century capitalism*, edited by Nelson Lichtenstein, 107–42. New York: New Press.

Phillips, N. 2013. "Unfree labour and adverse incorporation in the global economy: Comparative perspectives from Brazil and India." *Economy and Society* 42, no. 2: 171–96.

Phillips-Fein, Kim. 2010. *Invisible hands: The businessmen's crusade against the New Deal.* New York: W. W. Norton.

Pick, Adam. 2006. "Foxconn takes number one rank in EMS [Electronics Manufacturing Services]." Last updated May 30, 2006. http://www.emsnow.com/npps/story.cfm?ID=19523.

Piore, Michael. 1997. "The economics of sweatshops." In Ross, *No sweat*, 135–42.

Piore, Michael J., and Andrew Schrank. 2006. "Trading up: An embryonic model for easing the human costs of free markets." *Boston Review* 31: 1–22.

——. 2008. "Toward managed flexibility: The revival of labour inspection in the Latin World." *International Labour Review* 147, no. 1: 1–23.

Pires, R. 2008. "Promoting sustainable compliance: Styles of labour inspection and compliance outcomes in Brazil." *International Labour Review* 147, nos. 2–3: 199–229.

Piven, Frances Fox. 2014. "Interdependent power: Strategizing for the occupy movement." *Current Sociology* 62, no. 2: 223–31.

Polaski, Sandra. 2003. "Protecting labor rights through trade agreements: An analytical guide." *Journal of International Labor and Policy* 10, no. 13: 13–25.

Posthuma, A. 2010. "'Beyond regulatory enclaves': Challenges and opportunities to promote decent work in global production networks." In Posthuma and Nathan, *Labour in global production networks in India*, 57–80.

Posthuma, A., and D. Nathan, eds. *Labour in global production networks in India*. New Delhi: Oxford University Press.

Pou Chen. 2015. "Footwear Business." http://www.pouchen.com/index.php/en/business/footwear-business. Accessed October 26, 2015.

Prieto-Carron, M., P. Lund-Thomsen, A. Chan, A. Muro, and C. Bhushan. 2006. "Critical perspectives on CSR and development: What we know, what we don't know and what we need to know." *International Affairs* 81, no. 3: 499–513.

Pun, Ngai. 2005. *Made in China: Women factory workers in a global workplace*. Durham: Duke University Press.

Pun, Ngai, and Jenny Chan. 2012. "Global capital, the state, and Chinese workers: The Foxconn experience." *Modern China* 38, no. 4: 383–410.

———. 2013. "The spatial politics of labor in China: Life, labor, and a new generation of migrant workers." *The South Atlantic Quarterly* 112 no. 1: 179–90.

Pun, Ngai, Yuan Shen, Yuhua Guo, Huilin Lu, Jenny Chan, and Mark Selden. 2014. "Worker-intellectual unity: Trans-border sociological intervention in Foxconn." *Current Sociology* 62, no. 2: 209–22; and *The Asia-Pacific Journal* 12, no. 11: 1–31. http://www.japanfocus.org/-Pun-Ngai/4093.

PVH. 2011. "A shared commitment." http://www.pvh.com/pdf/corporate_responsibility_shared_commitment.pdf. Accessed May 9, 2015.

———. 2012. "PVH Corp. announces landmark agreement with coalition of NGOs and Bangladesh labor unions on fire and building safety." http://www.pvh.com/investor_relations_press_release_article.aspx?reqid=1674827. Accessed May 15, 2015.

Qi, L. 2014. "Yue Yuen Strike is estimated to cost $60 Million." *The Wall Street Journal*, April 28. http://online.wsj.com/news/articles/SB10001424052702304163604579528504234144092. Accessed May 13, 2015.

Quinteros, Aida Carolina. 2000. "Organizaciones sociales y la lucha reivindicativa en torno a la maquila en Centroamérica." http://unpan1.un.org/intradoc/groups/public/documents/icap/unpan045111.pdf. Accessed May 11, 2015.

Quan, K. 2008a. "Use of global value chains by labor organizers." *Competition and Change* 12, no. 1: 89–104.

———. 2008b. "Evolving labor relations in the women's apparel industry." In *New directions in the study of work and employment: Revitalizing industrial relations as an academic enterprise*, edited by Charles J. Whalen, 194–210. Northampton, MA: Edward Elgar.

Quynh, Chi Do. 2015. "The challenge from below: Wildcat strikes and the pressure for union reform in Vietnam." https://web.warwick.ac.uk/russia/ngpa/ChallengefromBelow.doc. Accessed May 11, 2015.

Radio Free Asia. 2013. "Conditions in Cambodia's garment industry worsen: ILO." http://www.rfa.org/english/news/cambodia/garment-07182013175956.html. Accessed May 12, 2015.

Rahman, Waliur. 2005. "Bangladesh tops most corrupt list." *BBC News*, October 18. http://news.bbc.co.uk/2/hi/south_asia/4353334.stm. Accessed May 12, 2015.

RAIS. 2012. "Annual Statistical Yearbook of Social Information." http://www.rais.gov. br. Accessed May 12, 2015.

Ratha, D. 2010. "Diaspora bonds for development financing during a crisis." The People Move blog, October 26. http://blogs.worldbank.org/peoplemove/node/1303.

Raworth, Kate, and Thalia Kidder. 2009. "Mimicking 'lean' in global value chains: It's the workers who get leaned on." In *Frontiers of commodity chain research*, edited by Jennifer Bair, 165–89. Stanford, CA: Stanford University Press.

Reich, Robert B. 1997. *Locked in the Cabinet.* New York: Vintage Books.

Reimann, Kim. 2006. "A view from the top: International politics, norms, and the world-wide growth of NGOs." *International Studies Quarterly* 50, no. 1: 45–67.

Reporters Without Borders. 2013. "2013 World press freedom index: Dashed hopes after spring." http://en.rsf.org/press-freedom-index-2013,1054.html. Accessed May 23, 2013.

Reuters. 2014. "IBM China workers strike over terms in $2.3 billion Lenovo deal." Reuters.com, March 6. http://www.reuters.com/article/2014/03/06/us-china-ibm-strike-idUSBREA250ZB20140306. Accessed May 13, 2015.

Robbins, Allie. 2013. "The future of the student antisweatshop movement: Providing access to U.S. courts for garment workers worldwide." *American University Labor & Employment Law Forum* 3: 131–36.

Robinson, Ian, Rachel Meyer, and Howard Kimeldorf. 2013. "The strengths of weak commitments: Market contexts and ethical consumption." In *Workers' rights and labor compliance in global supply chains: Is a social labor the answer?*, edited by Jennifer Bair, Marsha Dickson, and Doug Miller. New York: Routledge.

Rodriguez-Garavito, C. A. 2005. "Global governance and labor rights: Codes of conduct and anti-sweatshop struggles in global apparel factories in Mexico and Guatemala." *Politics & Society* 33, no. 2: 203–33. doi:10.1177/0032329205275191.

Rogers, Brishen. 2010. "Toward third-party liability for wage theft." *Berkeley Journal of Employment and Labor Law* 31: 1.

——. 2012. "Passion and reason in labor law." *Harvard Civil Rights-Civil Liberties Law Review* 47: 313–69.

Rogers, Joel. 1990. "Divide and conquer: Further 'reflections on the distinctive character of American labor laws.'" *Wisconsin Law Review* 1: 1–147.

Rosen, Ellen. 2002. *Making sweatshops.* Berkeley: University of California Press.

Ross, Andrew, ed. 1997. *No sweat: Fashion, free trade and the rights of garment workers.* New York. Verso.

Ross, Robert. 2002. "The new sweatshops in the United States: How new, how real, how many, and why?" In Gereffi, Spender, and Bair, *Free trade and uneven development*, 100–122.

——. 2004. *Slaves to fashion: Poverty and abuse in the new sweatshops.* Ann Arbor: University of Michigan Press.

——. 2006. "A tale of two factories: Successful resistance to sweatshops and the limits of firefighting." *Labor Studies Journal* 30, no. 4: 65–85.

——. 2009. "China, Asia and labor standards after the MFA." In *Asia and the transformation of the world-system*, edited by Ganesh Trichur, 99–116. Boulder, CO: Paradigm Publishers.

——. 2013. "American clothing retailers should put up or shut up." *Milwaukee Journal Sentinel*, May 23. http://www.jsonline.com/news/opinion/

american-clothing-retailers-should-put-up-or-shut-up-b9917630z1-208747871. html?ipad=y. Accessed June 1, 2013.

Ross, Robert, and Kent Trachte. 1983. "Global cities and global classes: The peripheralization of labor in New York City." *Review* 6, no. 3: 393–431.

——. 1990. *Global capitalism: The new Leviathan.* Albany: State University of New York Press.

Rossi, A. 2011. "Economic and social upgrading in global production networks: The case of the garment industry in Morocco." PhD diss., Institute of Development Studies at Sussex University, Brighton.

Rossi, A., A. Luinstra, and J. Pickles, eds. 2014. *Towards better work: Understanding labour in apparel global value chains.* Geneva: International Labour Organization and Palgrave Macmillan.

Ruggie, John. 1982. "International regimes, transactions, and change: Embedded liberalism in the postwar economic order." *International Organization* 36: 379–415.

——. 2013. *Just business: Multinational corporations and human rights.* New York: W. W. Norton.

Sabel, Charles F. 2014. Contribution to "Review symposium: On Richard M. Locke, *The promise and limits of private power: Promoting labor standards in a global economy*" (New York: Cambridge University Press, 2013). http://www2.law. columbia.edu/sabel/papers/On%20Richard%20Locke.pdf. Accessed May 11, 2015.

São Paulo City Council. 2006. "Testimony to the São Paulo City Council Commission to investigate workers in conditions analogous to slave labor in the apparel industry, 2013." ("O relatório final da Comissão Parlamentar de inquérito para apurar a exploração de trabalho análogo ao de escravo.") http://www1.camara. sp.gov.br/central_de_arquivos/vereadores/CPI-TrabalhoEscravo.pdf. Accessed February 14, 2014.

Schlesinger, Emil. 1951. *The outside system of production in the women's garment industry in the New York market.* New York: The Hecla Press.

Schmidt-Hebbel, K., S. B. Webb, and G. Corsetti. 1992. "Household saving in developing countries: First cross-country evidence." *The World Bank Economic Review, The World Bank Group* 6, no. 3: 529–47.

Schneiderman, David. 2008. *Constitutionalizing economic globalization.* Cambridge: Cambridge University Press.

Schorr, Juliet B. 2011. "Ethical consumption is a route to activism." *Boston Review.* http://www.bostonreview.net/BR36.6/ndf_juliet_b_schor_ethical_consumption. php. Accessed May 10, 2015.

Schrank, A. 2009. "Professionalism and probity in a patrimonial state: Labour inspection in the Dominican Republic." *Latin American Politics and Society* 51, no. 2: 91–114.

Scott, R. E. 1999. *China can wait: WTO accession deal must include enforceable labor rights, real commercial benefits.* Washington, DC: Economic Policy Institute.

——. 2012. "The China toll: Growing U.S. trade deficit with China cost more than 2.7 million jobs between 2001 and 2011, with job losses in very state." Economic Policy Institute, August 23. http://www.epi.org/publication/ bp345-china-growing-trade-deficit-cost/.

Seidman, Gay. 2007. *Beyond the boycott: Labor rights, human rights, and transnational activism.* American Sociological Association Rose Series in Sociology. New York: Russell Sage Foundation.

———. 2009. "Labouring under an Illusion? Lesotho's 'sweat-free' label." *Third World Quarterly* 30, no. 3: 581–98.

Seidman, Joel. 1968. "The I.L.G.W.U. in the Dubinsky period." *Labor History* 9: 55–68.

Selden, Mark. 1997. "China, Japan, and the regional political economy of East Asia, 1945–1995." In *Network power: Japan and Asia*, edited by Peter J. Katzenstein and Takashi Shiraishi, 306–40. Ithaca, NY: Cornell University Press.

Selden, Mark, and Elizabeth J. Perry. 2010. "Introduction: Reform, conflict and resistance in contemporary China." In *Chinese society: Change, conflict and resistance*, edited by Elizabeth J. Perry and Mark Selden, 1–30. 3rd ed. London: Routledge.

Shailor, B. 2005. "Skirting the facts on China: Barbara Shailor responds to Kent Wong." *New Labor Forum* 14, no. 1: 105–8.

Shamir, R. 2004. The de-radicalization of corporate social responsibility. *Critical Sociology* 30, no. 1: 669–89.

Shea, Anna, Mariko Nakayama, and Jody Heymann. 2010. "Improving labour standards in clothing factories: Lessons from stakeholder views and monitoring results in Cambodia." *Global Social Policy* 10: 85–110.

Shi, Qiu. 2008. "The story of Shenzhen Uniden workers' protests" (in Chinese). *Workers' Forum*, April 28. http://grbbs.net/thread-2590-1-1.html.

Short, Kevin. 2013. "5 reasons American companies refused to sign Bangladesh Safety Accord." *Huffington Post*, July 11. http://www.huffingtonpost.com/2013/07/11/rival-bangladesh-factory-safety-plans_n_3574260.html. Accessed May 12, 2015.

Shotwell, James, ed. 1934. *Origins of the International Labor Organization*. New York: Columbia University Press.

Silver, Beverly J. 2003. *Forces of labor: Workers' movements and globalization since 1870.* Cambridge: Cambridge University Press.

Sims, Emily. 2013. "Getting the most out of company efforts to protect workers' rights: A view from the ILO helpdesk for business." Paper presented at the Workers Rights in a Global Economy conference, Bellagio, Italy, July 7.

Smith, Sandy. 2013. "ILO launches program aimed at improving safety in Bangladesh garment industry." *EHS Today*, October 22. http://ehstoday.com/safety/ilo-launches-program-aimed-improving-safety-bangladesh-garment-industry. Accessed May 12, 2015.

Smith, Ted, David A. Sonnenfeld, and David Naguib Pellow, eds. 2006. *Challenging the chip: Labor rights and environmental justice in the global electronics industry.* Philadelphia: Temple University Press.

SOL's Europe. 2013. "Sustainable development." http://www.sols-europe.com/ESA/esa/Marque.jsp?@where.ID@comp.SelectContenuSeul=14&idC=11. Accessed May 28, 2013.

Sousa Lima, A. M. 2009. "As faces da subcontratação do trabalho: Um estudo com trabalhadoras e trabalhadores da confecção de roupas de cianorte e região." PhD diss., Institute of Philosophy and Human Sciences, University of Campinas, São Paulo, Brazil.

Stanford University Law School. 2013. "Monitoring in the dark: An evaluation of the International Labour Organization's Better Factories Cambodia monitoring and reporting program." https://humanrightsclinic.law.stanford.edu/wp-content/uploads/2013/03/Monitoring-in-the-Dark-Stanford-WRC.pdf. Accessed May 11, 2015.

Staritz, C., G. Gereffi, and O. Cattaneo, eds. 2011. "Shifting end markets and upgrading prospects in global value chains." *International Journal of Technological Learning, Innovation and Development* 4, no. 1–3: 13–257.

Starosta, Guido. 2010. "The outsourcing of manufacturing and the rise of giant global contractors: A Marxian approach to some recent transformations of global value chains." *New Political Economy* 15, no. 4: 543–63.

Stein, Leon. 1977. *Out of the sweatshop: The struggle for industrial democracy.* New York: Quadrangle.

Stevis, Dimitris, and Michael Fichter. 2012. "International framework agreements in the United States: Escaping, projecting, or globalizing social dialogue." *Comparative Labor Law & Policy Journal* 33, no. 1: 667–90.

Stillman, S. 2013. "Death traps: The Bangladesh garment-factory disaster." *The New Yorker,* May 1. http://www.newyorker.com/news/news-desk/death-traps-the-bangladesh-garment-factory-disaster. Accessed May 13, 2015.

Streeck, Wolfgang. 2005. "The sociology of labor markets and trade unions." In *The handbook of economic sociology,* edited by Neil J. Smesler and Richard Swedberg, 254–83. 2nd ed. Princeton, NJ: Princeton University Press.

Strom, Stephanie. 1996. "A sweetheart becomes suspect: Looking behind those Kathie Lee labels." *New York Times,* June 27. http://www.nytimes.com/1996/06/27/business/a-sweetheart-becomes-suspect-looking-behind-those-kathie-lee-labels.html. Accessed May 16, 2015.

Sturgeon, Timothy, John Humphrey, and Gary Gereffi. 2011. "Making the global supply base." In Hamilton, Petrovic, and Senauer, *The market makers,* 231–54.

Su, Julie. 1997. "El Monte Thai garment workers: Slave sweatshops." In Ross, *No sweat,* 143–49.

Swenson, Peter. 1989. *Fair shares: Unions, pay and politics in Sweden and West Germany.* Ithaca, NY: Cornell University Press.

——. 2002. *Capitalists against markets: The making of labor markets and welfare states in the United States and Sweden.* Oxford: Oxford University Press.

Szasz, Andrew. 2011. "The costs of ethical consuming." *Boston Review.* http://www.bostonreview.net/BR36.6/ndf_andrew_szasz_ethical_consumption.php. Accessed May 10, 2015.

Tajgman, D. 2011. "Corporate social responsibility meets traditional supervision of fundamental labour rights: Why CSR needs social dialogue to fill the governance gaps." In *The role of labour standards in development: From theory to sustainable practice?,* edited by T. Novitz and D. Mangan, 188–223. Oxford: Oxford University Press.

Tao, Qingqing. 2012. "Ohms trade union voting for a trade union chair" (in Chinese). *Southern Daily,* May 30.

Taylor, Bill, Chang Kai, and Li Qi. 2003. *Industrial relations in China.* Cheltenham, UK: Edward Elgar.

Tedlow, Richard. 2003. *Giants of enterprise: Seven business innovators and the empires they built.* New York: Harper Business.

Teixeira, F. 2007. *The history of the São Paulo textile industry.* São Paulo: SINDITEXTIL.

Tickle, Cindy. 2009. "Top business schools integrating corporate social responsibility." *MatterNetwork,* October 22. http://www.matternetwork.com/2009/10/aspen-institutes-top-10-business.cfm. Accessed May 10, 2015.

Toffel, M., J. Short, and M. Ouellet. 2012. "Reinforcing regulatory regimes: How states, civil society and codes of conduct promote adherence to global labor standards." Harvard Business School working paper 13-045.

Tomlins, Christopher. 2015. "The presence and absence of legal mind: A commentary on Duncan Kennedy's 'Three globalizations of law and legal thought.'" *Law and Contemporary Problems* 78: 1–17.

Transparency International. 2013. "In Bangladesh corruption kills hundreds." http://www.transparency.org/news/feature/in_bangladesh_corruption_kills_hundreds. Accessed May 30, 2013.

Traub-Merz, Rudolf. 2012. "All-China Federation of Trade Unions: Structure, functions and the challenge of collective bargaining." In *Industrial democracy in China: With additional studies on Germany, South-Korea and Vietnam*, edited by Rudolf Traub-Merz and Kinglun Ngok, 11–60. Beijing: China Social Sciences Press. http://library.fes.de/pdf-files/bueros/china/09128/09128-english%20version.pdf.

Tucker, Eric. 2012. "Labor's many constitutions (and capital's too)." *Comparative Labor Law & Policy Journal* 33: 355–78.

UK DFID. 2013. "Capturing the Gains." http://www.capturingthegains.org.

Ullah Mirdha, R. 2014. "BGMEA opposes retailers' plan." *The Daily Star*, February 15. http://m.thedailystar.net/bgmea-opposes-retailers-plan-11401. Accessed May 13, 2015.

UNCOMTRADE. 2000–2013. "United Nations Commodity Trade Statistics Database." http://comtrade.un.org/db.

UNCTAD. 2013. "Global value chains: Investment and trade for development: World Investment Report 2013." http://unctad.org/en/PublicationsLibrary/wir2013_en.pdf. Accessed May 8, 2015.

Unger, J., and A. Chan. 1995. "China, corporatism, and the East Asian model." *The Australian Journal of Chinese Affairs* 33: 29–53.

Unger, Jonathan, Diana Beaumont, and Anita Chan. 2011. "Did unionization make a difference? Work conditions and trade union activity at Chinese Walmart stores." In Chan, *Wal-Mart in China*, 217–38.

UN Global Compact. 2015a. "About the UN Global Compact." http://globalcompactfoundation.org/about-ungc.php. Accessed May 11, 2015.

——. 2015b. "Frequently asked questions." https://www.unglobalcompact.org/AboutTheGC/faq.html. Accessed May 11, 2015.

——. 2015c. "How to participate: The corporate commitment." https://www.unglobalcompact.org/HowToParticipate/Business_Participation/index.html. Accessed May 11, 2015.

——. 2015d. "Integrity measures." https://www.unglobalcompact.org/AboutTheGC/IntegrityMeasures/index.html. Accessed May 11, 2015.

United Nations General Assembly and Human Rights Council. 2008. "Protect, respect and remedy: A framework for business and human rights." Report of the special representative of the Secretary-General on the issue of human rights and transnational corporations and other business enterprises, Professor John Ruggie. http://www.reports-and-materials.org/sites/default/files/reports-and-materials/Ruggie-report-7-Apr-2008.pdf. Accessed May 12, 2015.

University of Minnesota Human Rights Library. 2015. "The global Sullivan principles." http://www1.umn.edu/humanrts/links/sullivanprinciples.html. Accessed May 11, 2015.

US Bureau of Labor Statistics. 2012. "Consumer expenditure survey." http://www.bls.gov/cex/2011/Standard/quintile.pdf. Accessed May 25, 2013.

——. 2015. "Consumer price index." https://research.stlouisfed.org/fred2/release?rid=10. Accessed May 13, 2015.

US Department of Justice. 2011. "Business review letter regarding Worker Rights Consortium's proposed 'Designated Suppliers Program.'" Last updated December 16, 2011. http://www.workersrights.org/dsp/.

US Department of Labor. 1997. "Summary of apparel industry's partnership agreement." Last updated April 14, 1997. http://actrav.itcilo.org/actrav-english/telearn/global/ilo/guide/apparell.htm.

Verité. 2015. "Strengthening protections against in persons in federal and corporate supply chains." http://www.state.gov/documents/organization/237137.pdf. Accessed May 11, 2015.

VF Corporation. 2011. "Joint statement." http://vfc.com/VF/corporation/resources/ images/Content-Pages/Global-Compliance/joint-statement.pdf. Accessed May 13, 2015.

Vogel, David. 2006. *The market for virtue: The potential and limits of corporate social responsibility*. Washington, DC: Brookings Institution Press.

———. 2010. "The private regulation of global corporate conduct: Achievement and limitations." *Business and Society* 49, no. 1: 68–87.

Waldinger, Roger, Chris Erickson, Ruth Milkman, Daniel J. B. Mitchell, Abel Valenzuea, Kent Wong, and Maurice Zeitlin. 1998. "Helots no more: A case study of the justice for janitors campaign in Los Angeles." In *Organizing to win*, edited by Kate Bronfenbrenner, Sheldon Friedman, Richard W. Hurd, Rudolph Oswald, and Ronald L. Seeber, 102–19. Ithaca, NY: Cornell University Press.

Wall Street Journal. 2014a. "Four dead in Cambodia garment strike." Last updated January 3, 2014. http://www.wsj.com/articles/SB10001424052702304325004579 297511167310046.

———. 2014b. "Cambodia Sets Minimum Wage Below Union Demands." November 12, 2014. http://www.wsj.com/articles/cambodia-sets-minimum-wage-below-union-demands-1415789944

Walmart. 2012. "Standards for suppliers." http://corporate.walmart.com/global-responsibility/ethical-sourcing/standards-for-suppliers. Accessed May 28, 2013.

———. 2013. "Wal-Mart statement on IndustriALL Bangladesh factory labor proposal." http://news.walmart.com/news-archive/2013/05/14/walmart-statement-on-industriall-bangladesh-factory-labor-proposal. Accessed May 12, 2015.

———. 2014. "Global responsibility report." http://www.corporatereport.com/walmart/ 2014/grr/compliance_worker_safety.html.

Walsh, D., and S. Greenhouse. 2012a. "Inspectors certified Pakistani factory as safe before disaster." *The New York Times*, September 19. http://www.nytimes. com/2012/09/20/world/asia/pakistan-factory-passed-inspection-before-fire. html?pagewanted=all. Accessed May 13, 2015.

———. 2012b. "Certified safe, a factory in Karachi still quickly burned." *The New York Times*, December 7. http://www.nytimes.com/2012/12/08/world/asia/pakistan-factory-fire-shows-flaws-in-monitoring.html?hp&_r=0. Accessed May 13, 2015.

Wang, Haiyan, Richard P. Appelbaum, Francesca Degiuli, and Nelson Lichtenstein. 2009. "China's new labor contract law: Is China moving towards increased power for workers?" *Third World Quarterly* 30, no. 3: 485–501.

Washington Post. 1989. "For the record." Last updated January 24, 1989.

Weil, David. 2005. "Public enforcement/private monitoring: Evaluating a new approach to regulating the minimum wage." *Industrial & Labor Relations Review* 58, no. 2: 238–57.

———. 2010. "Improving workplace conditions through strategic enforcement." http:// www.dol.gov/whd/resources/strategicEnforcement.pdf. Accessed May 11, 2015.

———. 2012. "Examining the underpinnings of labor standards compliance in low wage industries." Report to the Russell Sage Foundation. http://www.russellsage.org/ sites/all/files/Weil.Final%20Report%202012.pdf. Accessed May 16, 2015.

———. 2014. *The fissured workplace: Why work became so bad for so many and what can be done to improve it*. Cambridge, MA: Harvard University Press.

Wells, Don. 2007. "Too weak for the job: Corporate codes of conduct, non-governmental organizations and the regulation of international labour standards." *Global Social Policy* 7, no. 1: 51–74.

Westervelt, A. 2015. "Two years after Rana Plaza, have conditions improved in Bangladesh's factories?" *The Guardian*, April 24. http://www.theguardian.com/sustainable-business/2015/apr/24/bangladesh-factories-building-collapse-garment-dhaka-rana-plaza-brands-hm-gap-workers-construction. Accessed May 13, 2015.

Wetterberg, Anna. 2010. "Harder soft law: Private labor standards in socially regulated markets." Paper presented at the annual meeting of the American Sociological Association, Atlanta, GA, August 14.

White, George, and Patrick McDonnell. 1997. "Sweatshop workers to get $2 million." *Los Angeles Times*, October 24. http://articles.latimes.com/1997/oct/24/business/fi-46054.

Whittaker, D. H., T. Zhu, T. Sturgeon, M. H. Tsai, and T. Okita. 2010. "Compressed development." *Studies in Comparative International Development* 45: 439–67.

Wolf, C. 2001. "China's capitalists join the party." *The New York Times*, August 13. http://www.nytimes.com/2001/08/13/opinion/13WOLF.html. Accessed May 13, 2015.

Wood, Z. 2010. "Child labor hotspots identified in 12 emerging economies." *The Guardian*, December 2. http://www.theguardian.com/business/2010/dec/02/child-labour-hotspots. Accessed May 13, 2015.

Worker Rights Consortium. 2008. "Assessment re Jerzees de Honduras (Russell Corporation)," November 7, 2008, http://www.workersrights.org/Freports/Jerzees%20de%20Honduras%2011-07-08.pdf.

———. 2012. "Saturday's devastating factory fire in Bangladesh and the urgent need for reform." http://www.workersrights.org/university/memo/113012.html. Accessed May 13, 2015.

———. 2013. "Global wage trends for apparel workers, 2001–2011." https://www.americanprogress.org/issues/labor/report/2013/07/11/69255/global-wage-trends-for-apparel-workers-2001-2011/. Accessed May 11, 2015.

———. 2014. "Crackdown in Cambodia: Workers seeking higher wages meet violent repression." http://www.workersrights.org/freports/WRC%20Report%20-%20Crackdown%20in%20Cambodia%203.24.14.pdf. Accessed May 12, 2015.

The World Bank. 2005. "Global economic prospects 2006: Economic implications of remittances and migration." http://www.worldbank.org/content/dam/Worldbank/GEP/GEParchives/GEP2006/343200GEP02006.pdf. Accessed May 11, 2015.

WRAP. 2015. "WRAP's 12 Principles." http://www.wrapcompliance.org./en/12-principles. Accessed September 12, 2015.

Wrinkle, Haley. 2011. "Better Factories Cambodia: Transparency and Workers Rights." Unpublished Masters thesis, University of California, Santa Barbara.

WTO. 2014. "Statsical database, online." http://stat.wto.org/StatisticalProgram/WSDBStatProgramHome.aspx?Language=E.

Xinhua. 2013. "Xi asks labor unions to protect workers' rights." Last updated October 23, 2013. http://en.acftu.org/28623/201405/12/140512173707181.shtml.

Yardley, Jim. 2012. "Horrific fire revealed a gap in safety for global brands." *The New York Times*, December 7. http://www.nytimes.com/2012/12/07/world/asia/bangladesh-fire-exposes-safety-gap-in-supply-chain.html?_r=0. Accessed May 11, 2015.

Ying, Zhaoping. 2003. "Trade union direct election: A process driven by foreigners to transform workers' rights" (in Chinese). *Southern Daily*, June 25.

Zhang, Xiang. 2015. "Foxconn's long hours causing workers' deaths: Union." *China Daily*, February 3. http://www.chinadaily.com.cn/china/2015-02/03/content_19477082.htm.

Contributors

Mark Anner is associate professor of labor and employment relations, and political science, at Penn State University. He directs the Center for Global Workers' Rights and Penn State's MPS Program in Labor and Global Workers' Rights, which is a part of the Global Labour University network. His recent research examines workers' rights, labor organizing and resistance, and pricing and sourcing dynamics in apparel global value chains in Central America, Vietnam, and Bangladesh.

Richard P. Appelbaum is the MacArthur Foundation Chair and Research Professor in Global and International Studies and Sociology at the University of California at Santa Barbara, and is on the faculty of Fielding Graduate University. He is currently engaged in two principal research projects: a multidisciplinary study of labor conditions in supply chain networks in the Asian-Pacific Rim, and a study of high-technology development in China and Latin America. He is faculty representative to the University of California Advisory Committee on Trademark Licensing, and chairs the Advisory Council of the Worker Rights Consortium.

Jennifer Bair is associate professor of sociology at the University of Colorado Boulder. Her research interests in political economy and development studies have a regional focus on Latin America and the Caribbean. Much of her work focuses on the dynamics of global production networks and their implications for firms and workers in developing countries. Together with Mark Anner and Jeremy Blasi, she is writing a book on labor regulation in international supply chains that focuses on lead firm liability in contracting relationships.

Renato Bignami is a labor inspector in Brazil and has worked in labor administration, industrial relations, and labor law. He is a former labor inspectorate adviser and the former deputy labor inspection secretary for the Labor Inspection National Secretariat, the central authority for labor inspection in Brazil. His main interests are the modernization of the employment relationship, intervention and control possibilities over the labor relationship and the workplace, international labor law, and labor markets integration.

Jeremy Blasi is a staff attorney for UNITE HERE Local 11 in Los Angeles and a nonresident research fellow at Pennsylvania State University's Center for Global Workers' Rights. He formerly served a judicial law clerk in federal district court and as director of investigations for the Worker Rights Consortium, where he coordinated investigations and led efforts to remedy labor rights violations at factories in Latin America, the Caribbean, Africa, and Asia.

Anita Chan is a visiting fellow at the Coral Bell School of Asia Pacific Affairs, Australian National University, and is coeditor of *The China Journal*. Her research focuses on Chinese labor and its relation to labor standards, occupational health and safety, labor rights, the Chinese and Vietnam trade union, and comparative labor.

Jenny Chan is a lecturer in sociology and China studies at the School of Interdisciplinary Area Studies, and an elected junior research fellow of Kellogg College, University of

Oxford. She was the Hong-Kong-based SACOM (Students and Scholars Against Corporate Misbehavior) chief coordinator (2006–2009), a Reid Research Scholar, and is currently a board member of the International Sociological Association's Research Committee on Labor Movements (2014–2018).

Jill Esbenshade is associate professor of sociology at San Diego State University. She teaches labor, race, immigration, and community-based research. She currently serves on the boards of the Worker Rights Consortium and the Center on Policy Initiatives. She has contributed to projects to reign in labor abuses and create more worker empowerment in the garment, taxi, hotel, and restaurant industries.

Gary Gereffi is professor of sociology and director of the Center on Globalization, Governance & Competitiveness at Duke University (http://www.cggc.duke.edu/). He recently completed a three-year project on economic and social upgrading in global value chains, financed by the UK's Department for International Development (http://www. capturingthegains.org/), and he is currently working on a book on the uptake of the global value chain paradigm by major international organizations in the economic and social development arena.

Jeff Hermanson has been an organizer for the Teamsters and Carpenters, the national organizing director for the International Ladies' Garment Workers' Union and UNITE, a field representative of the AFL-CIO Solidarity Center in Mexico, a senior adviser for the American Center for International Labor Solidarity, and the assistant executive director for the Writers Guild of America, West. He has represented the Central General de Trabajadores de Honduras in negotiations with Russell Athletic and Nike, and the PT Kizone Workers' Coordinating Committee in negotiations with adidas. He is currently coordinator of the International Union League for Brand Responsibility and director of global strategies for Workers United-SEIU.

Jason Kibbey is the CEO of the Sustainable Apparel Coalition. He was the CEO and cofounder of PACT, an apparel company combining design, sustainability, and philanthropy. He served as cofounder and interim executive director of Freedom to Roam, a nonprofit initiative that brings together people, organizations, and businesses to enhance and protect wildlife corridors and landscape connectivity in North America. He developed Freedom to Roam while working on environmental campaigns for Patagonia.

Nelson Lichtenstein is the MacArthur Foundation Chair in History at the University of California, Santa Barbara, where he directs the Center for the Study of Work, Labor, and Democracy. He is the author of *The Retail Revolution: How Wal-Mart Created a Brave New World of Business* (2010) and many other books.

Xubei Luo is a senior economist at the World Bank, where she is currently with Poverty and Equity Global Practices. She was a core team member of the World Development Report 2014, Risk and Opportunity, and led the work on the enterprise aspect. She has worked in the East Asia region, the Europe and Central Asia region, the Development Economic Network, the Poverty Reduction and Economic Management Network, the Independent Evaluation Group, and the chief economist's office of the Global Practices vice presidency at the World Bank.

Anne Caroline Posthuma is the specialist in employment and labour market policies in the Office of the International Labour Organization (ILO) in Brasilia, Brazil. She was a senior researcher at the International Institute for Labour Studies of the ILO in Geneva from 2006 to 2010, during which time she participated in a project on economic and social upgrading in global value chains (http://www.capturingthegains.org), financed by the UK government's Department for International Development. Her research interests include the governance of labor standards in global production, SME development policies, youth employment, and formalization of the informal economy.

Scott Nova is executive director of the Worker Rights Consortium, an independent labor rights monitoring and advocacy organization. The WRC played a central role in the conception, negotiation, and implementation of the Accord on Fire and Building Safety in Bangladesh. Nova is a leading expert on the intersection of labor rights and global commerce.

Ngai Pun is a professor in the Department of Applied Social Sciences and director of the China Development and Research Network at Hong Kong Polytechnic University. She recently coauthored and coedited several books on labor and social economy in Hong Kong and China (in Chinese).

Katie Quan is a senior labor specialist at the UC Berkeley Center for Labor Research and Education. Formerly chair and associate chair of the Labor Center, she specializes in research on global labor strategies and executive education for union leaders. In 2010 she cofounded the International Center for Joint Labor Research at Sun Yat-sen University in Guangzhou, China, and was its codirector until 2014. Prior to joining the staff of the Labor Center in 1998 she was a seamstress, organizer, and international vice president with the International Ladies' Garment Workers' Union and its successor, UNITE.

Brishen Rogers is associate professor of law at Temple University, where he teaches torts and various courses on domestic and international labor law. Both before and after law school he worked in the US labor movement, first for SEIU, then for the Change to Win Federation. Prior to joining the faculty at Temple he was a Climenko Fellow and lecturer in law at Harvard Law School.

Robert J. S. Ross is research professor of sociology and at the Mosakowski Institute for Public Enterprise at Clark University in Worcester, Massachusetts. He is a former chair of the Section on Political Economy of the World System of the American Sociological Association. He serves on the Board of Directors of the Sweatfree Purchasing Consortium.

Mark Selden is a senior research associate in the East Asia Program at Cornell University and a visiting researcher at the Asian/Pacific/American Studies Institute at NYU. A specialist on modern and contemporary geopolitics, political economy, and the history of China, Japan, and the Asia Pacific, his work ranges broadly across themes of war and revolution, inequality, development, regional and world social change, social movements, and historical memory.

Chris Wegemer is a high school educator in Santa Barbara, California, dedicated to youth activism and empowerment. He has primarily been involved in the labor movement as a local organizer for United Students against Sweatshops and as a research intern for the Worker Rights Consortium.

Index

A&P, 97

ABVTEX. *See* Brazilian Association of Apparel Retailers

Accord, the. *See* Bangladesh Accord on Fire and Building Safety

adidas, 6, 68, 236, 257, 264; and PT Kizone factory (Indonesia), 68, 147, 269; purchase of Reebok by (2005), 215; unions and, 256, 267, 268, 271; and university contracts, 68, 253–54, 257, 269

AFL-CIO, 47, 190, 206–7, 277n22, 283n12

agriculture, 162–63, 164, 167

Albert, John, 68

Alcatel, 175

Alliance for Bangladesh Worker Safety, 30, 151, 264; contrast of, with the Bangladesh Accord on Fire and Building Safety, 30, 31, 68–69, 79, 88, 110, 148; lack of enforcement provisions in, 30, 79, 88, 110; US corporations in, 30, 69, 88, 110

Alta Gracia label, 254, 285n15

Altshuler Berzon LLP, 269

Amalgamated Clothing and Textile Workers' Union (ACTWU), 262

American Federation of Labor (AFL), 39

Annan, Kofi, 40, 41, 42

Anner, Mark, 51–52, 54, 57, 61, 92, 319; chapter by, 239–58

anti-sweatshop movement, 4, 7, 35–38, 46–47, 211–12, 257–58, 267; and Bangladesh, 109, 264, 273; and Nike, 7–8, 35–37, 46, 257; and The Gap, 35, 38, 275n2; and universities, 7–8, 37, 46–47, 65 (*see also* United Students Against Sweatshops). *See also* Clean Clothes Campaign; International Labor Rights Forum; Worker Rights Consortium

Apparel Industry Partnership (AIP), 46–47

Appelbaum, Richard P., 319; chapters by, 1–14, 32–50

Apple, 8, 174, 175, 180, 185; in China, 8, 12, 174, 175, 178–85, 192; market power of, 2, 33, 282n2; at top of a global supply chain, 1, 12, 33, 98, 169

Asia Floor Wage campaign, 147–48

Asia Multinational Resource Center, 267

Asian Pacific American Legal Center, 38

Aspen Institute, 44–45

automobile industry, 96, 157–58, 223

Bair, Jennifer, 92, 319; chapter by, 239–58

Ballinger, Jeffrey, 36–37

Bangladesh, 108, 263; building collapses in, 76, 81–83 (*see also* Rana Plaza building collapse); corruption in, 90–91, 92, 111; growth of low-cost production in, 9, 18, 20–21, 26, 76, 78, 108, 160, 161, 241; monitoring in, 25, 48–49, 56, 58, 59, 88, 109; safety laws in, 18–19, 25, 26, 90; unions in, 20–21, 25, 27, 111, 148, 255, 256, 258, 264–65, 268; wages in, 21–22, 25, 89, 108, 264

—factory fires in, 17, 26–27, 29, 70–71, 76–78, 79–81, 83–86; deaths in, 29, 33, 76, 80, 83, 84, 86, 108; and weak monitoring, 25, 33, 80–81, 86–87. *See also* Tazreen Fashions factory fire

Bangladesh Accord on Fire and Building Safety, 11, 27–29, 91–92, 239; as binding agreement, 27, 28–29, 65, 109–10; contrast of, with Alliance for Bangladesh Worker Safety, 30, 31, 68–69, 79, 88, 110, 148; firms agreeing to, 27, 91, 108–9, 275n3; as a form of jobbers' agreement, 91, 239–40, 255–56; and joint liability, 258; most US firms' rejection of, 79, 88, 91, 110

—origins of, 9–10, 29–30, 108–9; and anti-sweatshop movement, 109, 264, 273

—provisions of, 27–29, 148, 239; limitations of, 110–11, 148, 256

Bangladesh Garment Manufacturers Association (GMAC), 100, 105, 106, 107, 108–9, 279n4

Batay Ouvriye union federation (Haiti), 270

Better Factories Cambodia (BFC), 11, 55–56, 59, 104–8, 109, 110, 265; limited impact of, 55–56, 64–65, 106–8, 265

Better Work Program (of ILO), 43, 163, 165; in Cambodia: *see* Better Factories Cambodia; in Vietnam, 54

Bignami, Renato, 319; chapter by, 112–36